Care Relations in Southeast Asia

The Intimate and the Public in Asian and Global Perspectives

VOLUME 8

The titles published in this series are listed at *brill.com/ipap*

Care Relations in Southeast Asia

The Family and Beyond

Edited by

Patcharawalai Wongboonsin
Jo-Pei Tan

TUTA SUB AEGIDE PALLAS · 1683 ·

BRILL

LEIDEN | BOSTON

Cover illustration: A modern Southeast Asian family, drawn by Patchara Wongboonsin.

Library of Congress Cataloging-in-Publication Data

Names: Patcharawalai Wongboonsin, editor. | Tan, Jo-Pei, 1977-editor.
Title: Care relations in Southeast Asia : the family and beyond / edited by Patcharawalai Wongboonsin, Jo-Pei Tan.
Description: Leiden ; Boston : Brill, [2019] | Series: The intimate and the public in Asian and global perspectives; 8 | Includes bibliographical references and index.
Identifiers: LCCN 2018043242 (print) | LCCN 2018046863 (ebook) | ISBN 9789004384330 (E-book) |ISBN 9789004384187 (hardback : alk. paper)
Subjects: LCSH: Older people--Care--Southeast Asia. | Caregivers--Family relationships--Southeast Asia. | Families--Southeast Asia. | Home care services--Southeast Asia.
Classification: LCC HV1454.2.S644 (ebook) | LCC HV1454.2.S644 C37 2019 (print) |DDC 306.8740959--dc23
LC record available at http://lccn.loc.gov/2018043242

Typeface for the Latin, Greek, and Cyrillic scripts: "Brill". See and download: brill.com/brill-typeface.

ISSN 2213-0608
ISBN 978-90-04-38418-7 (hardback)
ISBN 978-90-04-38433-0 (e-book)

This book is printed on acid-free paper and produced in a sustainable manner.

Contents

Preface

This volume of work, *Care Relations in Southeast Asia: The Family and Beyond*, aims at providing a better understanding of care relations, from the perspectives of intergenerational relations and transactions in elderly care and childcare within and beyond the family network. Taking a multidisciplinary approach, the volume is based on the nexus of demography, psychology, gender and family studies, as well as social welfare intertwined with care relations. It explored and examined these types of care relations and transactions across three middle-income Southeast Asian countries, namely the Federation of Malaysia, the Kingdom of Thailand and the Social Republic of Vietnam. These exemplify societies in transition due to prominent shift in their cultural, socio-economic, and demographic landscapes.

The volume comprises nine chapters. Chapter 1, which serves as the introductory chapter, presents key terminologies and a discussion of the conceptual frameworks as well as hypotheses that form the basis for all chapters in this volume. It also discusses the research methodologies and data collection while outlining the structure of the volume with an explanation how and why the volume is structured as such.

Thereafter, the volume is further divided into three main parts. Part 1 includes three chapters, which explored continuity and changes in care relations at the national-level perspective of the Federation of Malaysia, the Kingdom of Thailand and the Social Republic of Vietnam, respectively. The analysis was carried out against the cultural background and the changing demographic, socio-economic and political contexts of each country up to 2017.

Part 2 comprises three chapters that offer a comparative study of the attitude and practice of elderly care and childcare at the specific-area level of the capital city of the three countries. These are Kuala Lumpur, Bangkok Metropolis, and Hanoi. The study was based on the merged data of the three most recent family surveys carried out by these research institutions: Universiti Putra Malaysia, for the survey in Kuala Lumpur and Selangor, Malaysia in 2011; the College of Population Studies' Human Development & Migration Studies Centre, Chulalongkorn University for the survey in Bangkok Metropolis, Thailand in 2010; and the Institute for Family and Gender Studies, for the survey in Hanoi, Vietnam during 2010–2011. The surveys are part of Comparative Asian Family Survey (CAFS) project, which was launched in 2010 as a joint endeavour of the Kyoto University GCOE and Seoul National University with financial support from JSPS (Japan Society for the Promotion of Science) and Qatar

Foundation. The CAFS project aimed to enhance our knowledge of changing family dynamics, especially that of family values, intergenerational transactions, changing marriage forms and the gender division of labor in the Asian context. The surveys incorporated, with slight modifications according to local contexts, the 2006 East Asian Social Survey (EASS) family module, which was a collaborative work of the Chinese General Social Survey (CGSS), Japanese General Social Survey (JGSS), Korean General Social Survey (KGSS) and the Taiwan Social Change Survey (TSCS) launched in 2006. Please refer to EASSDA (www.eassda.org) for the details of EASS.

By doing so, this volume hopes to contribute to a better understanding of intergenerational family solidarity and evidence-based inputs from the three societies. The volume also seeks to offer policy recommendations and social innovations to address the current and future concerns in care relations for the three societies, which expect to attain their second demographic dividend rather than getting old before getting rich.

Part 3 is composed of two chapters. One revisits Part 2 from a synthesis perspective of convergence and divergence at the area-specific level so as to pave the way for the final chapter that follows. The final chapter comprises three sections: looking back, looking forward, and policy recommendations for moving forward. Challenges at the national level that were intertwined with those at the area-specific level are accordingly synthesised based on the findings of all previous chapters. Then, future challenges in decades to come are provided so as to lead to policy recommendations for the three countries to attain more viable caring societies while advancing their economies.

This volume of work is guided by three major frameworks to examine and understand the concept of care relations: the demographic dividend, intergenerational family solidarity, and the welfare care model. The analysis was based on the premise that the recent transitions in care relations were spill-over effects of modernisation, which were not necessarily being addressed by social policies. Despite the common belief of the 'nuclearisation' of families and of a welfarism trend, it is argued that the role of the extended family and other kin members were important in care provision. Together with the state, the roles of family, community and the market were changing care relations in terms of attitudes and practices of care. In spite of the stronghold of filial piety values, the traditional family support was expected to come more and more under pressure. The family cannot be expected to continue to play the same role as effectively in the future. With the increased demand for old-age support and affordable care for children and frail older persons, further commodification of care work can be expected in the Federation of Malaysia and the Socialist Republic of Vietnam, while the Kingdom of Thailand will rely more on a partnership approach engaging the community, the family, the state and the private sector in care provision. By having a combination of macro, meso and micro perspectives of care relations, the contents of this volume are expected to contribute to policy makers and scholars in the fields of demography, international relations and development studies, gender and family studies, political science, sociology and gerontology.

Finally, the editors and contributors in this current volume sincerely appreciate the significant contribution of EASS to CAFS. They also acknowledge the generous support, financial and/or technical, provided by Chulalongkorn University's ASEAN Studies Center, the Human Development & Migration Studies Center, the College of Populations Studies in Bangkok Metropolis, Kingdom of Thailand, the Universiti Putra Malaysia's Institute of Gerontology in Selangor, Federation of Malaysia, the Institute for Family and Gender Studies, the Vietnamese Academy of Social Science in Hanoi, Socialist Republic of Vietnam, the Department of Social Care and Social Work, Faculty of Health, Psychology and Social Care, Manchester Metropolitan University, United Kingdom.

We would like also to acknowledge these experts for their valuable comments and insights when the manuscripts were presented at a series of international seminars and workshops organized by the Human Development & Migration Studies Center, College of Populations Studies, Chulalongkorn University in Bangkok Metropolis, Kingdom of Thailand, in collaboration with ASEAN Studies Center, Chulalongkorn University, and the Kyoto International Consortium for Asian Studies, Kyoto University, from April 2014 to October 2017: Professor Emiko Ochiai from the Kyoto International Consortium for Asian Studies, Kyoto University, Japan; Prof. Yoko Hayami, Center for Southeast Asian Studies, Kyoto University, Japan; Professor Hachiro Iwai, Graduate School of Education, Kyoto University, Japan; Professor Fumiko Oshikawa, Japan Center for Area Studies (JCAS), Japan; Dr. Heiwa Date, Kyoto International Consortium for Asian Studies, Kyoto University, Japan; Professor Emeritus John Knodel from the Department of Sociology and Population Studies Center, University of Michigan; Professor Peter Xenos from the College of Public Health Sciences, Chulalongkorn University; Professor Dr. Gavin W. Jones, Director of JY Pillay Comparative Asia Research Centre, Global Asia Institute, Republic of Singapore; Professor Dr. Worawet Suwanrada from the Faculty of Economics, Chulalongkorn University, Kingdom of Thailand; Dr. Elke Loichinger, College of Population Studies, Chulalongkorn University, Thailand; Professor Dr. Trin Duy Luan, High Senior Researcher, Former Director, Institute of Sociology; Associate Professor Vu Manh Loi, Vice-Director, Institute of Sociology, Hanoi, Socialist Republic of Vietnam; Dr. Anjli Panalal Doshi, Deputy Director

General (Policy), National Population and Family Development Board Malaysia, Federation of Malaysia.

Patcharawalai WONGBOONSIN
Jo-Pei TAN
March 2018

Illustrations

Figures

Tables

Abbreviations

ARCPM	Association of Registered Childcare Providers Malaysia
ASEAN	Association of Southeast Asian Nations
BMA	Bangkok Metropolitan Administration, Thailand
CDR	Crude death rate
CHXHCNVN	Cộng hòa Xã hội chủ nghĩa Việt Nam (Socialist Republic of Vietnam)
DINK	Double Income, No Kids
DOSM	Department of Statistics of Malaysia
DSW	Department of Social Welfare, Malaysia
ECCE	Early Childhood Care and Education, Malaysia
EPF	Employees Provident Fund, Malaysia
EPU	Economic Planning Unit, Malaysia
GDP	Gross Domestic Product
HIV/AIDS	Human immunodeficiency virus infection and acquired immune deficiency syndrome
IEC	Information, Education and Communication
ILO	International Labor Organisation
IMS	Institute of Medical-Sociology, Vietnam
IPS	Institute of Population Studies, Thailand
JKM	Jabatan Kebajikan Masyarakat Malaysia (Department of Social Welfare)
KAP	Knowledge, attitudes and practices
LFS	Labor Force Survey, Thailand
LINUS	Literacy and Numeric Screening, Malaysia
MAMA	Malaysian Maid Employers Association (Persatuan Kebajikan Amah Malaysia)
MIPAA	Madrid International Plan of Action on Ageing
MOCST	Ministry of Science and Technology, Vietnam
MOF	Ministry of Finance, Malaysia
MOH	Ministry of Health, Vietnam
MOLISA	Ministry of Labor, Invalids and Social Affairs, Vietnam
MoPH	Ministry of Public Health, Thailand
MPI	Ministry of Planning and Investment, Vietnam
MPFS	Malaysian population and family survey
MSDHS	Ministry of Social Development and Human Security, Thailand
MUWHLG	Ministry of Urban Wellbeing, and the Housing and Local Government, Malaysia
MWFCD	Ministry of Women, Family and Community Development, Malaysia

NACSA	National Assembly's Committee for Social Affairs, Vietnam
NDP	New Development Policy, Malaysia
NEDS	National Education Development Schemes, Thailand
NEP	New Economic Policy, Malaysia
NESDP	National Economic and Social Development Plan, Thailand
NESDB	National Economic and Social Development Board, Thailand
NFPP	National Family Planning Programme, Malaysia
NPFDB	National Population and Family Development Board, Malaysia
NRC	National Research Council, Thailand
NSO	National Statistical Office, Thailand
NXB	nhàxuấtbản (publishing house), Vietnam
OAPF	Old Age Pension Fund, Thailand
OPP	Outline Perspective Plan, Malaysia
OWAFD	Office of Women's Affairs and Family Development, Thailand
PAPA	Persatuan Agensi Pembantu Rumah Asing Malaysia (Malaysian Association of Foreign Maid Agencies)
PLI	Poverty Line Income
PRS	Private Retirement Scheme, Malaysia
QIAS	Quality Improvement Accreditation System, Malaysia
RM	Ringgit Malaysia
RSK	Rumah Seri Kenangan, Malaysia
RWT	RumahWargaTua, Malaysia
SECAPT	Socio-Economic Consequences of Ageing of the Population in Thailand
SINK	Single Income, No Kids
SOCSO	Social Security Organisation, Malaysia
SOPT	Survey of Older Persons in Thailand
SRVG	Socialist Republic of the Vietnam Government
SWET	Survey of Welfare of the Elderly in Thailand
TB	Thai Baht
TRF	Total Fertility Rate
UN	United Nations
UNCRC	United Nations Convention on the Rights of a Child
UNDP	United Nations Development Programme
UNFPA	United Nations Population Fund (formerly the United Nations Fund for Population Activities)
UNICEF	United Nation Children's Fund
VCP	Vietnamese Communist Party
VCPHCSC	Vietnam population and housing census
VEA	Vietnam Elderly Association
VGP	Vietnam Government Portal

VGSO	Vietnam General Statistics Office
VNA	Vietnam News Agency
VWU	Vietnam Women Union
WW	World War

Notes on Contributors

Asmidawati Ashari
Ph.D., Malaysian Research Institute on Ageing (MyAgeing), Universiti Putra Malaysia, Malaysia

Ki Soo Eun / 은기수
Ph.D., Associate Professor of Sociology and Korean Studies, Seoul National University, Republic of Korea

Tengku Aizan Hamid
Ph.D., Professor in Social Gerontology, Malaysian Research Institute on Ageing, Universiti Putra Malaysia, Malaysia

Rahimah Ibrahim
Ph.D., Faculty of Human Ecology, Universiti Putra Malaysia, Malaysia

Thuttai Keeratipongpaiboon / ธัชไท กีรติพงค์ไพบูลย์
Ph.D., National Economic and Social Development Board, Thailand

Nguyen Huu Minh
Ph.D., Associate Professor, Institute for Family and Gender Studies, Vietnam

Pataporn Sukontamarn / ปัทพร สุคนธมาน
Ph.D., Deputy Dean, College of Population Studies, Chulalongkorn University, Thailand

Jo-Pei Tan / 陈若琲
Ph.D., Faculty of Health, Psychology and Social Care, Manchester Metropolitan University, UK

Tran Thi Minh Thi
Ph.D., Institute for Family and Gender Studies, Vietnam

Kua Wongboonsin / เกื้อ วงศ์บุญสิน
Ph.D., Professor of Demography, Sasin Graduate Institute of Business Administration of Chulalongkorn University, Thailand

Patcharawalai Wongboonsin / พัชราวลัย วงศ์บุญสิน
Ph.D., Professor of Demography, College of Population Studies, Chulalongkorn University, Thailand

CHAPTER 1

Introduction

Patcharawalai Wongboonsin and Jo-Pei Tan

In the past, Asian parents were expected to take care of their children and in return, children were expected to reciprocate by caring for their parents, particularly in their old age. However, the demographic transition in various parts in Asia, which began in the first half of the 20th century, was notable for the reduction of the fertility rate, the expansion of life expectancy, increased education attainment and a shift in female labor force participation. These had strong implications on support provision and transaction between family members. In addition, modernisation, technological advancement and changing social norms that include shifting patterns in family values, marital bonds and intergenerational ties dramatically altered the landscape of family life in Asian societies. In the new terrain, it is strongly believed that there is a convergence toward small families, increased individualism and the weakening function of the family, which has led to a drastic change in age structure and family characteristics, as well as profound implication for the familial role in care provision. This is especially the case in traditional Southeast Asian societies where the public support system is limited. As they strive to cope with weakening family ties and young as well as old age support, governments are under increasing pressure to formulate policies that help to meet the challenges of care relations and old age support in the societies. This volume examines some of the most pressing issues in family life and intergenerational relations that affect support for older persons and children in modern times across developing Southeast Asian societies. It also examines current strategies and seeks to offer alternative and innovative policy responses to these developments.

Southeast Asian societies are noted for their diversity of cultural and religious traditions, having adherents of all the major belief systems. Thus, the amalgamation of traditional culture and religious beliefs is expected to diversify family forms, kinship systems and intergenerational ties, which have shaped the provision of care for older persons and children across Southeast Asian societies. The following sections present definitions of pivotal concepts that include the definition and concept of family, care, and kinship systems and how they relate to care relations. These are discussed within the context of Southeast Asian and are essential to understand the context and background of the volume.

 | DOI:10.1163/9789004384330_002

1 Key Terminologies

1.1 *Family*

1.1.1 Definition and Concepts of Family

While family is widely perceived as a primary social group, there is also a wide variation of definitions when looked at from different theoretical and cultural perspectives and studied in cross-disciplinary research between sociologists, psychologists, economists and political scientists. Georgas, Berry, Vijver, Kagitçibasi & Poortinga (2006) noted that the term *family* has cultural connotations, and is often labelled by many Western sociologists and psychologists as synonymous with *nuclear family*, the immediate family structure that includes a father, a mother and at least one child. Meanwhile, others see family as a social group encompassing a wider network of family members beyond the immediate family structure (Klein & White 1996). The notion is relevant to many Asian countries, even though in certain cases unrelated persons may be considered as part of the family.

Thus, this volume defines *family* within Southeast Asian communities as a manifestation of a *social unit network*, whereby it has a wide web of networks that encompass parents or elderly parents as the core element with adult children and other family members living in the same or different households. The discussion in the following sections aims to provide a general definition of family from multiple disciplines before delving into the more regional-specific definition, in light of the variation of kinship systems and family types in societies across Southeast Asia.

1.1.2 Features and Forms of Family

During the rapid socio-demographic transition amongst Southeast Asian societies, the notion of family was constantly challenged and reshaped by the changing social, economic and political tides of the last few decades. Family sociologist, Quah (2008) asserted the existence of a multiplicity of family forms and supported the notion raised by Levy (1949; 1945) of two distinguished family forms: *ideal* and *actual*. The *ideal family* refers to a vision of the family structure and relationships that one wishes to have in terms of parents, spouse, desirable number of children and the best family living arrangement, forged by the community's prevalent cultural values and political or religious ideology. While, the family form in practice or the *actual family* refers to the type of family ordinary people in the community can afford to have, given the real constraints of their socioeconomic, and political situation.

Relevant literature suggests that, dictated by different culture and traditions, there is variation across Southeast Asia. Certain communities are inclined to regard their *ideal family* as the extended family. This is the case, for example, in Malaysia (Ngin & DeVanzo 1999), Philippines (Medina 1991), Singapore (Quah 1998), Thailand (Schvaneveldt, Young, & Schvaneveldt 2001) and Vietnam (Thi 1999; Knodel, Friedman, Anh, & Cuong 2000). Over the decades, the rapid social, political and economic development across Southeast Asia challenged and reshaped such a concept.

Cultural anthropologists, who are interested in small societies throughout the world, have developed their theoretical perspectives to identify a broad spectrum of different family types, roles, kin relationships, and relationships with their societies. Based on cultural anthropological studies, *family* is considered as a social arrangement based on marriage (Stephens 1963, 8), despite others arguing against its oversimplification. For example, according to Valsiner (2000) in collective societies in African, Mediterranean and Asian regions where a particular household may include parents and children, there is also active interaction with the grandparents in a separate household in the same town that allows regular visits on a daily or weekly basis. Based on the interactions, the definition of *family* is expanded and ambiguous; 'Are we talking about two families, distributed over two households?' or 'Are we talking about one family, over two households?' In other words, the notion reflects a relatively fluid definition of the family.

This raises the question, 'Within Southeast Asian communities, who can be considered to be a family?' The expanded definition of family in Southeast Asia may reflect the overlap in relations between family and household. In fact, the characteristics of family as a wide social unit network are apparent among communities in the region. For example, Dube (1997) describes a Malay family as a household basically supposed to include a conjugal pair along with a network of supportive kin, with women maintaining close links with their kin. The significance of *kinship* among Malay communities is also reflected during a *divorce*. It is recorded that one of the conditions that freed a woman from the marital bond included keeping or taking her away from her kin, as well as physical violence, and the husband's failure to provide for the conjugal family. Setiadi (2006) adds that the divorcee tended to return to live with her parents.

An approach relevant and useful to the study of family is the examination of the dynamics among the family members within and beyond the social network. The family system constitutes a dynamic and evolving social system formed by the network of social relationships between spouses, parents-children and sibling relationships (Whitechurch & Constantine 1993). The socialisation experience inculcated within and outside of the family has close relevance to the study of family. The socialisation agent, as argued by Coleman (1990, 590–592), is not exclusive to parents but may encompass a variety of adults, including kin and non-kin. The latter, for example, includes friends of the parents, teachers, neighbours or even adult youth leaders who play a significant role in parent-child relationship. Thus, in the family, children may experience nurturance from a multiplicity of socialisation agents, who may become their significant others and role models.

As Valsiner (2000) suggested, this combination of criteria provides a typology of families by way of the establishment of what constitutes a household or a residence in Southeast Asian cultures. *Family can be perceived as combining a shared household (and its locality) with marriage as a social bond* (Stephens 1963, 8). In general, from the perspective of *post-marital* residence, *patrilocality*, also known as *virilocality*, refers to a social system in which a married couple sides with or near the husband's parents. *Matrilocality*, also known as *uxorilocal* residence, they reside with or near the wife's family. In those types of social system, the power role of the elderly parents with whom the adult children share the residence is maintained. *Neolocality* involves establishment of a new, separate household when an adult child marries or even when a child reaches adulthood and becomes active, economically and socially.

Based on this literature, this volume looks at the family within the Southeast Asian region as a 'network' unit, comprising a web of familial social networks with elderly parents as the focal element and adult children residing in the same or a different household.

1.2 *Care*

1.2.1 Care as a Concept

In general, care is a multidimensional concept which varies depending on the discipline and cultural context. There is a large body of literature on care, mostly in psychological, health services, social politics, economic, sociological and social policy research. The meaning and elements of care vary even within one discipline, and according to how it is perceived. One may see it as a functional activity, such as one involving work, tasks, or labor, while others may see it as a relational process, involving loving, thinking, and doing (Leira 1992). In a book on care-giving in the East and the West, Liu & Kendig (2000b) divide the *nature of care* into four major and not mutually exclusive categories: medical care, personal care, help with instrumental activities of daily living, and other non-specific care tasks (i.e. staying with and watching over someone for personal safety). It also includes nursing care and care-giving through formal channels that involves help with transportation, arranging services and benefits on behalf of a care recipient.

In addition, the *nature of care* can be both paid and unpaid work (Lewis 1984, 1991; Leira 1993), and formal and informal. From the perspective of the social division of labor, according to Graham (1991), caring is perceived as the unpaid work of kin within the private domain of their family and involves the transaction of goods and services as well as psychological support. In some cases, the term *care* is used more for relationships in which instrumental and expressive supports are fused inseparably. Thomas (1993) further unpacked the concept of care from individual, social, economic and political dimensions. They include the identity of the care providers and recipients, the relationship between them, the social content of care, the economic character of the relationship and the institutional setting within which care is provided.

In sociological research, care as a relationship is characterised by interconnectedness and interdependence (Tronto 1993; Bubeck 1995). Familial care or care within the family boundary may extend beyond immediate family members. One may differentiate between caring about, taking care of, and care-giving and care-receiving (Tronto 1993).

In terms of the care-giving role, the *boundary ambiguity* is the uncertainty among family members concerning who is in or out of the family and who is performing what roles and tasks within the family system (Boss 1993, 164; Pasley 1987, 206). Within the family, the perceived salience of the parental role is higher for women than it is for men (LaRossa & Reitzes 1993, 145–146). Quah (2008) argued that one would expect that boundary ambiguity affects more the care role of a father than that of a mother because she would have more likelihood of being psychologically and physically present for the children. In Confucian-based societies in parts of Southeast Asia, a father wields greater decision-making power than does a mother; however, in care-giving, he plays a lesser role during infancy of a child and his role as disciplinarian only develops as the child matures (Ho & Kang 1984). According to Magnis-Suseno (1984), a mother in Javanese families is expected to spend more time with a child for the purpose of care and discipline. The father's role is often seen in the interaction with the community as the protector of the entire family. Zhou & Bankston (1998) found a tendency for Vietnamese mothers to possess a large share of power within the household domain than tthose in East Asia, through managing family finances and playing the role of *noi-tuong* or 'home-minister'. Dube (1997) adds that it is also the case among most Thai, Malaysian, Indonesian women and Filipina. This ambiguous boundary may have implications for the role division and responsibility in the household domain between father and mother within the Southeast Asian familial context.

Similar assumptions could be applied in the analysis of care-provision role within the family. This is particularly from the perspective of gender parity between male and female members of the family in care provision. Drawing from the experience of Javanese families, a father tends to be the head of the family as reflected in the interaction within the community. He is accordingly expected to be the main breadwinner and protector of the entire family, besides making important decisions such as regarding the marriage of children, purchasing property and in punishing grave misbehaviour of the children. A Javanese mother tends to play a significant role in maintaining relationships and the provision of emotional support to all family members, besides managing the family finances being influential in such decisions as the choice of schools, jobs, and spouses for the children (Magni-Suseno 1984; Setiadi 2006).

Liu & Kendig (2000b) argue that defining the *need and nature of care* or care-giving is twofold in the context of cultural comparisons. First, the concept of need is in itself a function of social values as well as political culture; in countries with strong public services' provision, the concept of need can be regarded as entitlement. In social politics, one tends to look at care from the perspective of the nexus between care work and gender in the welfare regimes (Knijn & Ungerson 1997b; Knijn & Kremer 1997a; Daly & Lewis 2000). Such a division of labor can also be perceived in the dimension of *patriarchy*, specifically in East and Southeast Asian cultural contexts (Huber & Spitze 1998). Furthermore, Glicksman (2000), highlighted the significance of cultural diversity even within one society with respect to the care of the elderly as reflected in their different expectations for families and governments. Within this cultural heterodoxy, he raises major questions on how the state can work sensitively in sharing aged care responsibilities with different communities. This cultural consideration may be relevant to a multicultural Southeast Asian country, such as Malaysia, which comprises different ethnic groups with a substantial sub-population of Malays, Chinese and Indians.

Second, there are also wide variations in the way people consider transitional stages in life. This life-span view may affect care-giving in some ways. For example, in East Asia, care-giving is a continuous and reciprocal process for support that emphasizes mutual dependency among certain family members throughout their life span (Liu & Kendig 2000b). The cut-off point as to when the young are mature enough to provide care to their parents while still in some ways being cared for by parents is not always clear (Fry & Keith 1982). In addition, care, both giving and receiving, can be interpreted differently across cultural contexts. In a society emphasising personal *independence*, ageing without decrepitating makes care-giving irrelevant and unnecessary (Glascock & Feinman 1986). Decrepitating then is perceived as the pre-requisite for needing assistance. On the other hand, in cultures that value *interdependence* decrepitating may not be required before care-giving is received or expected. Merely negotiating or the recognition of getting old is sufficient for the young to render and for the old to receive assistance.

The strong socio-cultural roots of interdependence among communities in Asia can be identified in childrearing from early childhood. This cultural value not only characterises the relationship between parents and children as intense, but is also based on a family system of reciprocity, defined by caring and mutual obligations (Chao & Tsang 2002). Thus, in terms of childcare, mothers are expected to be primarily responsible and devote for their children's early care (Wu & Tseng 1985). Children, in turn, are expected to fulfil obligations and responsibilities to their families. For example, Filipino families are guided by the concept of '*utung na loob*', which translates literally as 'internal debt' (Almirol 1982). In addition, children can expect to receive support and assistance from other family members while also are expected to fulfil responsibilities to the family (Chao & Tsang 2002; Ismail, Tan & Ibrahim 2009).

Moreover, Southeast Asian parents are found to often share the childcare responsibilities with grandparents, uncles, aunts and cousins (Maria 2002; Tapanya 2011), especially those who live in the same household or in proximity (Frankenberg, Chan & Ofstedal 2002). Grandparents, especially grandmothers often help with supervision of house chores and the children, especially for working parents (Setiadi 2006). This contributes to strong bonds between the grandparents and the grandchildren. These grandparents tend to be more indulgent with their grandchildren and do not take up the duty as disciplinarians. Setiadi (2006) noted that among Javanese families in Indonesia, when parents are old, children have the duty to care for them. In most families in rural area, daughters are supposed to help their parents with household chores while the sons help in fields, and older daughters often take over some of the mother's responsibilities in the house such as cooking, washing and taking care of younger siblings. Not only does the responsibility to care transfer from mothers to daughters, married children have the duty to take care of their parents even if they do not live in the same house, neighbourhood or city. Adult children are also expected to support their grandparents, grandchildren, uncles, aunts and cousins in times of need. However, the extent of support depends on the proximity of their residences and the frequency of contact (Geertz 1961). Setiadi (2006) also noted that the extended support network tends to be more common and expected from neighbours in the rural areas and in the lower income communities in the cities.

Lately, more literature has emerged, focusing on the institutional setting, or the *care regime*, in which care is delivered. This includes both the private and public domains. Esping-Andersen (1990) and Esping-Andersen, Gallie, Hemerijck, & Myles (2002) include the state, the market, and the family in their *welfare-triangle model*. Besides these three sectors, community, voluntary, non-market or non-profit care providers are added to form the *welfare diamond* model (Evers, Pilj & Ungerson 1994). The extent to which care, whether it is child care or aged care, is viewed as a private or a public responsibility, still varies from one country to another, with care for both generations perceived more as a public responsibility in Europe and relatively more as a private responsibility in North America (Walker 2000).

Within traditional Asian culture, the primary task in providing care and support for children and older people rests within the family system. It is conceptualised as a private responsibility related to the kinship system and connected with gender roles in Southeast Asia, especially during times of need or family crisis (Liu & Kendig 2000b; Quah 2008; Butts, Thang & Yeo 2012). The private care arrangement may extend to include kin to assist parents with child care in times of need. For example, this is the case when parents face long work and commuting hours as a spill-over effect of the increasing labor force participation among women and expanded job opportunities (Chan 2005; Yaacob 2004).

Drawing upon the above notion, this volume looks at care as both function and responsibility. The responsibility includes childcare and elderly care in both the private and public domains. This responsibility includes, for example, medical treatment of the elderly and nursing care, livelihood of the elderly, child rearing and care work, children's education costs. Particularly in the private domain, the function of care for livelihood of the elderly includes emotional support and functional support (i.e. financial assistance and household chores). This volume aims to decipher the multifaceted forms of care from the social division of caring functions across and within the private and public domains to the social identity and role of the caregiver and care recipients, including children and elderly parents.

1.3 *Kinship Systems in Southeast Asian Societies*

The kinship system is a very strong force in which the principle and role of kinship is particularly important for many parts in East, South and Southeast Asia. Amongst these societies, the kinship system, as asserted by Dube (1997), provides the principles for group organisation and social identity, marriage and conjugal relations, entitlement to inheritance and resources, socialization and rights over children, post-marital residence and women's relationships, and, authority and power within the family and community. Specifically, different kinship systems were found to have different implications for the *nature of care* and the *responsibility* to provide care, which is often intertwined with the issues connected to religion, the economy and politics.

Literature on kinship systems among communities in Southeast Asia documented a variety of kinship systems of three principle types: patrilineal, matrilineal and bilateral. One may argue that Southeast Asia is predominantly bilateral (Errington 1990), while others recognised a variety patterns and configurations of the systems (Dube 1997). For example, there is a significant presence of the matrilineal system among the Minangkabau of West Sumatra and the people of Negeri Sembilan in Malaysia as well as in some patrilineal communities, especially the diaspora of Chinese and Indian communities in Southeast Asia (Dube 1997; Thambiah 2016; Setiadi 2006).

Literature on family research in Southeast Asian societies is still limited. Thus in the following sections, the various kinship systems are examined in relation to social identity, marriage and conjugal relations, divorce, entitlement to inheritance, rights over children and living arrangements. The discussion draws on research on communities in Indonesia, Malaysia, the Philippines, Singapore, Thailand and Vietnam.

1.3.1 Bilateral Kinship Systems

Bilateral kinship systems comprise the presence of both matrilineal and patrilineal systems in which the relatives of both parents are viewed as being equally important and discrete clans and lineage identities do not exist (Djamour 1959; Nagata 1976). In bilateral societies, a child is reckoned to be the child equally of both its parents, despite the notion that the mother's biological role and close relationship with the child tend to make her more important and to establish her rights over her children. Social identity is derived from both parents and the ancestors of both are recognised as kin. According to Maeda (1975) and Kling (1995), the bilateral system among Malay families in Malaysia specifies the exact boundary at which the family circle ended, which emphasised the broad and flexible membership without clear cut and fixed boundary exclusive only to the immediate family. For example, Malay bilateral families would have recognisable cross-linkage with three sets of families: two sets of parental families and a set of children's own families. Kling (1995), also found that outside the circle of the immediate family, others were generally classified as *saudara-mara* (kindred) which included close, almost kindred, and distance relatives of unspecified degrees.

A feature of bilateral societies is that marriage does not obliterate the earlier identity of its participants; it simply means that the new kin of the spouse are added. In bilateral societies, legitimate paternity does have significance but a child born out of wedlock is not discarded. For example, among the Muslim Malay in Malaysia, Dube (1997) argued that there was less fuss and outrage over a child born out of wedlock that was seen in the patrilineal communities of South Asia. Dube (1997) also noted that in Thailand, children of unidentified paternity were often brought up by their maternal grandparents. Thailand seemed to be more liberal in this respect, perhaps because Buddhism has few prescriptions and proscriptions relating to family matters (Dube 1997).

It can be seen that Islamic influence and local custom (*adat*) contribute to an interesting dynamic and practice within Malay families in Southeast Asia. The intertwining of Islamic law and *adat* (indigenous) law isalso acknowledged in civil law, such as marriage and inheritance in Malaysia and Indonesia (Setiadi 2006). In bilateral Muslim Malay *adat* or custom enjoined that property be divided equally among sons and daughters and there was a greater tendency to follow *adat* than Islamic law. Only those conscious of adhering to Islam and those having considerable self-earned money wish to follow Islamic rules of the division of property. Gender parity and the absence of discrimination between brothers and sisters in the allocation of resources and in the transmission of property are characteristics of Filipino and Thai cultures, reflecting bilaterality in these societies (Thambiah 2016).

Another cultural feature linked to the bilateral system is the tolerance of divorce (Jones 1981). It was found that the divorce rate in Southeast Asia in the 1950s was the highest in the world (Jones 1981, 1997); and it was deemed to be a marriage model with a 'traditional high divorce' rate (Goode 1993). One of the explanations for the high divorce rate was related to the economic independence and financial activity among women in the region. It was also not uncommon for women to seek support from their natal families during and after divorce (Thambiah 2016). Additionally, there was no stigma in getting a divorce or moral prestige for staying in a marriage if it was unsatisfactory and the couple was unhappy. In addition, the arrival of Islam reinforced the expectation of the 'avoidance of premarital sex', which led to increased early marriage and therefore more divorce (Jones 1981; Tsubouchi 1975).

The cultural and religious disposition of a culture has implications for child care from the perspective of women. For example, among the Thai, Dube (1997) stated that divorce was not considered a serious matter and it was not compulsory for women to give up her children when she remarried. However, poverty was the main cause for Thai women to carry the burden of living and bringing up children without the help of a man. Similarly, divorce was not viewed as unilateral decision, as a Malay woman could show her unwillingness to continue with marriage (Dube 1997). In terms of child custody, under Islamic law, the mother tended to maintain custody of the children if they were under age, while older children could choose their custodian (Setiadi 2006). Among the middle class in Indonesia, on divorce the husband and wife tended to divide the earnings they had accumulated during their married life. However, among the less educated with low income, the husband tended to leave the wife and children without sufficient support. In a way, the depiction of the role women in informal settings and family affairs, complemented by social identity may have contributed to skewed care responsibilities for women. In the Philippines, women have a strong position in the financial affairs of the household, taking both domestic and extra-domestic decisions. Filipino conjugal relations showed an egalitarian ethos: authority was diffused and the bilateral ethos is maintained (Setiadi 2006).

Among bilateral families, living arrangements after marriage are characterised by flexibility rather than strict prescriptions (Keyes 1995; Tsubouchi 1975). A married couple can choose among *patrilocality*, *matrilocality* or *neolocality* as their post-marital living arrangement. The flexibility in bilateral societies also makes it possible for a couple to begin married life with one set of parents and later move to the other set or to establish a household of their own. Some of previous studies documented matrilocality as the most common post-marital residence within a bilateral kinship system (Keyes 1995; Goode 1993). However, evidence showed that improvement of economic conditions, infrastructure and communication enabled young couples to travel further and move away from their parents or area of origin. As a consequence, in certain societies there was a higher tendency to live separately from parents. Nevertheless, most still maintained close relationships with their parents through regular visits, and grandparents often provided care for grandchildren when the parents were working (Setiadi 2006).

In discussing the unique features of the bilateral system, scholars have identified discrepancies between the *ideal* and *actual* practice within family and community (Setiadi 2006; Thambiah 2016). For example, the majority of Indonesians, especially those who lived in Java, could be considered as bilateral in terms of lineal descent where men and women supposedly had the same rights in the family inheritance. In practice, however, sons tended to receive a larger share than daughters. Even though the nuclear family was the basic family unit, one finds many three generation families in Indonesia. In fact, they could be categorised into two main types: (1) the married son/daughter brings his/her family to live with the parents; (2) the elderly grandparents live with their son/daughter's family. In both types, the male – the grandfather in the first type and the father in the second type – was the formal leader of the family, especially in dealing with the community and external affairs. Meanwhile, the grandmothers or the mothers had a more significant role in domestic affairs (Setiadi 2006).

1.3.2 Matrilineal Kinship Systems

In *matrilineal communities*, children of both sexes acquire permanent membership of the mother's descent group, which consist of relatives connected through female links and share common blood. A child thus derives its social identity from its mother. In other words, membership of descent groups under *matriliny* does not change at marriage. For resources distribution, a woman in matrilineal communities can use her group's resources, a part of which would be devolved on her children.

In terms of post-marital residence, on marriage a man moves into the house shared by his wife with her female kin and their husbands. For example, among the matrilineal society of Minangkabau of *West Sumatra*, traditional houses and land were corporately held by the kin group (Dube 1997). Women had exclusive rights over the *longhouses*. Due to the flexibility of the family boundary in Southeast Asia, mostly, an unmarried sister, mother or other close relative of the wife may be included. Similar to bilateral societies, kin support is apparent when separated from husband as the women exercise considerable choice in their entry into and exit from, marriage and on remarriage asserting rights over children is easy.

In matrilineal societies, a conjugal pair form the nucleus of the family but as mentioned earlier, there is certain flexibility in the constitution of the household. Children can move from one family to another, being brought up by kin. Divorce does not necessarily cause a serious disruption in the lives of the persons concerned. In Indonesia, relevant literature argued that Javanese women were in full command of the domestic domain and were the main figure of authority for children, as well as having an independent income. The relationship with the husband was more equal, respect was shown for the husband with some formal deference as he was generally older, and there may have differences in education, formal position and class but these were not used as a basis for assigning a wife an inferior status. In rural areas, divorce was very common, as the Javanese did not believe in continuing a marriage in the face of constant conflict (Setiadi 2006).

Unlike the flexibility of the bilateral system, matrilineal families specifically narrow their linkages to those focused on the mother only. This has implications for remarriage, for example, 'if a man remarries, he is in no position to choose to live with his father because his step-mother may not be from his clan and he is himself from another clan and the children are from another clan' (Kling 1995, 53). However, the Islamic influence modified the Malay Minangkabau matrilineal system slightly, by insisting on the importance of the father in a family (Kling 1995). A father would otherwise be considered as an outsider in his own family of orientation. Specifically, Islam emphasised the importance of the structural position of the father, who was provided with the power to take care of his family and children. In cases of marriage and divorce, the father was empowered by Islam to give away his daughter in marriage or pronounce divorce, in the case of separation from his wife. At the same time, he was also the mother's brother who was empowered by *adat* (custom) to protect his sister's family. These Malay matrilineal family systems were regarded as the traditional *adat* systems in relation to the Islamic system, incorporating the Islamic patrilineal elements in their family organisation. As provided by *adat* principles, Islamic codes were to take precedence over *adat* (Kling, 1995). To a certain extent, therefore, custom and norms among Southeast Asia communities were changed and modified to accommodate religious rules which were based on patrilineal and bilateral principles.

1.3.3 Patriarchy and Patrilineal Kinship Systems

According to Szołtysek, Klüsener, Poniat, Gruber (2017), *patriarchy* is categorised into four dimensions: male domination, generational domination, *patrilocality* and son preference. It characterises a society of a *patrilineal* structure which traces descent through the paternal line. Stivens (1998) stated that the Asian family ideology was used to reiterate Asian and patriarchal culture in which the father is the protector and the mother is the care giver, reinforcing the role of women as mothers and nurturers in the domestic or private domain.

From the perspective of care giving, while the obligatory norm of filial duty is loaded on the son in a patrilineal family, a daughter-in-law, by virtue of her position as the wife of the son, normally assumes the domestic responsibilities of caring for both her husband's children and her husband's ageing parents (Liu 2000a; Yu, Lai, Wen & Liu 2000). Liu & Kendig (2000b) noted that in a society dominated by patriarchal lineage, the role of daughter-in-law and her relationship with her mother-in-law is a critical issue in understanding the institution of patriarchy. In this system, a girl is always socialised under the shadow of an imaginary mother-in-law (Dube 1997). As a mother, her affection and desire to care for her children is both natural and instinctual but as the wife of the son, her affinity to the mother-in-law is only significant in terms of the role structure of the system and may not necessarily significant with respect to affective relationships (Wong 2000).

Some literature based on anthropological studies depicted communities in Southeast Asia as predominantly bilateral (Dube 1997; Errington 1990; Djamour 1959; Nagata 1976). Others perceived Southeast Asia as less patriarchal than other parts of Asia (Thambiah 2016; Atkinson 1982; Kling 1995). It was argued that the arrival of world religion and belief systems reshaped the relationship between men and women within the bilateral kinship system in Southeast Asia and provided a template for gender norms, which emphasised the major role of the man in organising and accounting for kinship links. The influence of certain religious beliefs, such as Islam (Andaya 2004; Djamour 1959) and

Christianity (Thambiah 2016), is noted to have constrained opportunities for women in the region and modified the custom and flexibility of the bilateral kinship system in the region. It was also argued that some key features of patrilineal kinship systems were apparent within the cultural matrix of Southeast Asia from the amalgamation of custom, religion and the political system (Cheu 1993).

The above contradictory notions of Southeast Asian societies form the rationale for this volume to examine if patriarchy existed in the family system there in the context of care relations along two major dimensions with different family settings: gender and generational domination. The former refers to domination of men over women and the latter refers to domination of the older generation over the younger generation. It contends that the matrix of these two patriarchy elements may have different implications for the nature and function of care and support for older and younger generations across three selected societies, namely Malaysia, Thailand and Vietnam.

2 Conceptual Frameworks

This volume of work is guided by a nexus of four conceptual frameworks to examine and understand the concept of care relations and consider the ways in which they may be construed differently according to cultural prescripts, individual and societal expectations, and expectations of government. These guiding frameworks are the demographic dividend, *familism*, intergenerational family solidarity, and welfare models.

2.1 *The Demographic Dividend*

Developing countries in Southeast Asia such as Thailand, Vietnam and Malaysia were subject to demographic and societal transformation and continue to experience an increase in the proportion of the aging population, despite the variation in amplitude between countries. In particular, Thailand was the first developing country there to attain the status of an aging society. This was followed by Vietnam while Malaysiais about to experience such an aging process (Wongboonsin & Wongboonsin 2008, 2013). There was a common concern that the increase in the aging population wouldhinder economic development through an increase in the demand for older age resources such as *social protection* and *long-term care*. The combined effects of these challenges may not be limited to the *middle-income trap*, but may also extend to the *quality of life* of the population in other age groups.

The concept of the *demographic dividend* serves as the pivotal driver for this examination of care relations across Thailand, Vietnam and Malaysia. In general, the concept of the demographic dividend is based on the link between demographic changes and economic development. It refers to demographic contribution to accelerating *economic growth* (Bloom, Canning & Sevilla 2003; UNFPA 2015). This is particularly in terms of the effect of age structure on the economy via labor supply, labor productivity, and the behavior of labor on savings (Wongboonsin & Wongboonsin 2014). The concept was conceived following the United Nations International Conference on Population and Development (ICPD) held in Cairo in 1994. It came at a time when the world was focusing on the interplay between population structure changes, economic growth and development (UNFPA 2015).

Theoretically, there are two phases of the demographic dividend. The first phase of the demographic dividend, or the *first demographic dividend*, occurs during a demographic transition process when fertility begins to rapidly decline. It results in the working-age population growing more rapidly than the young and old dependents. The *support ratio* accordingly rises and per capita income correspondingly increases. The first demographic dividend can last about five decades or longer (Bloom, Canning & Sevilla 2003; Lee & Mason 2010). Later on, due to low fertility rates and stable mortality, life spans increase. Accordingly, the young as well as the working-age population grow more slowly while the elderly population increases in proportion. The increase in the old-age dependency ratio signals the fading away of the opportunity to capitalize on the demographic conditions for the first demographic dividend. The increase in the proportion of the elderly population may lead to a situation, which constitutes a burden on the economy. In the case of Japan, Ogawa, Kondo & Matsukura (2004) call the negative impact of such a demographic change a *demographic onus* (Ogawa et al. 2004). Wongboonsin & Wongboonsin (2014) argue that the demographic onus may also constitute a burden to the society, the family, and the individuals.

An economy can be subject to a *second demographic dividend*, or increased *capital accumulation*, rather than the demographic onus. This can be the case if during the first demographic dividend, workforce and families are well prepared for greater wealth accumulation and greater *human-capital* investments for young generations as well as for *old-age security*. This is based on the notion that lower fertility rates and increased life expectancy can lead to greater wealth. Moreover, with fewer children to care for, it should be more possible to have more resources to invest in each of them (Mason & Lee 2006; Lee & Mason 2010). The second demographic dividend is typically larger than the first one. The combined effects of both demographic dividends on the GDP growth per effective consumer – the number of consumers weighted for age variation in consumption needs – are forecasted to range as high as 1.9% yearly in East and Southeast Asia (Lee & Mason 2006).

This volume of work is of the notion that the current structure of care provision for both the elderly and the children across generations has significant implications for the prospects of Malaysia, Thailand and Vietnam to capitalize on their demographic dividends. Declining optimum conditions for a demographic dividend in Thailand and Vietnam since 2010 and Malaysia between 2025 to 2030 has raised numerous concerns fortheir future economy and human resources development (Wongboonsin & Wongboonsin 2013).

Economists argue that the contribution of *labor productivity* is a determining factor for economic growth. Previous studies, particularly those in the mainstream scholarship of the *population-development nexus*, maintain that the demographic dividend requires the intertwining of these *policy conditions* for a more productive workforce: (a) economic policy: open markets; (b) labor policy: flexible labor markets; human resource development policy: high-quality health care and education; and (c) financial system: investment and saving incentives (Bloom, Canning & Sevilla 2003; Wongboonsin & Guest 2005; Mason & Lee 2006). Other scholars (Wongboonsin & Wongboonsin 2007; Wongboonsin & Wongboonsin 2008; Wongboonsin 2015) further highlight the contribution of an appropriate *family policy* to the demographic dividends, while arguing that it must be in place before the first demographic dividend is fading away so that the second demographic dividend is attained in an ageing society.

Based on the above notion, we are of the opinion that familism and intergenerational solidarity serve as a basis for a society to ensure a demographic dividend. Given these challenges, this volume also focuses on exploring appropriate policies and mechanisms at the national level to capitalise on the first demographic dividend and to secure the second, taking into account the varied prospects along with the diversity in developmental paths, socio-economic conditions, political systems and cultures across the three Southeast Asian countries.

2.2 *Familism*

Familism is a theoretical and empirical concept of cultural value that emphasises an ideal for family relationships to be one that is supportive and that family be prioritized over self (Sabogal, Marin, Regina, Barbara Vanoss, & Perez-Stable 1987; Garzón 2000; Steidel & Contreras, 2003; Behnke, MacDermid,

Coltrane, Parke, Duffy, & Widaman 2008; Hernández & Bámaca-Colbert 2016). Familism was primarily understood as a cultural construct among Latino families, *familismo* (Parke & Buriel 2006). Later on, literature applied the concept to other societies across the globe, from different perspectives. As suggested by Lopez (2009), the word familism can hold different meanings in different cultures, however, and may manifest itself in different ways. In Asia, scholars tend to look at familism together with the notion of *filial piety*. This is from the perspective that they both are associated with living in close *proximity* or shared households with family and contributing to the family's financial well-being (Fuligni, Tseng & Lam 1999; Yeh & Bedford 2003). This is also the case in other parts of the world, such as the United States (Schwartz, Weisskirch, Hurley, Zamboanga, Park, Kim, Umaña-Taylor et al. 2010).

Within its diverse manifestation, it is important to note that familism is considered a measure of *family solidarity* (Heller 1970). According to Heller (1970) the following five dimensions of familism measure family solidarity: (a) a sense of belongingness to the family, where non-family members are perceived as outsiders; (b) integration of the activities of persons belonging to the family, meaning that individuals in the same family act in a synergic way to achieve the aims of the family; (c) management of the property, such that financial resources and other material goods are the property of the entire family; (d) familial continuity or strong interest in the perpetuation of the entire family, manifest for example, in children receiving help from their parents in order to start a business activity that is in keeping with the family's expectations; and (e) mutual help, involving the friendly exchange of help between parents and their married children.

Over the years, the concept of familism has been reexamined and redefined by several scholars. For example, according to Baca & Wells (2000), familism can be categorized into demographic (e.g., family size), structural (e.g., proximity to family), behavioral (e.g., contact with family), and normative or attitudinal domains (e.g., beliefs about family). Steidel & Contreras (2003) saw familism as comprised of four dimensions, namely: (a) priority of the family over its individuals; (b) familial interconnectedness; (c) familial reciprocity in time of need; and (d) familial honour, which refers to a family member's behaving in a way that upholds family honour. Later on, Mucchi-Faina, Pacilli & Verma (2010) argue that there are two faces of familism: support obligations and traditional norms. It appears that the manifestation of familism has an emphasis on its functionality as an assessment of solidarity or connectedness among family members through more divergent dimensions.

2.3 *Intergenerational Family Solidarity*

In this volume, *intergenerational solidarity framework* (Bengston & Schrader 1982) is used to explore the norms and practice of intergenerational support across the three Southeast Asian societies. This is to provide understanding of care and support transactions between generations at the family level. While the type of support generally is distinguished into practical, financial and social support, the construct of intergenerational solidarity characterizes the types of support with regards to the behavioural and emotional dimensions of interaction, and cohesion and sentiment across generations of parents and children, grandparents and grandchildren (Bengston & Schrader 1982; Bengtson & Oyama 2007). These multi-facets and multi-dimensions of intergenerational solidarity are reflected in six elements of cross-generational interaction: affectual solidarity, referring to positive attitudes and evaluations family members express about their relationship with other members; associational solidarity, relating to type and frequency of contact between family members; consensual solidarity, reflecting the degree of agreement on opinions, values, and orientations between generations; functional solidarity, referring to the giving and receiving of support across generations; normative solidarity, including expectations regarding filial obligations and parental obligations as well as the importance of *familistic values*; and structural solidarity, reflecting the 'opportunity structure' for cross-generational interaction such as *geographic proximity* between family members.

The deployment of this framework on intergenerational family relations aims to shed light on the direction of care provision and transaction, and its magnitude according to the types of support given. In developing societies, the role of children as a form of old age security is far more important than it is in western societies. It is often reflected in financial support to parents and that *coresidence* of parents and adult children is common in many developing countries (Demeny 2004).

One of the more important claims in the literature is that the flow of *intergenerational exchange* has been reversed as societies become more modern. However, rapid demographic and socio-cultural changes in recent decades across Southeast Asia have put the topic of the flow of support across generations on the academic agenda. Thus, it is crucial to explore whether the flow is still upward and to what extent and specifically, how intergenerational solidarity and interaction at the family level explained the care provision and support exchange in the three countries under investigation, and if family solidarity and cross-generation reciprocity there are still maintained despite distance and other social changes affecting the family. Therefore, we also consider that intergenerational family solidarity should be promoted in order to reap the benefits of the *second demographic dividend.*

2.4 *Welfare Models*

Against the background of an ageing population, care provision, especially for the elderly, has become an increasingly important issue in the current literature; and in this context, the family has emerged as one of the more important potential sources of care and consequently, for well-being of older people, next to having good health and a decent pension. *Informal care* – by neighbours, family, and friends – is also regarded as an important addition to the more formal and more expensive types of care such as paid care services. Given the burden of care shouldered by family members, the role of the state as a welfare provider becomes noticeable, not only in western countries, but also in Southeast Asia, albeit to a different degree, with a different scope and with different features.

Thus, this volume adopts the *welfare models* as a guiding framework to identify the sectors in which care services are provided in Malaysia, Thailand and Vietnam. These welfare models share the notion that *familial care* is provided on an informal and unpaid basis while the care market provides care in return for earnings or fees and incorporates various sectors in care provision, namely the state, the market, the family, and a heterogeneous cluster of the community, as well as voluntary, non-market or non-profit care providers (Esping-Andersen 1990; Esping-Andersen, Gallie, Hemerijk & Myers 2002; Razavi 2007). In particular, Razavi (2007) proposed four institutions as active individuals or institutions taking part in formal and informal care provision for the elderly and the children: family/household, markets, the public sector and the *not-for-profit* sector, including voluntary and *community* institutions. According to Razavi & Staab (2008), both care *market* and non-profit sectors provide different types of care whether it is formal, informal, home-based or centre-based services. Care provision by the state or the public sector is formal and may be directly in the form of publicly organized or financed centre-based services and/or indirectly by subsidizing the family/household, market, or non-profit providers to provide care. Regulating these *non-state care providers* is also part of the state's role in the realm of care.

Based on these models, this volume focuses on exploring the most responsible care provider taking part in formal and informal care provision for the elderly and the children within these societies. For the attitudes towards care provision, we investigate the *family-state balance* of responsibility regarding different aspects of elderly and child care based on the notion of *shared responsibility* between the family and the state raised in Daatland & Herlofson (2003) in modern welfare states. Thus, an investigation into the attitude of individuals towards care provision for the elderly and children can contribute to a better understanding of whether *familialism* prevails across the three societies or if *defamilizing care* can be instead expected.

3 Hypotheses

Quah (2008) asserted that there are vast challenges in family research in Southeast Asia. Firstly, Asian countries vary widely in terms of population and geographical size, ethnic composition, level of socioeconomic development and political systems, among other aspects. Second, a major constraint on comparative analysis is the absence of a standardised Asian wide databank on families, or the equivalent of comprehensive panel household surveys conducted in the United States or the European community by agencies such as the European Observatory on National Family Policies (Ditch, Barnes, Bradshaw & Kilkey 1998). In the most recent book by Quah (2008), data and information on the Asian family tend to focus on two general sources: *micro-level data* from published social science studies of the family from accessible research, and relevant *macro-level* (i.e. population) data published by international organisations and national governments. However, it was noted that the latter source was problematic due to unevenness in data reporting and of available population statistics (i.e. irregular and sporadic population characteristics and census data in some Asian countries).

On one hand, the data and findings presented this volume offer a fresh multidisciplinary perspective along a multilevel macro, *meso* and micro analysis of care relations in three ageing, middle income societies. It highlights the changes and continuity in care relations across different societies and time spans. On the other hand, it also addresses the literature gap by providing a nexus of different perspectives – cultural, demographic, socio-economic development and political – that are intertwined with care relations. It provides a better understanding of the context of care relations in three different Southeast Asian societies against the backdrop of modernization, socio-cultural changes and economic development.

Drawing on the discipline of demography, psychology, gender and family studies, and social welfare as well as findings from empirical data, this volume frames the emerging needs, changing expectations and new challenges that have an impact on care exchange and provision across generations. Four hypotheses are reintroduced in this volume. All the hypotheses are derived from the theoretical framework discussed above; while hypotheses 3 and 4 guide the analysis strategy to explore, in more depth, the associations between the characteristics of adult children, the characteristics of parents, familial factors, family-in-law and living arrangements, with care transactions for the three societies. All these hypotheses are examined in this volume using empirical data from the three societies in transition. These hypotheses also serve to open avenues of understanding and to stimulate debate about where the empirical findings might take us. The hypotheses tested for this volume are as follows:

(1) *Strong* family relationships led to care provision by family.
(2) Southeast Asian Families were *patriarchal* in the context of care relations;
(3) Care transactions within Southeast Asian families were more attributable to the *parent's characteristics* than the children's characteristics.
(4) There was a difference between *attitude* and *practice* for intergenerational support within Southeast Asian families.

This volume explores and examines care relations and transactions within and beyond the family network across Malaysia, Thailand and Vietnam. The main focus of the volume is to address changes in care relations across the three societies at both the national and specific-area levels. The latter refers to Kuala Lumpur in Malaysia, Bangkok Metropolis in Thailand, and Hanoi in Vietnam. It aims to provide a better understanding of care relations, from the perspectives of childcare and elderly care. It also seeks to offer policy recommendations and social innovations to address the current and future challenges in care relations for aging societies which expect to move away from the middle-income trap.

4 Structure of the Volume

The volume comprises nine chapters. Chapter 1 serves as the introductory chapter. It first looks at the definition of pivotal concepts that include family, the nature and needs of care, and the kinship systems, namely the bilateral, matrilineal and patrilineal system. These are discussed within the context of Southeast Asia and how they relate to care relations across the three middle-income societies under investigation. The chapter also discusses the guiding frameworks, which are the demographic dividend, familism, intergenerational family solidarity, and welfare models, that serve as drivers for the investigation of care relations and transactions within and beyond the family network.

Thereafter, the volume is divided into three parts: Part 1, covers cultural, demographic and socio-economic background of care relations; Part 2, attitudes and practices in care; and Part 3, provides a synopsis and way forward.

Part 1 includes three chapters exploring changes in care relations at the national-level perspective of Malaysia (chapter 2), Thailand (chapter 3) and Vietnam (chapter 4). Based on archival research, the analysis was carried out against the cultural background and the changing demographic, socio-economic and political contexts of each country. Each of the three chapters follows a similar outline of discussion for each respective country. They start with a discussion on the cultural background, followed by socio-economic and demographic changes therein. Each of the three chapters also documents the progress of the regimes and the changes in care relations for each respective country. In terms of cultural background, it explores the culture and custom, gender role in family relations, and child preferences. From the perspective of socio-economic development, it elaborates issues related to modernisation and economic development, urbanisation and migration, and employment and education in each country. The demographic transition of each country is discussed in relation to fertility, population structure, family composition and size as well as trends in marriage and divorce. Each chapter also provides an analysis of the changes and initiatives in policy and legislation in each respective country up to 2017. In the last section of each chapter, an overview of its care regime for children and elderly is provided. Besides the family network, the role of the state, market, not-for-profit and other sectors are discussed. The unique characteristics of each of the three countries in the above-mentioned aspects are the focus.

To contribute to a better understanding of intergenerational family solidarity, Part 2 comprises three chapters, each of which focuses Kuala Lumpur and Selangor, Bangkok Metropolis, and Hanoi. They are purposively selected as case studies of societies in transition.

Kuala Lumpur, or officially the Federal Territory of Kuala Lumpur, is commonly known as KL. According to the 2010 Population and Housing Census of Malaysia, or Census 2010 (DOSM 2011), it is the national capital of Malaysia as well as its largest city, with a population of 1.67 million in 2011, when the survey for this volume was carried out. It was the most densely populous state (6,891 persons per square kilometre), with a 100% level of urbanization. Kuala Lumpur was previously part of *Selangor*, currently an adjacent state. Selangor was the most populous state (5.46 million in 2011) in Malaysia, yet ranked much lower in terms of population density (674 persons per square kilometre) with a 91.4% level of urbanization.

Bangkok Metropolis, or *Bangkok* in short, is the capital and most populous city of Thailand. It had an estimated population of 8.31 million, or 12.5% of the total population in Thailand, according to data from the 2010 census, a 2.8% increase from the 6.3 million recorded in 2000 (NSO 2012). However, only

5.7 million of them were registered residents. The population density was 5,751.5 persons per km^2. During daytime, Bangkok Metropolis became more populous (15 million), due to the daytime population commuting from neighbouring provinces to work there. Bangkok is part of the so-called *Bangkok Metropolitan Area,* which is a political definition of an urban area comprising Bangkok Metropolis and five adjacent provinces. They are *Nakhon Pathom, Pathum Thani, Nonthaburi, Samut Prakan,* and *Samut Sakorn.* Those five adjacent provinces were excluded from the survey for this volume.

Hanoi, the capital of Vietnam, is the country's second largest city by population, comprising 1 town (181,831 population), 12 urban districts (3.4 million population), and 17 rural districts (about 4 million population), with an average annual urban population growth rate of 4.2% according to the 2009 Population and Housing Census (VCPHCSC 2010). Among the three societies under investigation in this volume, Hanoi had the lowest population density (1,926 persons per km^2).

The empirical evidences in Part 2 are primarily based on the merged data of the three most recent family surveys carried out in Kuala Lumpur & Selangor, Bangkok Metropolis, and Hanoi by these research insitutions: Universiti Putra Malaysia, Kuala Lumpur, Malaysia in 2011; College of Population Studies' Human Development & Migration Studies Center, Chulalongkorn University, Bangkok Metropolis, Thailand in 2010; and Institute for Family and Gender Studies, Hanoi, Vietnam during 2010–2011. All the three surveys were adapted from the standard questionnaires in the 2006 East Asian Social Survey (*EASS*) family module.

The family survey in Kuala Lumpur & Selangor followed a stratified multistage sampling method. The state of Selangor was stratified into urban and rural, while Kuala Lumpur only has an urban stratum. For each stratum, 78 Enumeration Blocks (EBs) were selected, totalling 234 EBs. For each EB, eight households were chosen, and one respondent from each household was interviewed. Multi-stage sampling was used to allow for ethnic and age group comparison. The sample's ethnic proportion was the ratio of 50:35:15 for Malays, Chinese, and Indians respectively. Out of the total 1,883 respondents aged 18 and above, 51% of them were female, and 49% were male. This part only analyses data from the 1,523 respondents who provided complete information on all the selected variables for this volume. For brevity, the analysis in Part 2 will refer to this survey just as the Kuala Lumpur survey, and Kuala Lumpur & Selangor as just Kuala Lumpur.

The Bangkok Metropolis family survey relied upon a stratified and clustered sampling technique along a multi-stage sampling approach, starting with districts in each part of Bangkok Metropolis, then sub-districts, zones, blocks/communities and households. The Bangkok Metropolis family survey covered 40 out of 50 districts in Bangkok Metropolis. It selected one sub-district from each district, one zone from each sub-district, one block from each zone in which about 35 households (or a range of 15–30% of all households) was selected from each block/community followed by one household member per household. To ensure equal ratios of gender, one male and one female household member in every alternate household were interviewed. However, when a male member of the household was not available, interviewers were permitted to substitute the male interviewee with a female interviewee and vice versa Overall, 1,092 respondents aged 18 and above were interviewed. 64% of them were female, while male respondents accounted only for 36%. For the analysis, specifically in Part 2, respondents with missing information were dropped, and this led to an analysis of 910 samples from Bangkok Metropolis.

Based on a cluster sampling approach, the Hanoi family survey was conducted in 24 wards/communes across three different regions whereby it included eight urban wards, eight communes bordering the inner city, and eight communes separated from the inner city in Hanoi. Fifty households were chosen randomly from each ward/commune. In total, 1,118 out of 1,219 respondents aged 18 years and above with complete information on all selected variables were included in the analysis. 54% of them were female, and 46% male.

Overall, the age range of the respondents in the analysis in Part 2 was between 18 and 96 years old, see Figure 1.1, Figure 1.2 and Figure 1.3. Despite the data shown in Figure 1.4 revealing that the respondents in the three societies belonged to different living arrangements, the majority of them lived in a 2-generation household. This was particularly the case in Kuala Lumpur. More than 30% of the respondents in Hanoi lived in a 3-generation household, compared to only 20% in Bangkok Metropolis and about 15% in Kuala Lumpur. The category called 'others', which included skip-generation household and a nuclear-family-with-sibling household, accounted for up to 19% of the respondents, the highest proportion among the three societies. This was followed with a slightly lower proportion by those in Kuala Lumpur (18% of the total respondents there).

Chapters 5 and 6 in Part 2 examine and compare the pattern of *care transactions* between adult children and parents as well as their *parents-in-law* in *coresident* and *non-coresident* families, respectively, in Kuala Lumpur, Bangkok Metropolis and Hanoi, based on a Bengston's intergenerational solidarity framework (Bengston & Schrader 1982). The analysis was carried out from the perspective of the effect of adult children and parents' characteristics and, filial norms and expectations that made care relations unique to the three societies. The comparative analysis included *t-test* and *ANOVA* across age,

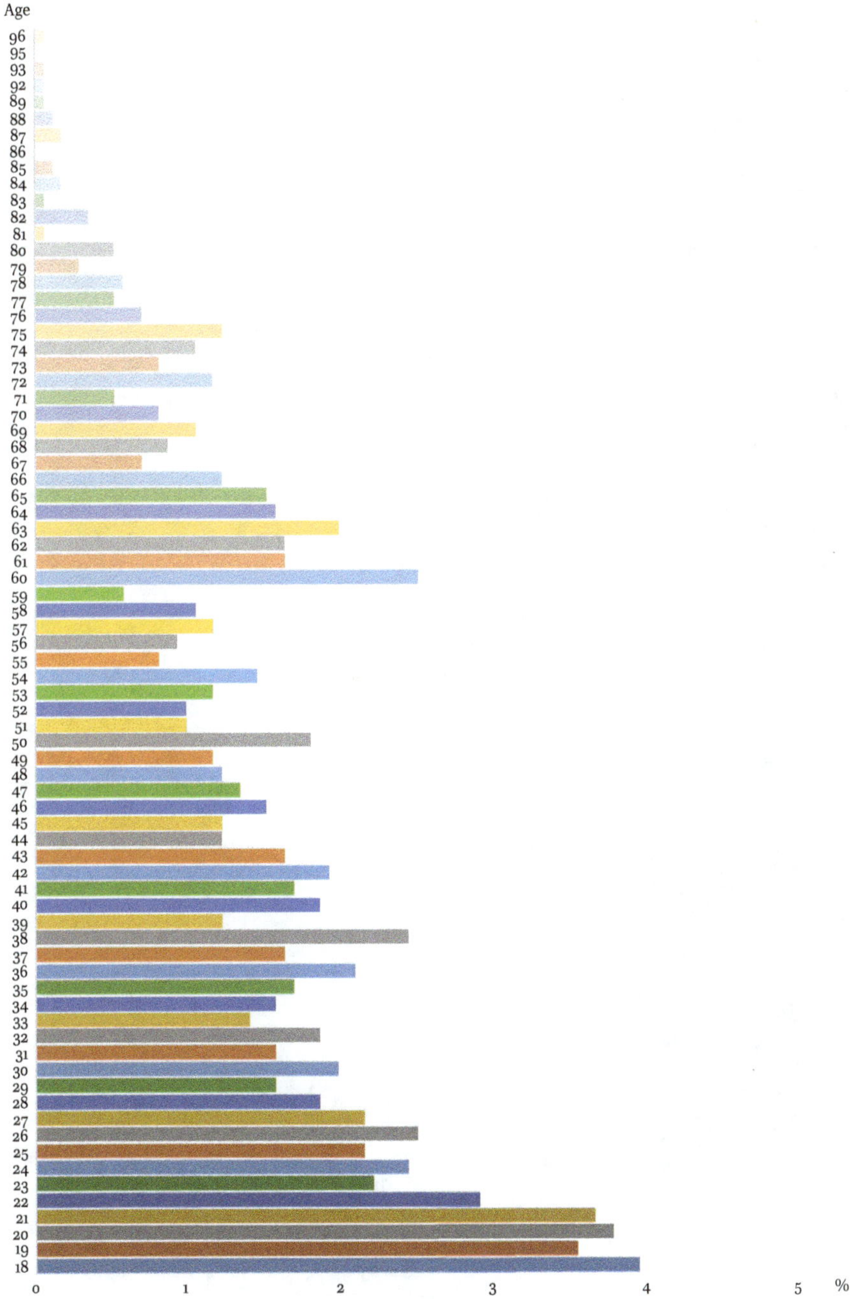

FIGURE 1.1 Age distribution of respondents in Kuala Lumpur
SOURCE: 2011 KUALA LUMPUR FAMILY SURVEY

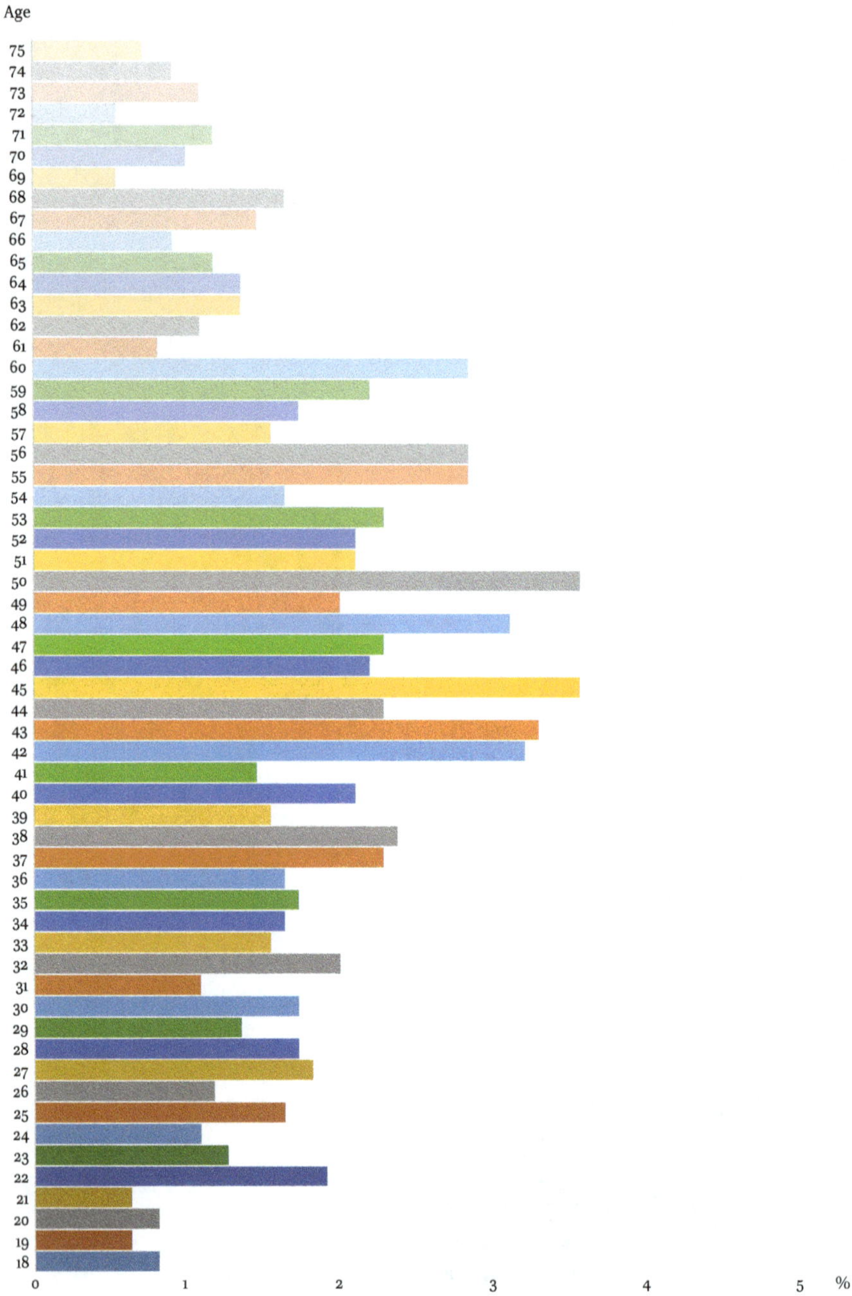

FIGURE 1.2 Age distribution of respondents in Bangkok Metropolis.
SOURCE: 2010 BANGKOK METROPOLIS FAMILY SURVEY.

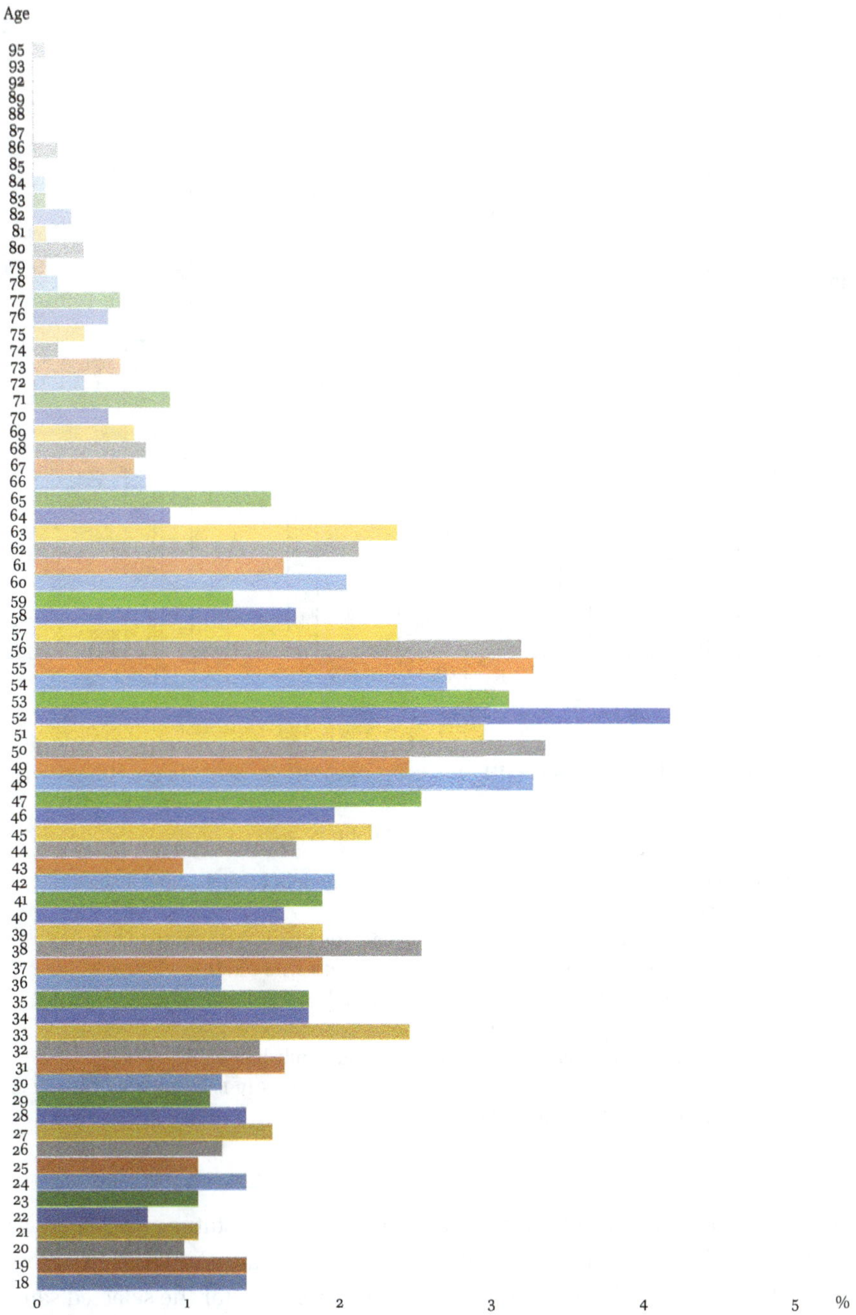

FIGURE 1.3 Age distribution of respondents in Hanoi.
SOURCE: 2010 HANOI FAMILY SURVEY.

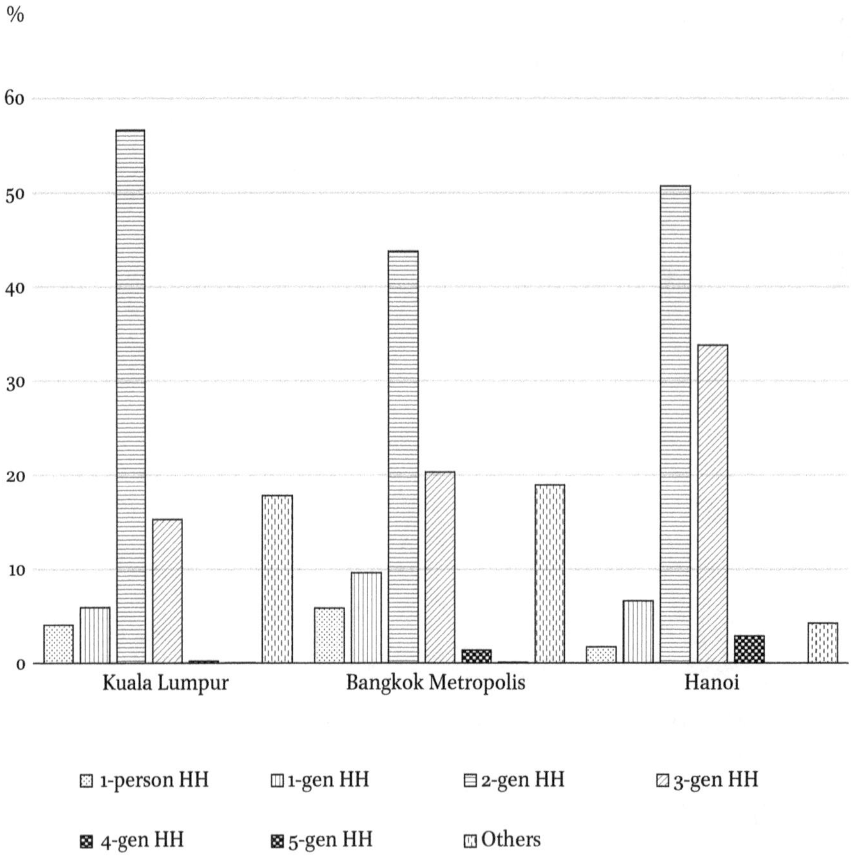

FIGURE 1.4 Percentage of respondents by living arrangement in Kuala Lumpur, Bangkok Metropolis and Hanoi.
Note: HH = Household: 1-gen HH = 1-generation household (husband + wife);
2-gen HH = 2-generation household (husband + wife + kid);
3-gen HH = 3-generation household; 4-gen HH = 4-generation household
6-gen HH = 5-generation household;
Others = Skip-generation household; nuclear family household + sibling.
SOURCES: 2011 KUALA LUMPUR FAMILY SURVEY; 2010 BANGKOK METROPOLIS FAMILY SURVEY; 2010 HANOI FAMILY SURVEY.

education, gender, marital status, interaction of marital status and gender, as well as health status among parents and parents-in-law. Comparison across strata, living standard and ethnicity was also carried out for the selected sample in Kuala Lumpur and Hanoi. Further *multivariate analysis* was performed to identify significant factors affecting intergenerational care relations in the three societies.

In chapter 7, besides elderly care, the practices and attitudes towards childcare in both formal and informal dimensions were also investigated. To do so, five different sectors involved in care provision and practice were analysed and they were the family, state, market, not-for-profit and others. The chapter further examined the attitudes towards the role and responsibility of the state and family from the family-state balance perspective for different types of elderly and childcare. They were, namely, elder's medical treatment & nursing care, elder's general livelihood, children's rearing & care work and children's educational costs. Further *logistic regression* analyses were performed to determine the unique factors affecting those attitudes for each society.

In Part 3, chapter 8 synthesised the empirical evidence from all the chapters in Part 2 to identify similarities and differences in intergenerational support and care provision in Kuala Lumpur, Bangkok Metropolis and Hanoi. Specifically, this chapter critically analysed findings from the three family surveys conducted in the three selected areas to address the previously discussed hypotheses derived from the literature. This chapter is divided into three sections. The first section, which focused on family relationships and care provision, identified the significance of family in care provision within the three societies. Yet, diversity existed in their attitudes of and practices in intergenerational support. The second section demonstrated evidence that challenged the notion of a common patriarchal family system and its association with care relations among coresident and non-coresident families across the three Southeast Asian societies. The final section revealed a stronger contribution of adult children's characteristics in comparison to parents' characteristics and familial factors in predicting intergenerational support from adult children to parents and parents-in-law among coresident and non-coresident families in Kuala Lumpur, Bangkok Metropolis and Hanoi. Furthermore, it evidenced the existence of reciprocal support which reflected an active downward support from parents to adult children across all three societies, regardless of living arrangement.

Finally, chapter 9 is divided into three sections: looking back, looking forward, and policy recommendations for moving forward. In doing so, it provided a synopsis of the findings care relations at the national level in Part 1 that are intertwined with key findings on the attitudes and practice of intergenerational care relations at the specific-area level, particularly those identified in chapter 8. While doing so, it argued that the economic, demographic and socio-cultural transition resulted in a complex dimension of care.Such complexity rendered difficulties for the adult children to sustain their role in familial care, particularly for the elderly, over the long-term. These notions led to the second section, which looked forward to further challenging structural transitions, especially from the perspective of demographic transition, which were foreseen to be more dynamic in the decades to come, together with socio-economic impacts in the three Southeast Asian countries. It argued that the three countries in this part of Southeast Asia are expected to be characterized as aging, aged and super-aged societies. Malaysia would become one of the speediest countries in the world to become an aging society in less than two decades from now, and to turn into an aged society within half a decade thereafter. By the time of Vietnam's becoming an aged society during 2030–2040, a super-aged society will have characterised Thailand. The changing landscape of the age structures in years to come are expected to further limit intergenerational family relations, especially in care provision. Chapter 9 further argued that such a demographic shift in the near future was a current concern at the policy making level of the three countries, for it can be expected to adversely affect old-age security and the economic development process. It highlights that the demographic transition in years to come would derail the possibility for a 2nd demographic dividend there if the prevailing approach of policy making in the three countries remains. Chapter 9 calls for Malaysia, Thailand and Vietnam to assure the prospects of being caring societies with sustainable welfare so as to benefit from the 2nd demographic dividend. To do so, it proposed that care should be regarded as a social investment, in which the other four sectors of care provision form a partnership to share the care responsibility for current and future generations to enjoy societal and economic well-being. Some of the policy measures were finally provided for future old-age financial security while minimizing the negative impacts of future structural transitions on the family.

References

Almirol, Edwin B. (1982). Rights and obligations in Filipino American families. *Journal of Comparative Family Studies*, 13, 291–305.

Andaya, Leonard Y. (2004). A very good-natured but awe-inspiring government: The reign of a successful queen in seventeenth-century Aceh. In Locher-Scholten Elsbeth, & Peter Rietbergen (Eds.), *Hof en handel: Aziatische vorstenen de VOC 1620–1720* (pp. 59–84). Leiden: KITLV Uitgerverij.

Atkinson, Jane Monnig. (1982). Anthropology. *Signs: Journal of women in culture and society, 8*(2), 236–258.

Baca, Zinn M., & Barbara Wells. (2000). Diversity within Latino families: New lessons for family social science. In David H. Demo, Katherine R. Allen, & Mark A. Fine (Eds.), *Handbook of family diversity* (pp. 252–273). New York: Oxford University Press.

Behnke, Andrew, Shelley MacDermid, Scott Coltrane, Ross Parke, Sharon Duffy, & Keith F. Widaman. (2008). Family cohesion in the lives of Mexican American and European American parents. *Journal of Marriage and Family, 70*(4), 1045–1059.

Bengtson, Vern, & Petrice S. Oyama. (2007). *Intergenerational solidarity: Strengthening economic and social ties.* New York: United Nations.

Bengtson, Vern, & Sandi Schrader. (1982). Parent-child relations. In David Mangen, & Warren Peterson (Eds.), *Research instruments in social gerontology* (Vol. 2), (pp. 115–186), Minneapolis: University of Minnesota Press.

Bloom, David E., David Canning, & Jaypee Sevilla. (2003). *The demographic dividend: A new perspective on the economic consequence of population change.* Santa Monica: Rand.

Boss, Pauline G. (1993). The reconstruction of family life with Alzheimer's disease. In P. Boss, W.J. Doherty, R. LaRossa, W.R. Schumm, & S.K. Steinmetz (Eds.), *Sourcebook of family theories and methods: A contextual approach* (pp. 163–166). New York: Plenum.

Bubeck, Diemut Elisabet. (1995). *Care, gender and justice.* Oxford: Clarendon Press.

Butts, Donna M., Leng L. Thang, & Alan H Yeo. (2012). Policies and programmes supporting intergenerational relations. White Paper. New York: Secretariat of the United Nations.

Chan, Angelique. (2005). *Formal and informal intergenerational support transfers in South-Eastern Asia.* Paper presented at the United Nations expert group meeting on social and economic implications of changing population age structures, Mexico City, Mexico.

Chao, Ruth, & Vivian Tseng. (2002). Parenting of Asians. In M.H. Bornstein (Series Ed.), *Handbook of parenting: Vol. 4. Social conditions and applied parenting* (pp. 59–93). Mahway, New Jersey: Lawrence Erlbaum Associates.

Cheu, Hock Tong. (1993). *Chinese beliefs and practices in Southeast Asia: Studies on the Chinese religion in Malaysia, Singapore and Indonesia.* Malaysia: Pelanduk Publications.

Coleman, James. (1990). *Foundations of social theory*, Cambridge, Massachusetts: Harvard University Press.

Daatland, Svein Olav, & Katharina Herlofson. (2003). 'Lost solidarity' or 'Changed solidarity': A comparative European view of normative family solidarity. *Ageing and Society, 23*, 537–560.

Daly, Mary, & Jane Lewis. (2000). The concept of social care and the analysis of contemporary welfare states. *British Journal of Sociology, 51*(2), 281–298.

Demeny, Paul. (2004). *Developing economic support systmes for the old-age population in Asia: Learning from the mistakes of Western welfare states.* Paper published as part of the international conference on the demographic window and healthy aging: Socioeconomic challenges and opportunities, Beijing, China.

Ditch, John, Helen Barnes, Jonathan Bradshaw, & Majella Kilkey. (1998). *A synthesis of national family policies 1996*. European observatory on national family policies. York: Social Policy Research Unit, University of York.

Djamour, Judith. (1959). *Malay kinship and marriage in Singapore.* London: The Athione.

DOSM. (2011). *2010 population and housing census of Malaysia.* Putrajaya: Department of Statistics, Federal Government Administrative Centre.

Dube, Leela. (1997). *Women and kinship: Comparative perspectives on gender in South and South-East Asia.* Tokyo: United Nations University Press.

Errington, Shelly. (1990). Recasting sex, gender, and power: a theoretical and regional overview. In J. Atkinson, & S. Errington (Eds.), *Power and difference: gender in island Southeast Asia* (pp. 1–58). Stanford, CA: Stanford University Press.

Esping-Andersen, Gøsta, Duncan Gallie, Anton Hemerijck, & John Myles. (2002). *Why we need a new welfare state.* New York: Oxford University Press.

Esping-Andersen, Gøsta. (1990). *The three worlds of welfare capitalism.* Princeton, NJ: Princeton University Press.

Evers, Adelbert, Marja Pilj, & Clare Ungerson (Eds.). (1994). *Payments for care.* Aldershot, UK: Avebury.

Frankenberg, Elizabeth, Angelique Chan, & Mary Beth Ofstedal. (2002). Stability and change in living arrangements in Indonesia, Singapore, and Taiwan, 1993–1999. *Population Studies, 56*, 201–213.

Fry, Christine L., Jennie Keith. (1982). The life course as a cultural unit. In M.W. Riley, R. Abeles, & M.S. Teitelbaum (Eds.), *Aging from birth to death: Sociotemporal perspectives* (pp. 51–70). Boulder, CO: Westview Press.

Fuligni, Andrew J., Vivian Tseng, & May Lam. (1999). Attitudes toward family obligations among American adolescents with Asian, Latin American, and European backgrounds. *Child Development, 70*, 1030–1044.

Garzón, Adela. (2000). Cultural change and familism. *Psicothema, 12*(Supl.), 45–54.

Geertz, Hildred. (1961). *The Javanese family: A study of kinship and socialization.* London: The Free Press.

Georgas, James, John W. Berry, Fons J.R. van de Vijver, Çigdem Kagitçibasi, & Ype H. Poortinga (Eds.). (2006). *Families across cultures: A 30-nation psychological study.* Cambridge: Cambridge University Press.

Glascock, Anthony P., & Susan L. Feinman. (1986). Treatment of the aged in non-industrial societies. In C.L. Fry (Ed.), *Aging in culture and society: Comparative viewpoints and strategies* (pp. 281–296). New York: J.F. Bergin.

Glicksman, Allen. (2000). The social context of the nature of care. In W.T. Liu, & H. Kendig (Eds.), *Who should care for the elderly? An East-West value divide* (pp. 68–77). Singapore: Singapore University Press.

Goode, William J. (1993). *World changes in divorce patterns.* New Haven, CT: Yale University Press.

Graham, Hilary. (1991). The concept of caring in feminist research: The case of domestic service. *Sociology, 25*(1), 61–78.

Heller, Peter L. (1970). Familism scale: A measure of family solidarity. *Journal of Marriage and Family, 32*(1), 73–79.

Hernández, Maciel M., & Mayra Bamaca-Colbert. (2016). A behavioral process model of familism. *Journal of Family Theory & Review, 8*(4), 463–483.

Ho, David Y., & Tsi Kit Kang. (1984). Intergenerational comparisons of childrearing attitudes and practices in Hong Kong. *Development Psychology, 20*(6), 1004–1016.

Huber, Joan, & Glenna Spitze. (1998). Trends in family sociology. In Neil Joseph Smelser (Ed.), *Handbook of sociology* (pp. 425–448). Newbury Park, California: Sage Publications.

Ismail, Nellie, Jo-Pei Tan, & Rahimah Ibrahim. (2009). The relationship between parental belief on filial piety and child psychosocial adjustment among Malay families. *Pertanika Journal of Social Science and Humanities, 17*(2), 215–224.

Jones, Gavin W. (1981). Malay marriage and divorce in Peninsular Malaysia: Three decades of change. *Population and Development Review, 7*, 255–278.

Jones, Gavin W. (1997). Modernization and divorce: Contrasting trends in Islamic Southeast Asia and the West. *Population and Development Review, 23*(1), 95–114.

Keyes, Charles F. (1995). Who are the Tai? Reflections on the invention of local, ethnic, and national identities. In Lola Romanucci-Ross, & George De Vos (Eds.), *Ethnic identity: Creation, conflict, and accommodation* (pp. 136–161), Walnut Creek, California: Alta Mira.

Klein, David M., & James M. White. (1996). *Family theories: An introduction*. Thousand Oaks, CA: Sage Publications.

Kling, Zainal. (1995). The Malay family: Beliefs and realities. *Journal of Comparative Family Studies, 26*(1), 43–66.

Knijn, Trudie, & Monique Kremer. (1997a). Gender and the caring dimension of welfare states: Toward inclusive citizenship. *Social Politics, 4*(3), 328–361.

Knijn, Trudie, & Claire Ungerson. (1997b). Introduction: Care work and gender in welfare regimes. *Social Politics, 4*(3), 323–327.

Knodel, John E., Jed Friedman, Truong Si Anh, & Bui The Cuong. (2000). Intergenerational exchanges in Vietnam: Family size, sex composition and the location of children. *Population Studies, 54*(1), 89–104.

LaRossa, Ralph, & Donald C. Reitzes. (1993). Symbolic interactionaism and family studies. In P.G. Boss, W.J. Doherty, R. LaRossa, W.R. Schumm, & S.K. Steinmetz (*Eds.*), *Sourcebook of family theories and methods: A contextual approach* (pp. 135–163). New York: Plenum.

Lee, Ronald, & Andrew Mason. (2006). What is the demographic dividend? *Finance and Development, 43*(3), 16–17.

Lee, Ronald, & Andrew Mason. (2010). Fertility, human capital, and economic growth over the demographic transition. *European Journal of Population, 26*(2), 159–182.

Leira, Arnlaug. (1992). *Welfare states and working mothers*. Cambridge: Cambridge University Press.

Leira, Arnlaug. (1993). Concepts of care: Loving, thinking and doing. In Julia Twigg (Ed.), *Informal care in Europe* (pp. 23–40). York: University of York.

Levy, Marion Joseph. (1949). *The family revolution in modern China.* Cambridge, Massachusetts: Harvard University Press.

Lewis, Jane. (1984). *Women in England, 1870–1950*. Brighton: Harvester Wheatsheaf.

Lewis, Jane. (1991). *Women and social action in Victorian and Edwardian England.* Aldershot: Edward Elgar.

Liu, William T. (2000a). Values and caregiving burden: The significance of filial piety in elder care. In W.T. Liu, & H. Kendig (Eds.), *Who should care for the elderly?* (pp. 183–200). Singapore: Singapore University Press.

Liu, William T., & Hal Kendig. (2000b). Critical issues of caregiving: East–west dialogue. In W.T. Liu & H. Kendig (Eds.), *Who should care for the elderly: An East–West value divide* (pp. 1–23). Singapore: Singapore University Press.

Lopez, Shane J. (Ed.). (2009). The encyclopedia of positive psychology. Hoboken, NJ: Wiley-Blackwell.

Maeda, Narifumi. (1975). Family Circle, Community, and Nation in Malaysia. *Current Anthropology, 16*(1), 163–166. Retrieved from http://www.jstor.org/stable/2740958.

Magnis-Suseno, Franz. (1984). *Etika Jawa: Sebuahan alias falsafi tentang kebijaksanaan hidup Jawa.* Jakarta: Gramedia Pustaka Utama.

Maria, Santa M. (2002). Youth in Southeast Asia: Living within the continuity of tradition and the turbulence of change. In B.B. Brown, R.W. Larson, & T.S. Saraswathi (Eds.), *The world's youth: Adolescence in eight regions of the globe* (pp. 171–206). Cambridge, UK: Cambridge University Press.

Mason, Andrew, & Ronald Lee. (2006). Reformand support systems for the elderly in developing countries: Capturing the second demographic dividend. *GENUS, LXII* (2), 11–35.

Medina, Belen T.G. (1991). *The Filipino family: A text with selected readings*. Deliman: University of the Philippines Press.

Mucchi-Faina, Angelica, Maria Giuseppina Pacilli, & Jyoti Verma. (2010). The two faces of familism: A cross-cultural research in India and Italy. *Psychological Studies, 55*(4), 365–373.

Nagata, Judith. (1976). The status of ethnicity and the ethnicity of status: Ethnic and class identity in Malaysia and Latin America. *International Journal of Comparative Sociology, 17*, 242–260.

Ngin, Chor Swang, & Julie DeVanzo. (1999). Parent-child coresidence and quasi co-residence in Peninsular Malaysia. *Southeast Asian Journal of Social Science, 27*(2), 43–64.

NSO. (2012). The 2010 population and housing census (Whole Kingdom). Bangkok: National Statistical Office, Ministry of Information and Communication Technology.

Ogawa, Naohiro, Makoto Kondo, & Rikiya Matsukura. (2004). *Japan's transition from demographic bonus to the demographic onus.* Paper presented at the international conference on the demographic window and healthy ageing: Socioeconomic challenges and opportunities, Beijing, China.

Parke, Raymond. D., & Ross Buriel. (2006). Socialization in the family: Ethnic and ecological perspectives. In N. Eisenberg, W. Damon, & R. Lerner (Eds.), *Handbook of child psychology: Social, emotional, and personality development* (pp. 429–504). Hoboken, NJ: John Wiley and Son.

Pasley, Kay. (1987). Family boundary ambiguity: Perceptions of adult stepfamily members. In K. Pasley, & M. Ihinger-Tallman (Eds.), *Remarriage and stepparenting: Current research and theory* (pp. 206–224). New York: Guildford.

Quah, Stella R. (2008). *Families in Asia: Home and kin.* Oxford: Routledge.

Quah, Stella R. (1998). *Family in Singapore: Sociological perspectives.* Singapore: Times Academic Press.

Razavi, Shahra. (2007). *The Political and social economy of care in a development context: Conceptual issues, research questions and policy options.* Geneva: United Nations Research Institute for Social Development, June.

Razavi, Shahra, & Silke Staab. (2008, September 19). *The Social and political economy of care: Contesting gender and class inequalities.* Paper presented at the equal sharing of responsibilities between women and men, including care-giving in the context of HIV/AIDS, the United Nations Division for the Advancement of Women.

Sabogal, Fabio, Gerardo Marin, Otero-Sabogal Regina, Marin Barbara Vanoss, Eliseo J. Perez-Stable. (1987). *Hispanic familism and acculturation: What changes and what doesn't?. Hispanic Journal of Behavioral Sciences, 9*, 397–412.

Schvaneveldt, Paul L., Margaret H. Young, & Jay D. Schvaneveldt. (2001). Dual-resident marriages in Thailand: A comparison of two cultural groups of women. *Journal of Comparative Family Studies, 32*(3), 347–360.

Schwartz, Seth J., Robert S. Weisskirch, Eric A. Hurley, Byron L. Zamboanga, Irene J.K. Park, Su Yeong Kim, Adriana Umaña-Taylor, Linda G. Castillo, Elissa Brown, Anthony D. Greene. (2010). Communalism, familism, and filial piety: Are they birds of a collectivist feather?. *Cultural Divers Ethnic Minor Psychology, 16*(4), 548–560.

Setiadi, Bernardette N. (2006). Indonesia: Traditional family in a changing society. In James Georgas, John W. Berry, Fons J.R. Van de Vijver, Çigdem Kagitçibasi, & Ype H. Poortinga (Eds.), *Families across cultures: A 30-nation psychological study* (pp. 370–378). Cambridge: Cambridge University Press.

Steidel, Angel G. Lugo, & Josefina M. Contreras. (2003). A new familism scale for use with Latino populations. *Hispanic Journal of Behavioral Sciences, 25*, 312–330.

Stephens, William N. (1963). *The family in cross-cultural perspective*. New York: Holt, Rinehart & Winston.

Stivens, Maila. (1998). Sex, gender and the making of the Malay middle class. In Krishna Sen, & Maila Stivens (Eds.), *Gender and power in affluent Asia* (pp. 86–126). London: Routledge.

Szołtysek, Mikołaj, Sebastian Klüsener, Radosław Poniat, & Siegfried Gruber. (2017). The patriarchy index: A new measure of gender and generational inequalities in the past. *Cross-Cultural Research, 51*(3), 228–262.

Tapanya, Sombat. (2011). Attributions and attitudes of mothers and fathers in Thailand. *Parenting, 11*(2–3), 190–198.

Thambiah, Shanthi. (2016, May 27). *Gender in Southeast Asia a fluid, contested and negotiable conceptual field.* Paper presented at the international conference of ISEAS/BUFS: Revisiting and reconstructing Southeast Asian characteristic, Institute of Southeast Asian Studies, South Korea.

Thi, Le. (1999). *The role of the family in the formation of Vietnamese personality*. Hanoi: The Gioi Publishers.

Thomas, Carol. (1993). De-constructing concepts of care. *Sociology, 27*(4), 649–669.

Tronto, Joan C. (1993). *Moral boundaries: A political argument for an ethic of care*. London: Routledge.

Tsubouchi, Yoshihiro. (1975). Marriage and divorce among Malay peasants in Kelantan. *Journal of Southeast Asian Studies, 6*, 135–150.

UNFPA. (2015). Demographic dividend. United Nations Population Fund. Retrieved September 24, 2017, from http://www.unfpa.org/demographic-dividend.

Valsiner, Jaan. (2000). *Culture and human development*. London: Sage.

VCPHCSC. (2010). *The 2009 population and housing census*. Hanoi: General Statistics Office of Vietnam.

Walker, Alan. (2000). Sharing long-term care between the family and the state – a European perspective. In W.T. Liu, & H. Kendig (Eds.), *Who should care for the elderly?* (pp. 78–106). Singapore: Singapore University Press.

Whitechurch, Gail G. & Larry L. Constantine. (1993). Systems theory. In P. Boss, W.J. Doherty, R. LaRossa, W.R. Schumm, & S.K. Steinmetz (Eds.), *Sourcebook of family theories and methods: A contextual approach* (pp. 325–352). New York: Plenum.

Wong, Odalia M.H. (2000). Children and children-in-law as primary caregivers: Issues and perspectives. In W.T. Liu, & H. Kendig (Eds.), *Who should care for the Elderly: An East–West value divide* (pp. 297–321). Singapore: Singapore University Press, National University of Singapore and World Scientific.

Wongboonsin, Patcharawalai (Ed.). (2015). *20-year long-term population plan (2015–2034)*. Final report (Vol. 2/5) research project on the outlining appropriate approaches to reduce inequities in the Thai society amidst demographic shift, submitted to Office of the National Economic and Social Development Board by College of Population Studies, Chulalongkorn University. Bangkok: Chulalongkorn University Printing House.

Wongboonsin, Kua, & Philip Guest (Eds.). (2005). *The demographic dividend: Policy options for Asia*. Bangkok: Chulalongkorn University Printing House.

Wongboonsin, Kua & Patcharawalai Wongboonsin. (2008). Modern population trends, m-curve labor-force participation and the family. In Emiko Ochai, & Barbara Molony (Eds.), *Asia's new mothers: Crafting gender roles and childcare networks in East and Southeast Asian Societies* (pp. 129–139). London: Global Oriental.

Wongboonsin, Kua, & Patcharawalai Wongboonsin. (2014). Demographic dividend and the future of Asia. In Emiko Ochiai, & Leo Aoi Hosoya (Eds.), *Transformation of the intimate and the public in Asian Modernity* (pp. 91–115). Leiden: Brill.

Wongboonsin, Patcharawalai, & Kua Wongboonsin. (2007). Modern population trends and the family. In A. Scott Loveless & Thomas B. Holman (Eds.), *The family in the new millennium: World voices supporting the "Natural" clan, Volume I, The place of family in human society* (pp. 153–162). London: Praeger, an Imprint of Greenwood Publishing Group.

Wongboonsin, Patcharawalai, & Kua Wongboonsin. (2013). Demographic dividend and the future of Asia. In Emiko Ochiai, & Leo Aoi Hosoya (Eds.), *Transformation of the intimate and the public in Asian modernity* (pp. 91–115). The Netherlands: Brill.

Wu, David. Y.H., & Wen-Shing Tseng. (1985). Child training in Chinese culture. In Wen-Shing Tseng, & David Wu (Eds.), *Chinese culture and mental health* (pp. 113–134). Orlando, FL: Academic Press.

Yaacob, Harun. (2004). *Malaysia: Papers on society and culture*, Wellington: Victoria University of Wellington.

Yeh, Kuang-Hui, & Olwen Bedford. (2003). A test of the dual filial piety model. *Asian Journal of Social Psychology, 6*, 215–228.

Yu, Elena S.H., Shihlong Lai, Zehuai Wen, & Yinglun Liu. (2000). Caregiving survey in Guangzhou: A preliminary report. In W.T. Liu, & H. Kendig (Eds.), *Who should care for the elderly?: An East-West value divide* (pp. 322–338). Singapore: Singapore University Press.

Zhou, Min, & Carl Bankston. (1998). *Growing up American: How Vietnamese children adapt to life in the United States*. New York: Russell Sage Foundation.

PART 1

Cultural, Demographic and Socio-economic Background of Care Relations

CHAPTER 2

Cultural, Demographic, Socio-economic Background and Care Relations in Malaysia

Rahimah Ibrahim, Jo-Pei Tan, Tengku Aizan Hamid and Asmidawati Ashari

1 Introduction

Malaysia encompasses an area of 330,803 square kilometres and shares its land borders with Thailand, Indonesia and Brunei Darussalam as well as the South China Sea maritime borders of Singapore, Vietnam and the Philippines. The country is divided into two parts: (1) Peninsular or West Malaysia situated to the south of Thailand and north of Singapore; and (2) East Malaysia, separated by the South China Sea, which is located on the island of Borneo bordering Brunei Darussalam and Kalimantan, Indonesia. The country is comprised of 13 states and three federal territories, of which 11 states and two federal territories, namely Kuala Lumpur and Putrajaya, are located in Peninsular Malaysia. Two other states, namely Sabah and Sarawak, and the federal territory of Labuan are located in East Malaysia. Kuala Lumpur is the nation's capital city and Putrajaya serves as a federal administrative centre. The state of Selangor is the most populous state with 5.46 million people.

As a former British colony, vestiges of the colonial period remain in Malaysia's political, legal and social systems. After gaining its independence in 1957, the federation of Malaya formed Malaysia along with Sabah and Sarawak in 1963. Malaysia practices parliamentary democracy, alongside a federal constitutional elective monarchy where the monarch is Head of State, a position rotated among nine hereditary rulers.

As one of the developing countries in the Southeast Asian region, Malaysia shares some of the demographic and social trends traversing many societies in the region. Asian families, including those in Malaysia, have been greatly romanticised for taking care of their own family buttressed by its generous welfare system (Mohd 2012), which is family based (Croissant 2004). In other words, both young and old people customarily rely on family for care and support, with an overarching notion of filial or religious obligation among family members, especially for old age support. However, these representations of the 'ideal family' have been challenged by the fast and drastic macro changes in

 | DOI:10.1163/9789004384330_003

its population structure, demographic transition, economic development and socio-cultural context leading to a phenomenon of compressed modernity which shapes the present welfare regime, policies and programs in the country within the context of care. Thus, this chapter presents a careful analysis of the historical, cultural, socio-economic, demographic, policy and legislative context, focusing on changes and continuity in the factors that can impact family and care relations in Malaysia.

2 Cultural Background

2.1 *Culture and Customs*

Early contacts across ethnic groups were established through strong trading links between Chinese and Indian traders with the Malays in the Peninsula (Hatin et al. 2011). Given its current diverse ethnic setting, people from Malay, Chinese, Aboriginal and Indian backgrounds have developed a cross-cultural socialisation in the country. The census in 2010 reported a population of 28.3 million people in Malaysia which was made up of: Malays and *Bumiputeras* (indigenous and native peoples) (67.4%), followed by the Chinese (24.6%), Indians (7.3%), and other ethnic groups (0.7%). According the 2010 census, the predominant ethnic group in Peninsular Malaysia was the Malays, constituting 63.1%. For Sabah, the predominant ethnic groups were the Kadazan/Dusun (24.5%) and Sarawak, the Ibans (30.3%). Major religions included Islam (61.3%), Buddhism (19.8%), Christianity (9.2%) and Hinduism (6.3%). The multi-religiosity in the country was fostered by its religious-freedom policy in which Malaysians had the right to practice their different religions. In addition, the people in Malaysia were multilingual, with Malay (Bahasa Malaysia), Chinese, Tamil and English being widely used of which Malay and English were the most prominent media of communication among the diverse ethnic groups. The demographic characteristics of Malaysia reflected its multicultural, multireligious and multilingual society. As a consequence of the multicultural, multireligious and multilingual cultural landscape, there were converging and diverging cultural conventions related to family life and care giving. The roles and responsibilities of family members were embedded across all religious beliefs, in addition to the strongly held cultural values of filial piety and family centred care (Hossain 2014; Ismail, Tan & Ibrahim 2009; Masud & Haron 2014). However, ethnic pluralism was initiated in the British colony through large-scale migration and spatial segregation among the groups and, hence, gave rise to a socially fragmented landscape and unequal multi-ethnic society (Aziz & Yusooff 2012).

Amongst the population in Malaysia, the Malays and Chinese made up more than two-thirds of the total population while almost 10% of the remaining population were Indians. Unlike some multicultural countries, Malaysia was not characterised by a dominant culture defined by a majority group to which other smaller ethnic groups assimilated. Not only the Chinese comprised a significant minority in Malaysia (37% in 1957; 28% in 1991; 26% in 2000; 24.6% in 2010), like the Malays, they had a strong desire to preserve and practise their cultural identity, traditional religion and customs. Similarly, the Indian population emphasised their identity development through religious practices, patriarchal family values and traditional customs. These factors not only buffered the assimilation effect of Malay culture but also led to divergence in family relationships and care support across these ethnic groups (DOSM 2011).

2.1.1 Kinship, Filial Obligation and Religiosity

Like most Asians, Malaysian families were nurtured with the mentality of having the 'family-as-centre' of all activities emphasising the importance of family, kinship systems, and family interdependence (Chao & Tseng 2002). In fact, within a variety of kinship systems across ethnic groups, a high value was uniformly placed on familial obligation and harmony with a core of filial duty which were shaped through religiosity. Despite increasing westernization (Daud, Chew, Lee & Quek 2001), filial behaviour was one of the topmost cultural practices in the majority of Asian families as well as in the Malaysian family system, and parents played a vital role in inculcating filial practices in the younger generation (Ismail, Tan & Ibrahim 2009). Filial piety was a central quality of cultural practices in a family which included obedience and honouring of one's parents and it was considered as the fundamental element to practice in the Malaysian family system.

The multi-ethnic groups in Malaysia embraced all the major belief systems: Malays practised the Islamic teaching, the Chinese generally were Buddhists or practised traditional Chinese religions, and majority of Indians practised Hinduism. Similarly, all these religious scriptures and scholarly treatise stressed the moral obligation of children to revere and respect their parents and provided for their support and care (Attwood & Croll 2006).

The pattern of family life and relationship among Malays was strongly shaped by the Islamic religion which ultimately determined the behaviour, values and beliefs among the Malays (Kling 1995). In Islam, the Quran stressed devotion for parents and the responsibility of children for their support and care (Philipps 1992) and children were perceived as 'gifts' from God requiring that parents provided for them. Thus, a family with many children was a 'prosperous' family, irrespective of their economic situation (Yaacob 2005).

This belief may have had implications on the family planning practices and the use of contraception, thus, explaining the larger household size among Malays compared to the Chinese and Indians. Guided by their traditional religious beliefs and practices, the care relations and support exchange among Chinese were shaped accordingly and the duties of children to revere and support parents were clearly set out (Philipps 1992). The majority of the Indians practiced Hindu and Sikh cultures, and one of the principal values was filial respect and support for parents, which remained strong in the Indian community in Malaysia. Filial obligation among Malaysian families involved mutual responsibilities across generations which emphasised the children's sense of indebtedness or obligations to parents in return for early care during childhood. Thus, the religious practice and traditional custom not only clearly defined the rightful attitudes and behaviours of children towards parents, but also obliged parents to support and provide for their children.

2.1.2 Age Hierarchies

Age hierarchy was another salient feature in the kinship system and intergenerational relations in Malaysian society. Seniority in age and social position were customarily accorded precedence and authority, thus ranking for, and support of, the older generation before all other obligations, or parent-care before child- or self-care (Attwood & Croll 2006; Yaacob 2014). Hence, a prominent feature of intergenerational care and support, combining obedience and sense of obligation, was the subordination of the younger generation to the will and welfare of parents and grandparents. A common ideal was centred on a prosperous old age surrounded and supported by many children in a multigenerational household. However, this ideal may not be feasible in contemporary Malaysian society which was challenged with drastic demographical changes and eroded filial obligations.

Age and seniority were traditionally very important aspects in family relationships in Southeast Asian communities. Among the Malays, the elder and senior members of the family were much respected and often hold the responsibility for all major family matters. They served as the source of advice and place for resolving family conflicts (Kling 1995). Younger family members were expected to show respect to the elderly in terms of obedience, proper manners, deference, body language and low-tone of language. In a Malay community, as kin members were often bound into cohesive family units, an elderly person was often expected to be taken care of by his/her kinship group or extended family members. An elderly Malay person, if he was alone, could either join his son's family or his daughter's family where he would be expected to become part of the family and involved in all aspects of family affairs (Yaacob 2014).

Maintaining close familial relationships was not only an obligation but also a religious duty. Guided by Islamic teachings, a person was considered unfaithful to the religion if he disregarded his kin and family members and turned them down in times of need, especially his parents and other members of the immediate family.

The concept of filial piety strongly influenced and guided family relations among Chinese families in Malaysia. Traditionally, filial piety entailed a system of age and patriarchy. Not only parents and elders had greater authority and should be treated with respect, children were expected to be obedient and consult their parents for guidance throughout their adulthood. Respect and the act of honouring elders was also reflected in their form of ancestor worship. This practice led to the belief among the Chinese that they would be cursed by their ancestors if they abandoned their duty to care for their elderly parents (Sokolovsky 2001). Similarly, among Indian society, family solidarity was based upon the hierarchical principle. Elders were more authoritative than younger persons and so were men compared to women. A woman's status and authority was largely dependent on her husband's position within the family. The wife controled domestic affairs but exerted a lesser authority compared to her mother-in-law who was a senior in social hierarchy (Kakar 1978). These cultural norms and values accounted for the fact that institutionalisation was provided as a last resort by the government for specific vulnerable groups

2.2 *Gender Role in Family Relations*

Although there were similarities in relation to care and support across generations among the Malays, Chinese and Indians in Malaysia, contrasts nevertheless existed with respect to their distinctive cultural values and custom. Thus, the family ideologies and expectations of children among these three ethnic groups may be distinctive, specifically regarding gender roles within family.

The differences in gender roles, especially the expected provision and return for sons and daughters, often shaped by traditional values and family system, tended to be clearer in certain ethnic groups compared to others. For example, Malay families were based on a bilateral system with equal expectations for both sons and daughters in providing care and support to parents while, patriarchal Chinese and Indian families set out a clearer expectation of sons over daughters. These unique and indigenous notions across different ethnic groups may have had implications on the care responsibilities and support exchange within a community.

The bilateral family system, such as that which was prevalent in Malay families, emphasised equal rights of inheritance and both genders were taken into consideration regarding living arrangements, filial obligations and support for parents. For example, elderly Malay parents were expected to either join his (married) son or (married) daughter's family; whereas married couples could decide to co-reside with the husband's or wife's family, with no specific residential rules. This may explain the fact that in general, there was no strong preference for either a son or daughter among Malays. However, matrilineal and matrilocal family was observed among the Minangkabau Malay in the state of Negeri Sembilan who practised a matriarchal family system which favoured daughters and family members from maternal side in inheritance and co-residence. There was often a greater tendency to follow traditional customs (*adat*) than Islamic law in relation to inheritance and the division of property (Yaacob 2014).

Chinese and Indian families in Malaysia were organised on the basis of a patriarchal system, which emphasised the dominance of male over female. Chinese families practised a patrilineal system whereby family lineage was only continued through male offspring and therefore, sons (especially the eldest) or children of sons were to be favoured in inheritance over the children of daughters. In addition, daughters-in-law tended to be treated more favourably in family relationships than daughters (Kuo & Hassan 1976). Sons, especially the eldest, were preferable to share residence with parents for old age support and care provision, reflecting patrilocal values among the Chinese. Similarly, among Indian families, men had greater authority within a patriarchal system and high expectations were set on sons, particularly the eldest, to take up core filial responsibility stressing obedience, sacrifice for and indebtedness to parents (Kakar 1978; Ranganath & Ranganath 1997).

The expectation of children was expressed in significantly different ways among the different ethnic groups. The Chinese and Indian had clear-cut obligations for their children, engendered by debt and financial contributions for their parents' well-being, while the Malays had more diffused obligations for children engendered by gifts and, the long-term return was expressed in a more subtle way (Li 1989). Remittance between parents and children tended to flow in both directions (Yaacob 2005). Malay parents supported children who were not economically independent; while working children were required to support aged parents and younger siblings when parents became incapable of financially supporting the needs of family.

Interestingly, the division of labor within the Malay, Chinese and Indian families followed the traditional sex-differentiated pattern where the male was seen as the breadwinner and protector of the family while the female was seen as the caregiver and caretaker of the household. Traditionally, boys were socialised and trained to inherit their family business while girls were nurtured to be good homemakers in preparation for marriage and motherhood.

For example, among traditional, rural families, there was a common scenario of women's economic dependency on men such as an unmarried girl on her father, a wife on her husband or an elderly mother on her son. The gendered role of care responsibility may have explained the growing trend among Malay women to leave employment or opt for early retirement as a result of the demands and pressures of familial matters (Yaccob 2005).

2.3 *Child Preferences*

Despite there being little evidence for child preference in Malaysia, Malay and Indian parents did not show a consistent sex preference while preference for a son was more pronounced among Chinese parents. The reason for preferring a son was commonly associated with traditional values of old age support, continuation of the family name and the completion of male tasks in the home (Callan & Kee 1981).

3 Socio-economic Background

3.1 *Modernisation and Economic Development*

Economic development in Malaysia was impressive after its independence in 1957, transforming from a resource-based economy dependent on agriculture and primary commodities to a modern industrial economy based on large-scale manufacturing and technological industries (Hill, Yean, & Mat Zin 2012). Under various national development plans, the country's Gross Domestic Product (GDP) grew from RM5.1 billion in 1957 to RM766 billion in 2010 (DOSM 2012b).

Industrialisation played a major role in the 1971–1990 New Economic Policy (NEP) and 1991–2000 New Development Policy (NDP) (Embong 1996; Jomo 2013; Shari 2000). The NEP was a key policy that led to government intervention in social restructuring to reduce socio-economic disparities among the ethnic groups through poverty eradication measures, as a response to the 1969 post-election race riots (Embong 1996; Jomo 2004). It shaped the First Outline Perspective Plan (OPP) to reduce poverty in Peninsular Malaysia from 49% to 16% between 1971 and 1990 (Jomo 2004; Mohd 2012). Succeeding the NEP was the NDP which guided the Second OPP (1991–2000) with greater emphasis on attaining rapid growth, industrialisation and structural change (Jomo 2004). In 1983, the government announced its initiatives on privatisation policy which led to the adoption of Guidelines for Privatisation in 1985 and the Privatisation Master Plan in 1991 (Nambiar 2009).Economic liberalisation and privatisation has undermined the role of the state in promoting economic growth, and restructuring the society since the mid-1980s (Embong 1996; Jomo 2013). The Third OPP (2001–2010), linked to the National Vision Policy (also known as Vision 2020), also focused on developing and modernising various economic sectors and generating high sustainable growth. As a result, the country's economic progress was built upon its political stability which hinges on delicate social fabric and inter-ethnic distributional policies (Doraisami 2012).

The interventionist nature of the Malaysian State along with the rapid growth in export-led industrialisation contributed to the success in poverty reduction (Shari & Mat Zin 1995). Historically, the nation had a long track record of combating poverty through specific social programs directed at certain groups that include farmers, fishermen, cash-crop smallholders, estate workers, agricultural laborers and indigenous peoples. The incidence of poverty, calculated as households with monthly gross income below the Poverty Line Income (PLI), declined to 3.8% for the poor and 0.7% for the hard-core poor (those living below the food PLI), totalling around 4.5% of all households in 2009. It was noted that the PLI had different cut off points for the different regions of West and East Malaysia. The PLI for Peninsular Malaysia (RM763) was lower than that for Sabah (RM1,048) and Sarawak (RM912). Urban and rural differences were also taken into account but the overall PLI calculation (in terms of food and non-food needs) for Malaysia in 2009 was RM800 per month (DOSM 2012b).

During the same period (2009–2011), household inequality was moderate (GINI ratio stood at 0.441 in 2009), yet there was a notable increase in total household debt (RM667 billion or 110% of disposable income in 2011). In 2009, the mean and median household income were at RM4,025 and RM2,641 per month (DOSM 2011, 2012a). During 2012, there was a growth in the household income of the general population with the highest growth in Kuala Lumpur. The 2012 Household Income Survey reported an increase of 7.2% to RM5000 and particularly in Kuala Lumpur, where there was a rise of 14.9% from RM5488 to RM8586 (DOSM 2012a).

Despite the nation's economic growth, becoming an upper middle-income country, average Malaysian families were struggling to make ends meet in the face of a high inflation rate, slower income rise (average of 2.4% per annum) and surging living costs. Those in the middle-income group, accounting for about 40% of total households in Malaysia (DOSM 2012b), tended to be burdened by more housing loans in comparison to the low-income households, comprising another 40% of the country's population. While the recent economic plan strategically aimed at improving the livelihood of the bottom 40% of households and empowering vulnerable groups (i.e. women, elderly and disabled population), the middle-income group was likely to be burdened by economic difficulties with minimal support from state-initiated programs. Amidst this desire for economic growth, the country faced significant fiscal challenges, including weak public finances, lower government debt ratings, and ongoing political tension (Gomez 2012; Hal 2010). This middle-income trap was going to continue under the 10th Malaysia Plan, which aimed at enabling the country to achieve the status of "prosperous economy" country by 2020. Furthermore, plans to reduce public subsidies for fuel and sugar, as well as plans to raise tariffs on electricity in 2014, could further burden the growth in the middle-income population who were likely to be sandwiched by the responsibilities of caring for the dependent children and ageing parents.

3.2 *Urbanisation and Migration*

In terms of *urbanisation*, through rapid development, the urban population in Malaysia increased from 9% to 71% between 2000 and 2010 (DOSM 2012b). Data from the Department of Statistics Malaysia also indicated that the two federal territories of Kuala Lumpur and Putrajaya had a 100% level of urbanisation, followed by other states, namely, Selangor (91.4%) and Pulau Pinang (90.8%). Lesser urbanisation levels were found in the east coast (i.e. Kelantan), central region (i.e. Pahang) and in Perlis of Peninsular Malaysia. Rapid urbanisation was closely linked with industrialisation and the rapid development in infrastructure, society and economy within those states that were more urbanised. In Malaysia, national development plans incorporated strategies for the country to become a fully developed nation with a high income by the year 2020 (Huff 2001). Migration intensified in the last few decades, in particular, internal migration.

Recent data indicated that 90% of total migration was internal and the remainder was immigration into Malaysia from other countries. The predominant migration was within the state (61.3%), followed by inter-state migration (28.5%); as for rural to urban intra-state migration, the rate increased by only 0.5% after 2010. Migration within states and across-state borders led to increased density in several states along the west coast of Peninsular Malaysia, which included Kuala Lumpur. According to DOSM (2012b), the capital Kuala Lumpur was the most densely populated state (6,891 persons/km^2), followed by Penang (1,490 persons/km^2) and the Federal Territory of Putrajaya (1,478 persons/km^2).

The national migration survey also found that the majority of the migrants were aged between 15 and 34 years. The migration of the younger generation was pulled by the opportunities of employment, socio-education infrastructure, tertiary education and career or personal development (Green & Canny 2003), and pushed by factors such as the lack of job opportunities, career development and public infrastructure in the states which were less urbanised. This population movement not only caused changes in living patterns among Malaysians but also caused breakdown of the circuit of care provision and familial support, especially among multigenerational households. In addition, migration of older generation into urbanised cities was reported for health reasons, loss of spouse, or care taking of grandchildren.

Furthermore, cross-country migration was also an issue highlighted in the national development policies. In 2010, there were 1.6 million (or 12.8% of total workers in the country) foreign workers in Malaysia compared with 0.8 million in 2000, the majority of whom tended to be low or semi-skilled workers (MOF 2013). Thus, it can be seen that urbanisation and migration had significant implications on the population distribution of the country.

3.3 *Education and Employment*

3.3.1 Education

Education was the core agenda for the National Development Plan of the country after independence in 1957. After the 2nd Malaysia Plan (1971–1975), in addition to general education, greater emphasis was given to establish vocational and technical training schools as a measure to alleviate youth unemployment, especially among those who were not interested in general education. The emphasis on the education sector was also reflected in public expenditure and the National Development Plan, which was proposed every 5 years. For instance, in 2011, a total of 5.9% of the country's GDP was spent on education, increasing from 4.3% in 1995. In addition, the most recent 10th Malaysia plan (2010–2015) aimed to strengthen the education system for further human capital development through programs for improving pre-school enrolment rates, identifying high performing schools, establishing a Literacy and Numeric Screening (LINUS) programme, and improving the quality of teaching professionals.

Improved education attainment was closely related to family life, in particular, employment opportunities, which subsequently led to changing expectations of their role among women, delayed age of marriage and motherhood. From 1970 to 2000, there was a decrease in terms of primary school enrolment, from 38.2% to 29.8% due to shrinking in the number of young children (aged 6–12 years). This was a reflection of the decrease in family size. There was also evidence of a narrowing gap in education attainment between sexes. It was recorded that the difference in attainment between the sexes declined from 5.5 percentage points (2000) to 4.7 percentage points (2010). The 2010 Census documented a change of trend in post-secondary education compared to the 2000 Census. Among the population aged 15 years and above, there was a higher percentage of females (68.9%) who obtained post-secondary school qualifications such as a certificate, diploma or degree than their male counterparts in 2010 (66.8%); while the trend was opposite in 2000 (male: 62.6%; female 57%). A similar pattern was reported across the main ethnic groups, where the largest gap between male and female in 2010 was among the Chinese (3.2%), followed by Bumiputera (1.6%) and Indians (0.4%). These changing trends have very important implications on family life among Malaysians.

In general, the opportunity to pursue a higher educational level increased the overall participation rate in the workforce, especially among women. While rapid economic development and growth in Malaysia boosted new employment opportunities benefiting both men and women, increased accessibility to the educational attainment of women enabled them to be gainfully employed in all economic sectors such as manufacturing, business, service and agriculture, in addition to their traditional role in the unpaid domestic sector of the economy.

3.3.2 Employment

Over the years, the Malaysian labor market expanded with higher rates of *employment* among people of the working age population of 16 to 64 years. The percentage of the economically active population has risen to 67.0% or 13.6 million in 2012 from 62.7% or 11.9 million in 2008, according to Table 2.1 In comparison, the employment rate was still considerably higher among males (79.0% in 2008 and 80.7% in 2013) than females (45.7% in 2008 and 52.4% in 2013). However, the Economic Planning Unit (EPU 2011) also reported a fourfold increase in workforce participation among women (6.7%) compared to men (1.7%) during the same period. The rise of employment levels of women over the last four decades was supported by governmental policies. The National Policy for Women (NPW) was used as a guide for women's participation in the development process and to integrate women in all sectors of national development, in line with their abilities and needs in order to improve the quality of life, eradicate poverty, abolish ignorance and illiteracy. In the 6th Malaysia plan (1991–1995), a special fund for the development of women became a significant and integral step towards empowering women in Malaysia.

As a result of educational attainment and employment opportunities for women, there was an increase in the number of dual-earner families with both husband and wife working. This scenario led to a change in the traditional family structure and challenged the male-breadwinner model that prescribed the division of labor between men and women among many Malaysian families. Thus, it can be seen that women not only had a key role as primary carer within the family but also played a vital economic role as well. Mahari (2011) argued

Table 2.1 Labor force participation by gender, 2008–2013

	Unit	2008	2009	2010	2011	2012	2013
Labor force	'000	11,968	12,083	12,361	12,646	13,119	13,634
Total[a]		62.7%	63.3%	63.4%	64.1%	65.5%	67.0%
Male		79.0%	79.5%	79.5%	79.8%	80.5%	80.7%
Female		45.7%	46.2%	46.5%	47.9%	49.5%	52.4%
Unemployment (% of labor force)		3.3	3.7	3.3	3.1	3.0	3.1

a Total number of people economically active as a percentage of total number in the working-age population of 15 to 64 years (estimate).

SOURCE: LABOR FORCE SURVEY REPORT (2008–2013) DEPARTMENT OF STATISTICS MALAYSIA (DOSM)

that while there were significant changes in relation to the role and status of women in society and participation in labor market, there was still a lack of support services which enabled women to combine family commitments and work responsibilities.

Figure 2.1 illustrates the labor force participation rate by age group from 1980 to 2010. The most active force in labor market participation was those between 25 to 45 years. Thus, it was expected that the most active age group in labor market would also likely be the 'sandwich generation' who would likely be a overwhelmed with financial responsibilities for their own families as well as with the duty to take care of elderly parents, especially parents who were old and frail. In addition, data from the recent Census in 2010 showed a trend towards delayed entry into the labor force market among the younger generation, while there was also an indication of early exit from active employment among the working population in Malaysia as compared to data from Census in 2000, 1990 and 1980. Delayed entry into the labor force may reflect a continuity of support from parents into their children's adulthood, which could translate to further a financial burden for the 'sandwiched' middle generation. Attwood & Croll (2006) argued that this was one way to reduce the odds and increase the likelihood of filial returns or repayment by the younger generation, given greater mobility, declining fertility, changing values and new social trends which weakened the possibility of old-support from children.

As the population structure was altered with the increasing proportion of older people, the trend of labor force participation from 1980 till 2010 reflected that participation tended to decrease with age among those who are over 50 years. Hamid, Momtaz, Ibrahim, Yahaya & Abdullah (2013) asserted

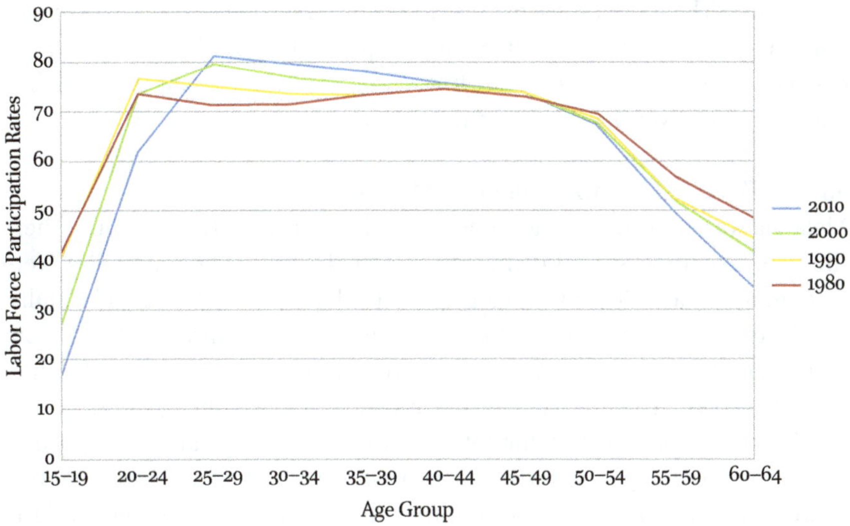

FIGURE 2.1 Labor force participation rates by age group, Malaysia (1980–2010).
SOURCE: DOSM, LABOR FORCE SURVEY REPORT (VARIOUS YEARS).

that continued employment was the most important form of social security in Malaysia, thus, decreased ability to generate economic income may cripple older persons' livelihood with limited coverage from the post-employment social protection system that included Employees Provident Fund (EPF) – a mandatory retirement savings plan, and the Social Security Organisation (SOCSO). Yet, it was the family (or household) which provided most of the personal social services and support to each other. The employment status among elderly persons was further examined with data from 2004 Malaysian Population and Family Survey (MPFS) which showed that a high percentage of 28.2% elderly (60+) were still working, a scenario which could be attributed to having an 'average health status'; however, the majority were working in agriculture and the fishery sector (46.8%), which may not have generated an adequate income to sustain the provision of old age support (NPFDB 2005). This may have led to poverty, especially among the elderly who were alone or widowed with no spouse or children.

4 Demographic Background

Since the beginning of the twentieth century, demographic change in Malaysia can be divided into three stages (Mahari 2011). The first stage occurred from 1911 until 1927 (16 years), during which there were low birth rate and high death rates. The nation subsequently entered the second stage in 1928 to 1957 (29 years) with the birth rate reaching its peak of 46.2, whereas death rates decreased. The third stage began from 1958 until the present day, which is marked by relatively low birth and death rates.

4.1 *Fertility, Life Expectancy and Mortality*

Malaysia was in the third stage of demographic transition (Hamid 2012) where the two basic processes of demography, namely fertility and mortality, were beginning to show signs of converging with a declining birth rate and stabilising death rate. In general, the *Total Fertility Rate* (TFR) of Malaysia fell from almost 5 children per woman in 1970 to 2.3 children per woman in 2010 (Mahari 2011). As shown in Figure 2.2, there was a sharp decline in the TFR in the country. Between 1950 and 1965, the total fertility rate was 6.2, and it dropped to 5.2 in 1970, 3.6 in 1990 and further decreased to 2.7 in the period 2005–2010. It is projected that the TFR of the country will fall below the replacement level by 2050.

The declining rate of TFR was attributed to several factors. Tey (2007a) suggested that the changes in TFR between 1966 and 1985 were closely related to

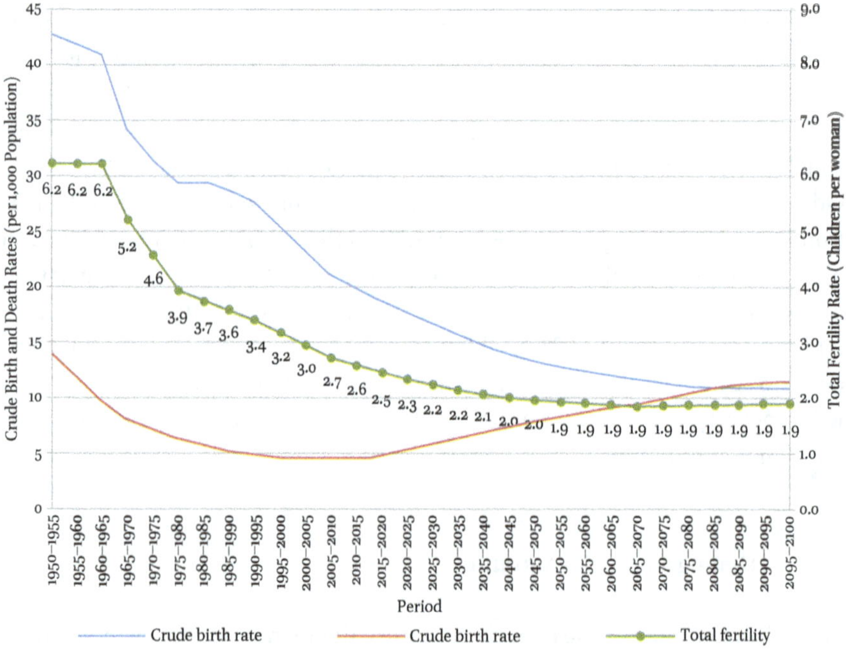

FIGURE 2.2 Crude birth rate, crude death rate, and total fertility rate in Malaysia, 1950–2100.
SOURCE: WORLD POPULATION PROSPECTS: THE 2010 REVISION (UN 2011).

the sharp rise of the contraceptive prevalence rate from 8% to 50% following the National Planning Program in 1966. Projections foresaw a downward trend of fertility levels in the country over the next two decades. The pro-natalist policy of 1984 did not successfully reverse the trend.

Although there was a steady decline in fertility rate among Malaysians, differences in the rate of decrease among the various ethnic groups were detected. The demographic transition in Malaysia began before 1965. In 1960, the TFR was found to be highest among Indians with 7.2 children per woman followed by Chinese (6.5) and Malays (5.9). However, from 1965, the fertility rate began to decline in Malaysia whereby the TFR of the Malays was higher than that of Chinese and Indians. While the average number of children born to a Malay woman (or TFR) showed a gradual decline, it was still relatively higher than the national average from 1970 onwards (i.e. 5.2 in 1970 and 2.3 in 2010) (Figure 2.3). The TFR among Malays were reported at 5.0 in 1970, 3.4 in 2000 and 2.7 in 2010.

The changing and diverse trend in fertility and mortality among the three major ethnic groups in Malaysia was closely related to various social, economic and cultural factors. Family planning was highlighted in a past study, which

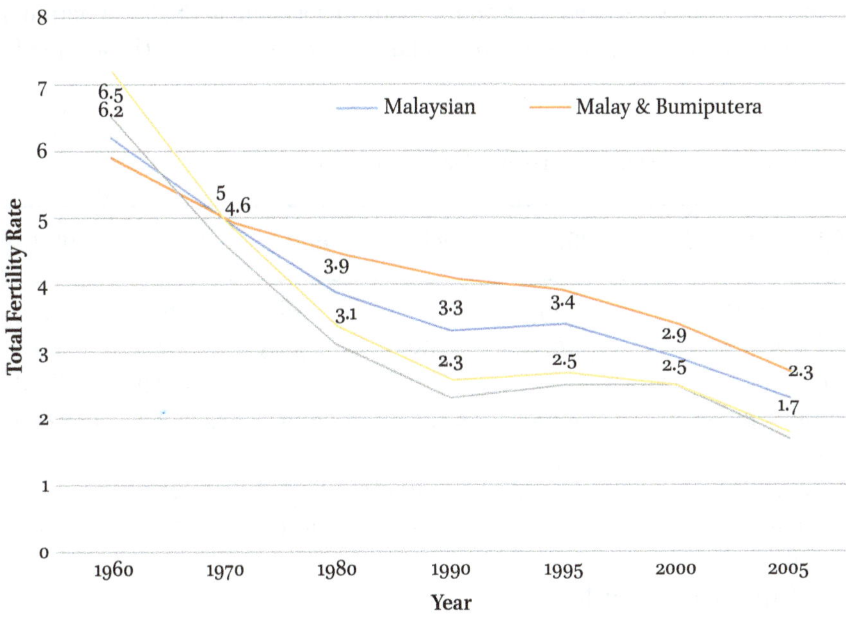

FIGURE 2.3 Fertility, mortality and total fertility rate in Malaysia, 1950–2100.
SOURCES: POPULATION PROFILE, MALAYSIA (NPFDB 1999); VITAL STATISTICS TIME SERIES, MALAYSIA, 1963–1998 (DOSM 2011B); VITAL STATISTICS, MALAYSIA, 2003 (DOSM 2003A); VITAL STATISTICS MALAYSIA, SPECIAL EDITION, 2001 (DOSM 2006).

reflected on the lower use of an efficient method of contraception among the Malays. The Malaysian Population and Family Survey-4 found that a large proportion (70%) of women in the survey used contraception; the highest rate was among Chinese (almost 80%), while the Malays and Indians were more or less around 65.0%. In addition, the desire to have more children was found to be stronger among Malays compared to Chinese and Indians who did not seem to aspire to have many children. The relatively larger number of children among Malays was also supported by religious and cultural notion that children ware 'gifts of god' and a family with many children was a 'prosperous' family, irrespective of their economic conditions (Yaacob 2005).

The Department of Statistics, Malaysia (2006; 2010) recorded a growing population from 10.4 million in 1970 to 28.3 million in 2010, with an increasing trend in a sex ratio of 102 (males to 100 females) in 1970 to 106 (males to 100 females) in the latest 2010 census (see Table 2.2). Meanwhile, Malaysia experienced almost a three-fold increase in the population over the last four decades.

Like many countries in Asia, life expectancy continuously increased among both males and females in Malaysia. In 1970, life expectancy at birth for males and females was 62 and 66 years respectively. After four decades, these figures (see Table 2.3) have soared to 70 and 75 years in 2000 and in the latest national census year 2010, the figures rose to 72 and 77 years respectively. The gap in life

TABLE 2.2 Basic demographic trends in Malaysia, 1970–2010

Age group (%)	1970	1980	1991	2000	2010
Young (0–14)	44.9	39.6	36.8	35.4	31.7
Adult (15–64)	52.0	56.8	59.5	62.6	63.6
Old (65+)	3.1	3.6	3.7	3.9	4.7
Total Population ('000)	10,439.4	13,136.1	18,379.7	23,274.7	28,334.1
Median Age	15.5	16.0	20.3	20.6	27.6
Sex Ratio (per 100 female)	102	101	103	104	106
Life Expectancy at Birth					
Male	61.6	66.5	69.2	70.0	72.0
Female	65.6	71.0	73.4	74.6	77.1

SOURCE: DOSM 2012B

TABLE 2.3 Life expectancy at birth (year) by ethnic group and sex, Malaysia, 1970–2011

Year	Total		Malay & Bumiputera		Chinese		Indian	
	Male	Female	Male	Female	Male	Female	Male	Female
1970	61.6	65.6	60.8	62.7	64.0	71.3	59.0	61.3
1980	66.4	70.5	66.5	68.9	68.0	74.0	62.1	67.0
1985	67.7	72.4	67.9	71.2	69.5	75.5	63.0	68.8
1990	68.9	73.5	69.0	72.4	70.6	76.3	64.4	70.4
1995	69.4	74.1	68.7	72.6	71.8	77.2	64.8	72.4
2000	70.2	75.1	69.2	73.5	72.4	78.0	65.7	74.4
2005	71.5	76.2	70.2	74.8	73.6	78.8	67.4	75.4
2006	71.5	76.3	70.2	74.7	73.8	79.1	68.0	75.6
2009	71.6	76.5	70.2	74.8	74.0	79.5	67.9	75.8
2010	71.7	76.8	70.2	75.1	74.2	79.8	68.0	76.1
2011	72.0	77.1	70.5	75.4	74.5	80.0	68.0	76.8

SOURCE: DOSM, 2003A, 2007, 2008, 2010 (YEARBOOK OF STATISTICS)

expectancy between sexes slightly widened; for the year 2000, it was 4.6 years while for year 2011, it was 5.1 years (DOSM 2010).

In 2016, the national census reported that, of the 31.7 million Malaysians, 6.0% of the population were elderly (age 65 or above) and 7.8 million or 24.5% were children (age 0 to 14 years old). Meanwhile, the median age of the population increased from 15.5 years in 1970 to 20.6 years in 2000 and further up to 28.0 years in 2016, reflecting an age structure transition from a 'very young' to 'mature' type of population. Based on the 2010 national census, the median age of the head of family also rose from 43.2 years in 2000 to 46.1 years in 2010. The transition of these demographic indicators was in line with the shift of population structure towards an aging society in Malaysia (DOSM 2010).

A similar trend was observed across the main ethnic groups in Malaysia from 1970 until 2011. Among males, the highest life expectancy at birth in 2011 was recorded by the Chinese at 74.5 years, followed by the Bumiputera (70.5 years) and the Indians (68.0 years). While among females, the highest was also recorded by Chinese (80.0 years), followed by Indians (76.8 years) and Bumiputera (75.4 years) (See Table 2.3). The differences across gender and ethnic groups may have been due to lifestyle and dietary difference or discrepancies in the knowledge, attitudes and practices (KAP) in health but this is yet to be further investigated in Malaysia. More importantly, the demographic transition in Malaysia implied the feminisation of ageing and diversification across ethnic groups.

Malaysia achieved remarkable progress in social development with improvements in educational levels, health status and the standard of living. As a result of health development strategies aimed at improving the infrastructure and delivery of health system (Hamid, Rashid & Salleh 2006), the *mortality rates* reduced to a fairly low level. The Crude Death Rate (CDR) dropped from 5.3 persons per 1000 populations in 1980 to 4.4 in 2005. In terms of ethnic group comparison, while the general pattern of CDR rates for different ethnic groups was coherent with the national pattern, statistics from the DOSM noted that the mortality rate was higher among Indians (7.0 in 1980, 5.2 in 2005) as compared to the Chinese (5.4 in 1980, 5.0 in 2005) and Malays (5.1 in 1980, 4.5 in 2005). The mortality rate difference may be attributed to the lifestyle and cultural practices of the ethnic Malays, Chinese and Indians in Malaysia (Hamid 2012).

In Malaysia, the trend of mortality rates among the elderly was on the decrease, an indication of a larger proportion of elderly in the coming decades. The continuous effort of the government on development and improvement of health care was evident. In the 2011 Malaysia budget, the government provided 5% of the government social sector development budget for public health care, which showed an increase of more than 47% compared to the previous budget. Due to the decreasing trend of mortality rates, there was an urgent need for the government to plan for and develop health programs to support more elderly people in the coming years.

4.2 *Proportion of Older People and Children and Dependency Ratio*

Malaysia experienced a gradual shift in the young-old balance over the last four decades. The 2010 national census reported that the total population of the country was 28.9 million of which 9.2 million were below 15 years old. While the total population soared from 10.4 million in 1970, the proportion of those below the age of 15 years (or young children) decreased to 31.7% in 2010 compared to 44.9% in 1970, 39.6% in 1980 and 35.4% in 2000. DOSM (2012b) projected that the downward trend of the below-15 young population would continue, and it was estimated that it would be 19% of the total population by 2040.

On the contrary, the elderly population (aged 60 or over) increased steadily over the last few decades (See Figure 2.4). The latest Census in 2010 reported a total of 2.3 million or 8% of the total population were elderly (aged 60 or

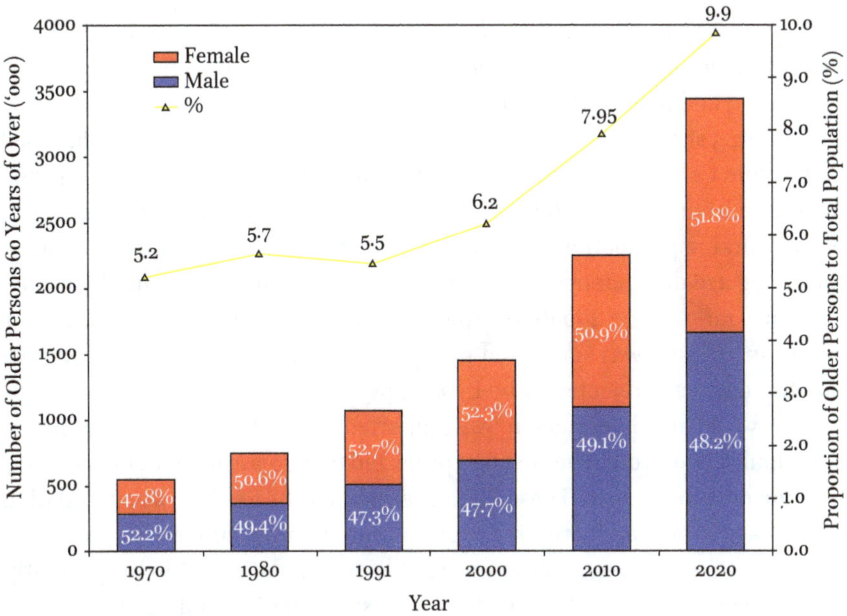

FIGURE 2.4 Rise of the older population, Malaysia (1970–2010).
SOURCE: DOSM 2011, 2012B.

over) which soared from 0.5 million or 5.2% in 1970. Specifically, data from the DOSM (2006, 2010) showed a steadily increasing share of population aged 60 or over, from 5.7% in 1950 to a rapid increase of 6.2% from the year 2000 onwards. The figure was projected to increase more than two-fold to 4.4 million or 10% of the total population by 2020 and by 2040, the percentage of older persons aged 65 and over was projected to soar to 11.4%. In other words, by 2020, one in ten Malaysians would be an older person aged 60 and over. In terms of gender differences, there was a larger proportion of male (52.2%) than female (47.8%) in the older population in 1970; however, after 1980, the pattern reversed where the females outnumbered the males with a gap of 1.2% in 1980, 5.4% in 1991, 4.6% in 2000 and 1.8% in 2010. In addition, it was projected that there would be 51.8% females and 48.2% males in the older population by 2020.

The *dependency ratio* is a rough indicator of the financial cost that the working population (15–64 years old) is facing to support the economically inactive population that include (1) children aged below 15 and (2) older persons aged 65 and over. Hamid (2012) noted that since the mid-1960s, the total dependency ratio for Malaysia fell due to the shrinking proportion of the young population. However, the country would experience an expansion of the aged population and contraction of the youth population as a result of declining fertility and mortality rate as well as increased longevity. In the 2000 Census, it was found that one older person was supported by 15 productive aged members of the population and in 2010, the number decreased to 14 (DOSM 2005, 2011).

Figure 2.5 shows the projected population support ratios of Malaysia based on the 2010 Census. It indicates that the total dependency ratio was projected to decline from 47.8 to 44.9 for the period of 2010 to 2040. This increased cost of the working population in Malaysia was further reflected in the decline in the young age dependency ratio from 40.4 to 28.3 and increase in old age dependency ratio from 7.4 to 16.6 during the same period. In other words, in 2010, one young person was supported by 2 persons of the productive age population but this was projected to be 1 young person to almost 4 working persons in 2040; while one older person was supported by 14 persons in the productive age population in 2010. The cost was projected to increase to 1 older person to 7 working persons in 2040. These figures reveal that the working age population would have to bear an increasing support from their dependents, in particular, the increasing number of those in the old age population. More importantly, the increasing number of family members surviving into old age means that the population would require more personal care. The demand for care would intensify with old age and deteriorating health status. However, given the smaller number of families which were available to share the responsibility, as well as the geographical distance, the question of whether or not the family was ready to provide this type of care remained to be answered.

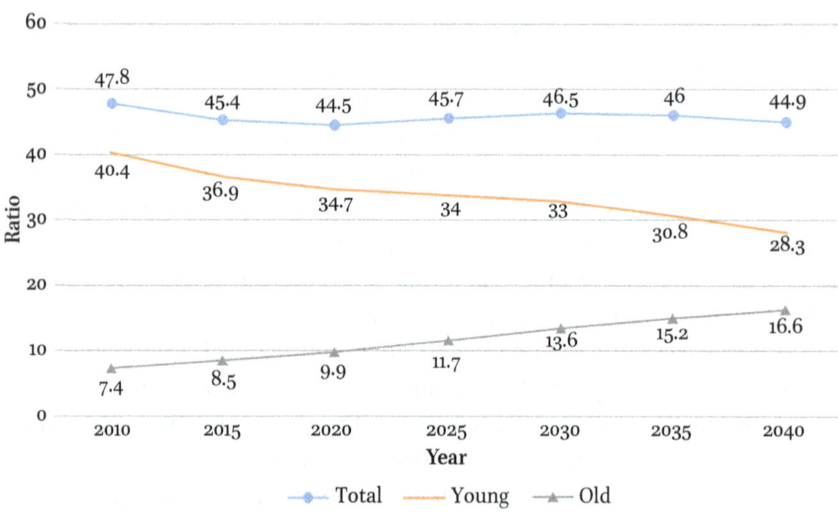

FIGURE 2.5 Dependency ratio, Malaysia, 2010–2040.
SOURCE: DOSM 2012B.

4.3 *Family/Household Composition and Size*

4.3.1 Changes in Family Composition

Malaysia was a developing country, having started off with an agrarian economy before successfully transforming to a modern industrialised economy. The country achieved remarkable economic progress and modernisation since its independence in 1957. Over the last four decades, Malaysia experienced a significant change in family landscape in terms of composition, size, structure and functions, as a result of demographic transition and socio-cultural shift. Family structure also diversified from traditional two-parent families to include a significant proportion of single-parent, blended, step and dual-earners families (Doshi 2010; Strong, DeVault & Cohen 2011) and this had an impact on the functions of family and relationships between generations. The fundamental changes in the composition and structure of families among the Malay, Chinese and Indian communities differed, given their unique socio-cultural characteristics. The following summarises the key trends and characteristics of the families in Malaysia, with details in the sections that follow.

(1) The significant proportion of nuclear household in Malaysia was steadily growing with a narrowing gap between urban and rural areas.
(2) Increasing proportion of single-person/one generation households.
(3) Increasing proportion of nuclear household with older persons.
(4) Decreasing family and household size.

4.3.2 Shrinking Family Size and Prevalence of Nuclear Household

Demographic transition in Malaysia reflected the change from a large family size with short lifespans to a small family size and longer lifespans. Census data provided a clear indication that there was a continuous decline in family size. The average family size was reported to be at 5.2 in 1980 and it had dropped to 4.3 in 2010. Similarly, the average household size reported a downward trend where the average number of persons per private household in Malaysia was reported to have decreased from 5.2 (1980) to 4.2 (2010).

As indicated in Tables 2.4 and 2.5, the nuclear family which consisted of two parents and at least one unmarried child, remained the predominant family living arrangement in Malaysia. It also remained the most frequently reported type of household as compared to others that included extended households, single person households and living with relatives. According to the National Census and 2004 Malaysian Population Family Survey (MPFS), there was an increased percentage of nuclear household families in which 70% of the households form a nuclear family as compared to 65.4% in 2000. However, this figure has dropped to 62.8% in 2010. A similar descending trend was observed

TABLE 2.4 Household types (%) by Stratum, Malaysia (1980–2010)

Year	Total		Urban		Rural	
	Nuclear	Extended	Nuclear	Extended	Nuclear	Extended
1980	55.2	27.8	50.4	29.3	57.7	27.0
1991	59.9	26.4	58.7	27.2	61.1	25.7
1994	68.0	26.0	67.0	26.0	69.0	27.0
2000	65.4	20.3	65.9	19.3	64.6	22.1
2004*	70.3	20.3	70.1	19.3	70.7	21.8
2010	70.0	18.0	n/a	n/a	n/a	n/a

* Peninsular Malaysia only.
SOURCE: DOSM 2012B

among extended family households where the total percentage dropped to 18.0% in 2010 from 27.8 in 2000. The percentage difference in nuclear households between rural and urban areas was more apparent between 1980 and 1994; while from 2000 onwards, the proportion of nuclear households was almost equal between the rural and urban stratums. While there was a decline in extended family households, past research asserted that there was relatively a high proportion of the elderly in Malaysia who continued to co-reside with their adult children and other family members (DaVanzo & Chan 1994; Chan & DaVanzo 1996; Ngin & DaVanzo 1999).

4.4 *Growing Single Person and Older Person Household*

While there was a decrease in the percentage of nuclear households to 62.5% in 2010, single person households have shown a slight increase in percentage. The proportion of single person households has grown to 8.7% in 2010 from 7.1% in 2000. Looking at the subset of households with older persons, about one-third of them were nuclear households while more than half tend to be extended households (Table 2.5). There was also an increase of nuclear households with older persons (37.6%) in 2000 compared to 1990 (30.6%); while the number of extended households with older persons decreased during the same period of time. This may be an indication that given their increased longevity, older people were more likely to live with their spouse in a nuclear household as compared to co-residing with adult children who were living at a distance or in a different city.

TABLE 2.5 Living arrangement, Malaysia (1991 & 2000)

Types of household composition	Total Private household			Household with Older persons		
	1991 (%)	2000 (%)	2009/10* (%)	1991 (%)	2000 (%)	2009/10* (%)
Single-member	8	7	8.7	6.8	6.8	9.2
Unrelated member	3	4	0.3	1.4	1.0	0.3
Nuclear family	60	65	67.8	30.6	37.6	66.8
Extended family	26	20	23.8	57.8	49.2	23.8
Other related member	3	4	–	3.5	5.6	–
Total household (Thousands)	3,537.60	4,777.60	43.02	571.10	798.70	7.89

SOURCE: DOSM 2005, 2011

4.4.1 Diversified Family and Emergence of New Family Types

While statistics on divorce and marital dissolution, an indication of the stability of the family as an institution, indicate that the majority of Malaysian families tended to be stable, non-traditional families such as single parent, blended and step-families were on the rise in the current society. As shown in Figure 2.6, the divorce rate increased steadily from 0.58 cases per 1000 population in 2000 to 1.02 in 2005 and slipped slightly to 0.93 in 2008. Moreover, there was a disparity between the number of divorce cases among non-Muslims and those among the Muslim population. Among non-Muslims, the number of divorces increased rapidly by 2.7 times (9,020 cases) in 2012 from just 3,291 cases in 2004. In comparison, the number of divorces between Muslim couples increased more than twofold within 10 years in which the number of cases increased from 13,536 in 2000 to 20,529 in 2007 and further soared to 27,891 in 2009 and 33,239 in 2010. In addition, 20.7% of the 135,548 registered marriages resulted in divorce in the year 2010 alone (DOSM 2006, 2010).

While the divorce rate steadily increased among both Muslim and non-Muslim couples, the rates of marriage tended to be higher between Muslims (M) than non-Muslims (NM) couples (2000: M=14.7%, NM=2.6%; 2003: M=15.2%; NM=5.6%; 2005: M=15.5%; NM=7.2%). Comparing the three dominant ethnic groups, Chinese Malaysians had the lowest divorce or separation rate (2.2%),

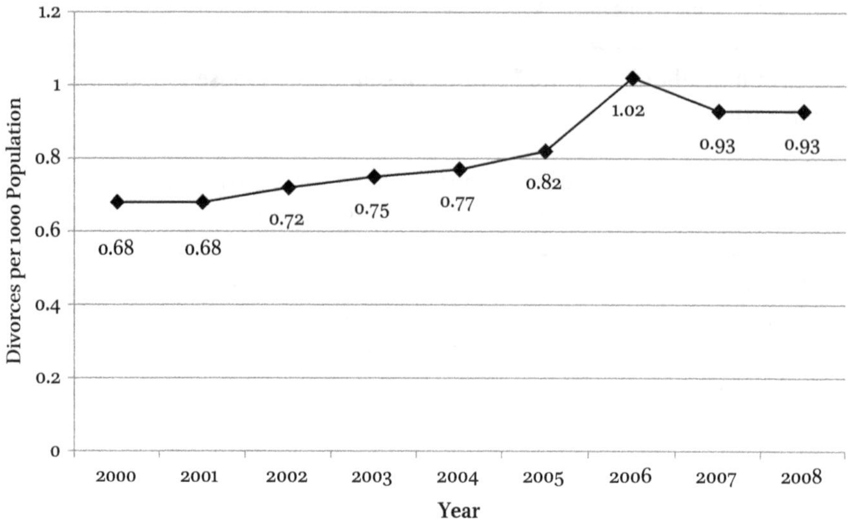

FIGURE 2.6 Divorces in Malaysia, 2000–2008 (per 1000 population).
SOURCE: DOSM 2006, 2010.

followed by Indians (2.9%), and Malays (8.4%). In 1989, only 19.9% of divorced women in general remarried, but the rate was 78.7% for Malay women. It was widely perceived that these higher rates of divorce and remarriage in large part simply reflected the fact that divorce and remarriage tended to be far more socially acceptable among Malays than among the other ethnic groups (DOSM 2006, 2010).

The MPFS 2004 found that reasons for divorce included misunderstandings (41.6%), irresponsible husbands (11.6%) and in-law interference (8.9%). Other causes may have included poor parent-child relationships, failure to solve family issues, domestic violence and, lack of communication and commitment to the family (Doshi 2010). Following divorce, mothers typically received primary custody of the children. This could have had a significant impact on the father-child relationship and also the financial standing of the mother. Marital dissolution also led to other issues including severance of marital bonds, establishment of a new lifestyle, economic stressors, negotiation of custody arrangements, adjustments in parenting, and changes in social support systems. This phenomenon no doubt caused changes in the structure and dynamics among families in Malaysia such as the issues related to single mothers, the rise of women-headed households and, the adjustment of, and relationship between, divorced parents and their children (Doshi 2010).

Progressive economic development in the country which provided increased opportunities for employment and education, specifically among women, combined with changing family values and high cost of living, led to the emergence of several new types of family in Malaysian society such as dual-career families, DINK (Double Income, No Kids) families and commuter families. *Dual career* or dual earner families referred to families where both parents were actively engaged in full time employment and contribute to the economic well-being of the household. Within dual-career households, both parents were constantly challenged by the demanding roles of worker, parent and spouse. They also juggled issues on role conflict and role overload that included problems with child care arrangement, time management and balancing the demands of work and family life, emotional stress, and the need for support from the family and the workplace (Doshi 2010). Another significant implication of an increased female labor participation within Malaysian society was the emergence of "*DINK Syndrome/Lifestyle*" (Double Income, No Kids), where some couples may have decided not to have children at all. "*Househusbands*" may have also increased and this would have implications for family relationships and the traditional gender roles and responsibilities of husbands and wives (Doshi 2010).

The phenomenon of the *commuter family* became a concern in Malaysian society since their living style was entirely different from the conventional family model in Malaysia. A *Commuter family* was defined as a weekend family whereby one of the married couple stayed far away from the nuclear family and they met regularly but only once a week, twice a month or once a month. The commuter lifestyle either on a voluntary or an obligatory basis was often related to increasing households with dual-career couples, financial and societal demands, career enhancement, deployment by employer and potentially higher incomes. This new type of family emerged as a direct result of shifting demographical trends and socio-cultural values that might have had long-term implications for family relationships across generations and care networks in Malaysia. The emergence of various unconventional family models challenged the traditional gender ideology of 'father as primary breadwinner and mother as primary caregiver' in a nuclear family; and thus, their impact on the fast ageing society of Malaysia had a considerable impact on the development of the social protection programme and policy (Doshi 2010).

4.4.2 Decreasing Two-generation and Increasing One-generation Families

The rapid development and urbanisation process in Malaysia accelerated the outmigration of the younger generation for education, employment and marriage leaving the older population remaining in the rural areas. As such it impacted on the decrease of two generations and increase in one generation families. MPFS-5 (NPFDB 2014) survey found more than 66% of households being nuclear family households as compared to only 20.8% of the population living in extended family households. Adding to that, the mean household size was four persons and 82% of households are headed by male (Doshi 2010).

Concurrently, this scenario brought the older generation to next stage of family life, the so- called empty nest. The term empty nest referred to the situation where the elderly person was living alone or living together only with their spouse after their children migrated elsewhere. A recent national survey shows that 9.0% of the elderly are living alone and 20.9% are living only with their spouse (Doshi 2010). These elderly ones may be experiencing the empty nest syndrome. This kind of situation must be given special attention as it may affect the emotional, health and economic stability of the elderly.

4.5 *Marriage and Divorces*

Demographic changes significantly affected the marriage trend in Malaysian society. Greater access to education and more opportunities in the labor force market delayed marriage and family formation among Malaysians. Some of the major trend and characteristics included:

(1) Delayed marriage and child birth.
(2) Growing single or unmarried population.
(3) Diversified and emergence of new family types.

4.5.1 Delayed Marriage and Child Birth

There was a clear trend of men and women in Malaysia getting married at a later age, in particular, among women. Statistics showed that among women, the *mean age at first marriage* has increased from 23.5 years in 1980 to 25.1 years in 2000, and 25.7 years in the 2010 census; while among men, the *mean age of first marriage* also rose from 26.6 years in 1980 to 28.6 years in 2000 and 28.0 years in the latest 2010 census. A similar pattern was reported among Malays, Chinese and Indians (Doshi 2010).

Delay in marriage may be strongly associated with improvement in education attainment and employment opportunities. The achievement of women in education was remarkable with the increment of those in secondary education rising from 10% to 39.2% between 1970 and 2000; tertiary education reached 6.2% in 2000; and a reduction in the percentage of 'never attended school' from 51.0 to 22.8% was reported. The Malaysian Population and Family Survey-4, conducted in 2004 also revealed that age at first marriage increased with the educational level among women whereas women with no schooling showed the lowest age at first marriage (20.6 years) while those with tertiary education reported the highest age at first marriage (25.6 years). The effects of educational level tended to be more evident on marriage postponement among the Chinese as compared to Malays and Indians (NPFDB 2005). Specifically, Tey (2007b) noted that in comparison to their Malay and Indian counterparts, Chinese women who were tertiary-educated tend to marry 5 years later, or more, than those who only received primary education; while this gap was much smaller among the Malays (1.3 years) and Indians (2.4 years) (NPFDB 2005).

4.5.2 Rise of Single or Unmarried Population

Among the *single or unmarried population*, their percentage distribution across different age groups was also changing. The percentage of the population who were never married in the age groups of 15 to 19 and 20 to 24 was higher but moving toward a decreasing trend from 1980 to 2000 while those who were never married in the age groups of 30 to 34 and above was on the rise during the same period of time. Specifically, the proportion of never-married people aged 20–34 increased from 43.2% in 1991 to 48.1% in 2000. The figures of single females between the ages of 20 to 34 increased to 68.5% in 2000, compared to only 60.2% in 1991. This pattern was found to be consistent among males and females between the ages of 25 to 34 (DOSM 2003a).

The 2004 MPF Survey (MPFS-4) also showed that the tendency to postpone marriage may be explained by the relatively high level of education in which more single females (34.7%) attained tertiary education qualifications than single males (25.7%) and, their economy stability where the majority are in employment whether as employees (79.5%), self-employed (15.9%), employers (2.6%) and unpaid family worker (1.9%). Only a minority (18%) indicated that they have 'no intention to get married' due to financial constraints (NPFDB 2005). In terms of ethnic comparison, at ages 30 to 34, there were almost one third of Chinese women with tertiary education level who were still unmarried and the proportion of married Malay women was also higher compared with Chinese and Indians across most age groups. While it was recognised that the proportion of the population who were never married has doubled in the last decade, the changing values and expectation of the society together with rising education level, career opportunities and options in life contributed to the increase of the single, unmarried population in Malaysia. Those who remained unmarried in their 30s may be encouraged by economic independence, availability of other options than marriage from increased employment, career development and greater freedom in life. This emergence of 'SINK' (Single Income, No Kid) lifestyle reflected a new trend in Malaysian society where both men and women in the working age group remained single without children.

5 Changes in Policy and Legislation

5.1 *Five Phases of Policy Regimes along Demographic Change*

Malaysia underwent a series of policy and legislative changes to promote economic growth and social development. Some of these policies directly or indirectly affected family structure and its function in protecting and caring for dependent family members. Lower fertility associated with rapid economic growth allowed the government to focus national investments in social development which include family planning, education, and health care programs (Robey 1991). In addition to lower fertility rates, economic developments also brought improvements in medical technology, public health and nutrition that led to increased well-being and increased life expectancy (Bongaarts & Sinding 2011; Robey 1991).

After its independence in 1957, the country implemented a total of ten national development plans which have guided the country's developmental planning strategies and contributed to a significant reduction in the incidence of poverty, and to a more equitable distribution of income. Policies concerning children and the elderly were scattered and largely incorporated into various general policies until early 2000s. A diversity of family-related policies and legislation were also implemented in Malaysia to address the need for different laws which cater to the Muslim and non-Muslim population.

Drawing upon these contextual backgrounds, this section aims to provide explanations for care relations in Malaysia, focusing on national development strategies and the shift in relevant policies as well as their implications for population structure and care relations and support for young and old within the family and beyond.

5.1.1 Phase I: Population Growth in 1950s and Introduction of Family Planning Policy in the 1960s

Between the period from 1950 to 1955, Malaysia continued to have high fertility rates with a total fertility rate of 6.8 births per woman (Bach 1981). Family planning was not included in national development plans until the early 1960s (Tey 2007). The reason behind this lag was because during the 1950s, family planning was perceived negatively by the federal government. High fertility rates and rapid population growth following Independence were necessary to fast-track economic growth. Despite that, the government allowed the services to be carried out by private entities, comprising various Family Planning Associations at state level, whose services were mainly available in large urban areas and to those who could afford such services (Tey 2007).

With economic problems looming, the government became increasingly apprehensive of the impact of high population growth on the society, the economy and the health fabric of the country (Chong, Sia, Lim & Ooi 2011). In particular, as a result of the economic slump from falling rubber prices and increasing unemployment, the government was concerned about whether the standard of living could be maintained unless there were improvements in employment and economic production. By 1964, the government changed its approach and decided to adopt family planning as a policy based on the report on "The Population, Development and Welfare in Malaysia".

When the First Malaysia Plan (1966–1975) came into effect in 1966, one of the specific targeted areas was population control and family planning (First Malaysia Plan 1966–1975). Parliament passed the Family Planning Act (Act No. 42) that led to the establishment of the National Population and Family Development Board (NPFDB) to provide the required leadership in the coordination and implementation of a National Family Planning Programme (NFPP) (Yoon & Cha 1999). Family planning became a tool to curb population growth rate and increase the average annual per capita income. By the early 1970s, family planning services were extended to various parts of the country (with the exception of Sabah and Sarawak which came much later) through integration with the maternal and child health programs under the Ministry of Health (Tey 2007). Thus, the change in national policy towards the adoption of family planning marked the triumph of economics and health over politics and religious fundamentalism in a country with a multi-ethnic society and Islam as a main religion (Inhorn & Sargent 2006; Tey 2007). In relation to childcare, the earliest policy of the National Education Policy, was on matters related to children, which focused on promoting preschool education for children. This reflected the government's initial efforts in human capital development through opportunities for education. This policy and legislative development have gradually led to a significant change in family size and population growth rates in the country.

5.1.2 Phase 2: Fertility Transition and New Economic Policy in the 1970s

The NFPP has effectively changed fertility levels in the population through its programs on family planning and limiting child births. Between 1970 and 1979, Malaysia's TFR had declined to 5.2 births per woman (Bach 1981). Ethnic differences in the acceptance of the NFPP were consequential in the diverging fertility trends among the main ethnic groups in Peninsular Malaysia (Abu Bakar, Tan, Tey & Rohani 1985; Yoon & Cha 1999). As the average annual population growth rate declined from 3.2 (1960–1965) to 2.4 (1970–1975) (DaVanzo & Starbird 1991), population growth was no longer featured in policies.

Under the Second Malaysian Plan (1971–1975), there was greater emphasis on rapid economic growth through greater opportunities for education, employment and higher income for those in disadvantaged groups. The New Economic Policy (NEP), drawn up after the May 1969 ethnic riots, combined all development planning with intensified implementation of poverty reduction programs to offset economic imbalance and create social unity. Improvements in economic indicators have led to fertility decline across all ethnic groups, with the Chinese and Indians having a much accelerated decline compared to the Malays (Bach 1981). Through the NEP, there was also a growing Malay middle class from the greater opportunities for urban migration, employment, education and affirmative action on quotas for business participation (Leete 1996). The policy's underlying motive of economic growth through income redistribution and affirmative action was noted as a reason for the variations in fertility decline among the ethnic groups due to differential opportunities afforded in education and employment.

5.1.3 Phase 3: Pro-natalist Policy for Population Growth and Increase in Productivity in the 1980s

The period of the 1980s saw enormous economic and social changes due to economic liberalisation and industrialisation in response to recessionary pressure at the beginning of the decade. Under the newly-elected Prime Minister, Dr. Mahathir Mohamad in 1981, the government introduced the Look East Policy, which resulted in privatisation and an aggressive industrial policy with a heavy emphasis on industrialisation in the national development strategies. The formulation of the Industrial Master Plan in 1985 has transformed Malaysia's industrial landscape into one that is capital intensive, high-tech and knowledge-based (EPU 1986). As a result, labor shortages began to emerge with industrialisation and the foreign labor market burgeoned (Ariff 1998). In the Mid-Term Review of the Fourth Malaysia Plan (1981–1985), a pro-natalist policy was developed and family planning was de-emphasised and Information Education and Communication (IEC) activities were discontinued. This was also supported by resurgence of Islamic fundamentalism in the 1970s. Thus, Malaysia was able to maintain fertility levels at a medium range compared to other Southeast Asian countries (Gubhaju & Moriki-Durand 2003; Sanderson & Tan 1995; Tey 2007).

The Fourth Malaysia Plan (1980–1985) not only promoted the agenda on women and included integration programs of women in development, but also included expanded programs for medical and health services to promote family development, women and child well-being, from infancy until they leave school. In relation to childcare services, the provision of maternity and child health services was expanded to previously underserved urban and rural centres as well as specific areas such as estates and mines (*Fourth Malaysian Plan 1981–1985*, 254). A review of the National Population Policy (NPP) in 1984 led to a major shift from family planning to family and human resource development, to achieve an ultimate population of 70 million by 2100 and to raise the quality of the population through education and human resource development. The NFPP was renamed the National Population and Family Development (NPFD) Programme with an expansion of programs on reproductive health, gender issues, marriage, parenting and counselling (Mahari 2011). The NPFD Board developed strategies and programs on family welfare in order to achieve a target population of 70 million by 2100, guided by more family-focused principles of the NPP: Attainment of a quality education, the role of woman in development, family support of the elderly, encouraging family and community and the government to support vulnerable/disadvantage groups and programs for child protection and survival.

In 1989, the National Policy on Women was introduced to enhance the role of women and warrant their integration into the development process including promotion of health services to women and children (Kahar & Mohd Zin 2011). In the same year, important legislation related to family development such as the *Child Care Centre Act 1984* (CCCA 1984) was introduced to regulate the quality of child care services for children below the age of four, and Early Childhood Care and Development training were provided to service providers and parents. The *Islamic Family Law (Federal Territories) Act 1984* contains the provisions for the rights of a Muslim child to be provided with maintenance by the parents until the age of 18 or until the completion of higher education/training. The Act also stipulates matters pertaining to the custody and welfare of children, including children who are born out of wedlock. Thus, in terms of family and child care, Muslim and non-Muslim women are governed separately by various laws such as the *Islamic Family Law Act* for Muslims and *The Law Reform (Marriage and Divorce) Act 1976* and *Married Women and Children (Maintenance) Act 1968* for non-Muslims. The implementation of diverse family- and child-related policies and legalisation is unique in the Malaysian context; nonetheless, an absence of child-focused and family-focused policy affects their smooth implementation in terms of upholding and supporting child care and family well-being (Kahar & Mohd Zin 2011). In terms of childcare, the *Care Centres Act 1993* governs the registration, control and inspection of the day and residential care centres which provide care for four or more persons over an extended period of time. Together with the *CCCA 1984*, these two Acts are crucial for the provision of child care services and quality control of child centres by both private and public sectors.

Policies implemented at the beginning of 1990 carried impacts on fertility rates and shortened childbearing spans for women and have contributed, through better education, and later marriage, and the country's vision, towards nation building and development of quality human resources. This lead to the introduction of the National Social Welfare Policy in 1990 with a focus on policies that promote the concept of a stable and 'caring society' for the well-being of people. The National Social Welfare Policy (1990) also addressed the need of older persons for care within the family and community, a commitment that was further emphasised in the National Policy for the Elderly (1995) (Ambigga et al. 2011).

5.1.4 Phase 4: Increased Emphasis on Social Development from 1996

The rapid economic progression that followed aggressive national industrialisation strategies in the 1990s has raised concern on the impact of economic growth on the individual, family and community development. The Seventh Malaysia Plan (1996–2000) reflected a significant paradigm shift in the national development plan with a greater precedence of social over economic development. With an increased budget allocation for a social agenda, the national development plan aimed for a more balanced development to create a resilient society with strong family values, greater self-discipline and an appreciation for culture (Seventh Malaysia Plan, 5). As proposed in the Vision 2020 plan (1990), national strategies were shifted to a stronger emphasis on economic resilience and quality of life with positive social and spiritual values (Seventh Malaysia Plan, 4), strengthening the nation's focus on developing quality human resources through the solidification of the family institution. In addition, this renewed emphasis also included efforts on promoting relationships between family members and across generations though the National Development Plan (NDP), replacing the NEP in 1991, for more integrated and holistic human resources development.

While there is still no child-focused policy in Malaysia, family-friend social policies for child care and family support are embedded in various general policies and legislation. For example, the *Education Act 1996* represents a strong government commitment to childcare, upholding the rights of every child of school age to free education for a period of eleven years. Under the Islamic Family law, the establishment of the Family Support Unit is the most recent policy introduced by the government in order to address the issues of maintenance, including children's educational support, (Kahar & Mohd Zin 2011), in addition to the *Baitul Mal* scheme which provides financial disbursement to the divorced, as well as economically deprived Muslim women whose ex-husbands could not afford to pay for their maintenance. It has been argued that the care and financial support for children under the *Islamic Family Law Act 1984* was more advanced than the civil courts, which governed the welfare of non-Muslim children (Kahar & Mohd Zin 2011).

The Child Act 2001 (CA 2001) was enacted when Malaysia realised that many of its statutes did not conform to the United Nations Convention on the Rights of a Child (UNCRC). The *CA 2001* is very comprehensive and covers all areas of law relating to children, from ill-treatment, neglect, abandonment or exposure of children to moral danger, child prostitution or begging to children left without reasonable supervision. In 2006, both the *CCCA 1984* and *CCA 1993* were amended to monitor the operation and quality control of childcare centres, including those at workplace and community centres. Compulsory Certification on Registration of Child Care Centre was issued to all qualified service providers. Following public concerns regarding children's safety, quality of care and training of child minders, the Department of Social Welfare was given more authority in monitoring the administration of centres with support from the Health Department, Fire and Safety Department and the Local Authority. The provision of childcare services, often privately owned, is often viewed by authorities as a business enterprise where the permit has to be renewed on a yearly basis rather than on the basis of the best interests of the child. Thus, this may have implications for children safety and the quality of child care services. Nonetheless, the National *Permata* Policy for early childhood care and education in rural areas and areas with lower socio-economic income groups has been implemented at government kindergartens and nurseries for children under 4 years old. This reflects the government's efforts and serious intent in the creation of policies and implementation of laws on childcare in Malaysia.

Major policies addressing the needs of older persons were also introduced from the 1990s namely the National Policy for the Elderly (1995) which was later revised in 2011. In 2003, the National Social Policy was used to consolidate all social development policies and strengthen other action plans in previous social policies (Kahar & Mohd Zin 2011). The government, through the Ministry of Health, also developed the National Plan of Action for the Health Care of Older Persons in 1997.

5.1.5 Phase 5: Approaching Replacement Level 2007 and Onwards

As the fertility rate is approaching replacement level, the government's view on fertility has changed from 'too high' in 1996 to 'satisfactory' in 2007. Thus, the population policy on fertility was reviewed and revised from one that sought to lower it, to one with no intervention, but with the emphasis on raising the quality of the population through education and human resource development.

The 1995 National Policy for the Elderly, which was revised in 2011 based on Madrid International Plan of Action on Ageing (MIPAA), was set to re-examine strategies for incorporating the reintegration of older persons into society, in order to promote healthy, active and productive ageing. These were pressing issues as Malaysia is approaching the fertility replacement level and transforming into an aging society at a much faster rate than expected, including increased life expectancy, a soaring population of older people, estimated to reach 15% by 2030 from 8% at present, under-utilisation of human resources, care and support for dwindling extended families, inadequate social protection, and the high cost of long term care. The introduction of the policy has led to several changes:

- Raising the mandatory retirement age to 60 in both the public and private sector.
- Tax relief up to RM5,000 to those who are providing care for the elderly which includes day care costs, a salary for maids who are specifically hired for the care of elderly and the cost of daily needs for encouraging family care.
- 100% tax rebate on costs to retrain older persons.
- Financial assistance for older people amounting to RM300 to assist the elderly poor to remain in their families or communities.
- The first University of the Third Age (U3A) in Malaysia was set up, affiliated to the Institute of Gerontology to encourage learning for leisure among the elderly.
- Through We Care Services, the Central Welfare Council of Peninsular Malaysia and Department of Social Welfare provide free transportation as a medium of accessibility to older person with disabilities to hospitals/clinics for health treatment and services.
- *Rumah Seri Kenangan* (home for the elderly), *Pusat Activiti Warga Emas* (senior activity centres) and home help services for elderly persons living alone, and partnerships with NGOs were set up to provide care and protection for the elderly who are in need and to encourage active aging.

In addition, the need for effective, coordinated and comprehensive health care for the elderly population led to the development of the National Health Policy for Older Persons in 2008. These governmental efforts were translated into services provided at Health Centres that included health promotion and education, health assessment, medical examinations, home visits and home nursing and rehabilitation, and at the hospitals, services include acute medical care, long term care, discharge plans, psycho geriatric care, counselling and clinical pharmacy. In addition, recognising the importance of the family as social and production units, and its important role in nurturing the future generation and the care of older people, a National Family Policy was introduced in 2010. It was used as the blueprint for family services and encompasses housing, education, health and community development. It advocated the concept of 'Family Well-being' based on family values, to impart positive values from generation to generation, and thus the importance of family solidarity development.

In terms of child care, many family policies were reviewed and revised to accommodate the emerging needs of changing Malaysian society. After 2011, maternity leave, addressed in the Employment Act 1955, increased from 60 days' leave to 90 days for civil servants, with other institutions and multinational companies beginning to follow the 90 days of leave. Paternity leave for civil servants increased from 3 days to 7 days in 2003. Under the *Children Act 2011*, Cash Allowances were provided for the following: (1) civil servants with a household income of less than RM5,000; (2) parents with a household income of not more than RM900 who sent their children to private childcare centres registered under the Social Welfare Department; and (3) tax relief of RM1,000 per child under the *Income Tax Act 1967*.

Several main social security programs were developed over the years which offered protection for old age support and ensure income security in old age, but much of the focus was on the national provident fund which managed a mandatory retirement savings scheme for private sector workers. The two main programs are the Employees Provident Fund (EPF), established in 1951 and governed by the *Employee's Provident Fund Act 1991*, which is a mandated defined contribution plan for private and non-pensionable public sector employees with a full withdrawal at age 55, and the Public Service Pension which was a pension payment for civil servants which was calculated based on the last drawn salary and number of years in service. It was perceived as a good scheme as compared to EPF because it buffered against inflation risks as it was adjusted in tandem with the civil service pay review. Other schemes which were given less attention include the Older Persons Assistance Scheme which started in the 1980s. This was a means-tested social assistance to support the poor elderly aged 60 years or over to sustain their livelihood in the community. In 2008, the government escalated their efforts through an active campaign to locate those in need of aid and this boosted the number of recipient by 7 times in 2010 compared to 2005.

Other schemes for specific populations included the Armed Forces Fund for military personnel below the rank of commissioned offers; the Private Retirement Scheme (PRS) which was a voluntary long term investment plan to boost retirement savings and was complimentary to saving with the EPF; the Malaysia Retirement Savings Scheme in 2010 targeting self-employed individuals and workers in informal sectors with fixed incomes including housewives; and the

Merdeka Savings Bond which was a risk-free, highly liquid, 3-year tenure bond issued by the Bank Negara Malaysia to boost retirement savings.

6 Changes in Care Relations

6.1 *Child Care*

In the last quarter of a century, Malaysia experienced rapid changes economically and socially. There was an emerging trend of contemporary social changes such as the rise of dual-worker households, sandwich families and commuter families, growing numbers, and higher rates, of family breakdown in the current society as well as economic problems (Ortega, Abdullah & Roslan 2014; Roslan, Li & Ahmad 2013) and (Roslan et al. 2013). Added to that, the increasing in education and labor force participation of women, and the dual earner couple emerged as the norm rather than the exception, and in the Malaysian context, women form a substantial force in the labor market. Thus, this new social economic transition had a significant impact on childcare.

6.1.1 Role of Family and Kin

One of the main functions of the family was to provide care for the young. The central and crucial role of family in the care of young children was prominent in traditional society. In Malaysia, child rearing that included instilling cultural values and norms to children was often not perceived as the sole responsibility of family, but was shared with other kin members (Yaacob 2014). Traditionally, children were primarily cared by the mother, but grandmothers and other familial or non-familial members may also be involved. The most recent national survey indicated that the care of young children was also provided by other family members, namely grandparents (60.4%), other relatives (22.5%), and older siblings (17.1%) (NPFDB 2014). For example, young children were being looked after by grandparents or an unmarried aunt when the parents were working. In line with this, Chinese parents were found to rely more on extended family members and grandparents for child-care and this may have also provided a better sense of security and assurance to parents that their babies were well cared for (Roopnarine, Lu & Mohammad 1989) while Malay parents tended to rely on other kin members for childcare.

Previously, a review of early childhood care and family policies in Malaysia by Kamerman (2002) highlighted a study by the National Planning and Development Board in 1998 on "Childcare and Parenting Styles among Working Parents". The study reported that working parents were profoundly dependent on alternative childcare services even though they would have preferred to provide the care themselves (14.6%) or to have family members play a role in co-parenting while they work (30.6%). Among family members, grandparents play an important role as care providers (60.4%) followed by other relatives (22.5%) and older siblings (17.1%). The survey also noted that working parents were also obtained care from neighbours and friends which accounted for another 15% of childcare services.

These changing demographic trends re-established intergenerational links and encouraged a more integral grandparental role to family functioning and intergenerational solidarity (Bengtson & Oyama 2007). More importantly, the unique role and contribution of grandparents and the fact that elderly parents played an increasingly significant role in downward support to their children and grandchildren in Asian societies, was recognised. (Butts, Thang, Yeo & Jefferson 2012; Tsai, Motamed, Elia & Rougemont 2011) Therefore, the potential importance and contribution of intergenerational relationships for the development of family and grandparents became increasingly recognised.

6.1.2 Role of State

There were three main ministries namely the Ministry of Women, Family and Community Development (MWFCD), the Ministry of Education (MOE) and the Ministry of Health (MOH) that were responsible for social welfare, health and education in childcare. They played an important key role in providing social welfare services, education and primary healthcare to children and families in order to ensure that family and community perspectives are incorporated in the formulation of policies and plans as well as in the implementation of programs.

In addition, the Malaysian government placed a strong emphasis on Early Childhood Care and Education (ECCE) and formulated the National Policy for Early Childhood Education (Boon 2010). Under this policy, programs were introduced to meet the various needs of the vital early years of children until the age of six. These programs provided a solid foundation for healthy growth and development which expose them to activities in nation building and enhance their readiness for primary school education (Boon 2010). There were several initiatives to make early childhood programs more accessible and available, especially for less fortunate children and those in less urban areas. Early childcare and education (ECCE) in Malaysia was divided into two age groups, which were 0–4 years and 4–6 years old. The first group (0–4 years), came under the Ministry of Women, Family and Community Development (MWFCD) which coordinated national programs on the growth and development of children ("Early Childhood Care & Education (ECCE) in Malaysia at a Glance (for newborns to 6–year olds),"). Through its Department of Social Welfare, MWFCD maintained registration of all childcare centers (also known as taska) in the country. Pre-school education for the second group (4–6 years) came under three ministries/agencies namely the Ministry of Education, the Ministry of Rural and Regional Development, and the National Unity Department and were offered through two types of institutions, namely childcare centres or nurseries or *taska*, and preschools or kindergartens or *tadika*.

In 2006, the *Permata* Early Childhood Education and Care programme with the theme 'Every Child a Jewel' was initiated to provide integrated quality care and early education services based on the needs of the local community to children below five years old. This program was implemented in childcare centres of the Community Development Department of the Ministry of Rural Development all over the country, childcare centres of the National Unity Department, and some institutions which were community-based childcare centres. It adopts the community-based integrated approach practised by Pen Green Corby, United Kingdom under the SureStart Programme. Under this approach, the centres offer childcare services, outreach programs, parenting courses, counselling, and healthcare services to help the local community develop a healthy lifestyle. Facilities included a community resource centre and library; and some may offer the services of a speech therapist and nutritionist. The founding principles of *Permata* ECEC Centres were: "Every child is a jewel for the country; Every child is precious; Every child is a part of the human capital of the country; Every child needs the best education; and Education must start from young/birth."

6.1.3 Role of Local Governments, Communities, and Other Not-for Profit Providers

In 1982, a study was jointly conducted by the Ministry of Social Welfare and the United Nation Children's Fund (UNICEF) which indicated the need to enhance the quality of childcare among childcare providers especially in the aspects of food handling, environment, mental development and training for childcare providers. As a result, the Childcare Centre Act 1984 was passed to maintain required minimum standards in childcare centres across the country. Besides its aim of providing care and education to preschool children, the Act included directives on registration; monitoring and inspection of the childcare centres; and protecting the interests and safety of the children against any form of abuse or neglect.

Thereafter, the Childcare Centre Act 1984 was reviewed and updated by Parliament giving rise to the Childcare Centres (Amendment) Act 2007. Government-supported community childcare centres, subsidized workplace childcare centres and a Quality Improvement Accreditation System (QIAS) were also implemented. The Association of Registered Childcare Providers

Malaysia (ARCPM) was one of the non-profit organizations that worked towards ensuring that the children received quality care by professional child-care providers and/or their parents. In Malaysia, a legislative-approved child-care centre was defined as any premise where four children or more from a household were received to be looked after for a fee with childcare services ranging from a half-day to full day basis. The objectives of the childcare centre are (i) to assist working parents so that their children get good care while they were at work, (ii) enhancing the standards of living of the family, (iii) to provide opportunities for people who love children to work in the childcare centres and (iv) encouraging involvement of society in the caring and nursing of the children. The childcare centres fell into four categories:

- Government-owned childcare centres
- Workplace childcare centres
- Institution-based childcare centres with 10 children or more
- Home-based childcare centres with fewer than 10 children

Under the Childcare Centre Act, all childcare centres needed to be registered with the Department of Social Welfare (DSW), more popularly known as *Jabatan Kebajikan Masyarakat Malaysia* (JKM), under the Ministry of Women, Family and Community Development (MWFCD). MWFCD was responsible for the approval and establishment of childcare centres in the country whilst the Department of Social Welfare served as the main regulator and coordinator of ECCE programs. In the plantation sector, childcare centres were provided under the Standard Act, Minimum Housing and Workers Facilitation 1990 and monitored by the Ministry of Human Resources. The Association of Registered Childcare Providers Malaysia (ARCPM) was a registered national association that plays roles in implementing programs and providing consultancy & training services to childcare providers, organizations and individuals who worked with children.

6.1.4 Day Care Services by Profit and Not-for Profit Providers

During the 1950s, child care services were limited to those provided by the churches (Chiam 2008). Fortunately, the extended family could still be relied upon at that time to supplement the role of parents in providing childcare. Nevertheless, significant rural-urban migration led to the breakdown of extended families and coupled with the unprecedented entry of women into the labor market, the care of children was beyond what the family could cope with. For these reasons, child care services were made available by the late 1970s (Chiam 2008).

As Malaysia was increasingly moving towards becoming a developed nation by 2020 and look to boost its female workforce participation, the establishment of high-quality child care centres became an imperative. Awareness of the demand for childcare kept increasing as most parents, especially those from urban areas, are both active in the work force. However, the National Family and Population Board's survey in 1999 reported that affordability became a significant factor for parents to want to use childcare services.

Therefore, in the *Ninth Malaysian Plan* 2006–2010, the Malaysian government initiated community childcare centres in urban and rural areas with the objective of providing quality childcare services that was more accessible and affordable to the local community especially for targeted groups. The centres used a curriculum set by MWFCD which was based on the active participation of the local community, parents, children, governmental agencies as well as private organizations.

Besides that, workplace childcare centres were another alternative that provide child rearing services. In line with the National Plan of Action for Children for the establishment of child care centres to be set up at, or near business premises, which operated during the usual work hours of the employer towards providing care for children aged 0–4 years, as specified in the Child Care Centre Act 1984, MWFCD encouraged employers to set up childcare at the workplace. For instance, the government provided incentives in the form of a RM 80,000 grant for the establishing of childcare centres within government offices. In addition to encouraging working mothers to utilise these centres, a subsidy of RM180 per month was given to government servants with monthly salaries below RM2000 who sent their children to these centres. MWFCD also encouraged the private sector to provide childcare facilities at the workplace for their employees. Incentives included a 10% tax exemption on the cost of building the childcare centres for a period of 10 years.

Despite the local community and government providing several schemes and incentives to encourage participation of mothers in labor force, the rate of workforce participation among Malaysia women (aged 15–64) remained well below that of other countries in Southeast Asia, ranging between 44–47% for the last three decades. The low rate of Malaysian women's participation in the workforce was mainly due to inflexible working arrangements, family commitments and child rearing responsibilities (MWFCD 2014). As such, work-family balance became a common issue related to early resignations among women workers (NPFDB 2014). The recent 5th Malaysian Families Survey (MFS-5) highlighted childcare problems as the highest reason for leaving the workforce among Malaysia women, accounting for 32.4%. . As such, the cost of childcare could be one of the reasons for women to stop working. In Malaysia, a local study found that on average the cost of childcare ranges from RM350 up to RM1,200 per month excluding necessities such as clothes, diapers and food or formula milk which might cost up to RM3,000 per month. The fees for childcare centres commonly depend on the location, type of childcare service, age of child, the length of time that the services were required, whether these were used on a full day or half day basis. Another option for childcare was through employing a live in domestic helper a so called "*bibik*" which may have costed up to RM22,400 per year including fees for domestic workers' agency that ranged between RM8000 and RM18,000 (Baby Centre 2015).

6.2 *Elderly Care*

6.2.1 Role of Family and Kin

The family was considered the main institution for the livelihood and care of older persons. This was based on with its traditional role of directly caring for their aged relatives. In line with Asian values of filial piety and religious values of respecting and caring for older parents, society's younger members, out of their sense of duty and filial piety, care for elderly family members (Alavi, Sail, Idris, Samah & Omar 2011; Hossain 2014). Institutionalisation was frowned upon because it implies irresponsible and ungrateful children dumping their parents in the old folks or nursing homes (Kua 2007).

Family members, especially adult children, remained the main support for the elderly in Malaysian society (Ong & Hamid 2010; Teh, Ng, Tey & Siti-Norlasiah 2013). A local study on living arrangement preference among elderly parents noted that almost all the respondents refused to stay at nursing homes, regardless of ethnicity (Alavi et al. 2011). The study reported that Malay and Indian parents indicated that since they had taken care of their children, when the parents were fragile and unhealthy would be the time for the children to reciprocate such care. A nearby accommodation was perceived to be helpful for provision of personal, emotional and physical support, especially in times of crisis. In addition to care provision from children/family, support from ones' spouse is another source of care among older persons, although this tends to differ across ethnic groups (Hamid 2012). The majority of elderly Malays and Indians had support from their children, whereas elderly Chinese got support from their partners. In fact, many elderly Chinese reported having at least one child living abroad compared to Malays or Indians (Hamid & Yahaya 2008). Given the smaller number of children among the Chinese, this scenario would translate as the unavailability of children as family caregivers.

The family provided a variety of assistance and care to its aged members to ensure their socio-economic wellbeing. Economic wellbeing included providing food, clothing, shelter; and financial assistance. On average, family caregivers spent up to RM900 per month to purchase medical supplies, dietary supplements as well as disposable items for elderly parents; while social wellbeing includes family care, housekeeping, socio-emotional support, and personal care. This range of care, which was provided round the clock, forms a part of everyday family interaction and is addressed by the caregiver on an individual basis. Nonetheless, the extended family structure, which made such care giving possible is gradually disintegrating and changing towards the nuclear family system. This transformation was due to the modernisation process, rapid development, urbanisation, and rural-urban migration.

In Malaysia, the changes in care provision for the elderly may have been attributed to the intertwining of three major factors, namely demographic, economic and epidemiological shifts. First, demographic shifts affected family size and composition. Fertility decline and smaller family sizes diminished the pool of children and with that, the potential source of social and financial support for elderly parents. Family size was also shrinking as families transform from the extended into the nuclear form to fit current economic conditions and modern lifestyles. At the same time, high co-residence between older persons and their children remained the norm (Sulaiman & Masud 2012). Longer life expectancy and the high cost of housing also changed family composition to become multi-generational (Antonucci, Birditt, Sherman & Trinh 2011; Izuhara & Forrest 2013). The family adapted to changing social circumstances to increase its survival, for example, through structural adaptation as in 'beanpole families' which had more surviving family members but with smaller numbers from each generation (Aziz & Yusooff 2012), and functional adaptation by 'women in the middle' (Jones & Leete 2002), who continued to provide protection and care to older members despite shifting social conditions.

Second, economic growth and urbanisation also curbed family size and family networks, introducing economic values that negated interdependence and collective responsibility (Lee, Ong & Smith 1973), and brought modern pressures on the individual and family. Families invested in the higher education of their children to improve the family's economic conditions and allowed the younger generation to pursue career mobility to urban areas at the expense of extended family ties. Increased educational opportunities and greater participation of women in the formal labor force also meant a steady decline in the pool of daughters as traditional carers in the family system, and therefore, increased the demand for the provision of institutional support for the elderly (Chee & Barraclough 2007).

Third, demographic and epidemiological shifts also affected the capacity of informal carers to provide care for older family members. Longer life expectancy and high disability due to co-morbid conditions among older Malaysians pushed family members to their limit and stepped up the demand for formal long-term care services that could manage the changing health circumstances of older persons. Added to that, increased life expectancy also contributed to the emergence of the 'sandwich family' in today's society. In 'sandwich families,' adult children of working age not only had to provide care and support to their children but also to elderly parents. The pressure of providing care and support to both young and old generations was more apparent especially among time-poor, young dual-earner couples when economic resources were limited (Ambigga et al. 2011). In addition, the old-age dependency ratio which reflected the burden of working adults to support the elderly increased from 14 adults:1 elderly to 11 adults:1 elderly (MPFS-4 2010). The escalating cost of social protection and demands for aged care services came to the attention of the government, necessitating greater collaboration across sectors for long-term sustainability.

6.2.2 Role of State

The government, through the collaboration and participation from the stakeholders such as the Ministry of Women, the Family and Community Development (MWFCD), the Ministry of Health (MoH), the Ministry of Urban Wellbeing, and the Housing and Local Government (MUWHLG), was a major provider of public-funded services and regulates major functions such as social and welfare services, public healthcare facilities and services, affordable housing and urban planning. The MWFCD was a government ministry that plans and implements social policies and oversees the direction of government ministries and agencies in achieving the goals of gender equality, family development and a caring society. The MWFCD, through the Department of Social Welfare, provided institutional (residential care) and non-institutional services (financial assistance, activity centres) for older persons. In addition, the MUWHLG provided for affordable housing schemes, regulates various areas pertaining to physical planning and housing, and guides local government agencies in delivering municipal services, recreational and socio-economic facilities.

There were 14 government-funded old folks' homes, known as *Rumah Seri Kenangan* (*RSK*) and *Rumah Warga Tua* (*RWT*) which provided shelter and protection for 2553 residents. Eleven of the *RSK*s are in Peninsular Malaysia and Sarawak[1] whereas there were three *RWT*s in Sabah. The residents of these homes had to fulfil the admission criteria which included being Malaysian citizens of age 60 and older who lacked the means to support themselves. They were also required to be free of mental illness and any contagious diseases. The lack of

1 There were two old folks' homes, or *Rumah Seri Kenangan* in the state of Sarawak located in Kuching and in Sibu. The facilities were undergoing reconstructions and residents were temporarily relocated to other nearby welfare institutions while the project was being completed.

family support was generally the basis of the decision to stay or be admitted to the old folks' homes. This was because older persons who were poor but having family members to take care of them were supported through the financial assistance schemes for the elderly (*Bantuan Orang Tua*) of RM300 per month.[2] The Department of Social Welfare also operated two homes for the chronically ill (*Rumah Ehsan*) and two social rehabilitation centres for beggars and the destitute (*Desa Bina Diri*) which were not age-specific.

Other than providing primary, secondary and tertiary healthcare, the MOH was also actively involved in monitoring the National Health Policy for Older Persons (2008) and more recently, in the development of the new Private Aged Health Facilities and Services Bill. The new bill was presented to the lower house (*Dewan Rakyat*) and was yet to be passed by the Senate of the Parliament. Until the new law was gazetted, the present regulatory mechanism separates private healthcare facilities and nursing homes which are licensed by the Ministry of Health, whereas the old folks' homes were to be registered with the Department of Social Welfare.

Other government agencies and departments such as the Civil Service Department, Armed Forces Fund Board, Employee Provident Fund, Social Security Organization dealt with government- or employment-related social security programs and schemes. The government also provided some tax relief for Malaysian citizens, through the Inland Revenue Board of Malaysia, for the medical expenses of parents, limited to RM5,000 for both parents or RM1,500 for one parent, and the purchase of basic supporting equipment for parents up to RM6,000, which was borne by adult children. Inasmuch as population ageing entered the political discourse in Malaysia, gender issues was central in the social security system with regards to health, financial support and welfare. With the longer life expectancy of women and the cumulative disadvantages over their lifespan, the addition of the demographic dimension piqued the issue of the quality of life and the needs for social protection and long-term care for a growing segment of the population.

Malaysia's social security system was made up of an assortment of programs and schemes under public health, welfare, employment, and education systems, in addition to rural and urban development plans in poverty eradication. As such, there were gaps in the social security programs that provide basic protection through contributory and non-contributory schemes. The system caters for healthcare and essential needed for livelihood in old age, but did not necessarily address the need for long-term care. In addition, financial assistance was not substitutable for long-term care and there was still a strong focus

2 The amount of financial assistance was raised to RM350 in the 2018 Budget.

on the family to provide support and care, regardless of whether it was going to be provided by the family network or paid formal services.

The institutional arrangement of social security programs/schemes and care services was presently being reviewed. The government also strengthened its regulatory mechanisms for the emerging aged care industry through a new act that consolidates the regulation of private nursing homes and care centres for the elderly under a single body. Over the long term, these programs and schemes would not be sustainable in view of the rapidly ageing population that was expected to become double and triple in magnitude in the next few decades. Thus, there was a need to expand the social protection floor and long-term care for the elderly and to use innovative approaches that enable the distribution of the care burden and cost-sharing of care across individuals and family, the community/voluntary sector, the market and the government.

6.2.3 Role of Local Governments, Communities, and Other Not-for-profit Players

Local governments in Malaysia generally fell under the purview of the state government but the federal ministries, namely the Ministry of Urban Wellbeing, Housing and Local Government and the Ministry of Federal Territories and Urban Wellbeing, oversight in formulating, executing and monitoring all laws related to local government. There were three types of local government with a range of responsibilities reflecting their size and capacity: city councils (in the Federal Territory of Kuala Lumpur and in Sabah and Sarawak), municipal councils, and district councils. The scope of their authority was related to urban planning, the development of basic facilities and infrastructure, monitoring development, public health, waste management, business licensing, maintenance of peace and landscape, and promoting the local economy. The local authorities derived their income from taxes, non-tax revenue and federal or state government allocations. However, due to the centralized federalism or the significant intervention of the federal ministries, the local governments' functions were diluted by other levels of government (Berman 2017).

The community was represented by a spectrum of civil society actors on ageing in Malaysia. Based on a recent engagement of the Malaysian Institute of Ageing with the third sector on the 12th of October 2017, it was found that there were many individual actors with important roles with regard to ageing and the elderly. We identified a core role of the actors but their actual activities may not necessarily be limited to these roles. The roles included:

- Research institutions in various academic institutions
- Professional bodies
- Retiree associations Disorder / Disease / Health support

- Senior citizen clubs
- Advocacy / welfare groups
- Learning / education groups
- Faith-based groups
- International groups

The discussion and deliberation of issues among the civil society organizations highlighted several issues regarding the existing structure and modus operandi of civil society organizations. Some of these issues were: (a) not many of older adults' groups were registered or collaborate with each other, even the registered groups might be inactive regarding older adults' engagement, (b) the third sector on aging was not active in terms of enumerating their resources or sharing their experiences to develop intra- or inter-sectional collaborations, (c) the main focus for quality of care and regulatory compliance was still on residential facilities and services, and day care or mobile care were presently beyond legal reach. Service providers need to join their voice for the rapidly developing aged care industry, (d) there was a large gap between public funding, autonomous capacity and service coverage, and (e) there was a lack of understanding of the issues which led to failure to respond to the new opportunities for civil society growth. These issues signalled the need for the aggregation and coordination of civil society organizations at the national level to promote collaboration and more efficient responses to the needs of older population.

6.2.4 Elder Care Services by Profit and Not-for-profit Providers

Families seeking support to care for the elderly requiring long-term health and daily physical assistance had to rely on the services by the for-profit and not-for-profit providers. The for-profit sector played a major role in supplying full-time domestic workers, residential and non-residential aged care services that included nursing or personal care for the more dependent elderly. The not-for profit sector was better known for their role in providing financial assistance, companionship and helped with some household chores, learning and social activities as well as accommodation with some level of personal care for the elderly who were poor and lack family support. Other support services provided included awareness and advocacy, as well as the development of financial products for retirement (Malaysian Digest 2017).

6.2.5 Full-time Domestic Workers

Time-poor adult children tended to hire a live-in domestic worker to act as a primary caregiver to their elderly parents. In general, these full-time 'foreign maids' worked around the clock to feed, washed, dressed and accompanied the elderly; the more dedicated ones were able to perform more technical tasks including wound dressing, suction of phlegm and basic physiotherapy or rehabilitation exercises. It became quite common to see patients of all races in the geriatric ward being accompanied by a female domestic worker from neighbouring countries such as Indonesia, Myanmar and Cambodia. Nevertheless, not all families could cope with the exorbitant fees of hiring foreign domestic workers (Malaysian Digest 2017).

The cost of hiring a live-in foreign domestic worker was approximately RM18000 per annum. With the additional agency fees ranging from RM 12000 to RM18000 in the first year, the total cost for employers could come up to RM36000 (or approx. USD9000) ("Implement the New Maid Hiring Policy Quickly" 2017). In addition, employers also had to bear additional charges including an annual levy of RM600 along with another RM100 for their maids' annual medical examination. Yet, in the absence of more affordable alternatives including community-based day care centres and mobile care services, the hiring of a live-in foreign domestic maid offered a quick fix for the recurrent and highly intensive care needs of households with not just very old members, but also with very young children. The guilt and stigma of sending parents to old folks' homes or nursing facilities (Malaysian Digest 2017) may have also contributed to the employment of live-in foreign domestic workers becoming a common approach for well-to-do families.

A study on immigrants in Malaysia (Munoz Moreno, Del Carpio, Testaverde, Moroz, Carmen, Smith, et al. 2015) highlighted significant challenges in Malaysia's approach to migration including fragmentation, lack of coordination, and the inability to meet market needs. The on-going system of hiring foreign maids through a middle party was also seriously vulnerable to abuse by unscrupulous agencies. For instance, the current recruitment fee for Indonesian maids was set by the government at RM7800; however, agents were known to mark up the price to as high as RM12000 and to charge an additional fee of RM5000 to replace a maid who absconded or was deemed unsuitable for the job. It was also reported that agency fees skyrocketed due to growing demands, amidst the dire shortage in the supply of domestic workers. Ill-treatment of domestic workers and human trafficking caused countries, such as Indonesia and the Philippines, to suspend the supply of domestic workers into Malaysia. The countries supplying the domestic workers, particularly Indonesia, insisted on sending upskilled domestic helpers who had specific skills and are provided with better wages, which fed into the cost of hiring domestic workers by households.

The announcement of a government policy which allowed foreign domestic workers to be hired directly without necessarily using agency services in the 2018 Budget brought some relief to households. Nonetheless, for this strategy to work, there must be more coordinated implementation of policies between the government agencies and the private sector and a stronger legal framework to protects the rights of the employers and the employees, instead of merely tinkering with the procedures. The role of the not-for profit sector in the domestic worker arena was exemplified in the establishment of The Malaysian Association of Foreign Maid Agencies (*Persatuan Agensi Pembantu Rumah Asing Malaysia* or *PAPA*) as a platform to address employers' and public grievances towards its members, comprising of agencies licensed under the Department of Manpower, Ministry of Human Resources Malaysia and registered with the Malaysian Immigration Department. Another not-for-profit group, the Malaysian Maid Employers Association (*Persatuan Kebajikan Amah Malaysia* or *MAMA*) was formed in 2011 to look after the interests and the rights of the employers and the welfare of the maids. Aside from providing awareness and training, *MAMA* also aimed to be of assistance to the government of the supplier and receiving countries in providing an amicable solution on the issue of maids.

6.2.6 Residential Aged Care by the Non-for-profit and For-profit Sectors

Shelters for the vulnerable elderly run by missionary groups were among the earliest form of residential aged care to exist followed by those operated by the federal government. As a case in point, the Penang Silver Jubilee Home for the Aged was established in 1935. The Central Welfare Council of Malaya (*Majlis Pusat Kebajikan Malaya*) was established in 1946, after World War II to attend to those afflicted by the war, and has been providing shelter and support for the elderly since the 1950s. The Central Welfare Council's report in 2013 provided a description of the history of the association and the types of elderly services provided by it. *Rumah Sejahtera*, or residential homes for the elderly, began in 1954 under the resettlement scheme to address the Malayan Emergency, to cater for elderly peasants, many of whom had no kin relations.

Another type of residence provided by the Central Welfare Council is *Pondok Sejahtera*, which was initiated in 1973 to respond to the elderly Malay peasants who refused to move to new resettlement areas in order to continue their religious studies in the rural areas. The *pondok* establishments in Malaysia, like the *pesantren* in Indonesia, represent the traditional Islamic educational institutions that began in the 18th century in rural areas on the north of Peninsular Malaysia. This set up was also part of the non-formal of adult learning within the community in pursuing religious education and become a new residential option amenable to the needs for a sociable and supportive environment among the Muslim elderly (Merriam & Mohamad 2000).

These residential set ups of old folks' homes and traditional learning institutions (*pondok*) created distinct models of institutional care that were fundamentally welfare-orientated. Homes for the elderly that were operated by the not-for-profit sector remain under the purview of the Department of Social Welfare, at the federal level, whereas the Islamic religious institutions belonged under the jurisdictions of the Islamic Religious Councils of each state. The *pondok* system was presently running in the absence of laws and regulations to govern the establishment, or the rights to operate such institutions from either the federal or state governments sides. These conditions, in turn, could have led to problems in ownership, accidents or negligence within the system (Merriam & Mohamad 2000).

In more recent decades, residential aged care also became a demand that was capitalised upon by business. The first nursing home run by the private sector was established in 1983. Nursing homes were mainly concentrated in the urban areas and affordable to those with high income. According to newspaper reports and government documents, there were a growing number of nursing homes. These homes were mainly located on the west coast of Peninsular Malaysia and in urban centres in Sabah and Sarawak. However, there were numerous small-sized homes with 10 beds or less mainly located in bungalows and other private premises. All the nursing homes offered full-time nursing care for people with various needs, including disabled people and older adults. As the quality of the services provided by the nursing homes was not consistent, they cannot be considered as formal facilities for long-term care. Although the detailed services provided by different homes differ, the basic facilities remain the same. From the numerous operating residential aged facilities in Malaysia, there were only 17 nursing homes that were licensed by the Ministry of Health facilities for the elderly or mixed population (Ong, Phillips & Hamid 2009).

As was demonstrated above, the demand regarding establishing nursing homes for older adults was increasing. Furthermore, subsidies for the aged population resulted in an increase in government debt, thus there was an urgency for the governments to find more adequate solutions. Hence, developing senior living business concepts based on the Economic Transformation Program were encouraged by governments. Moreover, as Malaysia about to reach 2020 soon, more innovative, affordable private sector provided solutions with higher quality were the pressing issue. Additionally, due to an increase in chronic and lifestyle disease rates, the aging population in both developed and developing countries, and a growth in the number of middle class citizens with adequate incomes to spend on services in developing areas, the demand for healthcare was rising fast. Therefore, more private sector-based facilities were required to address the needs of the Malaysian aging population.

As part of the Government's Economic Transformation Programs to propel the growth of the nation's private pension industry, the Private Retirement Scheme (PRS) was initiated in 2012 to improve retirement savings. With the approval by the Securities Commission Malaysia, this scheme was established as the third pillar of a voluntary saving scheme under Malaysia's multi-pillar pension framework, protecting members' interests and educating the public on retirement planning. Other initiatives by the private sector included, concessions in service fees and preferential treatment (e.g., special lanes, parking, resting areas) for retirees/ senior citizens.

Malaysia had the right conditions for senior living concepts due to its own aging population and the introduction of the "Malaysia My Second Home" programme. Retirees from other countries were encouraged to live in Malaysia because of the low cost of living and the climate of the country.

It should be taken into consideration although the demand of the aging population was significantly increasing, the adequacy and adoptability of other countries' models should be evaluated carefully. And developers willing to provide services and care in terms of retirement homes or nursing homes for older adults had to consider the Malaysian culture and the stigma related to sending an older adult to live in a nursing home. Moreover, considering the type of services and the target service users was essential. More often, older adults from the highest income bracket were capable of maintaining their own homes and getting services delivered to them in their own premises whereas the middle income would be more inclined to choose residential care to optimise costs.

In terms of non-residential care for the elderly, the not-for profit sector also provided day care, rehabilitation centres, home help, and caregiver support groups. The Central Welfare Council of Malaysia and the National Council of Senior Citizen's Organizations in Malaysia, through their associations' members, provided senior activity centres and clubs to promote active ageing among the older population. Besides that, lifelong learning initiatives in the community was also initiated by the Universiti Putra Malaysia in 2007 and expanded through collaborations with the Department of Social Welfare, Civil Service Department and the community colleges. While civil society support for the elderly has been strong, the capacity of the sector must be further developed to expand the scope and reach of services in the community.

7 Conclusion

Within the context of care relations in Malaysia, it is interesting to note that the family existed as a microcosm, within which changes in human relationships and arrangements for care, were reflective and responsive to the larger cultural, demographic, economic, social and political developments. The temporal aspects, depicting continuities and changes in the different development timelines, were also discussed. The section on history and culture demonstrated that at the centre of ethnic pluralism, instigated by British colonisation, was an amalgam of family practices that were based on cultural notions of good childhood and parenthood. The religious institution also had an influence on the family in terms of fertility and family planning, family size, gender roles and expectations as well as the rights and responsibilities between parent and children. The discussion on socio-economic conditions illustrated that despite improvements in economic indicator, the growth in the economy favoured smaller, alternative family forms and promoted female labor participation that created the demands for universal social pensions, affordable child care services and availability of child care at workplace. There were also increasing economic pressures on dual career families as the nation braces itself through several economic crises and struggles under the circumstances characterised by the middle income trap. The primacy of economic growth in national development plans affected fertility levels, with some differences across ethnic groups, and opened the first demographic window for the population to increase its productivity. In spite of the paradigm shift in policies for welfare to social development approach, families remained an important pillar in the protection and care of children and older persons. The paradigm change should also be related to intensification in the government's investments in human capital, through education and training, in order to reap the benefits of the demographic dividend.

References

Abu Bakar, Noor Lailybinti Dato, Nai Peng Tey Boon Ann Tan, & Abdul Razak Rohani. (1985). *Ethnicity and fertility in Malaysia.* Singapore: Institute of Southeast Asian Studies.

Alavi, Khadijah, Rahim Sail, Khairuddin Idris, Asnarulkhadi Abu Samah, & Mustaffa Omar. (2011). Living arrangement preference and family relationship expectation of elderly parents. *Pertanika Journal of Social Science and Humanities, 19*(SPEC. ISSUE), 65–73.

Ambigga, Krishnapillai, Anis Safura Ramli, Ariaratnam Suthaha, Norlaili Tauhid, Lyn Clearihan, & Colette Browning. (2011). Bridging the gap in ageing: Translating policies into practice in Malaysian Primary Care. *Asia Pacific family medicine, 10*(1), 2.

Antonucci, Toni, Kira Birditt, Carey Sherman, & Sarah Trinh. (2011). Stability and change in the intergenerational family: A convoy approach. *Ageing and Society, 31*(7), 1084–1106.

Ariff, Mohamed. (1998). The Malaysian economic experience and its relevance for the OIC member countries. *Islamic Economic Studies, 6*(1), 1–31.

Attwood, Gaynor, & Paul Croll. (2006). Truancy in secondary school pupils: prevalence, trajectories and pupil perspectives. *Research Papers in Education, 21*(4), 467–484. doi:10.1080/02671520600942446.

Aziz, Rahimah Abdul, & Fatimah Yusooff. (2012). Intergenerational relationships and communication among the rural aged in Malaysia. *Asian Social Science, 8*(6), 184.

Baby Center. (2015). *Childcare centre (nurseries)*. Retrieved December 27, 2017, from https://www.babycenter.com.my/a537554/childcare-centres-nurseries#ixzz52QDE2neF.

Bach, Robert. (1981). Migration and fertility in Malaysia: A tale of two hypotheses. *International Migration Review, 15*(3), 502–521.

Bengtson, Vern, & Petrice Oyama. (2007). *Intergenerational solidarity: Strengthening economic and social ties*. New York: United Nations Headquarters.

Berman, Evan. (2017). *Public administration in Southeast Asia: Thailand, Philippines, Malaysia, Hong Kong, and Macao*. Boca Raton, FL: Taylor & Francis.

Bongaarts, John, & Steven Sinding. (2011). Population policy in transition in the developing world. *Science, 333*(6042), 574–576. doi:10.1126/science.1207558.

Boon, Ng Soo. (2010). Governance of education related ECCE policies in Malaysia. *International Journal of Child Care and Education Policy, 4*(1), 45–57. doi: 10.1007/2288-6729-4-1-45.

Butts, Donna, Leng Leng Thang, Alan Hatton Yeo, & Thomas Jefferson. (2012). *Policies and programmes supporting intergenerational relations*. Background paper. UNDESA, New York.

Callan, Victor J., & Poo-kong Kee. (1981). Sons or daughters? Cross-cultural comparisons of the sex preferences of Australian, Greek, Italian, Malay, Chinese and Indian parents in Australia and Malaysia. *Population & Environment: Behavioral & Social Issues, 4*(2), 97–108.

CCA, Child Care Centre Act. (1984). *LAWS OF MALAYSIA*. Retrieved from http://www.agc.gov.my/agcportal/uploads/files/Publications/LOM/EN/Act%20308%20-%20Child%20Care%20Centre%20Act%201984.pdf.

Chan, Angelique, & Julie DaVanzo. (1996). Ethnic differences in parents' coresidence with adult children in Peninsular Malaysia. *Journal of Cross-Cultural Gerontology, 11*(1), 29–59. doi:10.1007/bf00116264.

Chao, Ruth, & Vivian Tseng. (2002). Parenting of Asians. In M.H. Bornstein (Ed.), *Handbook of parenting: Social conditions and applied parenting* (pp. 59–93). Mahwah, NJ, US: Lawrence Erlbaum Associates Publishers.

Chee, Heng Leng, & Simon Barraclough. (2007). *Health care in Malaysia: The dynamics of provision, financing and access*. New York: Taylor & Francis.

Chiam, Heng Keng. (2008). Child care in Malaysia: then and now. *International Journal of Child Care and Education Policy, 2*(2), 31–41.

Chong, Shyue Chuan, Bik Kai Sia, CheeSeong Lim, & Bee Chen Ooi. (2011). Are the urban Malaysian selfish, altruistic, dynastic, or social norms and tradition?. *European Journal of Social Sciences, 27*(1), 96–103.

Croissant, Aurel. (2004). Changing welfare regimes in East and Southeast Asia: Crisis, change and challenge. *Social Policy & Administration, 38*(5), 504–524. doi:10.1111/j.1467-9515.2004.00404.x.

DaVanzo, Julie, & Ellen Starbird. (1991). Correlates of short interbirth intervals in peninsular Malaysia: Their pathways of influence through breastfeeding and contraceptive use. *Studies in Family Planning*, 241–254.

DaVanzo, Julie, & Angelique Chan. (1994). Living arrangements of older malaysians: Who coresides with their adult children?.*Demography, 31*(1), 95–113.

Daud, Fatimah, Sing Buan Chew, Kiong Hock Lee, & Ai Hwa Quek (Eds.). (2001). *Education and work: the state of transition.* Kuala Lumpur: Faculty of Education, University of Malaysia.

Doraisami, Anita. (2012). Economic crisis and policy response in Malaysia: the role of the new economic policy. *Asian-Pacific Economic Literature, 26*(2), 41–53. doi: 10.1111/j.1467-8411.2012.01348.x.

Doshi, Kokila. (2010), Sustainability and impact of microfinance institutions: A case study of ACCION San Diego. In Tojo Thatchenkery, David L. Cooperrider, & Michel Avital (Eds.), *Positive design and appreciative construction: From sustainable development to sustainable value (Advances in appreciative inquiry, Volume 3)* (pp. 275–295). Bingley: Emerald Group Publishing Limited.

DOSM. (2003a). Vital statistics, Malaysia, 2003. Putrajaya: Department of Statistics of Malaysia.

DOSM. (2005). *Population and housing census 2000, General report.* Putrajaya: Department of Statistics of Malaysia.

DOSM. (2006). *Vital statistics Malaysia, Special Edition, 2001.* Putrajaya: Department of Statistics of Malaysia.

DOSM. (2007). *Yearbook of Statistics.* Putrajaya: Department of Statistics of Malaysia.

DOSM. (2008). *Yearbook of Statistics.* Putrajaya: Department of Statistics of Malaysia.

DOSM. (2010). *Yearbook of Statistics.* Putrajaya: Department of Statistics of Malaysia.

DOSM. (2011). *Population distribution and basic demographic characteristics 2010.* Putrajaya: Department of Statistics of Malaysia.

DOSM. (2011b). *Vital statistics time series, Malaysia, 1963–1998.* Putrajaya: Department of Statistics of Malaysia.

DOSM. (2012a). *Household income survey.* Putrajaya: Department of Statistic Malaysia.

DOSM. (2012b). *Malaysia economic statistics – time series, 2011.* Putrajaya: Department of Statisticsof Malaysia.

Embong, Abdul Rahman. (1996). Social transformation, the State and the middle classes in post-independence Malaysia. *Southeast Asian Studies, 34*(3), 524–547.

EPU. (1986). *Fourth Malaysian plan 1981–1985*. Kuala Lumpur: Economic Planning Unit.

EPU. (2011). *Ninth Malaysian plan 2006–2010*. Putrajaya: Economic Planning Unit.

Gomez, Edmund Terence. (2012). The politics and policies of corporate development: race, rents and redistribution in Malaysia, *Malaysia's development challenges: Graduating from the middle* (pp. 63–82). London, u.a.: Routledge.

Green, Anne, & Angela Canny. (2003). *Georgraphical mobility: Family impacts*. Bristol: The Policy Press.

Gubhaju, Bhakta, & Yoshie Moriki-Durand. (2003). Fertility transition in Asia: Past experience and future directions. *Asia-Pacific Population Journal, September*, 41–68.

Hamid, Tengku Aizan, & Nurizan Yahaya. (2008). 6. National Policy for the Elderly in Malaysia: Achievements and Challenges. In Hock Guan Lee (Ed.), *Ageing in Southeast and East Asia: Family, Social Protection, Policy Challenges* (pp. 108–133). Singapore: ISEAS–Yusof Ishak Institute.

Hamid, Tengku Aizan, Sharifah Norazizan Syed Abdul Rashid, Mohamad Salleh. (2006). *Older population and health care system in Malaysia: A country profile*. Serdang, Malaysia: Universiti Putra Malaysia Press.

Hamid, Tengku Aizan. (2012). Population ageing: Past, present and future trends. In Tengku Aizan Hamid, Husna Sulaiman & Siti Farra Zillah Abdullah (Eds.), *Profile of Older Malaysians: Current and Future Challenges* (pp. 3–32). Serdang, Malaysia: Universiti Putra Malaysia Press.

Hamid, Tengku Aizan, Yadollah Abolfathi Momtaz, Rahimah Ibrahim, Mariani Mansor, Asnarulkhadi Abu Samah, Nurizan Yahaya, & Siti Farra Zillah Abdullah. (2013). Development and psychometric properties of the Malaysian elder abuse scale. *Open Journal of Psychiatry, 3*, 283–289. doi: 10.4236/ojpsych.2013.33027.

Hal, Hill. (2010). *Malaysian economic development: Looking backwards and forward*. (NBER Working Paper No. 2010/13). Canberra: The Australian National University, Arndt-Corden Department of Economics.

Hatin, Wan Isa, Ab Rajab Nur-Shafawati, Mohd-Khairi Zahri, Shuhua Xu, Li Jin, Soon-Guan Tan, Mohammed Rizman-Idid, Bin Alwi Zilfalil, & The Hugo Pan-Asian SNP Consortium. (2011). Population genetic structure of Peninsular Malaysia Malay sub-ethnic groups. *PLOS ONE, 6*(4), e18312. doi: 10.1371/journal.pone.0018312.

Hill, Hal, Tham S. Yean, & Ragayah H.M. Zin. (2012). Malaysia: A success story stuck in the middle?. *The World Economy, 35*(12), 1687–1711. doi: 10.1111/twec.12005.

Hossain, Ziarat. (2014). Parental beliefs and fathers' and mothers' roles in Malaysian families. In Helaine Selin (Ed.), *Parenting across cultures: Childrearing, motherhood and fatherhood in non-western cultures* (pp. 77–90). Dordrecht: Springer Netherlands.

Huff, Tony. (2001). Globalization and the internet: Comparing the middle Eastern and Malaysian experiences. *Middle East Journal, 55*(3), 439–458.

Inhorn, Marcia, & Carolyn Sargent. (2006). Introduction to medical anthropology in the Muslim world. *Medical anthropology quarterly, 20*(1), 1–11.

Ismail, Nellie, Jo-Pei Tan, & Rahimah Ibrahim. (2009). The relationship between parental belief on filial piety and child psychosocial adjustment among Malay families. *Pertanika Journal of Social Sciences & Humanities, 17*(2). 215–224.

Izuhara, Misa, & Ray Forrest. (2013). 'Active families': Familization, housing and welfare across generations in East Asia. *Social Policy & Administration, 47*(5), 520–541. doi: 10.1111/spol.12002.

Jomo, Kwame Sundaram. (2004). *The new economic policy and interethnic relations in Malaysia.* Identities, conflict and cohesion programme paper number 7. Geneva, Switzerland: UNRISD.

Jomo, Kwame Sundaram. (Ed.). (2013). *Industrializing Malaysia: Policy, performance, prospects.* Oxon: Routledge.

Jones, Gavin, & Richard Leete. (2002). Asia's family planning programs as low fertility is attained. *Studies in Family Planning, 33*(1), 114–126. doi: 10.1111/j.1728-4465.2002.00114.x.

Kahar, Rojanah, & Najibah Mohd Zin. (2011). Child related policy and legislative reforms in Malaysia. *International Journal of Social Policy and Society, 8*, 6–36.

Kakar, Sudhir. (1978). *The inner world: Childhood and society in India.* Delhi and New York: Oxford U. Press.

Kamerman, Sheila B. (2002). Early childhood care and education and other family policies and programs in South-East Asia. *Early Child hood and Family Policy Series(4).* Paris: UNESCO's workshop.

Kling, Rob. (1995). Controversies about electronic journals and scholarly communication: An introduction. *The Information Society, 11*(4), 243–246.

Kua, Ee Heok. (2007). *Dignity and grace of ageing.* Singapore: Armour Pub.

Kuo, Eddie, & Riaz Hassan. (1976). Some social concomitants of interethnic marriage in Singapore. *Journal of Marriage and Family, 38*(3), 549–559. doi:10.2307/350423.

Lee, Eddy, Michael Ong, & Thomas Edward Smith. (1973). Family planning in West Malaysia: the triumph of economics and health over politics. In Thomas Edward Smith (Ed.), *The politics of family planning in the third world* (pp. 257–290). London: George Allen and Unwin.

Leete, Richard. (1996). Malaysia's demographic transition: Rapid development, culture and politics. Kuala Lumpur, Malaysia: Oxford University Press.

Li, Tania. (1989). *Malays in Singapore: Culture, economy, and ideology.* USA: Oxford University Press.

Mahari, Zarinah. (2011). *Demographic transition in Malaysia: the changing roles of women.* Paper presented at the Conference of Commonwealth Statisticians Ismail, Delhi, India.

Malaysian Digest. (2017, December 2). *Indonesian maids too costly.* Retrieved from http://malaysiandigest.com/news/526030-indonesian-maids-too-costly.html.

Masud, Jariah, & Sharifah Azizah Haron. (2014). Income disparity among older Malaysians. *Research in Applied Economics, 6*(2), 116–131. doi:10.5296/rae.v6i2.5578.

Merriam, Sharan, & Mazanah Mohamad. (2000). How cultural values shape learning in older adulthood: The case of Malaysia. *Adult Education Quarterly, 51*(1), 45–63.

MOF. (2013). *Economic performance and prospects, economic report 2012/2013*. Putrajaya: Ministry of Finance.

Mohd, Saidatulakmal. (2012). Welfare regime, social protection and poverty reduction. In Koo Boo Teik (Ed.), *Policy regimes and the political economy of poverty reduction in Malaysia* (pp. 107–144). Hampshire, UK: Palgrave Macmillan.

Munoz Moreno, Rafael, Del Carpio Ximena Vanessa, Mauro Testaverde, Harry Edmund Moroz, Loo Carmen, Rebekah Lee Smith, Caglar Ozden, Kamer Karakurum-Ozdemir, & Pui Shen Yoon. (2015). *Malaysia – economic monitor: immigrant labor.* Washington, D.C.: World Bank Group.

MWFCD. (2014). *Study to support the development of national policies and programmes to increase and retain the participation of women in the Malaysia labor force: Key findings and recommendations.* Putrajaya: Ministry of Women, Family and Community Development.

Nambiar, Shankaran. (2009). Revisiting privatisation in Malaysia: The importance of institutional process. *Asian Academy of Management Journal, 14*(2), 21–40.

Ngin, Chor Swang, & Julie DaVanzo. (1999). Parent-child coresidence and quasi-coresidence in Peninsular Malaysia. *Asian Journal of Social Science, 27*(2), 43–63.

NPFDB. (1999). *Population profile, Malaysia.* Kuala Lumpur: Population and Family Research Sector National Population and Family Development Board.

NPFDB. (2005). *Report on key findings fifth Malaysian population and family survey (MPFS-4).* Kuala Lumpur: Population and Family Research Sector National Population and Family Development Board.

NPFDB. (2014). *Report on key findings fifth Malaysian population and family survey (MPFS-5).* Kuala Lumpur: Population and Family Research Sector National Population and Family Development Board.

Ong, Fon Sim, David Rosser Phillips, & Tengku Aizan Hamid. (2009). Ageing in Malaysia: Progress and prospects. In Fu Tsung-hsi & Rhidian Hughes (Eds.), *Ageing in East Asia: Challenges and policies for the twenty-first century* (pp. 138–160). London: Routledge.

Ong, Fong Sim, & Tengku Aizan Hamid. (2010). Social protection in Malaysia-current state and challenges towards practical and sustainable social protection in East Asia: A compassionate community. In Mukul G. Asher, Sothea Oum and Friska Parulian (Eds.), *Social protection in East Asia – Current state and challenges* (pp. 182–219). ERIA Research Project Report 2009-9, Jakarta: ERIA.

Ortega, Adriana, Haslinda Abdullah, & Samsilah Roslan. (2014). The emerging commuter families and changes in psychosocial and health behaviour profile. *Pertanika Journal of Social Sciences & Humanities, 22*(4), 1021–1032.

Phillips, David Rosser. (Ed.). (1992). *Ageing in East and Southeast Asia.* London: Edward Arnold.

Ranganath, Vijayalakshmi Mandayam, & Veena Kittane Ranganath. (1997). Asian Indian children. In Gloria Johnson-Powell, Joe Yamamoto, Gail E. Wyatt, & William Arroyo (Eds.), *Transcultural child development: Psychological assessment and treatment* (pp. 103–125). Hoboken, NJ, US: John Wiley & Sons Inc.

Robey, Bryant. (1991). Economic development and fertility decline: Lessons from Asia's newly industrialized countries. *Asia-Pacific Population & Policy, March* (16), 1–4.

Roopnarine, Jaipaul, Maureen Lu, & Ahmeduzzaman Mohammad. (1989). Parental reports of early patterns of caregiving, play and discipline in India and Malaysia. *Early Child Development and Care, 50*(1), 109–120.

Roslan, Samsilah, Siaw Yan Li, & Noorlila Ahmad. (2013). Commuters' psychosocial profile and their involvement in child rearing at home. *Procedia-Social and Behavioral Sciences, 82*, 477–481.

Sanderson, Warren C., & Jee-Peng Tan. (1995). *Population in Asia.* Washington D.C.: The World Bank.

Shari, Ishak. (2000). Economic growth and income inequality in Malaysia, 1971–95. *Journal of the Asia Pacific Economy, 5*(1–2), 112–124. doi: 10.1080/13547860008540786.

Shari, Ishak, & Ragayah Mat Zin. (1995). *Economic growth and equity in Malaysia: Performance and prospect.* Paper presented at the Fifth Tun Abdul Razak conference, Athens, OH, USA.

Sokolovsky, Jay. (2001). Living arrangements of older persons and family support in less developed countries. *Population Bulletin of the United Nations*, 42/43, 162–192.

Strong, Bryan, Christine De Vault, & Theodore F. Cohen. (2011). *The marriage and family experience: intimate relationships in a changing society.* Belmont, CA : Wadsworth/ Cengage Learning.

Sulaiman, Husna, & Jariah Masud. (2012). Determinants of income security of older persons in Peninsular Malaysia. *Pertanika Journal of Social Sciences & Humanities, 20*(1), 239–250.

Teh, Jan K.L., Sor Tho Ng, Nai Peng Tey, & Ismail Siti-Norlasiah. (2013). *Ethnicity and support for parents in Malaysia. Asian Women, 29*(4), 51–72.

Tey, Nai Peng. (2007a). The family planning program in Peninsular Malaysia. In Warren C. Robinson & Jonh A. Ross (Eds.), *The Global family planning revolution: Three decades of population policies and programs* (pp. 257–276). Washington, D.C.: The World Bank.

Tey, Nai Peng. (2007b). Trends in delayed and non-marriage in Peninsular Malaysia. *Asian Population Studies, 3*(3), 243–261.

Tsai, Feng-jen, Sandrine Motamed, Nadia Elia, & André C Rougemont. (2011). Evolution in intergenerational exchanges between elderly people and their grandchildren in Taiwan; data from a multiple round cross-sectional study from 1993 to 2007. *BMC Public Health, 11*(1), 639.

UN. (2011). *World population prospects: The 2010 revision.* New York: United Nations.

Yaacob, Harun. (2005). Unity in Malay family. *Journal Pengajian Melayu, 16*, 187–199.

Yaacob, Harun. (2014). Factors influencing relationships in Malay family. *Scottish Journal of Arts, Social Sciences and Scientific Studies, 20*(2), 154–163.

Yoon, Hyunsook, & Heung-Bong Cha. (1999). Future issues for family care of the elderly in Korea. *Hallym International Journal of Aging, 1*(1), 78–86. doi: 10.2190/HA1.1.g.

CHAPTER 3

Changes in Family Composition and Care Relations in the Kingdom of Thailand

Patcharawalai Wongboonsin, Thuttai Keeratipongpaiboon and Kua Wongboonsin

1 Introduction

The Kingdom of Thailand, or Thailand in short, was known during the premodern period as *Siam*.[1] The Kingdom is located in the heart of Southeast Asia, with Bangkok Metropolis as the capital city. Covering an area of nearly 513,115 square kilometres (approximately 198,455 square miles), Thailand shares land borders with the Republic of the Union of Myanmar in the north and west, the Andaman Sea in the west, Lao People's Democratic Republic or Laos in the north and north-east, the Kingdom of Cambodia and the Gulf of Thailand in the east, and the Federation of Malaysia or *Persekutuan Malaysia* in the south.

Thailand adopts a four-region classification system. In 2010, the semi-arid plateau in the Northeast was identified with the largest proportion of population (18.8 million, or 28.7% of the total population), followed by the Central region (18.1 million, or 27.7% of the total populations) in the fertile plain area, where Bangkok Metropolis, the capital city or Bangkok in short, is located. In the Northern region which occupies multiple mountainous and upland areas incised by steep river valleys, 11.5 million or, 17.5% of the total population are located. This is followed by the Southern region (8.9 million, or 13.5% of the total population). In 2010, the whole kingdom covered 76 provinces, 928 districts, 7,416 sub-districts and 61,032 villages. Among all provinces in Thailand, Bangkok was identified with the largest proportion of the population (8.2 million or 12.6% of the total population). From the whole kingdom perspective, the latest population and housing census carried out on September 1, 2010, recorded Thailand with 65.5 million people living in 20.5 million households. This compared to only 8.4 million households during the 1980 Population and Housing Census, when there were 44.8 million people living there. 95.1% of the

1 During the fourteenth century up to 1939, the Kingdom of Thailand was called *Siam* (สยาม).

 | DOI:10.1163/9789004384330_004

recorded population in 2010 were Thais (62.3 million) and 51.0% were female (33.4 million). Thailand was, accordingly, ranked as the fourth largest in population size in Southeast Asia, after Indonesia (240 million), the Philippines (92 million), and Vietnam (88 million), respectively (NSO 2012, 14–15). Thailand was also experiencing a fertility transition and transformed into an aging society as the country modernised from the pre-modern era, traditional agrarian economy.

Given the above, one would expect to find a changing family system and weakening family ties in Thailand. Relying upon documentary research of existing archives, this chapter accordingly aims to investigate whether there were changes or continuities in family composition and care relations. The analysis is made against the backdrop of modernisation and economic development, based on the hypothesis that the current transitions in care relations were spill-over effects of modernisation, which are not necessarily being addressed by social policies. In addressing the literature gap in family relationships by providing a nexus of different perspectives – cultural, demographic, socio-economic development and political – that were intertwined with care relations, this chapter is divided into six sections. Before turning to the changes in family composition and care relations in Thailand, it provides cultural, socio-economic and demographic background, which is followed by changes in policy and legislation relevant to care relations in Thailand. The concluding remarks are provided in the final section.

2 Cultural Background

2.1 *Culture and Customs*

As mentioned earlier, the 2010 Population and Housing Census recorded 95.1% of the population in Thailand as being Thais (NSO 2012). Despite the people there being mainly ethnic Thai, Thailand was said to home to more than 70 other ethnic groups of diverse history, dialect, physical appearance, culture and customs. The next largest ethnic group after the ethnic Thais was found to be the ethnic Chinese (Ramsay 2001; Luengthongkum 2007). Most of the non-ethnic Thais are descendants of immigrants to Thailand from around the 13th–14th centuries onward. They have been integrated through assimilation and acculturation into Thai society. Such an integration process can be traced back to the early 1900s when Thai nationalism prevailed. This is in addition to the common practice of inter-ethnic marriage within the Thai people (Wongboonsin 2013).

Against the above-mentioned background, there are certain cultural values and customs shared among different people in Thai society. Among them, these are inter-related and relevant to family values and care relations:

2.1.1 Buddhism

Buddhism is the predominant religion practiced in Thailand. According to the 2010 Population and Housing Census (NSO 2012), Buddhists constituted up to 93.6% of the population. About four percent of the population was Muslim residing mainly in the south along the Malaysian border. Besides Christians, which were about two percent of the population, other religious groups include Taoists, Hindu and Sikhs. Animism also exists in Thailand (Kitiarsa 2005; Wongboonsin & Chimmamee 2017).

Despite differences in religious belief, people in Thailand tend to share certain key characteristics and core values, some of which are deeply rooted in Thai society. Among them are hierarchy in interpersonal relations, both in terms of social position and age perspectives, and of family values. Both are interrelated.

2.1.2 Hierarchical Society

Since the pre-modern period, hierarchy in Thailand explains relationships, particularly in terms of authority, respect, protection, support and reciprocity expressed through rights and responsibilities verbally, morally, or in deeds, between and among people in both the intimate and public spheres. Besides a strong sense of relationship between super-ordination and sub-ordination, seniority is widely recognized in Thai society (Wongsith 1991, 73).

Previous literatures maintain that parents ranked as superior in social position and age in Thai society. Family was accordingly expected and institutionalised to be the cornerstone of society and was expected to play an important role in childrearing. This was the case after the Sukhothai period (1238–1438), according to Wongboonsin & Entz (1991). There was also a general expectation for seniors to take care of the juniors and subordinates, and the latter to be grateful and to take care of the seniors in return. In the relationships among family members, Thai parents were accordingly expected to take care of their young children and to be taken care by the latter when they turned old or frail. This was expressed in terms of expected responsibility to support, in both cash and kind. Co-residence with elder parents was also expected for at least one adult child (Knodel, Chamratrithirong & Debavalya 1987; Wongsith 1991; Knodel, Chayovan & Siriboon 1996).

However, conflicting notions were found during 2000s regarding whether it was to prioritize the elderly or the children at times of limited resources. As Thailand was ageing and moving further towards an aged society, society became concerned about the sustainability of the welfare system as the proportion of the elderly increases. Anti-ageism and social equity become a focus in discussing the issues of fair and equal distribution of resources and opportunities among different age-groups (Hanvoravongchai 2008, S79–S82; Prasartkul, Chuanwan & Thianlai 2012). In 2016, there was also a campaign mounted on the International Day of Older Persons raising awareness of the contribution of older people in social development, with a view to prevent ageism in the future.

2.1.3 Notions of 'merit,' 'demerit' and 'gratitude'

According to Wongsith (1991, 72–73), the Thai people generally adhered to 'merit' and 'demerit' notions. The former was especially connected to the notion of gratitude, which was another core cultural value called 'บุญคุณ' (*bunkun*) in Thai society, while the lack of it reflected a demerit. The *bunkun* core value applied throughout a person's life cycle in both intimate and public spheres. It was not bound to time or distance, according to Komin (1991). At the intimate sphere level, it was connected to family value, and encompasses filial piety. However, variations in practice existed to a certain extent. Some argued that they tended to be subject to modernization, as reflected in those between rural and urban areas, while others saw little difference (Wongsith 1991; Knodel 2009; Knodel & Chayovan 2009).

2.2 *Gender Role in Family Relations*

Thai culture viewed generational coresidence as part of filial piety. During the 1990s, co-residence with elder parents was expected for at least one adult child in Thailand (Hareven 1996). Filial caregiving in Thailand was also facilitated through quasi-coresidence. According to Ofstedal, Knodel & Chayovan (1999), the latter referred to a separate residence adjacent to, or within the same compound/building as the parents' residence, or within a distance that allowed daily visits between them.

Among the elderly living with any children was conditioned on availability; Ofstedal, Knodel & Chayovan (1999) found the highest incidence of these were living with single adult daughters (63.3% of the samples). This is followed by those living with single adult sons, married adult daughters, and married adult sons (58.2%, 40.4%, and 23.7% of the samples, respectively). An in-depth interview with key informants who defined themselves as unmarried between 30 and 44 years of age and residing in Bangkok Metropolitan, found them spending their time looking after their elderly or frail parents considering themselves unlikely to get married and prioritizing their elderly parents above a married life (Wongboonsin Sukontaman, Pothisiri & Kowantanakul 2013).

Among the elderly living with married children, the 1995 survey documents a slightly higher proportion living with married daughters (67.1% of the samples) than married sons (57.4%), according to Ofstedal, Knodel & Chayovan (1999). Accordingly, from the perspective of post-nuptial coresidence, one may note that the above findings from the 1995 Survey of the Welfare of the Elderly in Thailand seemed to support the evidence of previous studies on matrilocality as a predominant pattern of the family systems in Thailand (Podhisita 1984; Bentley, Pietrusewsky, Douglas & Atkinson 2005; Bowie 2008). This was the case despite other studies arguing for the existence of patrilocality and bilateral family systems there (Pongsapich 1990; Besaggio et al. 2007; Pongsapich 1990).

2.3 *Child Preferences*

Prachuabmoh & Knodel (1977) analysed a national longitudinal survey conducted in 1972–1973 by the Institute of Population Studies, Chulalongkorn University and found that most Thai urban people, both Chinese and Thai ethics, preferred to have sons to daughters. Son preference was more clearly in evidence among men than among women, given the mean ideal numbers of sons was higher among men (2.16) than among women (1.81). The mean ideal numbers of daughters was less than those of sons, amounting to 1.54 and 1.58 among men and women respectively. Regarding the ethnics, son preference was more pronounced among the Chinese than the Thais. In addition, the desire to have mixture in the sex composition of children, especially in large families, was found in society which coexisted with a tendency for son preference.

Later on, Wongboonsin & Ruffolo (1995) argued that there was no sex bias in child preferences there. The notion is based on an application of Coombs scale on these indicators (Coombs 1974): sex combination preference among women with two children, the percentage of second-birth intervals below 3 years old by the sex of the first birth, or the sex ratio of child mortality. The findings support previous studies during the 1980s, including Kamnualsilpa, Chamratrithirong & Knodel (1982) who maintained that a couple tended to continue child-bearing if their first two children were of the same sex in the hope of a child of the other sex.

3 Socio-economic Background

3.1 *Modernisation and Economic Development*

Thailand underwent a remarkable transformation from a rural-based subsistence agrarian economy of 8.27 million people as recorded in the 1st nationwide population census in 1911,[2] to industrialisation and urbanisation after the

2 Thailand's 1st census was called the "Household Survey 1911." It was carried out by the Ministry of Interior. Even though the census was organised in 1909 and data collection took place over a period of time, the reference time period for all data documented in the 1st census was assigned to 1 April 1911. Similarly, the reference time for the 2nd–5th censuses, or household

postwar era. Real GDP increased 19 times from 1961 to 2010 along a growth-orientated economic model, followed by a human resources development approach (Wongboonsin, Sermcheep & Srisangnam 2012, 2–3).

The 11th 5-year National Economic and Social Development Plan (NESDP) of 2012–2016 was written with the aim of enabling Thailand to climb up the development ladder to become a high-income, country with well-balanced development, and a sustainable sufficiency economy; the plan envisioned "a happy society with equity, fairness and resilience" (NESDB 2012a, ix). It was a medium-term strategic plan aimed at achieving the vision of the year 2027, which was that "Thai people are proud of their national identity, in particular hospitality." This was partly to deal with the emerging challenges of a sustained welfare system in the aging society of consumerism, and the resulting increase in public health expenditure at the expense of other investments (NESDB 2012a; NESDB 2012b).

This particularly referred to the concern that Thailand would get old before getting rich, particularly from the demographic dividend perspective of deficit life cycle income. As reflected in the study by Phananiramai & Chawla (2007) using information from the National Transfer Flow Account during 1981–2004, the average consumption per capita was higher than the average income per capita for a life cycle (0–90 years), in other words, there was a gap between income and consumption. The typical trend of people, at the individual level in Thailand, was to consume, despite the lack of income, until the age of 15. The income of Thai people tended to increase thereafter and to drop after the age of 60, when their income declined gradually while their consumption kept on rising. This was so despite a surplus at the national level, as the national income remained higher than rates of national consumption, which was attributable to the universal welfare programmes related to health and social services for all population groups. Furthermore, people in the workforce tended to be under pressure due to work overload, from regularly working from 8 hours/day to

---

surveys by the Ministry of Interior were assigned to 1 April 1919, 15 April 1929, 24 April 1937 and 25 April 1947, respectively. The 6th census, called the "Population Census 1960" was carried out by Central Statistical Office, National Economic and Social Development Board (NESDB), with the reference time of 25 April 1960. This was in accordance with the United Nations' recommendation for the national census to be undertaken every 10 years in the year ending with 0 (zero) for the purpose of international comparison. Thailand started conducting the 1st housing census simultaneously with the population census, with the reference time of 1 April 1970, "Population and Housing Census 1970" or the 7th census in short. The reference time for the 2010 Census was 1 September 2010. The 2010 Census represents the 11th round and marks the 100 year anniversary of the first Thai census. As in many countries, each census is said to undercount the population. For example, according to Grabowsky (1993, 58), the 1st–5th censuses each undercounted the population by 5–10%.

10–12 hours/day. Besides their health deterioration in general, their availability for the family was infringed on a remarkable basis (NESDB 2012a, 9).

In addition, the concerns raised were socio-structural problems across broad areas, including weakening social cohesion, particularly in the areas of child-rearing, elderly care and the care-provision role of working-age family members. The result of these problems was an increasing trend of the following: the increased proportion of school-age children adopting risky behaviours including drug use, unprotected sexual activity, unintended pregnancy and dropping out of school; the increased proportion of children who did not live with their parents; the increased numbers of teenage pregnancies and abortions; the increased numbers of low birth weight infants, particularly among teenage pregnancies; and the increased numbers of abandoned elders and children (NESDB 2012a, iii, v; NESDB 2012b, 2–10). These trends were supported by the 2013 report by the Office of Women's Affairs and Family Development (OWAFD), the Ministry of Social Development and Human Security (MSDHS) on family solidarity in Thailand indicating that 74.5% of families nationwide experienced weak family solidarity (OWAFD 2014).

These concerns were pronounced despite earlier empirical evidence against the assumptions of declining intergenerational solidarity from a series of six nationally representative surveys of older persons in private households. They include the 1986 Survey of Socio-Economic Consequences of Ageing of the Population in Thailand (SECAPT) conducted by the Institute of Population Studies, Chulalongkorn University. The 2011 Survey of Older Persons in Thailand (SOPT) was the most recent one, following those conducted by the National Statistical Office in 1994, 2002 and 2007, besides the 1995 Survey of Welfare of the Elderly in Thailand (SWET).

Based on an analysis of those surveys, Knodel & Chayovan (2009) and Knodel (2009) suggest that intergenerational relations between elderly parents and their adult children remained pervasive, and that filial material and financial support remained substantial, and that desertion of elderly parents was quite rare. This was the case in spite of an increase in the migration of adult children, declining co-residence and an increase in state support for older persons. Larger remittances were found to be from adult children who had moved to urban areas, especially to Bangkok, than from those who had moved to other destinations in Thailand. In many cases, grandchildren and grandparents in the areas of origin took care of one another. Besides this, there was a slight increase in non-monetary material support from non-coresident adult children in the form of food, clothes or goods. Knodel & Chavovan (2008) also find the elderly in Thailand living in better constructed houses with more appliances and amenities. More interestingly, while 2007–2011 saw a decrease in adult children as the main source of income, there was an increase in the percentages of elderly parents giving money to their adult children. Knodel (2009) was of the opinion that the increasing intergenerational solidarity was partly contributed to by the recent shift to universal old age allowance coverage.

3.2 *Urbanisation and Migration*

Urban growth, known as urbanization, accelerated dramatically in Thailand with the beginning of industrialisation in 1970s. At that time, large numbers of rural people moved to big cities in search of jobs and a better standard of living. These three phenomena – urbanisation, industrialisation and migration – are important factors in causing the change of living patterns in Thai society.

Due to industrialisation, the proportion of family businesses declined and family members, especially the young generation, became more financially dependent on waged employment outside the family (Mason 1992). Thus, there was a loss of parental power over the younger generation, which resulted in the breakdown of joint households. In addition, industrialisation created more employed jobs in an economy, which also increased the number of women participating in the job market. This resulted in increased female labor force participation in employed jobs. When the proportion of family-run enterprises decreased, the cost of home production then increased. Any goods previously produced in the household became more efficiently produced in factories, resulting in the increased need for laborers in the factories and as a consequence the opportunity cost of maintaining wives as full-time house-workers rises. Hence, a number of married women chose to participate in the labor market instead of doing housework. This increased the ability and desire of the younger generation to form separate households rather than to continue living with their parents.

Ubanisation caused a breakdown of multi-generational households. People in big cities generally lived in a small place due to the high price of accommodation and lack of housing. Thus, households in big cities, especially in Bangkok, were smaller than those in other areas. Migration involved the physical separation of older and younger generations and resulted in a reduction of multi-generational households in society.

Apart from internal migration, international movement was another interesting issue. It seemed unlikely to help in offsetting the impact of the population ageing as was the case of Thailand. As the natural decline rate was expected to start in the early 2020s where the number of deaths would be higher than the number of births, net migration at that time was predicted to be very low, amounting to only 19,000 migrants per year (United Nations 2014), which would not be sufficient to balance the changing demographic structure.

International migration was predicted to be on a downward trend; the figure was expected to be less than one thousand migrants per year by 2100 (United Nations 2014).

Nevertheless, some people were still interested in migrating into Thailand, especially those from neighbouring countries, i.e. Cambodia, Lao PDR and Myanmar. Their aim was to search for employment opportunities and a better standard of living. These migrants may have helped to relieve the problem of a smaller and older labor force for the next few decades. However, one may note that these migrated people may be required to move back to their home countries to re-participate in the labor force when the population of their countries begins to age.

3.3 *Education and Employment*

3.3.1 Education

Education became an important issue in Thailand in 1932 when the country shifted from an absolute to a constitutional monarchy. The National Education Development Schemes (NEDS) have been implemented since 1960. The first two NEDS (1960–1968 and 1969–1976) emphasised primary education, resulting in a drastic decrease of the primary school dropout rate from 60% of total enrolment in the 1960s to 42% in 1997 (Sattar 1984, 11). The NEDS of 1977–1991 changed the structure of Thai education from 4:3:3:2 to 6:3:3 where six-year primary education was compulsory.

In the 1980s, universal primary education was an ultimate goal. Tertiary education was also promoted considerably, so that private universities and colleges in the provinces were allowed to establish institutions around the country for the first time. During this period, however, secondary education was neglected to such an extent that, in 1990, the cabinet approved, in principle, the extension of compulsory education from six to nine years. Almost ten years later, the official nine-year compulsory education finally came about under the enactment of the National Education Act 1999. The Act enforced parents to keep their children in school until they had finished lower secondary schooling (Limanonda 2012).

In addition, education was one of the key factors causing the delay in marriage. A number of research papers found that the higher the rates of female education, the lower the fertility rate was. This was because well-educated women were likely to practise contraception for longer periods than lower-educated women do. Cochrane & Nandwani (1981) found that each additional year of schooling was likely to increase the women's age at marriage by a significant 0.24 year. In Bangkok, Limanonda (1989) found that well-educated women tend to get married at older ages compared to those with lower education.

Another reason for the decline in fertility was the changing economic value of children and the associated decrease in the demand for children in modern society. The new creative economy relied on manpower as much as the old resource-based economy.

3.3.2 Employment

As the world ages, the increasing proportion of older populations typically caused a shrinkage in the size of the global labor force. It unintentionally forced businesses to hire a greater number of older workers and forces the elderly to stay longer in the workforce. This was happening in Thailand. The labor force participation rate of ageing people was increasing over recent decades. The Labor Force Surveys (LFS) revealed that the proportion of economically active elderly people in Thailand's labor force was 7.0% in 2006, increasing from 3.7% and 5.1% in 1986 and 1996 respectively. In other words, approximately one-third of Thai senior citizens were found in the workforce in 2006 (Ministry of Labor 2007, 35–37). Thailand's elderly labor-force participation rates were higher if compared with most developed countries, but were low when compared with the rates in Africa and Oceania as showed in Table 3.1.

Fujioka & Thangphet (2009, 5) identified a dramatic decrease in Thailand's labor-force participation rates at the age of sixty, which was the legal retirement age in the public sector and state enterprises. In 2005, there were 80.8% of people aged 50–59 participating in the workforce; the percentage dropped to only 38.8 among people aged 60 or above. The number of elderly employed was still high compared to other developed nations. The main reasons of high labor-force participation rate among the ageing population were (1) improved health that allowed people to work longer and (2) expanded employment opportunities as a result of labor shortages. Most elderly workers were in the informal and agricultural sectors, where there is no formal age of retirement (NESDB 2009).

Labor Force Surveys (LFS) revealed that, besides the above notion of the increasing share of the elderly in the workforce, nowadays female elderly persons were also increasingly active. Figure 3.1 shows that 26.4% of the female elderly were found in the labor force in 2005. The statistics increased to 26.8% and 27.5% in 2007 and 2010, respectively. Part of the explanation was that they intend to relieve their family's financial problems (Ministry of Labor 2007). Self-employment and family-operated businesses were the most preferred jobs for Thai elderly persons due to work flexibility. Besides, well-educated persons had a higher probability of employment and earned higher wages than poorly-educated persons.

TABLE 3.1 Labor force participation rates, world, regions and age, 2005

Region/Country[a]	Age Group					
	25–54		55–64		65+	
	Men	Women	Men	Women	Men	Women
World[a]	95.1	66.7	73.5	38.7	30.2	11.3
Developed Countries[a]	91.9	75.3	63.9	44.9	13.4	6.3
Economies in Transition[a]	90.7	81.3	52.6	31.2	14.2	7.8
Africa[a]	96.2	61.0	86.5	48.3	57.4	25.8
Asia[a]	96.3	64.2	77.6	35.4	38.0	13.2
Latin America and the Caribbean[a]	94.3	64.3	76.1	37.2	37.2	13.7
Oceania[a]	87.4	73.3	76.0	60.6	51.4	33.4
Thailand[b]	95.9	82.2	81.8	65.7	41.0	21.7

Remark: By the definition of the United Nations, the developed countries include European Union, Iceland, Norway, Switzerland, Japan, United States of America, Canada, Australia and New Zealand. The economies in transition are those in the South-Eastern Europe and the Commonwealth of Independent States (CIS). The developing countries are those in Latin America and the Caribbean, Africa and Asia and the Pacific (excluding Japan, Australia, New Zealand and the member States of CIS in Asia).

SOURCES:

a United Nations (2007, p. 61, Table IV.2), *Development in an ageing world*;

b Authors' calculation from the ILO's data, http://laborsta.ilo.org/ accessed on 12 March 2012.

Unit: percentage of population in each age group.

Regarding areas of residence, it was found that people in the South are most likely to work beyond the age of sixty; approximately 43.7% were economically active in 2007 compared to 20.9% in Bangkok (Keeratipongpaiboon 2012). One of the main reasons for the difference in the number of elderly employees between Bangkok and other regions was job characteristics. Agricultural jobs i.e. fishery and rubber plantation in the South and rice farming and livestock in the Central, North and Northeast naturally allowed people to work beyond the official retirement age. Most people in these four regions worked on their own account and many of them were active until their 70s or 80s, unlike those in Bangkok who mainly worked in the formal sector and were usually asked to retire when they reached the age of 55 or 60.

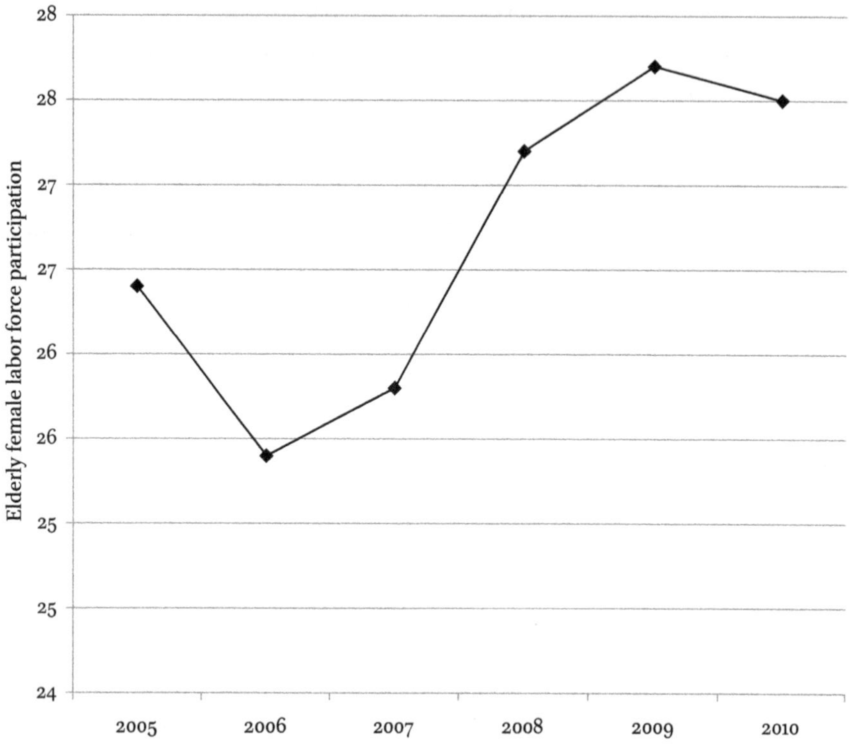

FIGURE 3.1 Elderly female labor force participation, Thailand, 2001–2016.
SOURCE: NATIONAL STATISTICAL OFFICE, LABOR FORCE SURVEY (LFS) 2005–2010.

4 Demographic Background

4.1 *Fertility, Life Expectancy and Mortality*

Based on the 2010 national census (NSO 2012), Thailand had a population of 65.98 million persons on 1 September 2010, of which 50.9% were female and 49.1% male, with a sex ratio of 96.2 (males to 100 females). As shown in Figure 3.2, despite the fact that there has been an increase in the number of the population over time, the annual growth rate of the population was declining from 3.2% in 1960 to around 2% in 1990 and to 0.8% by the time the 2010 national census was conducted. The population in Thailand had been only 8.2 million in 1911 and increased slowly during WW I at 1.2% annually to 9.2 million in 1919. During WW II, the annual growth rate of population dropped dramatically from 2.9% in 1937 to 1.9% in 1947 when Thailand had 17.4 million people.

Few decades ago, a number of countries in the world experienced a demographic transition from high to low levels of fertility. In most developed

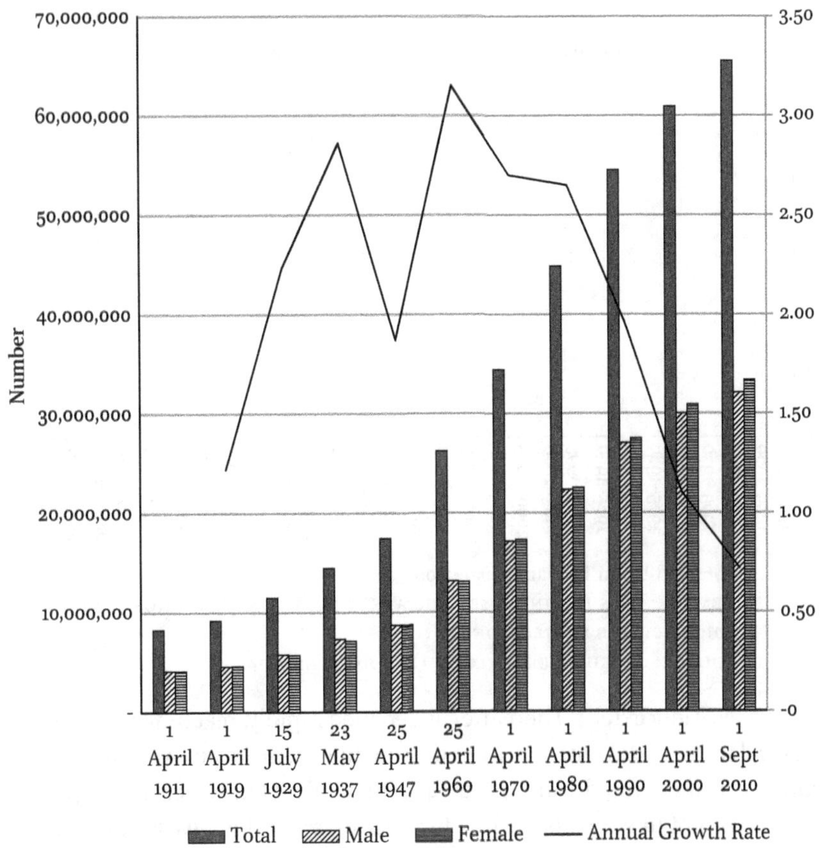

FIGURE 3.2 Census population by sex, number and rate of population growth, 1911–2010.
SOURCE: CALCULATED FROM NSO 1962, 1970, 1980, 1990, 2000, 2009, 2012.

countries, their fertility rates fell and remained below the replacement level. In less developed countries, the fertility rates have declined rapidly, which many of them already reached the replacement level (United Nations 2013). Thailand was one of the countries facing a drastic decline in the fertility rate.

As shown in Figure 3.3, this chapter argues that Thailand's fertility transition can be divided into five phases: Phase I, high fertility (before 1961); Phase II, the beginning of the fertility decline (1961–1971); Phase III, sharp fertility decline (1972–1996); Phase IV, below the replacement level (1997–2016); and Phase V, around the replacement level (2017 onward).

During Phase I of the fertility transition, before 1961, the total fertility rate (TFR) was very high, amounting to more than six births per woman. According to the national census, Thailand's TFR started to decline during 1961–1971,

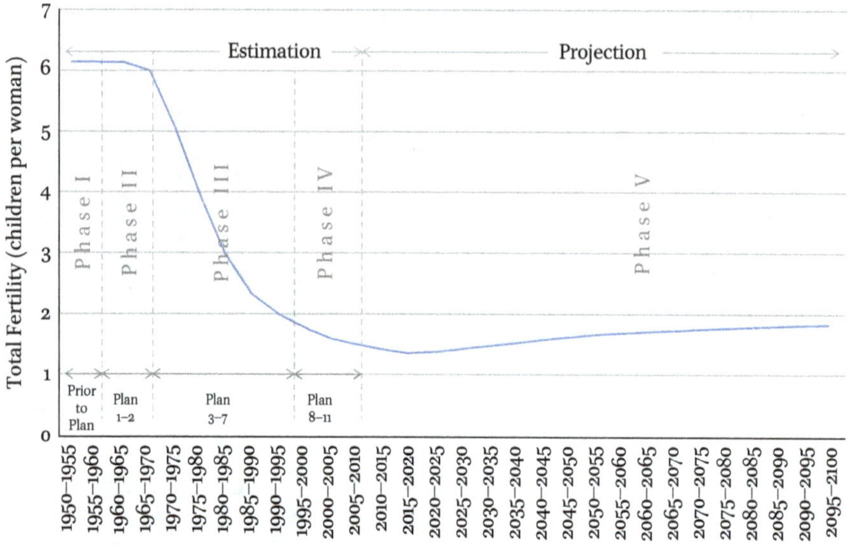

FIGURE 3.3 Total fertility in Thailand, 1950–2100.
REMARK: TFRS DURING 1950–2010 ARE ESTIMATIONS AND THOSE BETWEEN 2010–2100 ARE PROJECTIONS.
SOURCE: CALCULATED FROM UNITED NATIONS 2014.

albeit at a very low extent. Thereafter, it declined rapidly, reaching the replacement level in the 1990s with a further decline to 1.82 births per woman in 2000. According to the United Nations (2014), Thailand's TFR, which was 1.41 children per woman in early 2000s, was forecast to reach the lowest point at 1.36 children per woman by the year 2020, and to increase gradually thereafter, due to population momentum to 1.82 children per woman in 2100.

The evidence revealed that the TFR of the South was higher than other regions, amounting to 2.25 births per woman in 2000 compared to 1.17, 1.53, 1.76 and 2.15 births per woman in Bangkok, the Central region, the North and the Northeast respectively. It was noticed that the fertility rate of the North decreased quite sharply, dropping from 6.47 births per woman during 1964–1965 to 3.74 during 1974–1976. This was because an unofficial family planning programme was introduced in the Northern areas, i.e. Chiang Mai province, prior to other regions. Beginning in the early 1960s, the northern people learnt about contraception, prior to the implementation of the government's Voluntary Family Planning Programme in the year 1970 (Wongboonsin 1995).

According to the United Nations (2014), the life expectancy at birth in Thailand is now on an upward trend. It was as low as 51.6 years in 1950–1955 but the figure increased gradually to 73.3 years in 2005–2010. Assuming the medium variance, it was expected to increase to 80.5 years by 2050 and 86.4 years by

2100. Similarly to other countries, the life expectancy of Thai females tended to be higher than that of males. In 2005–2010, the life expectancy at birth of Thai women is 77.2 years, while that of men was only 71.0 years.

The increase of longevity was due to interacting factors. First, medical advances enabled people to live longer. People lived in closer proximity to healthcare services, which likely lowered the risk of death due to serious illnesses and diseases, compared to those in the past. Second, technological innovation resulted in better quality food. This in turn resulted in a better quality of life. Third, people were more likely to focus on their well-being as could be seen from the boom in the fitness business and the supplementary food market (Keeratipongpaiboon 2012).

The infant mortality rate in Thailand decreased dramatically over these few decades. In 1950, there were 119.7 infant deaths per 1,000 live births. Due to medical advances, the rate decreased to 11.8 by 2010 and is expected to be 2.3 by 2100. Similarly, the under-five mortality rate decreased drastically from 177 to 14 deaths per 1,000 live births during 1950–2010; it is forecast to be three deaths by 2100. Considering the crude death rate (CDR), it gradually decreased from 14.9 to 7.1 deaths per 1,000 populations during 1950–2010 (United Nations 2014). However, the CDR started to increase after the year 2010 due to the higher frequency of death of aged people, not the deterioration of medical services.

The 1996 national mortality data indicated that approximately half of Thai elderly people died because of senility. It revealed that heart diseases and cancers were common causes of death. The number of old persons who died from diabetes, kidney and liver diseases, paralysis, and pneumonia was on an upward trend. The increasing number of elderly deaths was potentially a consequence of changing lifestyles and dietary practices among Thai people. Modernisation transformed people's lifestyles, leading to (1) a change of eating patterns, from consumption of cereal-based and low-fat food to more animal products, fats and sugars, and (2) a change of working patterns, from non-stationary to sedentary styles (Keeratipongpaiboon 2012).

In reality, it cannot be concluded that in the future people who live longer will stay in better health. However, the increasing number of older persons will undoubtedly increase the demand for healthcare services. The situation of the ageing population, therefore, determines the supply of health services. If the period of morbidity associated with older age can be delayed or compressed, demands for healthcare services will be correspondingly reduced.

4.2 *Proportion of Older People and Children and Dependency Ratio*

The demographic structure of Thailand has changed rapidly. The number of children and working-age people is now on a downward trend at the same time, the number of elderly persons is on an upward trend. The proportion of children in Thailand was 19.8% in 2010 and it is expected to be 12.8% in 2040; during the same period, the proportion of working-age persons is projected to decrease from 67.0% to 55.1%. On the other hand, the proportion of the population aged 60 or over to total population was 13.2% in 2010. The figure is projected to reach 32.1% by 2040. By that time, the old-age dependency ratio is expected to be 58.3%, which implies that two working persons will have to take care of one old person (decreasing from seven persons in 2000). Table 3.2 shows the numbers and proportions of the population in Thailand during 2010–2040. Table 3.3 further reveals the estimated and projected proportions of Thai elderly persons and old-age dependency ratios by region during that same period of time.

Recently, the proportion of elderly people and the old-age dependency ratio of the North was the highest compared to other regions. In 2010, the ratio of the elderly living in the North was 15.5% and the old-age dependency ratio was 23.8%; while the ratios of Bangkok, the Central, Northeast and South regions were 13.4%, 19.7%, 23.0% and 18.7%, respectively. The North will be a region with the highest old-age dependency ratio for some decades. It is projected to reach 40.3% by 2020, which is higher than the country's average of 29.8%. The total fertility rate of the North decreased sharply from 6.4 births per woman during 1960–1964 to 4.7 during 1970–1974. On the other hand, Bangkok and its vicinities have, and are expected to have, the lowest elderly proportion and old-age dependency ratio over the next three decades. This is because a number of people, especially among the young generation, are migrating to such areas for employment opportunities and, probably, for a better standard of living.

In 2010, not all provinces in Thailand were ageing; there were nine of 77 provinces below the threshold of 10% elderly at aged 60 years and above. It will continue to be so until 2030 when all provinces will have the percentage of

TABLE 3.2 Numbers and proportions of population by age group, Thailand, 2010–2040

	2010	2020[e]	2030[e]	2040[e]
Total Number (million persons)	*63.8*	*66.0*	*66.2*	*63.9*
Children (0–14 years)	19.8%	16.8%	14.8%	12.8%
Labor (15–59 years)	67.0%	64.1%	58.6%	55.1%
Elderly (>60 years)	13.2%	19.1%	26.6%	32.1%

Remarks: [e] is projected number of population using assumption type 3 (normal decreasing trend of fertility).
SOURCE: NESDB 2014.

TABLE 3.3 Proportion of the elderly and old-age dependency ratio, Thailand, by region, 2010–2040

Region	Proportion of the elderly (%)					Old-age dependency ratio (%)				
	2010	2020[e]	2030[e]	2035[e]	2040[e]	2010	2020[e]	2030[e]	2035[e]	2040[e]
Whole Kingdom	13.2	19.1	26.6	29.6	32.1	19.7	29.8	45.3	52.3	58.3
Bangkok and vicinities	10.2	15.0	22.8	27.1	–	13.4	20.9	34.5	42.7	–
Central (exclude Bangkok & vicinities)	13.4	18.2	24.7	27.5	–	19.7	27.9	40.6	46.4	–
North	15.5	24.2	32.9	35.1	–	23.8	40.3	61.7	68.0	–
Northeast	14.3	21.5	29.7	32.8	–	23.0	35.9	56.3	65.3	–
South	12.2	16.3	22.7	25.7	–	18.7	25.9	38.5	44.7	–

Remarks: [e] is projected number of population using assumption type 3 (normal decreasing trend of fertility).
SOURCE: NESDB 2014.

elderly persons above 10% of the total population. At that time, 69 provinces will be aged as the proportion of their elderly population being over 20%, and the other eight provinces will be in the ageing category as the proportion of their elderly population ranging between 10% and 20% (Figure 3.4).

The estimates show that the province of Chai Nat had the highest old-age dependency ratio in 2010 (31.5%); while, the province of Samut Sakorn had the lowest old-age dependency ratio at 10.7%. In 2030, Uthai Thani and Chonburi are projected to be the provinces with the highest (77.3%) and the lowest (23.1%) old-age dependency ratios in Thailand. It should be noted that some provinces, i.e. Phuket, Rayong, Samut Sakorn and Krabi, are also projected to have relatively low old-age dependency ratios in the next three decades. This is contributed to by an emerging economy which attracts in-flows of the young workforce for employment opportunities (Table 3.4).

4.3 *Family/Household Composition and Size*

The concept of family and household in Thailand is interchangeable. Some may colloquially refer to the latter as *krobkrua* (ครอบครัว), a kin group living in the same residence and sharing day-to-day activities. Accordingly, one may interpret the concept of family in Thai society broadly, beyond just a group consisting of parents and their children. The members of the family may include

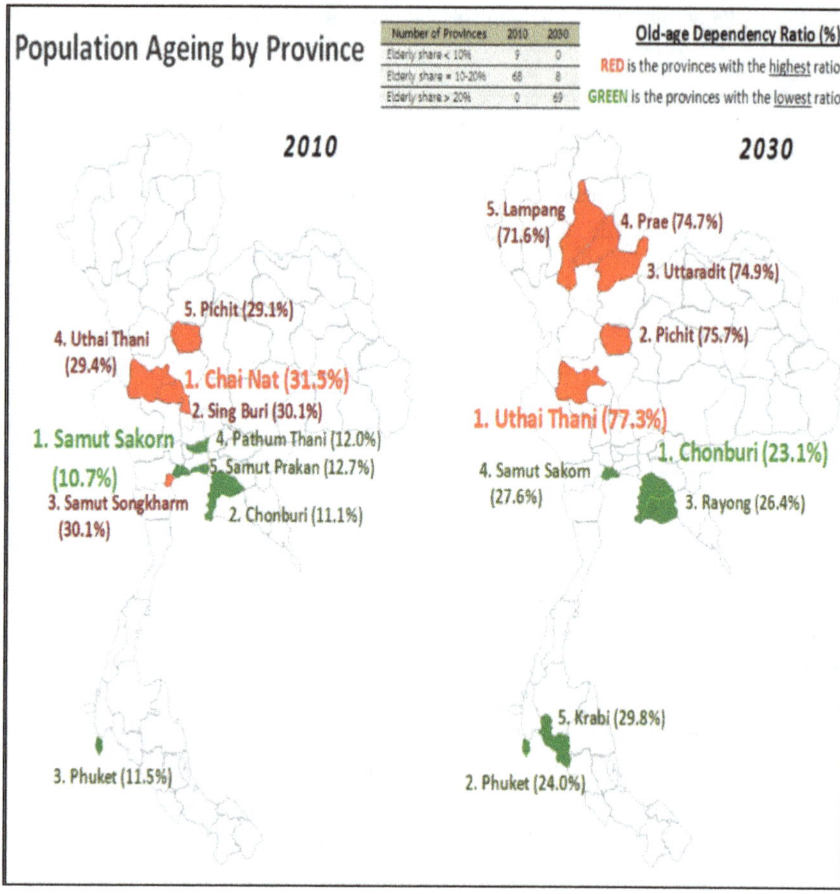

FIGURE 3.4 Population ageing in Thailand, by province, 2010–2030.
SOURCE: KEERATIPONGPAIBOON 2013.

parents and children, grandparents both maternal and paternal, uncles, aunts, in-laws, and grandchildren. In some families, non-relatives such as workers or maids who have lived in the house for an extended period of time may be counted as family kin (Jiumpanyarach 2012).

Based on the conventional modernisation theoretical framework, one would expect extended families to prevail in a pre-modern society, and to decrease as the people in the society become oriented to modernisation, when industrialisation, urbanisation, geographical as well as occupational mobility turn families to nuclearise and households to downsize, neo-localise and become solitary (Goode 1963; Cowgill & Holmes 1972).

Thailand was an example of a developing country, where the modernisation thesis could only partially explained the situation of families. Thailand

TABLE 3.4 Top 5 of Thai provinces with the highest and lowest old-age dependency ratio, 2010–2030

Highest old-age dependency ratio				Lowest old-age dependency ratio			
2010		2030[e]		2010		2030[e]	
1.	Chai Nat (31.5%)	1.	UthaiThani (77.3%)	1.	SamutSakorn (10.7%)	1.	Chonburi (23.1%)
2.	Sing Buri (30.1%)	2.	Pichit (75.7%)	2.	Chonburi (11.1%)	2.	Phuket (24.0%)
3.	SamutSongkhram (30.1%)	3.	Uttaradit (74.9%)	3.	Phuket (11.5%)	3.	Rayong (26.4%)
4.	UthaiThani (29.4%)	4.	Prae (74.7%)	4.	PathumThani (12.0%)	4.	SamutSakorn (27.6%)
5.	Pichit (29.1%)	5.	Lampang (71.6%)	5.	SamutPrakan (12.7%)	5.	Krabi (29.8%)

Remarks: [e] is projected number.
SOURCE: KEERATIPONGPAIBOON 2013.

underwent a modernisation process in both socio-economic and demographic terms, as reflected in transformation from the pre-modern era of being a traditional agrarian society to modernity while also turning into an aging society. The socio-economic and demographic development during the past decades joined with changes in family composition and intergenerational family relationships to an extent while certain family cultures were maintained. The following lists the key characteristics of families in Thailand:

(1) The changes were NOT that Thailand transformed from extended to nuclear families, as one may have expected. Up to 2010, nuclear families prevailed in both rural and urban areas, albeit in a decreasing proportion after 1980 when that of extended families was on a slow rise.
(2) While multi-generational households remained relatively constant in proportion, 1980 was identified as the turning point towards these new trends:
    a. Decreasing household size
    b. Decreasing prevalence of male-headed households
    c. Declining number of children per household on average
    d. Increasing numbers of older persons per household on average
    e. Increasing trend of skip-generation households

f. Increasing trend of one-generation households, including those with just the elderly and their spouse
g. Declining trend of two-generation households
h. Thai elderly mainly living in an extended family household, but a declining trend of those in three-generation households

The details of the analysis are provided below.

4.3.1 Nuclear Family Prevalence, Extended Family Households on the Rise

In the pre-modern period, literature provides an evidence-based notion that Thai people lived in nuclear families in small villages. Each family size was about 3–5 persons (Grabowsky 1993, 27; Podhisita 2011; Wongyannava 2011, 36–54).

According to Prachuabmoh, Knodel, Prasithrathsin & Debavalya (1972, 14–16), during the late 1960s and the early 1970s, when the average size of the households increased to 6.2 across the kingdom, the nuclear type of families was still made up the majority of households, 63.8%, 63.6%, and 56.1% of total households in the rural, urban, and Bangkok metropolitan areas based on a longitudinal study of social, economic, and demographic change. The notion referred to that comprising husband and/or wife with unmarried children, if any, but at least two persons in total. Unmarried relatives at the generation level of the children may be present as non-related persons.

Among the extended family types of households, stem families were more common than joint families, according to Thailand's National Statistical Office (NSO 1970–2000, 2010). The former were those with husband and/or wife with one married child and/or one married grandchild and possibly another unmarried child and grandchild. Unmarried relatives at the generation level of a child or a grandchild as well as a non-related person may also be present. The stem-family type of households accounted for 19.5%, 17.2%, and 17.5% of total households in the rural, urban, and Bangkok metropolitan areas. Joint families were those with husband and/or wife and at least one other married relative (usually a sibling) at the same generation level. Unmarried children or grandchildren may also be present as well as unrelated persons. There were also stem-joint families, which refer to those with husband and/or wife with two or more married children and/or two or more married grandchildren, or those with husband and/or wife with at least one married or unmarried relative (usually a sibling) at the same generation level and at least one married child or grandchild, according to Prachuabmoh, Knodel, Prasithrathsin & Debavalya (1972, 16). There were more stem-joint families in rural areas (9.0%) than in urban and metropolitan areas (1.2% and 3.8%, respectively). The household

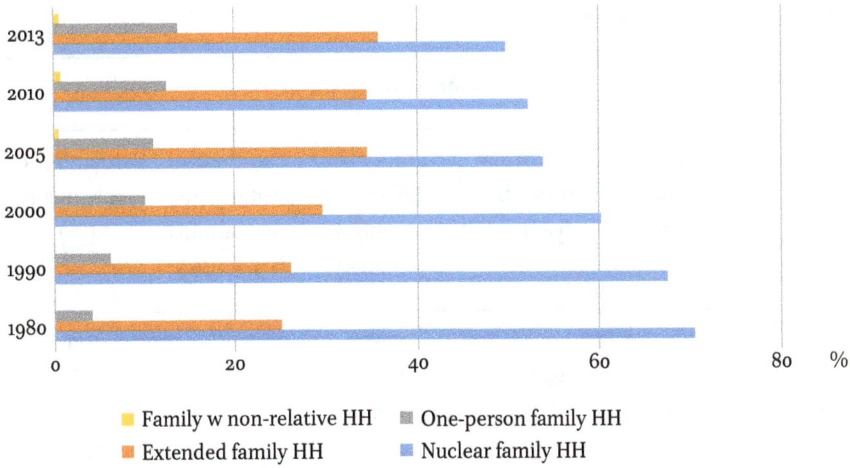

FIGURE 3.5 Types of household living arrangement in Thailand, 1980–2013.
SOURCE: CALCULATED FROM NESDB 2017A.

size ranged from one to more than nine persons Prachuabmoh, Knodel, Prasithrathsin & Debavalya (1972, 16).

Based on data from the NESDB (2017a), Figure 3.5 shows an increase in the proportion of nuclear families[3] to 70.6% of the total number of families in Thailand in 1980. Then, it decreased continually to 67.6%, 60.3%, 53.9%, 52.3% and 48.3% in 1990, 2000, 2005, 2010, and 2013, respectively. This compares to a steadily increasing proportion of extended families from 25.2% in 1980 to 26.2%, 29.6%, 34.5% in 1990, 2000, and during 2005–2010, respectively. In 2015, the proportion of extended families decreased to 32.9% of the total number of households in Thailand. This is due to a drastic increase of one-person households, which rose from 4.2% in 1980 to 6.2%, 10.1%, 11.1%, 12.6% and 18.3% in 1990, 2000, 2005, 2010 and 2013, respectively.

4.3.2 Smaller, More Female-Headed and Older Family Households

Considering the family size shown in Table 3.5 from 1980 up to 2007, one would argue that Thai families reached the turning point towards downsizing, from 5.2 persons on average in 1980 to 3.3 persons during 2006 and 2007. According to the 2010 Population and Housing Census (NSO 2012), the average size of a private household kept on decreasing further to 3.1 persons.

3 An extended family was categorized into three types: (1) a family comprising a family head and spouse, (2) a family comprising a family head and spouse and children, and (3) a family comprising a family head and children.

TABLE 3.5 Family composition, Thailand, 1980–2007

	Average households				
	Average household size (persons)	Average age of heads (years)	Numbers of children per households (persons)	Numbers of elderly per households (persons)	Percentage of male heads (%)
1980[a]	5.20	n/a	n/a	n/a	n/a
1988[b]	4.12	45.48	1.33	0.32	79.87
1990[b]	4.09	46.14	1.22	0.34	79.78
1992[b]	3.89	46.34	1.14	0.35	79.82
1994[b]	3.77	47.23	1.04	0.37	76.36
1996[b]	3.67	47.83	1.00	0.39	75.78
1998[b]	3.73	48.15	0.98	0.41	74.28
2000[b]	3.61	48.54	0.93	0.43	74.13
2002[b]	3.51	48.59	0.89	0.42	72.09
2004[b]	3.44	49.66	0.85	0.44	70.15
2006[b]	3.34	49.56	0.81	0.45	68.95
2007[b]	3.33	50.74	0.79	0.47	68.33

[a]Source 1980 Population and Housing Censuses by the NSO;
[b]Authors' calculation from the 1988–2007 SES data;

The decreasing family size was attributable to the fact that the people in Thailand tended to have fewer children and to live separately from their parents. Table 3.5 also reflects a declining number of children per household. In 2007, there were only 0.8 children in one family, compared to 1.3 in 1988 and 0.93 in 2000. Meanwhile, as Thailand was becoming an ageing society, the number of older persons in a family was on the rise. On average, 0.5 older persons were found in Thai families in 2007, an increase from 0.4 and 0.3 persons in 2000 and 1988, respectively.

The average age of the family head was also increasing. It was 45.5 years in 1988, rising to 48.5 years and 50.7 years in 2000 and 2007, respectively. Furthermore, despite the prevalence of male-headed households, the decline in their share from 79.87% to 68.33% during 1980 and 2007 implies that women had a more prominent role in leading families in Thailand (Table 3.5).

4.3.3 Decreasing Two-generation and Increasing One-generation Households

In the past two decades, the living patterns of Thai families were also clearly changing. Previously, people tended to live alone or just with their spouse. The national survey reveals that one-generational households increased dramatically from 17.3% in 1990 to 30.6% in 2007, of which 11.2% were one-person households and 19.3% were households comprising only a household head and his/her spouse.

The proportions of people living in multi-generational households were continually decreasing as can be seen from Table 3.6. The percentage of two-generational households dropped from 62.2 in 1990 to 49.8 in 2007. The evidence shows that about 40% of two-generational households were nuclear families (defined as head/spouse and their children). Another interesting finding was a drastic increase in the number of skip-generation households in Thailand; more children living with just their grandparents compared to those in the past. In this pattern of living, there was no middle generation because of either migration or death. In 1990, approximately 2% of Thai households were found to be grandchildren-grandparent households; however, the figure increased twice to 4% and 7% in 1998 and 2007, respectively. It was expected to increase continually as migration was still a trend in Thailand. Such skip-generation households were more likely to be found in the Northeast rather than in other regions. In 2007, about 15% of Thai elderly people in the Northeast lived in a skip-generational household compared to 2.1%, 8.6%, 12.4% and 8.9% of the elderly living in Bangkok, the Central, the North and the South, respectively. These were some possible explanations: (1) the trend that people have no or fewer children, (2) out-migration of young adults, (3) back migration of urban retirees from big cities to their hometowns, and (4) the expansion of HIV/AIDS in this area in the 1990s (Fujioka and Thangphet 2009, 25).

While the proportion of the elderly living alone in a household rose from 3.6% in 1994 to 10.4% in 2014, as shown in Figure 3.6, Keeratipongpaiboon (2012), argued that the majority of Thai ageing people (more than 60%) were still in the extended family, implying that the family relationship between the old and the young was still close. The average household size of Bangkok was the smallest (3.2 persons in 2004) compared to other regions. Table 3.7 shows that the two-generational household was a prominent living arrangement for older persons in the capital city. However, the proportion of elderly people living with just their spouse increased from 11.0% in 1990 to 15.6% in 2007 and the proportion of one-person households increased more than twofold from 3.30% to 7.40% over the same period. In the meantime, the percentage of elderly

TABLE 3.6 Living arrangement, Thailand, 1990–2007

	Year					
	1990	1994	1998	2004	2006	2007
All Households	100.00	100.00	100.00	100.00	100.00	100.00
4-Generational Household	0.57	0.33	0.50	0.47	0.50	0.55
3-Generational Household	19.88	19.73	22.10	20.22	18.89	19.13
– *Young 3-Gen Household*	*16.05*	*16.37*	*17.96*	*16.03*	*14.78*	*15.28*
– *Old 3-Gen Household*	*3.83*	*3.36*	*4.14*	*4.19*	*4.11*	*3.85*
2-Generational Household	62.21	59.25	55.18	50.95	50.09	49.75
– *Young Immediate Household (Head/Spouse & Children)*	*58.88*	*54.39*	*49.54*	*43.29*	*41.71*	*40.51*
– *Old Immediate Household (Head/Spouse & Parents)*	*0.99*	*1.02*	*1.53*	*2.04*	*1.99*	*2.06*
– *Skip-generation Household (Head/Spouse & Grandchild)*	*2.34*	*3.84*	*4.11*	*5.66*	*6.39*	*7.18*
1-Generational Household	17.34	20.69	22.22	28.36	30.52	30.57
– *One-person Household*	*6.61*	*7.79*	*8.27*	*10.26*	*11.06*	*11.24*
– *Household comprising of only a household head and his/her spouse*	*10.73*	*12.90*	*13.95*	*18.10*	*19.46*	*19.33*

Source: Keeratipongpaiboon 2012.

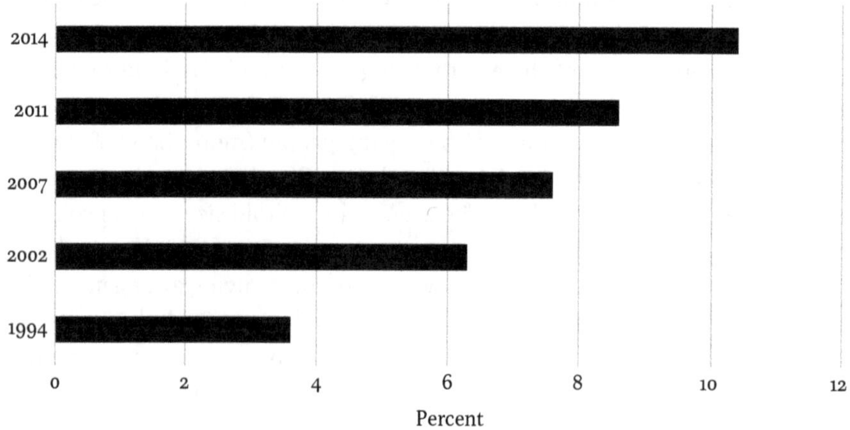

FIGURE 3.6 Percentage of the elderly living alone in a household, 1994–2014.
SOURCE: CALCULATE FROM NSO 2015.

persons in three-generational household decreased continually. Nevertheless, the three-generational household was still a prominent living arrangement for elderly persons in the Central and the Northeast (about 35–40% of the elderly in these regions living in households comprising three generations); meanwhile, the one-generational household was a prominent living arrangement for the elderly in the North as 31.4% of them were found in such households in 2007.

Living patterns of the elderly in the South did not change greatly over these two decades. One-third of them live in three-generational households and one-fourth stay in two-generational households. The evidence also showed that the percentage of elderly persons living in skip-generation households was on a downward trend, dropping from 12.1% in 1998 to 8.9% in 2007. On the other hand, the ratio of one-generational households was on an upward trend, increasing by 5.9 percentages points during the period of 1990–2007. This is mainly because the southern elderly people tend to live in head-and-spouse households. In 2007, about one-fourth of all senior citizens in the South were found in this living arrangement, a ratio which was much higher than for other regions (Keeratipongpaiboon 2012).

4.4 *Marriage and Divorces*

People in Thailand during the past few years tended to stay single compared to those in the past. Based on the census, the proportion of singlehood at age 45–54 increased from 1.95% for males in 1970 to 8.76% in 2010. For females, it rose from 2.77% to 8.84% during that time (Figure 3.7). Given the unlikeliness for the single female population in this particular age group to be get married, one may expect them to be permanently single throughout the rest of their life.

The young generation tended to live independently from their parents; they aimed to live on their own without creating any new financial dependants along the so-called 'Single Income No Kid (SINK)' lifestyle. A number of young couples were also living with the pattern of 'Double Income No Kid (DINK),' causing a significant decrease in Thailand's TFR (Wongboonsin 2010). The increasing DINK and SINK trends during 2001–2013 are reflected in Figure 3.8.

The percentage of ever-married women aged between 15–49 years old decreased from 71% in 1960 to 68% in 2000 and continued to decrease to 67% in 2010 (NESDB 2012b, 10). On the other hand, the proportion of women aged 50 and above who have never married has increased from 2.3% in 1960 to 5.8% and 7.6% in 2000 and 2010, respectively.

Delayed marriage was evidenced in the Population and Household Census of Thailand with the mean age of first marriage increasing from 24.4 to 27.2 years for men and 22.0 to 24.0 years for women during the period of 1970–2000.

TABLE 3.7 Living arrangement by region, Thailand, 1990–2007

	1990	1994	1998	2004	2007
THAILAND	**100.00**	**100.00**	**100.00**	**100.00**	**100.00**
4-Generational Household	2.88	1.04	1.26	1.42	1.71
3-Generational Household	40.06	37.85	40.61	38.87	35.21
2-Generational Household (excluding Skip-generation Household)	26.53	24.49	22.01	24.83	23.48
Skip-generation Household	8.62	12.54	11.39	9.52	11.27
1-Generational Household	21.91	24.08	24.73	25.36	28.33
– *One-Person Household*	*6.39*	*6.90*	*6.89*	*7.43*	*8.04*
– *Household comprising of only a household head and his/her spouse*	*15.52*	*17.18*	*17.84*	*17.93*	*20.29*
BANGKOK	**100.00**	**100.00**	**100.00**	**100.00**	**100.00**
4-Generational Household	1.92	0.51	0.46	0.98	0.74
3-Generational Household	32.54	32.53	35.15	33.20	29.98
2-Generational Household (excluding Skip-generation Household)	45.47	33.89	32.06	40.38	44.23
Skip-generation Household	5.74	7.31	3.49	1.39	2.07
1-Generational Household	14.33	25.76	28.84	24.05	22.98
– *One-Person Household*	*3.30*	*9.84*	*4.60*	*7.55*	*7.40*
– *Household comprising of only a household head and his/her spouse*	*11.03*	*15.92*	*24.24*	*16.50*	*15.58*
CENTRAL (Excluding Bangkok)	**100.00**	**100.00**	**100.00**	**100.00**	**100.00**
4-Generational Household	1.42	0.83	1.41	1.75	1.20
3-Generational Household	37.19	33.80	35.44	39.44	34.93
2-Generational Household (excluding Skip-generation Household)	26.12	28.78	21.90	25.72	26.25
Skip-generation Household	11.55	12.55	10.39	8.40	8.61
1-Generational Household	23.72	24.04	30.86	24.69	29.01
– *One-Person Household*	*6.04*	*8.38*	*8.84*	*7.65*	*9.27*
– *Household comprising of only a household head and his/her spouse*	*17.68*	*15.66*	*22.02*	*17.04*	*19.74*

	1990	1994	1998	2004	2007
NORTH	**100.00**	**100.00**	**100.00**	**100.00**	**100.00**
4-Generational Household	2.86	0.67	0.72	1.44	1.58
3-Generational Household	35.39	36.05	35.52	31.80	30.07
2-Generational Household (excluding Skip-generation Household)	23.06	23.99	22.83	23.33	24.51
Skip-generation Household	9.60	11.09	14.50	11.25	12.40
1-Generational Household	29.09	28.20	26.43	32.18	31.44
– *One-Person Household*	*8.42*	*7.03*	*8.45*	*8.79*	*9.52*
– *Household comprising of only a household head and his/her spouse*	*20.67*	*21.17*	*17.98*	*23.39*	*21.92*
NORTHEAST	**100.00**	**100.00**	**100.00**	**100.00**	**100.00**
4-Generational Household	5.13	1.48	2.07	1.32	2.67
3-Generational Household	49.96	44.84	49.59	45.73	41.04
2-Generational Household (excluding Skip-generation Household)	23.28	19.17	20.16	19.27	15.62
Skip-generation Household	5.99	14.65	11.06	12.17	15.14
1-Generational Household	15.64	19.86	17.12	21.51	25.53
– *One-Person Household*	*5.34*	*5.63*	*5.13*	*6.29*	*6.28*
– *Household comprising of only a household head and his/her spouse*	*10.30*	*14.23*	*11.99*	*15.22*	*19.25*
SOUTH	**100.00**	**100.00**	**100.00**	**100.00**	**100.00**
4-Generational Household	0.26	1.20	0.35	1.36	0.77
3-Generational Household	33.15	31.14	38.04	36.03	31.56
2-Generational Household (excluding Skip-generation Household)	29.33	28.69	20.01	29.46	25.75
Skip-generation Household	10.12	11.70	12.12	7.33	8.93
1-Generational Household	27.14	27.27	29.48	25.82	32.99
– *One-Person Household*	*8.38*	*6.09*	*6.60*	*7.63*	*8.69*
– *Household comprising of only a household head and his/her spouse*	*18.76*	*21.18*	*22.88*	*18.19*	*24.30*

Source: Keeratipongpaiboon 2012.

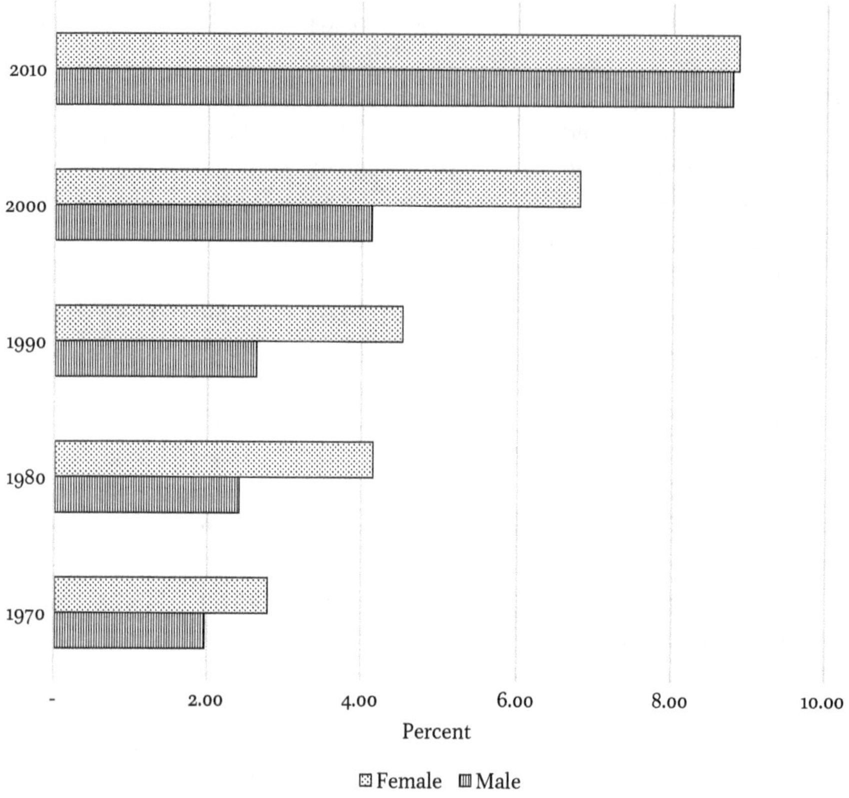

FIGURE 3.7 Percentage of singlehood at age 45–54, 1970–2010.
SOURCE: CALCULATE FROM NSO 1970, 1980, 1990, 2000, 2010.

The evidence also showed that in 2010, the percentage of never-married women aged between 20–24 years old was 56.0, increasing from 48.2 in 1990 and 38.0 in 1970. For those aged between 40–44 years old, the percentage was 9.3 in 2000, increasing from 7.0 in 1990 and 3.0 in 1970 (Prachuabmoh & Mithranon 2003).

According to the marriage and divorce registration data of the Ministry of Interior, the divorce rate of Thailand increased continually from 3.7 couples per 1,000 households in 1996 to 5.3 couples per 1,000 households in 2008 (NESDB 2012b, 11). Despite the possibility of the data being under-reported,[4] family disintegration was expected to affect other social problems in Thailand.

4 Previous studies argued that marital unions in Thailand were complex. They included legal registration, 'de facto' and/or religious marriages, while co-habitation was also a trend (Cherlin & Chamratrithirong 1988; Richter & Podhisita 1992). According to the Marriage and Family law in Thailand, which was governed by the Civil and Commercial Code book 5, 'de facto' marriages, religious marriages, nor same sex marriages, were recognized. Previous studies

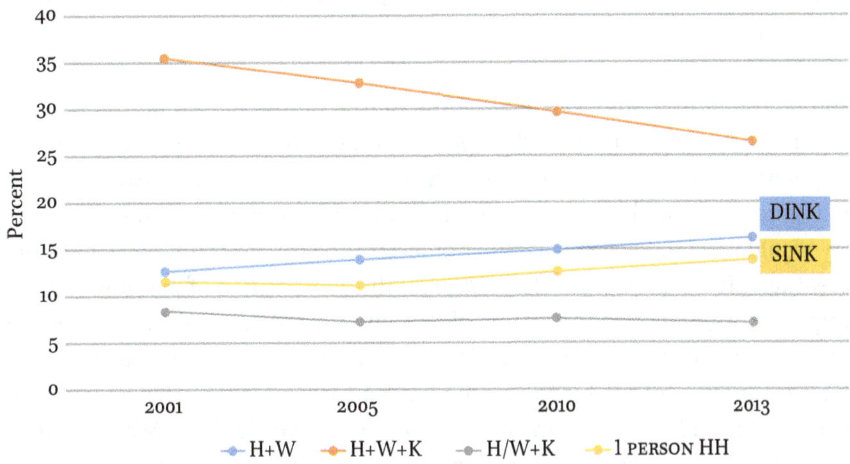

FIGURE 3.8 Nuclear family living patterns: DINK and SINK trends, 2001–2013.
SOURCE: CALCULATED FROM OWAFD 2013.

Mahaarcha & Kittisuksathit (2009) found that the children of divorced families were less likely to enrol in school than those living with married couples. Parental divorce typically disrupts family routine and affected ways of living of family members. Therefore, they became more prone to social problems and economic hardships with less likeliness to continue their studies.

5 Changes in Policy and Legislation

5.1 *Five Phases of Policy Regimes along Demographic Change*

In Thailand, family composition was related to reproductive behaviour and demographic structure. A shift in one dimension effected changes in others, particularly through government policies, which in turn also affected intergenerational care relations within the family and beyond. From the 1960s onward, Thailand was guided by the National Economic and Social Development Plans (NESDP) to provide directions for development. So far, a total of 12 NESDPs were implemented. They were regularly revised to keep up with the challenges of time and progress. This section accordingly provides explanations for care relations in Thailand through the lens of the NESDP and relevant

also maintained that divorce was common in Thailand (Richter & Podhisita 1992; Knodel, Debvalya, Chayovan & Chamratrithirong 1984). Based on the above notions, those not legally registering their marriage did not register their divorce.

policy measures affecting fertility transition and care relations within family and beyond.

5.1.1 Phase I: High Fertility (before 1961)

Given the above-mentioned slow population growth and the number of the population being below twenty million people during the early 1940s as shown in Figure 3.1, it was declared, by the then Prime Minister in 1942, that the country would need to have at least 100 million people in order to achieve national greatness. This was based on the notion of the contribution of manpower as an important source of economic development. A number of pro-natalist policy measures were then introduced. They were, for example, bonuses for large families and incentives for those who had an early marriage. This policy measure was intended to encourage Thai people to have children (Wongboonsin 1995). This was the case when urbanisation was not much expanded and the migration rate was not high. As a result, the population increased 3.2% annually to 26.3 million in 1960, and people tended to stay in an extended family comprising three or four generations.

With regards to childcare, although the importance of childrearing was recognised, there were no distinctive rules for childrearing practices. It was not until the first national education plan was introduced in 1898 that a standardised childrearing plan for infants and children's education was formulated and the first government kindergarten school, La-or Uthit School, was established. The first private schools with kindergartens were Rajini School, Wattana Wittaya Academy, and Mater Dei School (Wongboonsin & Entz 1991, 1).

5.1.2 Phase II: Beginning of the Fertility Decline (1961–1971)

The first plan was introduced in the year 1961, known as the First National Economic Development Plan (1961–1966). The Plan focused solely on the promotion of economic development, particularly on investments in infrastructure and public utilities services (NESDB 1967a). During the First Plan, some scholars, academia and policy makers began to realise that an excessively high population growth rate would bring about the adverse effects of development as suggested by the World Bank Economic Commission. Therefore, three government agencies namely the Ministry of Public Health (MoPH), the National Economic and Social Development Board (NESDB), and the National Research Council (NRC) were assigned by the cabinet to study the problems and facts of demographic changes in order to initiate population policies for the country. However, a population target was not yet mentioned and the government had no policy for controlling the number of births (Wongboonsin 1995). Therefore, the country's TFR was still high at the end of the Plan.

During the Second NESDP (1967–1971), the Voluntary Family Planning Programme was implemented. The government placed more importance on the social aspect and focused more on human resource development. Consequently, Thai people were eager to control birth volumes and practised contraception as guided by government and non-government agencies. The TFR therefore dropped to six births per women at the end of the Plan (NSO 1970). The Second Plan additionally suggested that the country distribute development benefits to the entire nation, in particular to the rural and remote areas. However, the result at the end of the Plan was the massive relocation from the rural areas to the cities and rising unemployment problems. A number of young people migrated to the big cities seeking better employment opportunities. Unfortunately, a number of elderly parents were left behind with children in remote areas. This was the beginning of the change of family composition and living patterns (NESDB 1967b).

5.1.3 Phase III: Sharp Fertility Decline (1972–1996)

The Third Plan 1972–1976 (NESDB, 1972, p. 41) set the reduction of population growth as the 7th objective of the plan. While it was the first time for the NESDP to include a population target, the plan also marked the inauguration of the National Family Planning Programme to meet the target to decrease the annual population growth rate from the level of 3.0% to 2.5%. This shifting approach was based on population projections carried out by the NESDB together with the Institute of Population Studies, Chulalongkorn University, and the National Statistical Office prior to the Third Plan (NESDB, IPS & NSO 1970).

This development model continued up to the Seventh Plan (1992–1996), which targeted a 1.2% population growth rate by the end of the plan (NESDB 1977, 1982, 1987, 1992). Policy measures were accordingly introduced both to reduce the population growth rate and to increase the quality of life for the population with better education and healthcare systems. Compulsory education was extended from 6 to 9 years. Long-term policy on the elderly was adopted. Thailand also started a monthly living allowance for the elderly in 1993. Revolution in reproductive behaviour nationwide was the result and the fertility rates reached the replacement level in early 1990s (Knodel, Chamratrithirong & Debavalya 1987; Lee, Walt, Lush & Cleland 1995, 64; Wongboonsin 1995; Knodel, Ruffolo, Ratanalangkarn & Wongboonsin 1996).

Among others, there were policy measures to educate and to encourage people to practise contraception nationwide. A Health-for-All policy was also adopted. Therefore, Thailand experienced a gradual decline of TFR at the end of the Third Plan. The plan also promoted economic growth in rural areas to reduce the gap in the standard of living and income. This led to policy measures to diversify social, health and educational services as well as manpower and employment development along with the first National Long-term Plan of Action for the Elderly (1986–2001) (NESDB 1972, xiii–xvi).

In 1990, the Thai government also designated April 14 as the nation's Family Day to underline the role of the family as an important institution for the development of Thai society. Moreover, the Social Security Act of 1990 mandated social security programmes in Thailand to cover private enterprises employing at least one or more workers, civil servants and self-employed professionals. Unemployed persons were not covered under the insurance programme. The insurance programme covered a range of benefits including:

- Sickness or Injuries Benefit: free medical treatment at a registered hospital and cash benefits for sick leave
- Maternity Benefit which consists of lump sum cash benefit for delivery
- Benefit for loss of physical organ and loss of physical or mental capacity to the extent that such employee is unable to work: medical treatment and a cash benefit
- Death Benefit which consists of a funeral grant and survivors' allowance
- Child Allowance, i.e. a monthly allowance paid to the first two children, under 6 years of age, of the insured person
- Old Age Benefit: a lump sum or monthly pension. The insured person receives an old age lump sum benefit or old-age pension benefit.

The pension system in Thailand was different for the private and public sector. The compulsory defined benefits scheme for the private sector (establishments with one or more employees) was called the Old Age Pension Fund (OAPF). This fund did not cover self-employed persons, persons working in the informal sector, and teachers in private schools. The Social Security Act defined the combined contribution rate for old age pension and child allowance to be collected from 3 parties: employer, employee and the government, at a rate which altogether did not exceed 9% of wages (employer 4%, employee 4% and government 1%) (Government Pension Fund 2012).

With regards to childcare, the 1977 National Education Plan prioritized pre-school education. The government had expedited and promoted pre-elementary child care and training both in the formal and non-formal school systems through the establishment of childcare centres or pre-school centres. Despite the government's serious initiatives and support, pre-school education was hindered by inadequate government budgets. It was the private sector that stepped in and filled this gap; a large number of pre-school centres were founded for both charity as well as commercial purposes (Wongboonsin & Entz 1991, 1–2).

5.1.4 Phase VI: Below the Replacement Level (1997–2016)

The Eighth Plan (1997–2001) started shifting to a people-centred development paradigm using a holistic and integrated approach to create a balance in the development of the economy, society, and environment. Instead of a downsizing population target as in the previous Plans, maintenance of the fertility rate at replacement level was planned. The family planning project was withheld in the areas with low TFRs, while continued operating in the areas with high TFRs. Yet, in practice, the restoration of the economy and reduction of the impact of the 1997 Asian Financial Crisis was prioritised and continued in the Ninth Plan (2002–2006). The 1997 Constitution covered child and youth development, while emphasising early childhood education. Several programmatic initiatives for children and families were accordingly launched to deal with child welfare and protection of the rights of children. Moreover, there were policy measures to deal with poverty and to improve the quality of life of people through the expansion of health services and better health insurance (NESDB 2007, 1–2).

Due to rapid ageing and the declining proportions of children and working age members of the population, an elder care regime was the focus of these policies. This was reflected in the Second National Plan for Older Persons (2002–2012), the 2003 Older Persons Act, and the 2007 Constitution when sections relevant to care regimes were launched, following the 1997 Constitutional provisions for the elderly with insufficient income to obtain State supports, and the establishment of the National Commission on the Elderly in 1999.

The Second National Plan for Older Persons (2002–2012) provided strategies on long-term care provision which covered a wide range of activities, including the promotion and support of informal care within the family, the provision of health and social services in both home/community and institutions, and the development of shelter/accommodation services, and environmental adaptation. The 2002 National Health Security Act guaranteed all Thai people the right to access quality health care services under the universal healthcare coverage scheme. Currently, most elderly persons in Thailand can access free medical services under this scheme. The National Commission on the Elderly, chaired by the Prime Minister was established to follow up the implementation of the National Plan and to oversee the policies and measures regarding older persons.

A child protection law was enacted in 2003. It covers child treatment, assistance, and welfare protection, child protection funds, and proper behaviour promotion to maximise child benefit without unfairness and discrimination. Child rearing, cultivation and development is to be performed by the guardian in reasonable manner with regard to local customs and culture, but to no less than the minimum standard as prescribed by the Ministerial Regulation. It mandated in Sections 52 that nurseries, primary shelters, assistance units, and development and rehabilitation units were to be licensed.

The 2003 Older Persons Act stipulated that the elderly shall be entitled to protection, promotion and support in various areas including medical and health services. A Parents Allowance Scheme was also launched in 2003 by the Ministry of Finance to encourage people to take care of their ageing, (financially) unproductive parents. Under the scheme, those in charge of looking after their dependent elderly parents were entitled to acquire a deduction in income tax, of 30,000 Baht per ageing person. In terms of spouses, income-tax concessions are available in the case where a spouse and his/her parents were not self-sufficient. Unemployment Benefit came into force on 1 January 2004. The laid-off insured person would receive an allowance of 50% of wages for not more than 180 days in 1 year. In 2005, an Announcement of the Ministry of Public Health on Medical Service for the Elderly stipulated for all hospitals to have an elderly clinic to serve as a special express service channel for the elderly. Special hospital staff must also be provided to assist the elderly while they were awaiting service.

The 2007 Constitution, Article 51, granted all persons an equal right to standard public health service while Article 53 grants those over 60 years of age, without sufficient income for living, the right to receive public welfare, public facilities and appropriate aids from the state. In 2009, the Government initiated and implemented a universal monthly subsistence allowance scheme, from which 6 million older persons without a pension can benefit to sustain their well-being.

Beginning on 1 January 2011, employee benefits in the form of contributions made by employers in relation to providing childcare facilities were exempted from Thai tax. The exemption only applied to the employee's natural children, as opposed to adoptive children, and the childcare facilities must be licensed to operate as part of an employee benefit scheme under the 2003 Child Protection Act.

It was at the end of the Tenth Plan (2011) when the concern on the changing demographic trend towards an aging society coincided with that on the changing socio-economic contexts, which could be expected to contribute to a further rapid pace in fertility decline towards an ultra-low level in subsequent decades, caused by changing family patterns and the changing lifestyle of individuals, as seen in a rising trend of double-income-no-kid (DINK) families, and a single-income-no-kid (SINK) lifestyles. A further rapid pace in fertility decline was expected to jeopardise the prospects for Thailand to reposition its socio-economic development towards sustained international competitiveness in decades to come, and to result in Thailand's prematurely facing the challenge of "getting old before getting rich" phenomenon. Those concerns led to the drafting of the Thai Population-Development Plan Guidance for 2012–2016, which outlined an appropriate approach towards a population-development plan in line with the 11th National Economic and Social Development Plan of 2012–2016 to address the issues of the first and second demographic transitions; the changing social context into a risk society; changing attitudes and values of people at the individual levels in the society into individualism; human development; and the first and second demographic dividends in the context of the ASEAN Economic Community (Wongboonsin & Pothisiri 2012).

In late 2012, the Population-Development Plan Guidance turned into a new population plan as part of the Eleventh National Economic and Social Development Plan (2012–2016), which envisions that all Thai citizens should be born with good prospects for a quality life. They are entitled to public support for human development at all stages of life to enable them to be the driving force of the country's growth. It also envisions the role of the family and communities in ensuring old-age financial security in a sustainable social welfare system.

The missions of the new population plan are threefold: (1) to promote reproductive health at all ages of the population so as to contribute to quality births and to promote fertility among married couples who are ready for childbearing; (2) to ensure appropriate development for the population at all ages in physical, mental, intellectual, and ethic aspects; and (3) to promote a post-retirement self-reliant approach along with family and community engagement to allow for the provision of better quality social services with increased coverage (NESDB 2012b, 13).

The Twelfth National Economic and Social Development Plan (2017–2021) also further targets on the quality of the Thai population rather than on its quantity. One of the goals is to prepare Thai people to live sufficiently and efficiently in the 21st century, by equipping them with practical knowledge, enhancing their working and analytical skills, supporting their health and wellness, and developing their mind and soul. The plan focuses on developing people at every single age group while leaving no one behind (NESDB 2017b, 65–67).

5.1.5 Phase V: Around the Replacement Level (Future of Thailand)

The Office of the National Economic and Social Development Board along with other governmental agencies were tasked to come up with a longer-term plan (10–20 years), with human development strategies that were consistent with the changing economic structure and the regional integration in Southeast Asia, or the so-called ASEAN Community. A 20-year long-term population plan was accordingly being drafted. It was expected to cope with the challenge of the TFR in Thailand being unlikely to increase beyond the replacement level in the next 20 years. The size of the population was not expected to change too much but the proportion of the working-age population would fall and that of the elderly population would rise significantly (College of Population Studies, Chulalongkorn University 2015).

Based on the 2010 Population and Housing Census conducted by the National Statistical Office, the Office of the National Economic and Social Development Board, Thailand made a 30-year projection of population growth and forecasted that, by 2040, there would be 20.5 million people over 60 years of age or equivalently 32.12% of the total population. On the other hand, the number of people in the working age and that of children are projected to decline from 42.74 million and 12.6 million in 2010 to 35.18 million and 8.2 million, respectively, in 2040. The TFR was projected to continue declining from the below replacement level of 1.6 births per Thai women in 2010 to 1.3 in 2040. The demographic transition was seen likely to destabilise the Thai economy and society at large, hindering the sustainability of long-term economic growth. Given the projection that the proportion of the working-age population would fall from 63% in 2022 to 55% in 2040, the shrinking workforce would negatively affect the economy as a whole, unless adjustments being in place in terms of labor productivity and a structural shift towards technology and innovation-driven production (College of Population Studies, Chulalongkorn University 2015).

The 20-year long-term population plan was also expected to address the adverse impact of the future demographic transition on economic growth, old-age security, and Thai families as a whole. This was based on the notion that without innovative policy interventions, Thailand would inevitably have to absorb the adverse effects of the aforementioned demographic change. The Thai economy would, accordingly, be expected to experience (a) a slower economic growth, (b) an ever-shrinking workforce and (c) a higher incidence of elder neglect (College of Population Studies, Chulalongkorn University 2015).

6 Care Relations

6.1 *Child Care*

6.1.1 Role of Family and Kin

The traditional family-based childcare patterns shifted towards diversification, involving profit and non-profit oriented providers in the public and private sectors since 1898, when the first national education plan was introduced and the standardised childrearing plan for infants and children education was formulated in response to the recognition of the importance of pre-school education.[5] Three major factors responsible for these changes were (Wongboonsin & Entz 1911, 1996):

- A decrease in family size and an increasing recognition of the importance of education, induced parents to send their children to schools rather than keeping them at home to care for their younger siblings. Consequently, there was a shortage of older brothers or sisters who could stay at home to care for younger siblings or help out with the housework.
- An increasing opportunity for women to work and earn cash income following the expansion of the modern economy, therefore, creating a push factor for a decrease in child care provided by non-working mothers.
- A trend towards a decline in the extended family structure, leading to a decrease in child care provided by relatives when mothers work.

Despite the changing trend towards diversification in childcare providers, available empirical evidence during the past decades suggested that the majority of child care providers for children of pre-school age were mothers and kin. A household survey of 1515 ever-married women in Bangkok Metropolis in 1990–1991 finds mothers as the most preferred choice for children below one year of age, compared to a few to prefer both parents. Kin, particularly maternal grand-parents, are the alternative in case of the unavailability of maternal care (Richter, Podhisita, Soonthorndhada & Chamratrithirong 1992). The general perception in support of the traditional role of women in childcare was the major explanation. Wongsith (1991) also found that childcare was the main role of mothers, followed by kin in rural areas. While neighbors were also relied upon when mothers and relatives were unavailable, distrust of nonrelative and formal care was found in Bangkok Metropolis (Wongsith 1991, Richter, Podhisita, Soonthorndhada & Chamratrithirong 1992).

6.1.2 Role of State

In Thailand by 2017, there were a number of ministries responsible for the provision of childcare. Among them were included, the Ministry of Public Health, Ministry of Education, Ministry of Interior, Ministry of Labor, and the Ministry of Social Development and Human Security. The latter served as the key agency responsible for providing social welfare services to children.

5 The first government kindergarten school was La-or Uthit (ละอออุทิศ) School. The first private schools with kindergartens were Rajini (ราชินี) School, Wattana Wittaya Academy (วัฒนาวิทยาลัย), and Mater Dei School.

The focus starts with welfare for the less privileged and protection for the vulnerable. Child and youth welfare, protection and development in families and communities was a form of service to enable children and youth to live happily with their families and communities, to have a better quality of life, and to be provided with welfare protection. Periodic surveys were carried out to locate children who were not properly brought up by their families, and who were homeless, abandoned, abused or exploited. Social workers or psychiatrists were also sent to accompany the police in the mission against child abuse and exploitation. Child welfare protection police officers were, in addition, dispatched to monitor and give advice to families and children in communities.

In the meantime, public, financial transfers to support pre-school children could be considered very limited. According to the National Transfers Account for Thailand in 2011 by NESDB (2012) shown in Figure 3.9, the expense of young children's consumption was mostly financed by private transfers, when

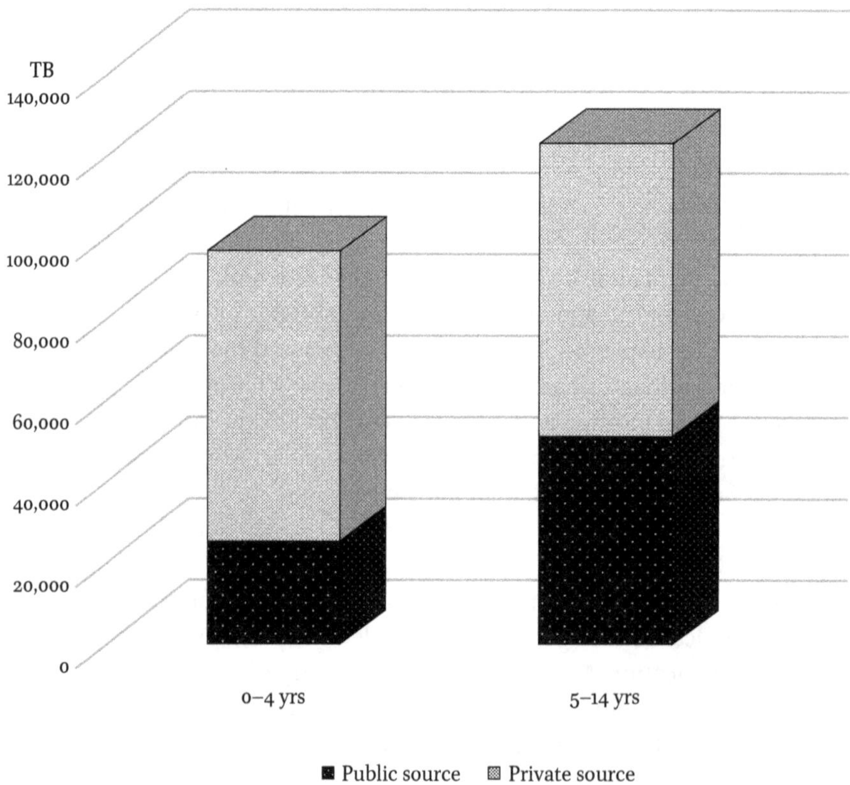

FIGURE 3.9 Public-private sources of consumption expense for children aged 0–4 and 5–14 Years.
SOURCE: CALCULATED FROM NESDB 2012.

compared with public sources. This was particularly the case for those in the 0–4 years of age group. Such an expense for young children included education, health, and other needs.

Role-sharing between the public and other sectors was part of the government's approach by 2017 towards the well-being of children and their families. Partnership and involvement of all sectors became the focus of the government. The government also relied upon the so-called community-based, rights-based and people-centred approach of social welfare management. To achieve this, each relevant ministry was mandated to develop and strengthen social development networks participated in by all sectors at all levels and to increase their potential to perform tasks with full awareness and responsibility to ensure better coverage of services and activities. Among others, financial support and close collaboration with the National Children and Youth Council, as well as the establishment of Children and Youth Council at all provinces an umbrella of more than 60 Thai non-governmental organizations across Thailand, were part of the efforts (See also below). It aimed at involving children and youth in social development.

6.1.3 Role of Local Governments, Communities, and Other Not-for Profit Players

The key player in social welfare for children and women in the community was local administrative organizations. The Tambon Administrative Organization, the key mechanism at the sub-district level, was instituted with the authority to direct and oversee development activities in their jurisdiction through their local offices. Besides their community infrastructure and detecting social problems detrimental to the well-being and safety of its people, this sub-district mechanism was in charge of social programmes for children under their supervision.

Communities became one of the most important social units in Thailand. The role of local communities in childcare was a governmental effort after the recent economic crisis. This refers to a project to encourage them to establish Family Development Centres. The project aimed at family empowerment, i.e. to establish caring and strong families as a basis for economic recovery and to provide greater immunity to social problems.

As afore mentioned, the National Council for Child and Youth Development was an umbrella of Thai NGOs dedicated to child and youth development. It has been established since 1984, as a national coordinating body for child and youth development.

For the children and youths to be important stakeholders in society, this council and its provincial and district counterparts served as a forum for them to voice their concerns on youth-related policies, in cross-sector partnerships with the government ministries & departments, sub-regional & provincial governments, as well as businesses (Thaiarry 2008).

6.1.4 Day Care Services by Profit and Not-for Profit Providers

According to a qualitative study in 1990–1991 by Richter, Podhisita, Soonthorndhada & Chamratrithirong (1992), among the very small proportion of those relying upon non-kin providers when mothers were unavailable, a live-in domestic helper was the choice for a family of a higher socio-economic status, while a neighbour was the choice for blue collar families. Few years ago, informal employment of domestic help in childrearing included both local and migrants, with the latter seeing an increase in demand (Anderson 2015). Among key explanations were the growing middle class and economic expansion, dual-earning families, and the decline of the extended family, according to Muttarak (2004). Some of these domestic helpers were treated as "part of the family" or the so-called fictive kin while others were on an employment contract via recruitment agencies. Lately, those in the latter group were more professionally trained and so the costs were relatively high, ranging between TB12,000–25,000 per month, eight hours a day, which was the legal working day for standard workers.

Childcare centres in Thailand were provided both by profit and not-for profit providers. Day care centres for children aged 0–3 years were less popular in Thailand. Part of the explanation was that quality childcare centres remained limited there. During the past decades, available childcare centres for children aged 0–3 years were able to accommodate only approximately 5% of the children in this age group, and 22% of kindergarten-age children were actually enrolled in kindergartens (Wongboonsin & Entz 1991; Nantamonkolchai, Isranurak, Kaewsiri & Pothisubsuk 2005).

Based on the 1992 Social Statistical Survey on Children and Youth conducted by the Social Statistics Bureau of National Statistical Office in May 1992, Wongboonsin & Entz (1996) find the following:

- The types of childcare providers were influenced by residence area. The highest proportion of children who were cared for in schools in both urban and rural areas were children aged 3–5 in the northern region. The highest proportion of children with child care provided by parents was found in the north-eastern region. The inequality of the variables such as the preparedness of childcare centres, culture, and the family's economic status in each region were responsible for this phenomenon.
- The number of household members could not explain the differences in the choice of child care provider in the way that the study expected. However,

the differences in the patterns of child care could be explained by this variable, which was statistically significant except for the urban area population since the number of household member variable did not specify who the household members were. If better information on household structure, such as the existence or inexistence of other members apart from the mother, was available, this variable may provide better explanation for childcare patterns.

- The influence of the parent's level of education on the types of child care providers was quite obvious, especially in urban areas. The proportion of children with child care provided by parents was higher in the group of children whose parents did not have any education. This proportion decreased progressively as the parent's educational level increased.
- Both the father's and mother's occupation had an influence over the types of child care providers. Agriculture provided the best opportunity for child care provided by parents. Occupations that did not allow parents to work at home or required unsuitable working hours force parents to depend on others for childcare or to put the child in a child care centre that they could afford.
- There was a correlation between parent's/parents' work status and the types of child care providers. If parents worked in a family business or were themselves employers, they had the time and convenience of providing child care for their own child. However, children with parents who were private employees or civil servants had the highest rate of being cared for in schools.

6.2 *Elderly Care*

6.2.1 Role of Family and Kin

Industrialisation, urbanisation and migration significantly affected the care of elderly people in society. When industrialisation generates economic growth, it also increased years of schooling. The consequences of higher education were lower fertility, deterioration of filial piety, and an increase in the survivorship rate of children. The first two effects could have lowered the availability of caregivers; the elderly could be less taken care of, by younger generations. Because of medical advances, there are more child survivors nowadays, which possibly results in more elderly care-givers (Mason 1992).

In most Thai families, older persons were looked after by their adult children, spouse, and kin of younger generations in a home environment. From the gender perspective, data from 1995 Survey of the Welfare of the Elderly in Thailand and 2014 Surveys of Older Persons in Thailand conducted by the National Statistical Office confirm the incidence of the elderly preference for daughters in care giving. Knodel, Teerawichitchainan & Pothisiri (2016)

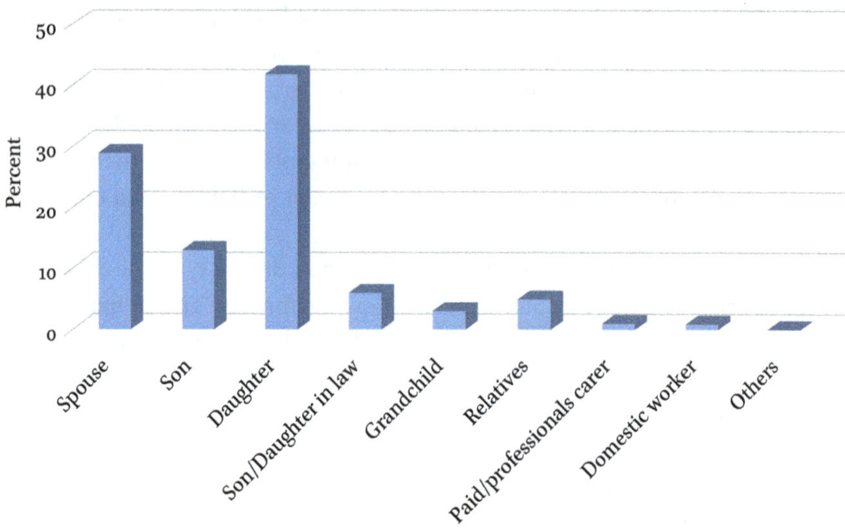

FIGURE 3.10 Providers of assistance in daily living activities of the elderly aged 60+, 2014.
SOURCE: CALCULATED FROM NSO (2015).

based on the 2014 Survey of Older Persons in Thailand also found relatively high happiness scores associated with men who have a daughter as their main caregiver.

Based on the data provided in the Preliminary Report Survey of Older Persons in Thailand 2014 (NSO 2015), Figure 3.10 shows that familial support was the main source of assistance for the elderly's daily living activities. It was the daughters who predominate in care provision for the elderly (42%) in practice, followed by spouse, son, son-/daughter-in-law, 29%, 13%, and 6%, respectively. Reports of relatives providing care to the elderly indicated this to amount to only 5%. Meanwhile, grandchildren providing care to their grandparents are up to 3%.

Given an increase in the proportion of the elderly, a decline in the proportion of elderly people living with children, and an increase in the proportion of elderly people living alone or with spouses, it was a concern that it was impossible for the elderly to be taken care of solely by the family and kin. Knodel, Prachuabmoh & Chayovan (2013) also found a decline, from 52% to 40%, in the elderly relying on their adult children for their old-age financial security. Currently, given the minimum pension to cover basic needs, about four million or around 36% of the elderly over 60 were still working (NSO 2016). This was not only for their own old-age security, but also to contribute to the well-being of their family members.

Intergenerational family relation in remote areas in Thailand was marginally investigation. The first study of such an issue among hill tribe people was carried out by Sutinyamanee and Wongboonsin (2016) in northern Thailand, an area with the highest level of ruralisation in the country. The study covered 1,285 sample households in a survey in 2016 of four major hill tribe groups, namely Karen, Hmong, Akha and Lahu in the provinces of Chiang Mai, Chiang Rai, Mae Hong Son, and Nan. From the perspective of elderly care, the study found intergenerational family relations there were relatively very strong, when compared to previous national surveys. Adult children are found to prioritize support and care to their adult children regardless of their working status, and the reverse is true of elderly parents with regard to their adult children. The study also found intergenerational solidarity characterized by effective communication, to be a key factor for increasing intergenerational economic and non-economic supports among family members.

6.2.2 Role of State

As noted earlier, for the elderly population, several policies and plans were put in place. Yet, two thirds of about 11 million elderly Thais were found to be without savings while the other third are in debt. Concerns arose regarding how the Thai elderly could be helped to be better-off, and how the welfare schemes could be made sustainable in years to come.

According to a study on the National Transfers Account for Thailand in 2011 by the NESDB (2012), Figure 3.11 shows that consumption expense in old age was more financed by private than public transfers. Such expenses for the elders included health and other needs. Nevertheless, Figure 3.12 shows that the old-age allowance superseded adult children in providing old-age financial security, while asset income receipt, income earned from economic activities, and pensions were on the rise in 2011 and then fell in 2014.

For example, under the Universal Healthcare Coverage scheme, government spending was sharply on the rise, from TB55.3 billion in 2003 to TB165 billion for the FY 2017. There was concerns regarding whether the scheme was sustainable or not. In 2014, the elderly welfare budget – which covered the old civil servant pension scheme, living allowances for the elderly and the government's contributions to the Government Pension Fund, the Social Security Fund and the National Savings Fund – amounted to 270 billion baht, or 2.1% of GDP. The budget was expected to increase to TB680 billion by 2024, accounting for about 3% of anticipated GDP by then. Moreover, the budget for pension-related schemes was expected to increase from TB287 billion currently to TB698 billion by 2024.

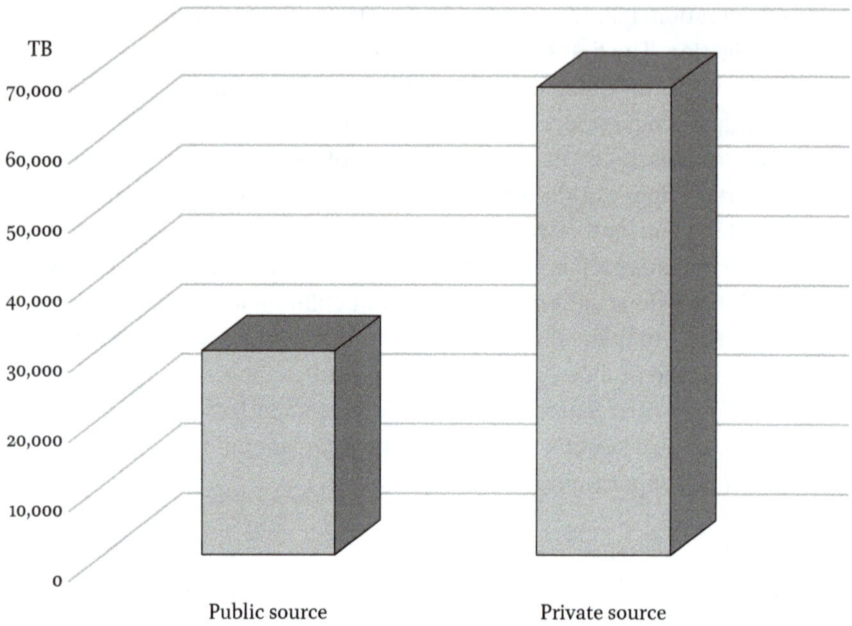

FIGURE 3.11 Public-private sources of consumption expense for the elderly aged 60+.
SOURCE: CALCULATED FROM NESDB 2012.

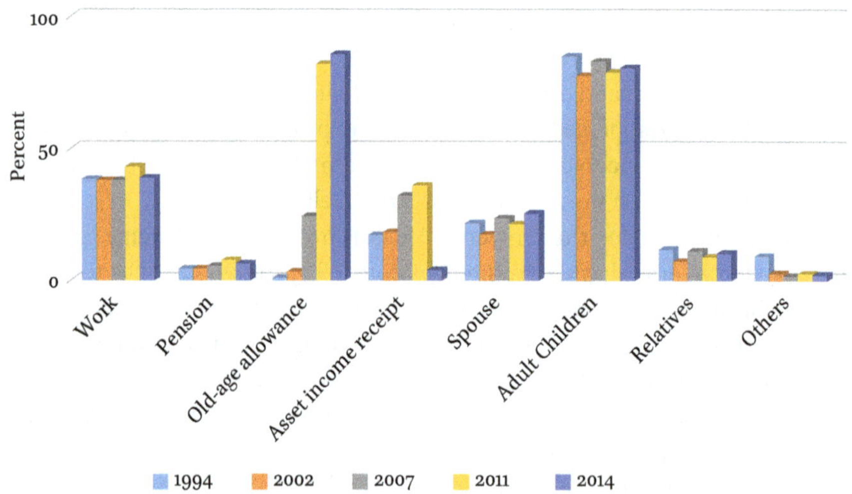

FIGURE 3.12 The elderly by main sources of income, 1994–2014.
NOTE: RESPONDENTS MAY REPORT MORE THAN ONE SOURCE.
SOURCE: CALCULATED FROM KNODEL, PRACHUABMOH, AND CHAYOVAN (2013) AND NSO (2015).

Accordingly, a partial welfare state was the current option besides new measures for providing a social safety net for security and quality of life in old age while easing the financial burden on the government as the proportion of the elderly increases.

(1) Old-age employment (Ministry of Labor 2016)
 (1.1) A tax break for employers of older citizens. They were subject to a double tax deduction on wages paid to elderly employees who earned up to TB15,000 a month. This is limited to employment of elderly people up to 10% of their workforce.
 (1.2) Vocational training for the elderly: there were a variety of practical courses organized free of charge by the Skill Development Department, Ministry of Labor, for older people. Records show elderly participants in certain courses earn TB2,735 a month, on average, after the training.

(2) Housing: a housing development plan for low-income and lower-middle earners nationwide was designed by a public-private partnership (PPP) since 2017 (Theparat 2017). A few years ago, the Bangkok Metropolitan Administration (BMA) launched a senior citizens' housing programme in Bangkok Metropolis. Currently, the capital city has 6 million registered residents, 12–13% of whom are aged 65 and above. However, studies tended to estimate the actual population to be above 10 million when those who relocated there for work or other purposes are included. The BMA estimated the proportion of elderly will reach 20% of the total population in the next decade (Fernquest 2011).

(3) An increase in reverse mortgage loans and elderly-friendly banking services: there was an attempt to increase reverse mortgage loans to the elderly who needed to borrow money against the equity of their home by a provider diversification approach, which also included private sector engagement. Previously, the Secondary Mortgage Corporation, a state-owned entity, was the only lender allowed to offer reverse mortgages. The Government Saving Bank served as another means for the elderly to access such a loan, which complements other elderly-friendly banking services provided by the Government Saving Bank, such as special interest rates (Shaj 2016; Kowitdamrong 2017).

Among measures for old-age security, those relating to the pension system were of relatively slow development. Several options were proposed, pending further investigation. They were, for example, the adoption of a more sophisticated tax system to allow universal pensions, and an increase in the eligibility age for the pension (HelpAge International 2011).

6.2.3 Role of Local Governments, Communities, and Other Not-for-profit Players

Thailand adopted a community-based system for long-term care. It was, nevertheless, at an early stage of building capacity. A "sub-district role model" was relied upon to strengthen community collaboration with other stakeholders, including families, local government, the private sector and government agencies, in the provision of services to dependent elderly people in the community and to serve the needs of the dependent population (Kasemsup et al. 2016).

Among the not-for-profit organizations actively participating in the policy-making process mentioned above for the elderly in Thailand, was the Association of Older Persons Councils of Thailand, under the Royal Patronage of Her Royal Highness the Queen Mother. Since its establishment in 1989, this association played a role in coordinating the elderly clubs in all provinces in Thailand while also contributing to the relevant legislative regimes and strategies. Policy inputs were also based on research on policy options and evaluations conducted by many research institutes and universities. Moreover, the Foundation for Older Persons' Development (FOPDEV) provided grants for the elderly, who formed a small group, for income-generating activities. About 30 groups of elderly reportedly registered for the grants (Saengpassa 2017).

6.2.4 Elder Care Services by Profit and Not-for-profit Providers

As shown in Figure 3.12 above, the role of paid/professional care workers and domestic workers in eldercare rather than by relatives, was less than 1% each according to the Preliminary Report Survey of Older Persons in Thailand 2014 (NSO 2015).

During the past few years, in-home care services by professional caregivers and senior-assisted living facilities and retirement centres in Thailand were mainly catering to foreigners rather than locals. However, given the increasing incomes which suggested a higher purchasing power in certain families, individuals had a higher chance to access private healthcare services. A number of elderly people were therefore well taken care of in private day-care centres. The demand for professional care facilities was expected to be on the rise, as well as that for professional caregivers. According to Zander (2017), the costs for in-home care varied greatly depending on the amount of care the individual requires. Full time caregivers, without a nursing degree could be hired for as little as TB8000–10,000 per month in Chiang Mai. The cost for a full-time registered nurse would be closer to TB20,000 per month. Hiring a live-in, qualified nurse available 24 hours a day, 7 days per week, or a qualified nurse with excellent English language skills may cost up to TB35,000 per month.

According to the recent measures adopted by the government on old-age security, the government allocated TB4 billion in loans for developers of "senior complex" projects for the elderly. The Treasury Department partnered with Mahidol University and Ramathibodi Hospital to develop such a complex as a pilot project. The senior complex was designed to be constructed on the 72 rai-plot owned by the Treasury Department in Samut Prakarn and to house a Hospice zone, Senior Housing Zone and Nursing Home Zone. This first state-owned "senior complex" was expected to be completed two years after construction begins. Thereafter, similar successive projects are planned to launch in Chon Buri, Chiang Mai, Chiang Rai and Nakhon Nayok provinces.

7 Conclusion

After periods of socio-economic and demographic shifts, the following were the major characteristics of Thailand: open middle-income economy; ageing and multi-generational society, below-replacement fertility; and varied types of families. The changes in family composition were not that Thailand was transformed from extended to nuclear families, as one may have expected. Nuclear families still prevailed in both rural and urban areas. While 1980 saw a slight increase in the proportion of extended families, these trends also became noticeable: decreasing family size; decreasing prevalence of male-headed households; declining number of children per household on average; increasing number of older persons per household on average; increasing trend of skip-generation households; increasing trend of one-generation households; declining trend of two-generation households; and increasing DINK and SINK patterns of lifestyle. While multi-generation households remained relatively constant in proportion, one can now find up to four generations in a household.

The living patterns of the elderly varied across regions. There was a decline in the elderly living in three-generation households while those living with just their spouse in a household were on the rise. One may, moreover, expect multi-generational households to further decline should the DINK and SINK patterns of lifestyle kept on rising. This was because those patterns of lifestyles can contribute to further fertility decline.

From the perspective of care relations, the study finds diversification in childcare providers, declining coresidence with older parents, an increase in state support for older persons, a decrease of adult children as the main source of income, and an increase of older parents providing financial support to adult children. Part of the downward support may be attributable to the fact that some were still working in their old age. While the Thai people expected the government to play a more important role in the welfare of the elderly, family remains the major childcare provider. Besides the relevant policy regimes, various cultural and religious values seemed to inter-relatedly counterbalance the negative impact of modernisation on intergenerational family solidarity, despite an increasing trend of non-coresidence and skip-generational households. Such a counterbalanced effect was also partly contributed to by state's policies to strengthen family relations through different policy measures.

One may expect the current trend to change to a certain extent in 2020 when 19.1% of the population will be aged 60 and above, and much more when Thailand turns from an ageing to an aged society. As shown in Table 3.2, by 2030 the elderly at 60 years of age and above will account for more than 20% of the total population. Without an appropriate policy intervention, the size of the family is expected to continue getting smaller. Yet, it remains to be seen if intergenerational family solidarity will decline more quickly as time passes, given the effect of the currently high proportions of a gender-free preference for children and of fathers taking part in childrearing.

References

Anderson, Bridget. (2015). *Worker, helper, auntie, maid?: Working conditions and attitudes experienced by migrant domestic workers in Thailand and Malaysia.* Bangkok: Internaional Labor Organizaion, Regional Office for Asia and the Pacific.

Bentley, R. Alexander, Michael Pietrusewsky, Michele T. Douglas, & Tim C. Atkinson. (2005). Matrilocality during the prehistoric transition to agriculture in Thailand?. *Antiquity, 79,* 865–881.

Besaggio, Davide, Silvia Fuselli, Metawee Srikummool, Jatupol Kampuansai, Loredana Castrì, Chris Tyler-Smith, Mark Seielstad, Daoroong Kangwanpong, & Giorgio Bertorelle. (2007). Genetic variation in Northern Thailand hill tribes: Origins and relationships with social structure and linguistic differences. *BMC Evolutionary Biology,7*(2), S12, doi: 10.1186/1471-2148-7-S2-S12.

Bowie, Katherine. (2008). Standing in the shadows: Of matrilocality and the role of women in a village election in northern Thailand. *American Ethnologist, 35*(1), 136–153.

Cherlin, Andrew, & Apichat Chamratrithirong. (1988). Variations in marriage patterns in central Thailand. *Demography,25*(3), 337–353.

Cochrane, Susan H., & Kalpana Nandwani. (1981). The determinants of fertility in 22 villages in Northern Thailand. *Population and human resource division.* Discussion papers no. 81–59. Washington D.C.: World Bank.

College of Population Studies, Chulalongkorn University. (2015). *Research project to outline appropriate approaches to reduce inequities in the Thai society amidst demographic shift.* Final report submitted to the Office of the National Economic and Social Development Board. Bangkok: College of Population Studies, Chulalongkorn University.

Coombs, Lolagene C. (1974). The measurement of family size preferences and subsequent fertility. *Demography,11*(4), 587–611.

Cowgill, Donald O., & Lowell D. Holmes. (1972). *Aging and modernization.* New York: Appleton-Century-Crofts.

Fernquest, Jon. (2011, May 31). Senior citizen housing projects. *Bangkok Post*, p. 1.

Fujioka, Rika, & Sopon Thangphet. (2009). *Decent work for older persons in Thailand.* Bangkok: ILO Regional Office for Asia and the Pacific.

Goode, William J. (1963). *World revolution and family patterns.* New York: Free Press.

Government Pension Fund. (2012). *Thai pension system.* Bangkok: Government Pension Fund.

Grabowsky, Volker. (1993). *An early Thai census: Translation and analysis.* Bangkok: Institute of Population Studies, Chulalongkorn University.

Hanvoravongchai, Piya. (2008). Health system and equity perspectives in health technology assessment. *J Med Assoc Thai,91* (Suppl 2), S74–S87.

Hareven, Tamara K. (1996). Introduction: Aging and generational relations over the life course. In Tamara K. Hareven (Ed.), *Aging and generational relations over the life course: A historical and cross cultural perspective* (pp. 1–12). New York: Walter de Gruyter & Co.

HelpAge International. (2011). *Pension watch: Briefings on social protection in old age.* London: HelpAge International.

Jiumpanyarach, Waruesporn. (2012). *Single-parent families in Bangkok, Thailand: factors affecting children living in single-parent families.* Unpublished doctoral dissertation, University of Kentucky, Lexington.

Kamnuansilpa, Peerasit, Apichat Chamratrithirong, & John Knodel. (1982). Thailand's Reproductive revolution: An update. *International family planning perspectives,8*(2), 51–56.

Kasemsup, Vijij, Thaworn Sakunphanit, Kanitta Bundhamcharoen, Sirinard Nipaporn, & Rassamee Tansirisithikul. (2016). Thai country Case Study, in WHO. *Population ageing, health and national development.* Geneva: WHO Western Pacific Region.

Keeratipongpaiboon, Thuttai. (2012). *Population ageing: Changes in household composition and economic behaviour in Thailand.* Unpublished doctoral dissertation, SOAS University of London, London.

Keeratipongpaiboon, Thuttai. (2013). *Population dynamic and changing household structure.* Paper presented at the 2013 NESDB Macroeconomic Annual Conference.

Kitiarsa, Patana. (2005). Beyond syncretism: Hybridization of popular religion in contemporary. *Journal of Southeast Asian Studies, 36* (3), 461–487.

Komin, Suntaree. (1991). *Psychology of the Thai people: Values and behavioral patterns.* Bangkok: National Institute of Development Administration (NIDA)

Kowitdamrong, Urisara. (2017, May 26). GSB to introduce reverse mortgages. *The Nation*, p. 1.

Knodel, John. (2009). *Is intergenerational solidarity really on the decline? Cautionary evidence from Thailand.* Paper prepared at the seminar on family support networks and population ageing, Doha, Qatar.

Knodel, John, & Napaporn Chayovan. (2008). *Population ageing and the well-Being of older persons in Thailand: Past trends, current situation and future challenges.* Bangkok: UNFPA Thailand and Asia and the Pacific Regional Office.

Knodel, John, & Napaporn Chayovan. (2009). Intergenerational relationships and family care and support for Thai elderly. *Ageing International, 33*(1–4), 15–27.

Knodel, John, Nibhon Debvalya, Napaporn Chayovan, & Apichat Chamratrithirong. (1984). Marriage patterns in Thailand: A review of demographic evidence. In Apichat Chamratrighrong (Ed.), *Perspectives on the Thai marriage* (pp. 31–68). Bangkok: Institute for Population and Social Research.

Knodel, John, Apichat Chamratrithirong, & Nibhon Debavalya. (1987). *Thailand's reproductive revolution: Rapid fertility decline in a third-world setting.* Madison: University of Wisconsin Press.

Knodel, John, Napaporn Chayovan, & Siriwan Siriboon. (1996a). Familial support and the life course of Thai elderly and their children. In Tamara K. Hareven (Ed.), *Aging and generational relations: Life-course and cross-cultural perspectives* (pp. 217–240). New York: Aldine de Gruyter.

Knodel, John, Vipan Prachuabmoh Ruffolo, Pakamas Ratanalangkarn, & Kua Wongboonsin. (1996b). *Reproductive preferences in post-transition Thailand: Implications for the future course of fertility.* Ann Arbor: Population Studies Center, University of Michigan.

Knodel, John, Vipan Prachuabmoh, & Napaporn Chayovan. (2013). *The changing well-being of the Thai elderly: An Update from the 2011 survey of older persons in Thailand.* Ann Arbor: Population Studies Center, University of Michigan.

Knodel, John, Bussarawan Puk Teerawichitchainan, & Wiraporn Pothisiri. (2016). *Caring for Thai older persons with long-term care needs.* Michigan: University of Michigan.

Lee, Kelly, Gill Walt, Louisiana Lush, & John Cleland. (1995). *Population policies and programmes: Determinants and consequences in eight developing countries.* London: UN Population Fund and LSHTM.

Limanonda, Bhassorn. (1989). An analysis of Thai marriage: Attitude and behavior, a case study of women in Bangkok Metropolis. *Journal of the National Research Council of Thailand, 21*(1), 21–51.

Limpanonda, Suphannada. (2012). *Provincial disparities in Thailand: Convergence, agglomeration economies and effects on poverty, 1988–2008.* Unpublished doctoral dissertation, SOAS, University of London, London.

Luangthongkum, Theraphan. (2007). The positions of non-Thai languages in Thailand. In Lee Hock Guan & Leo Suryadinata (Eds.), *Language, nation and development in Southeast Asia* (pp. 181–194). Singapore: Institute of Southeast Asian Studies.

Mahaarcha, Wanippol, & Sirinan Kittisuksathit. (2009). Impact of family structure, parental migration, and parental divorce on an adolescent's educational enrollment: Evidence from a longitudinal study on Kanchanaburi Province, Thailand. *Journal of Population and Social Studies, 18*(1), 1–21.

Mason, Karen Oppenheim. (1992). Family change and support for the elderly in Asia: What do we know?. *Asia-Pacific Population Journal, 7*(3), 13–31.

Ministry of Labor. (2007). *The situation of old-age employment in Thailand.* Bangkok: Department of Labor Protection and Welfare, Ministry of Labor.

Ministry of Labor. (2016). *Ministry of Labor promotes employment for the elderly.* Bangkok: Department of Labor Protection and Welfare, Ministry of Labor.

Muttarak, Raya. (2004). Domestic service in Thailand: Reflection of conflicts in gender, class and ethnicity. *Journal of Southeast Asian Studies, 35*(3), 503–529.

Nantamonkolchai, Sutam, Sirikun Isranurak, Duangporn Kaewsiri, & Saijai Pothisubsuk. (2005). phawawikrit naikhropkhrua kap kanopromliangdu lae phatnakan dekpotmawai lae wairian. *wansan satharanasuk laekanphatna, 3*(1), 1–7. [Family in crisis and child rearing and child development during early and schooling years of age. *Journal of Public Health and Development, 3*(1), 1–7].

NESDB. (1967a). *Evaluation of the first six-year plan (1961–1966).* Bangkok: Office of the National Economic Development Board, Office of the Prime Minister.

NESDB. (1967b). *The second national economic and social development plan (1967–1971).* Bangkok: National Economic Development Board, Office of the Prime Minister.

NESDB. (1972). *The third national economic and social development plan (1972–1976).* Bangkok: National Economic and Social Development Board, Office of the Prime Minister.

NESDB. (1977). *The fourth national economic and social development plan (1977–1981).* Bangkok: Office of the National Economic and Social Development Board, Office of the Prime Minister.

NESDB. (1982). *The fifth national economic and social development plan (1982–1986).* Bangkok: Office of the National Economic and Social Development Board, Office of the Prime Minister.

NESDB (1987). *The sixth national economic and social development plan (1987–1911).* Bangkok: Office of the National Economic and Social Development Board, Office of the Prime Minister.

NESDB. (1992). *The seventh national economic and social development plan (1992–1996)*. Bangkok: Office of the National Economic and Social Development Board, Office of the Prime Minister.

NESDB. (2002). *The ninth national economic and social development plan (2002–2006)*. Bangkok: Office of the National Economic and Social Development Board, Office of the Prime Minister.

NESDB. (2007). *The tenth national economic and social development plan (2007–2011)*. Bangkok: Office of the National Economic and Social Development Board, Office of the Prime Minister.

NESDB. (2009). *Integrated strategy on Thai elderly people*. Bangkok: Office of the National Economic and Social Development Board, Office of the Prime Minister.

NESDB. (2012). *NTA study 2011*. Bangkok: Office of the National Economic and Social Development Board, Office of the Prime Minister

NESDB. (2012a). *The eleventh national economic and social development plan (2012–2016)*. Bangkok: Office of the National Economic and Social Development Board, Office of the Prime Minister.

NESDB. (2012b). *Population plan during the eleventh national economic and social development plan (2012–2016)*. Bangkok: Office of the National Economic and Social Development Board, Office of the Prime Minister.

NESDB. (2014). *Population projection for Thailand 2010–2040*. Bangkok: National Economic and Social Development Board, Office of the Prime Minister.

NESDB. (2017a). *Khrong sang khongkhruaruean atra kanchotthabian somrot lae atra kan chotthabianya pi po so 2523–2558 raipi*. [*Structure of families, marriage registration rate and divorce registration rate 1980–2015 yearly*]. Bangkok: Office of the National Economic and Social Development Board, Office of the Prime Minister.

NESDB. (2017b). *The twelfth national economic and social development plan (2017–2021)*. Bangkok: Office of the National Economic and Social Development Board, Office of the Prime Minister.

NESDB, IPS, & NSO. (1970). *Population projections for Thailand, 1960–2000*. Bangkok: National Economic and Social Development Board, Institute of Population Studies, Chulalongkorn University, and National Statistical Office.

NSO. (1962). *Samnano prachakon haengprathetthai po so 2503 thuaratanachak. Krungthep: samnakngan sathitiklang samnakngan saphaphatnakan setatkit haengchat*. [*Population census of Thailand B.E. 2503 whole kingdom*]. Bangkok: Central Statistical Office, National Economic Development Board.

NSO. (1970). *1970 population & housing census, whole kingdom*. Bangkok: National Statistical Office, Office of the Prime Minister.

NSO. (1980). *1980 population & housing census, whole kingdom*. Bangkok: National Statistical Office, Office of the Prime Minister.

NSO. (1990). *1990 population & housing census, whole kingdom*. Bangkok: National Statistical Office, Office of the Prime Minister.

NSO. (2000). *2000 population & housing census, whole kingdom*. Bangkok: National Statistical Office, Office of the Prime Minister.

NSO. (2009). *Ruamchalong nuengroipi sammanoprachakon prathetthai sammano prachakonlaekheha pi po so 2553: napkhon nai prathet khrangthi 11*. [*Centennial celebration, population census in Thailand, 2010 population and housing census: 11th population counting in the country*]. Bangkok: National Statistical Office.

NSO.(2012). *2010 population & housing census, whole kingdom*. Bangkok: National Statistical Office, Ministry of Information and Communication Technology.

NSO. (2015). *Rayngan pol beungton sumruad prachakon sungayu nai prathetthai po so 2557*. [*Preliminary report, survey of older persons in Thailand 2014*]. Bangkok: National Statistical Office.

NSO. (2016). *Kan tumngan kong prachakon sungayu nai prathetthai po so 2559*. [*Employment of older persons in Thailand 2016*]. Bangkok: National Statistical Office.

Ofstedal, Mary Beth, John Knodel, & Napaporn Chayovan. (1999). *Intergenerational support and gender: A comparison of four Asian countries*. Ann Arbor: Population Studies Center, University of Michigan.

OWAFD. (2013). *Khomun satthitinaru phuea kanwikhro mitikropkhrua*. [*Interesting statistical data for an analysis of family dimension*]. Bangkok: Office of Women's Affairs and Family Development.

OWAFD. (2014). *Sathanakan khwamkhemkhaeng khong khropkhrua radapprathet (po so 2556)* samnakngan kitkansatri lae sathabankhropkhrua. Krasuang phatnasangkhom lae khwammankhongkhongomnut. [*Situation of family solidarity at the national level* (2013). Office of Women's Affairs and Family Development, Ministry of Social Development and Human Security]. Retrieved April 20, 2014, from http://www.owf.go.th.

Phananiramai, Mathana, & Amonthep Chawla. (2007). *Changing labor income, consumption and age reallocation in Thailand*. Paper presented at the national seminar on Asia's dependency transition: Intergenerational equity, poverty alleviation and public policy, UNFPA, Bangkok.

Podhisita, Chai. (1984). Marriage in rural northeast Thailand: A household perspective. In Apichat Chamratrithirong (Ed.), *Perspectives on the Thai marriage* (pp. 71–112). Bangkok: Sri Anata Press.

Podhisita, Chai. (2011). Kanplianplaeng khropkhrua lae khruaruean thai: rao (mai) ru arai? Nai Sathaban wichai prachakon lae sangkhom. *Prachakon lae sangkom 2554*. [Thai family and household changes: What we (don't) know? in Institute of Population and Social Research]. *Population and Society 2011* (pp. 24–41). Nakornpatom: Institute of Population and Social Research, Mahidol University. Retrieved

April 20, 2014, from http://www2.ipsr.mahidol.ac.th/ConferenceVII/Download/2011-Article-02.pdf.

Pongsapich, Amara. (1990). Changing family patterns in Thailand. In CWDS, UNESCO, & UNICEF (Eds.), *Regional workshop on changing family patterns and gender roles in Asia*, 7–10 May 1990, Surajkund, India. SHS/POP/UNIC/DWDS/90/07.

Prachuabmoh, Visid, & John Knodel. (1977). *Preferences for sex of children in Thailand: Result from the second round of a national survey*. Bangkok: Institute of Population Studies, Chulalongkorn University.

Prachuabmoh, Vipan, & Preeya Mithranon. (2003). Below-replacement fertility in Thailand and its policy implications. *Journal of Population Research*, *20*(1), 35–50.

Prachuabmoh, Visid, John Knodel, Suchart Prasithrathsin, & Nibhon Debavalya. (1972). *The rural and urban populations in Thailand: comparative profiles*. Bangkok: Institute of Population Studies, Chulalongkorn University.

Prasartsul, Pramote, Sutthida Chuanwan, & Kanchana Thianlai. (2012). Elderly: Inner people to be marginalised. In Kulapa Vajanasara, & Kritaya Archavanitkul (Eds.), *Marginalized population and justice in Thai society* (pp. 105–124). Institute of Population and Social Research, Mahidol University. Bangkok: October Printing.

Ramsay, Ansil. (2001). The Chinese in Thailand: Ethnicity, power and cultural opportunity structures. In Grant H. Cornwell, & Eve W. Stoddard (Eds.), *Global multiculturism: Comparative perspective on ethnicity, race and nation* (pp. 51–71). Oxford: Rowman & Littlefield Publishers, Inc.

Richter, Kerry, & Chai Podhisita. (1992). Thai family demography: A review and research prospects. *Journal of Population and Social Studies*, *3*(1–2), 1–19.

Richter, Kerry, Chai Podhisita, Kosol Soonthorndhada, & Apichat Chamratrithirong. (1992). *Child care in urban Thailand: Choice & constraint in a changing society*. Nakhonpathom: Institute for Population and Social Research, Mahidol University.

Saengpassa, Chularat. (2017, April 10). Livelihoods for elderly now a top priority. *The Nation*.

Sattar, Ellen. (1984). The drop-out problem in primary education: A regional overview. In Ellen Sattar (Ed.), *The drop-out problem in primary education: Some case studies* (pp. 1–18). Bangkok: UNESCO.

Shaj, Viraj. (2016, March 13). Fiscal policy office to increase reverse mortgage lending to elderly. *Business News*.

Sutinyamanee, Vasavat, & Patcharawalai Wongboonsin. (2016). Support and assistance: Bonds of intergenerational family solidarity among hill tribe people in Northern Thailand. *Journal of Demography*,*32*(2), 45–72.

Thaiarry, Srisak. (2008). *Dreamingbig in Thailand*. Bangkok: NCYD.

Theparat, Chatrudee. (2017, August 29). Thai government pushes public-private partnership for housing scheme. *Bangkok Post.*

United Nations. (2013). *World population ageing 2013*. New York: United Nations.

United Nations. (2014). *World population prospects: The 2012 revision.* New York: United Nations.

United Nations. (2017). *World population prospects: The 2017 revision.* New York: United Nations, Department of Economic and Social Affairs, Population Division.

Wongboonsin, Kua. (1995). *Population policy and programmes in Thailand: 1929-present.* Bangkok: Chulalongkorn University.

Wongboonsin, Patcharawalai. (2010). Kanlotlong khong atra cheroenphan: naito kanpanphon thangprachakon raya thi 2 yuk sangkhom siangphai. *warasan prachakonsat, 26*(2), 27–62. [Fertility decline: Implication for 2nd demographic dividend in a risk society. *Journal of Demography, 26*(2), 27–62].

Wongboonsin, Patcharawalai. (2013). Migration into Thailand: Change and continuity from a gender Perspective. In Dirk Hoerder & Amarjit Kaur (Eds.), *Proletarian and gendered mass migrations, A global perspective on continuities and discontinuities from the 19th to the 21st centuries* (pp. 365–381). The Netherland: Brill.

Wongboonsin, Patcharawalai, & Montakarn Chimmamee. (2017). Spiritualism of middle class in Thailand. *Shikoku Gakuin University Treaties, 151,* 49–71.

Wongboonsin, Kua, & Achara Entz. (1991). *Women's Work and the Need for Child Care among Prekindergarten Children in Bangkok Metropolitan Area.* Bangkok: College of Population Studies, Chulalongkorn University.

Wongboonsin, Patcharawalai, & Wiraporn Pothisiri. (2012). *Thai population development plan guidance for 2012–2016.* Unpublished report submitted to National Economic and Social Development Board. Bangkok: College of Population Studies, Chulalongkorn University.

Wongboonsin, Kua, & Vipan Prachuabmoh Ruffolo. (1995). Sex preference for children in Thailand and some other South-East Asian countries. *Asia Pacific Population Journal,10*(3), 43–62.

Wongboonsin, Patcharawalai, Sineenat Sermcheep, & Piti Srisangnam. (2012). *Toward a conceptualization of Thailand's economic development model: The analysis of national economic and social development plans (1961–2011).* Paper presented at the 5th Biennial Conference of the Korean Studies Association of Southeast Asia (KoSASA), University of Social Sciences and Humanities, Hanoi, Vietnam.

Wongboonsin, Patcharawalai, Pataporn Sukontaman, Wiraporn Pothisiri, & Rungratana Kowantanakul. (2013, 26 September–1 August). *Attitude and perceptions towards marriage and singlehood among Thai women.* Paper presented at the session 004: Transitions in the spousal selection process, The XXVI IUSSP international population conference 2013, International Union for the Scientific Study of Population, BEXCO Conference Center, Busan, Republic of Korea.

Wongsith, Malinee. (1991). Attitudes toward family values in Thai society. In Bhassorn Limanonda, Chai Podhisita & Malinee Wongsith (Eds.), *Report on a Thai family and household survey* (pp. 68–100). Bangkok: Institute of Population Studies, Chulalongkorn University.

Wongyannava, Thanes. (2011). The sound of sirens in social research on the intimate sphere in Thailand and its discontents. *Journal of Intimate and Public Spheres*, *1*(1), 36–54.

Zander, Ryan. (2017). *Care facilities of elderly assisted living in Thailand*. Retrieved November 17, 2017, from https://iglu.net/care-facilities-for-elderly-assisted-living-in-thailand/.

CHAPTER 4

Changes in Family Structure and Care Relations in Vietnam

Nguyen Huu Minh

1 Introduction

Vietnam is located in Southeast Asia, bordered by China to the north, Laos and Cambodia to the west, and to the east, by the East Sea. In 2010, it was the third most populous country in Southeast Asia, surpassed only by Indonesia and the Philippines, and it was the 13th most populous country in the world, according to Vietnam Central Population and Housing Census Steering Committee (VCPHCSC 2010). According to Vietnam General Statistics Office (VGSO 2015), the population of Vietnam increased from around 86 million in 2009 to 90.5 million in 2014 and was largely concentrated in the Red River Delta (in the North) and in the Mekong River Delta (in the South). With 70% of the population living in rural areas in 2015, Vietnam was primarily an agricultural country.

After more than one thousand years of Chinese domination, Vietnam regained her independence in 939 AD. Chinese cultural influences are found in some aspects of Vietnamese cultural and social life, especially at the high levels of government and among the elite of society (Taylor 1983; Tran 1991).

The French aggression and colonial rule over Vietnam which began in the late 19th century and lasted until the middle of the 20th century also left strong imprints on all aspects of social life, including family life. Right after President Ho Chi Minh proclaimed independence for Vietnam in 1945, Vietnam was once again thrown into the crucible of war for another 30 years, first fighting against the return of the French, a war which ended in 1954, and then the war against the American, which lasted until 1975. During the 1954–1975 period, Vietnam was temporarily divided into two parts with the Democratic Republic of Vietnam in the North and the Republic of Vietnam in the South. The human cost of the French colonial period, the Japanese occupation, and the thirty years of war from 1945 to 1975 included the untimely deaths of millions of Vietnamese people and the wounding of millions more (Banister 1993). The economic modernisation of Vietnam was impossible during these decades of war.

When the war ended in 1975, Vietnam was a battered nation that could not feed its own population. Although signs of economic renovation were evident

 | DOI:10.1163/9789004384330_005

from the late 1970s, it was not until 1986 that economic renovation began to significantly change Vietnam's socio-economic life. Today, Vietnam is engaged in efforts to rebuild the country and its economy in order to improve the living standards of its population.

The Red River Delta is located in North Vietnam and has socio-cultural characteristics rather different from those in the Central and South regions. It included two cities and nine provinces with a total population of about 20 million in 2009. It contained 6% of Vietnam's land area but 22.8% of her population. Its density was 930 persons/sq km (compared to a density of 259 persons/sq km for the whole country). Its sex-ratio [calculated as the number of males per 100 females at birth] in the 1979 Census was 82.3, in the 1989 Census it was 90.7%, and in the 2009 it was 97.2%, making it one of the regions with lowest sex-ratio in Vietnam (however sex-ratio at birth was 115.3, the highest among the regions). The Red River Delta had a medium fertility and low mortality rate compared with other regions of the country (VCPHCSC 2010). The region was long considered the cradle of Vietnamese culture where traditions of Vietnamese ethnicity were deeply preserved (Vu et al. 1991). Hanoi, the capital city of Vietnam is located in the heart of Red River Delta. The background information below, is related directly to the characteristics of the Red River Delta.

2 Cultural Background

2.1 *Culture and Customs*

2.1.1 Traditional Village and Family Life

The village played an important role in the life of the traditional Vietnamese family. Inhabitants of a Viet village lived in the same residential territory surrounded by cultivated land. They were not necessarily related to each other by blood. The mutual relationship between close-by neighbours in the same hamlet and neighborhood was very important as emphasised by the popular saying that "*ban anh em xa mua lang gieng gan*" [brothers living at a distance cannot equal close-by neighbours]. All the hamlets and neighborhoods in each village shared common village regulations called *huong uoc* [communal statutes] which helped maintain the village as a unique social unit. The *huong uoc* was a code governing the daily life of the village. Although the articles provided in the *huong uoc* concerned mostly individual behaviour, family responsibility was sometimes mentioned (Nguyen 1993). An individual's life in the traditional Viet village, therefore, was very much influenced by the existing customs and his/her relationship with others in the village. Regarding the care system, this tradition was advantageous because care of the elderly and children was carried out through and by the village system of neighbors.

Traditional Vietnamese families preferred to live in clusters, with members from different generations living near each other or together. However, a typical kind of Vietnamese family was not a "large patriarchal family" with many nuclear families of the same ancestry gathered under the same roof. The Vietnamese family system contained a majority of nuclear families and a number of "small families" [a term coined by Nguyen 1993]. The "small families" included the nuclear family of the oldest son (mostly, however, in a number of cases the youngest son), the parents and a number of younger brothers and sisters who were not yet married. This family structure was preserved over various periods perhaps because nuclear and small families were considered a productive unit fully compatible with pre-industrial rice cultivation (Nguyen 1993).

Each small family and nuclear family was a unit of a larger kinship system. The kinship system had an important role in a traditional Vietnamese village. Although familial relationships on both the mother's side and father's side were important, the Viet family is basically patrilineal. That was one reason why relationships on the father's side seemed closer and provided more opportunities to help each other than those on the mother's side. There were ways to keep and nourish the collective sentiments of membership among the families. Among family members there were regulations governing each person's responsibilities in the common activities of the lineage. The families used the "*gia pha*" [family record] – a kind of family tree which recorded all the names and important dates (births, deaths) as well as the position of the family's ancestors. The kinship system included a leadership composed of the "*toc truong*" [head of the lineage] and the "*chi truong*" [head of the branches]. There was also a system of rituals composed of ancestor worship and a family temple. Economic means such as the "*ruong ho*" [family paddy-fields] were established to support this form of worship. The importance of this kinship system was not merely for its function as a source of mutual aid, but also as a source of emotional and psychological comfort. Kinship solidarity was also a means for families to achieve political power in a commune (Nguyen 1993).

2.1.2 Traditional Marriage

In the traditional Vietnamese family, marriage was universal. There was a saying "*trai khon tim vo, gai khon tim chong*" [a wise man looks for a wife, and a wise woman looks for a husband]. Marriage to a person with a similar social and economic family background was preferred in traditional Vietnamese society. In addition to a match between families' social status, people paid much attention to the characteristics of the bride. The desirable qualities of a woman for marriage were gentleness and delicacy, her reproductive potential, and her potential contribution to household production.

Except for the prohibition of marriage within the lineage, which is still retained in modern law, there were no specific regulations about the match of the bride and the groom regarding residential background. However, Vietnamese people generally preferred to marry people from their own village or a neighbouring village (Nguyen 1993). This was a good foundation for the care system in villages in rural Vietnam.

The elderly people were usually cared for by their own family members. The social norm of filial piety required that children not only provide for their elderly parents' subsistence but also pay them respect and treat them with love so that they could live happily during their old age. Therefore, the common expectation was that children should not live far from their parental home while their parents were still alive so that they could take care of their parents.

Living arrangements were regulated by customs rather than by laws. However, norms of patrilocal co-residence were taken for granted and were implicit in the feudal laws. In the Le Code, for example, Article 321 stated that those wives who left *the husband's home* [my emphasis] without authorisation "shall be condemned to penal servitude as a serf assigned to kitchens" while Article 310 stipulated that if the wife violated one of 7 cases of repudiation, among them *not being filial to the parents-in-law* [my emphasis], but the husband did not force her out then he "shall be demoted in proportion to the gravity of the matter" (Vien 1991).

The eldest son was expected to live with his parents to support them in their old age. Younger sons, however, left their parents' house a short time after marriage to settle in a private house. This could be considered a custom of "rotation" in the living arrangements of Vietnamese families. As a reward, the eldest son inherited the *"huong hoa"* [incense-and-fire property], a special portion of property to be used for the expenses related to the cult of the family ancestors. Sometimes, if all the other children had already left home, the youngest would stay with the parental family. If the parents did not have a son, the eldest daughter may bring her husband into the parental home and might inherit the *"huong hoa"* to ensure perpetuation of the cult of the family ancestors (Nguyen 1993; Mai & Le 1978).

This pattern of co-residence not only reflects the traditional expectation that children are obliged to care for their elderly parents, but also expresses a desire among parents to help their children before they can afford to establish an independent household. Patrilocal residence also helps the new daughter-in-law become accustomed to being part of her husband's family and to meet the expectations of her parents-in-law. Traditional family patterns of co-residence reinforce the obligations of members of the younger generation toward their elders. These patterns are also a household strategy for mutual intergenerational support (Nguyen & Hirschman 2000). In other words, the "patrilocal residence pattern and its variation are useful for both the old and young generations." (Mai 2000, 40–41; see also Rydstrom & Drummond 2004). The persistence of traditional Vietnamese family structures has been confirmed by some recent empirical studies (Goodkind 1997a; Nguyen & Hirschman 2000; Mai 2000).

It has been suggested that modernisation, urbanisation, and industrialisation do not in themselves necessarily result in a linear development from extended or stem family to nuclear family. These results are related to findings from other countries in the region, which show persistence in patrilocal co-residence after marriage in recent decades (Freedman et al. 1994; Lavely & Ren 1992; Weinstein et al. 1994).

Co-residence of newly married children with the husband's parents usually only lasts for a short period of time. Younger sons are supported in establishing a new household, leaving only one son (usually the oldest son in the Red River Delta) to live permanently with, and take care of, old parents. This tradition has persisted almost unchanged in the Red River Delta and some other regions in Vietnam through the last several decades, although research findings show that there has been a reduction in the duration of patrilocal co-residence after marriage. In other words, young couples tend to leave their parental family earlier than before. Overall, among those persons who did co-reside with the husband's parents after marriage, about 50% of them continue to live with the husband's parents for more than three years (Nguyen & Hirschman 2000).

The maintenance of both the aforementioned trends reflects the different needs of parents and young couples regarding patrilocal co-residence. Behind these two trends are issues of social "logics" like parental support for the young couple in terms of economics when they first set up their own family and assistance in taking care of newborns, as well as the willingness of a young couple to leave the parental family in order to establish their own household, to live an independent life, and to make their own decisions.

2.1.3 Religion

Confucianism originated from China and was transferred to Vietnam in the 1st millennium AD when Vietnam was being occupied by China. Its spread on Vietnamese life had been continuously since then and most strongly from 15th century. The influence of Confucianism on the traditional Vietnamese family is rather strong. Confucianism highly values origins and descent; it also respects filial piety, parental care, and the worship of ancestors. It places a high premium on lineage and pays no attention to individual interests. The influence of Confucianism on Vietnamese families continued until Vietnam was transformed into a French colony. However, this influence was not uniform among different regions, or among different kinds of families, with the Red River Delta being considered to be most affected by Confucianism (Tran 1991).

For most Vietnamese, religious beliefs are an important dimension of cultural life. Of special significance in their life is a traditional custom "*Tho cung to tien*" [Ancestor worship] which has a strongly religious character. Vietnamese believe that one's own ancestors' spirits have influence on the lives of their descendants. Buddhism, the traditional religion of Vietnam, came to Vietnam sometime in the 1st century from China and India and was eventually adapted to fit with the existing traditional ancestor worship. This is why many people find it difficult to distinguish Buddhism from ancestor worship (Do 1991; Nguyen 1993; Nguyen 1997).

Christianity was introduced into Vietnam in the 17th century by Western missionaries. Its spread was impeded in its early years of development, particularly before the French colonisation of Vietnam, because it was considered to violate Vietnamese customs and challenge the King's power. During the French colonial period, Christianity spread dramatically. Christians tended to enjoy greater political power and economic privileges than non-Christians. The Vietnamese Christians became increasingly well organized (Tong Cuc Chinh Tri 1993). In the villages they tended to live in distinct neighborhoods, in clusters which were easily distinguished from the rest of the village. Christians appeared to have different views on marriage, family, reproduction, life, and death.

The major religions in the Red River Delta were Buddhism and Christianity. Since there was no significant difference between non-religious Vietnamese and followers of Buddhism (except for the monks), religious beliefs in the Red River Delta were in fact distinguished by belonging either to Christianity or Non-Christianity. This could be one reason why, in the Red River Delta, Christians and Non-Christians (Buddhists and non-religious people) were considered as two distinct groups, called the *luong* [non-Christians] and *giao* [Christians] in common language. It can be suggested that there is a clear difference between Christians and Non-Christians in terms of using the care system, since the Christians in Vietnam may be more influenced by Western systems with more individualistic thinking in their care systems.

2.2 *Gender Role in Family Relations*

Women had a complex position in the traditional family and social life. On the one hand, they were very effective in the family economy by their activities in farming and small trade activities. They brought home a significant amount of income. More importantly, Vietnamese women played a major role in the financial management of family resources once they became a wife and a mother. They were considered a *"Noi Tuong"* [Commander of the Interior, meaning a person who is responsible for everything within the family] or the person who *"nam tay hom chia khoa"* [held the key to the cash box] of the family. The women could also even exercise their influence in many other activities outside the family, as there was a saying *"lenh ong khong bang cong ba"* [His kettledrum cannot sound as loud as her gong]. However, as noted by several authors (Tran 1991; Nguyen 1993), the important role of women might most strongly be expressed among common peasant families.

On the other hand, under the influence of Confucianism, there was no basis of equality between males and females. In a Confucian society, the eldest man in the family is the head of the family. When unmarried, a girl must obey her father; after marriage, she must obey her husband; and when her husband dies, she must respect the guidance of her son who then becomes the head of the family. In relations with the outside world, only men can represent the family. Family chores are the responsibility of women. Vietnam was not an exception in these cultural precepts.

Although it is true that the Le Code once gave Vietnamese women property ownership rights equal with men, this fact should not be treated as indicating complete equality between men and women in the traditional Viet family. In addition, the right to inherit land granted to women by the Le Code legally existed for only a very short time. From the 16th century it was no longer practised in reality (Mai & Le 1978, 47) and later, in the early 19th century, daughters were excluded from inheritance of the family estate in the Gia Long Code (Nguyen & Ta 1987). The practice of passing an inheritance on to sons but not to daughters is taken for granted by many people in the Red River Delta up to the present time (Nguyen 1997). Even in the Le Code, which is notable for its advanced protections of women's rights compared to the later Gia Long Code in Vietnam or several Codes in other East Asian countries during the same period (Dinh 1968; Nguyen & Ta 1987), the husband still had more say in family matters. This practice would affect the elderly care system in Vietnam meaning that the son would be the person to take care of parents when they get old.

Few men were educated, but there were more educated men than women. One reason was that a daughter would join her husband's family later, so it was therefore economically irrational to educate her. In addition, since a woman's place was inside the house, she had little need for formal schooling. A man could study to become a scholar and statesman, but this was impossible for women because they were not allowed to take the examinations that afforded entry into the class of scholars (Tran 1991). In general, in traditional culture, the domination of men over women well expresses the patriarchal characteristics of Vietnam marriage and family patterns.

This patriarchal pattern of the Vietnamese family still remains today. The Vietnam Family Survey 2006 showed that in the modern Vietnamese family, the head of family has diversified, reflecting changes in family structure. It can be the wife, husband or both. However, in a general survey, respondents said that men are still the default head of the family. The Head of the family is generally the family member responsible for important decisions. In most cases, data suggested that wives more often make decisions on everyday work involving small amounts of money and husbands often decide larger things involving larger amounts of money. In urban, well-off households, wives are now making more important decisions, or are sharing these decisions with the husband more often than are women in rural areas, mountainous areas and poor households (MOCST et al. 2008). The Hanoi survey data in 2010 also showed that about 60% of the final decision of most important matters in the family was done by the husband, about 18% by the wife and 16% by both, the rest was by other persons in the family (Nguyen 2014a).

Traditional labor allocation according to gender is still common and survey data confirmed this. Most respondents said that the woman/wife is regarded as more suitable to work inside or near the house, doing work like domestic chores and taking care of family members and that men are more suitable to production, business and external relations. Where there was a more equal distribution of work between wife and husband it was generally among urban, well-off groups and more highly educated respondents. In households with both husband and wife working outside the home, more husbands shared the housework (MOCST et al. 2008). This pattern was similar in the Hanoi survey of 2010. About 61% respondents agreed that "A husband's job is to earn money; a wife's job is to look after the home and family", among them, the %age of those in rural areas who agreed was higher than those in urban area (68.2% vs. 49.1%) and females tended to agree more than males (63.6% vs. 58.2%).

The traditional patriarchal structure of Vietnamese society means that important property is generally in the name of the man/husband, and the survey found that this largely remains true today. This naturally gives husbands the final say in significant matters. Exceptions are the Ede and Kh'mer people, who have a matriarchal structure. (MOCST et al. 2008).

2.3 *Child Preferences*

To assure continuity of the patrilineage and to perform the rites of ancestor worship, which was the highest expression of Confucian filial piety, is among the most important values of the son in Vietnamese family. Per traditional thinking, the family with only daughters was considered as having no continuity of the patrilineage, "one son is considered as having a child, ten daughters are considered as having no child". The pressure to marry was also strong for women because of the common belief that they would only find a secure base from which to live and act within the framework of marriage (Marr 1981, 248).

If some traditional child values have changed dramatically in the context of profound industrialisation, modernisation and international integration, there is an aspect that remains very solid over time, which is the trend of son preference. The necessity to have a son is supported by a large proportion of population. The Vietnam Family Survey 2006 confirmed that, for the people, the meaning of son within a family has changed, however, there is still a significant proportion of people (36.7% of respondents of age 18–60[1]) supporting the necessity of having a son. Among many reasons, the purpose of continuing the family line and having support when getting old are important ones. (MOCST et al. 2008). In another words, it is supposed that son would be the person who would take care of elderly parents later on. It is noteworthy that this perception is even popular among the group of 14–25 years old, who are representatives of the young generation. According to the Survey of Vietnam Youth and Adolescent in 2009[2], 12.6% of young people reflected the need to have a son. Son preference is more popular in rural areas than urban areas. (Nguyen & Tran 2011).

3 Socio-economic Background

3.1 *Modernisation and Economic Development*

The centrally planned economy with a socialist model was implemented in North Vietnam beginning in 1954, after the end of the French war, and continued after the unification of the country in 1975. According to the socialist model, the state determined the direction of all important economic activities through a system of production and distribution plans based on strict regulation of pricing and interest rates. Vietnam's economy under this system proved to be inefficient and costly after unification. The weakness of this management mechanism was even more clearly revealed after foreign aid was reduced in 1979–80. This demanded a new solution for economic development.

1 With a random sample representative for a whole country, sample size is 9300 respondents.

2 With a random sample representative for a whole country, sample size is 10044 young people aged 15–24.

In December 1986, the Sixth Congress of the Communist Party of Vietnam announced a new policy called "Doi Moi" (Renovation). One of its main orientations was to shift Vietnam's economy from a centralised and subsidy-based economy strictly dependent on public and collective ownership, to a socialist-oriented multi-sector commodity economy under state management. Small and medium-sized private businesses received stimulus from the state (Vu 1995).

Doi Moi has been an important platform for change in all economic and social sectors in the country. As a number of strategies of economic and social development were implemented from 1986 up to the present, Vietnam's economy recorded good and relatively stable growth rates. The average annual GDP growth rate was around 7.26 percent in the period from 2001 to 2010. Economic structures shifted towards industrialisation and modernisation. GDP per capita was about US$1,168 in 2010, nearly three times that in 2000. The GDP growth rate was 5.9% in 2011, according to data from the Vietnam Communist Party (VCP 2011) and the Socialist Republic of the Vietnam Government (SRVG 2011). With this level of growth, Vietnam has moved from the group of poorest countries to the group of countries having low-to-average income levels. As a result of economic growth, investment in the social field, including the care system for children, has been increasing, especially for poverty reduction, universal education, health care development, health improvement for children and mothers. In recent years, the budget for regular education usually accounted for about 20% of GDP and for health care in 2016–2017 was about 6% (Nguyen 2017).

Despite encouraging achievements, Vietnam's economic and social development process is facing many difficulties. Total investment for the social development sector in 2013 was only 30.4%, the lowest level since 2000. This predicts that Vietnam will continue to face challenges in achieving and maintaining balance between economic growth and social development that includes childcare (National Assembly Economic Committee 2014). These include the challenges of maintaining macroeconomic stability, controlling inflation, the provision of social protection, ensuring sustainable development, enhancing economic competitiveness, raising per-capita income, reducing poverty, narrowing the gap between the rich and the poor[3], and disaster prevention.

3 As a result of rapid economic growth and implementation of a national poverty alleviation programme, the poverty rate has decreased substantially as mentioned earlier. However, the gap in living standards among resident groups has become bigger. In 1990, the richest 20% of the population had an income level that was 4.1 times higher than that of the poorest 20% of the population; in 1995, the gap was 6.99 times; by 2006, it had increased to 8.38 times (VGSO 2001, 2008, 613).

3.2 *Urbanisation and Migration*

3.2.1 Urbanisation

Urbanisation has taken place speedily in Vietnam. According to the National Census data, the proportion of the urban Vietnamese population had increased from 19.2% in 1979 to 19.4% in 1989 and 23.7% in 1999. It increased further to 29.6% in 2009 and 31.9% in 2012 and 33.1% in 2014. The %age of the urban population in the Red River Delta is not different from that of the whole country: 29.2% in 2009 and 33.8% in 2014 (VGSO 2010, 2015). As for Hanoi, the total population is more than 6.4 million, among them 40.9% living in urban areas (2009), which increased to 47.6% in 2014 (VGSO & UNFPA 2016). There are some important differences between urban and rural residents. Firstly, there is a matter of living standards. Differences are clearly reflected in housing quality, the availability of a hygienic water supply, sanitary conditions, and consumption of household goods by urban compared with rural residents. Significant gaps in education and levels of professional qualification exist between urban and rural residents; the more urbanised an area, the more its residents tend to be educated and professionally trained.

Differences in living standards, education, employment, etc. between urban and rural areas have created a lifestyle for urban inhabitants different from the rural lifestyle (Nguyen 2000). The popularity of the nuclear family, slackening kinship relations, diversity of economic activities outside the family, and higher education levels in urban areas influence urban inhabitants' ways of thinking about family, among them are elderly and child care. The development of the domestic work service sector has created advantages for people in caring for family members. Many people now are living far away from their parents, while also having fewer children and higher incomes. Therefore, having a domestic worker to help taking care of their elderly and children is a choice.

3.2.2 Migration

The 2009 Census data show that the migrant population, especially inter-provincial migrants, increased in both absolute and relative terms. In the past decades, migration has accelerated. The inter-provincial migrant population increased to 3.4 million people in 2009 from 2 million in 1999 and 1.3 million in 1989; the migration rate increased to 4.3% in 2009 from 2.9% in 1999 and 2.5% in 1989. In comparison with other regions, the Red River Delta attracted a large number of migrants (18.1% of total migrants from rural to urban areas), however it was less than the Southeast area (which accounted for more than 50%). During 2009–2014 Hanoi attracted more than 220,000 migrants from other provinces, and ranked the third in the country in terms of the number of migrants (VGSO 2015).

There was clear evidence of the "feminisation of migration" while the opposite trend is occurring for the non-migrant population. Females accounted for more than half of the migrant population in almost all types of migration and flows of migrants between urban and rural areas. Comparisons of age structure between migrant and non-migrant populations across the three Censuses (1989–2009) indicated that migrants, especially female migrants, had gotten younger while non-migrants had gotten older over the last three decades. The contrasting aging patterns between migrant and non-migrant populations suggest that the receiving areas are gaining young workers through migration while the sending areas are increasingly left to face problems associating with population aging such as the increase in the dependency ratio, reduction in productivity, and challenges of providing social security for the aged population (Nguyen & Nguyen 2011). This also creates difficulty for the care system that traditionally was the domain of females.

3.3 *Education and Employment*

Data from the National Censuses conducted in 1979, 1989, 1999, and 2009 indicate that the proportion of the adult population that has gone to school has increased gradually. Most of the urban population has gone to school, especially the men. In 2009, the literacy rate for the population aged ten or older was 94%, compared to 91.1% in 1999, 88.2% in 1989 and 85% in 1979. The difference in education levels between men and women has decreased gradually, especially with regard to young people. In 2009, the literacy rate for men was 96% and for women, 92% compared with 93% and 84% respectively in 1989. In general, gender inequality in basic education in Vietnam has almost been erased. Literacy rates in urban areas are higher than in rural areas. However, recently the urban–rural difference has reduced and is very low, 96.9% in urban areas and 92% in rural areas. The Red River Delta is the region with the highest literacy rate, about 97.1% in 2009 and 98.1 in 2014 (VCPHCSC 2010; VGSO 1991; VGSO 2015). In 2014, among the population aged 5 or above, 32.9% completed lower secondary school and 35.7% completed secondary school or higher. People in the Red River Delta receiving training from mid-level vocational education in 2014 was 8.2% and those having college education levels was 11.2%; the figures for Hanoi were 9.4 and 21.3%, respectively (VGSO 2015).

Economic development opened up non-agricultural employment opportunities for people, especially women, and significantly increased the economic independence of children from parents. The data from the 1999 general census showed a positive picture of women's participation in economic activities: 67.8% of women aged fifteen years and above participated in economic activities, according to Vietnam Central Population and Housing Census Steering Committee (VCPHCSC 2000, 75). The 2009 Census showed that 76.5% of the population aged fifteen or older participated in the labor force, 81.8% for males and 71.4% for females. The labor force participation rate for rural areas is fourteen percentages points higher than for urban areas (80.6% vs. 67.1%). The figures for 2014 are the following: 78% of the total population aged fifteen or older; 82.6% for males and 73.6% for females; 81.7% for rural areas and 70.5% for urban areas. As for the Red River Delta without Hanoi, the percentage of labor force participation was 80.0 for males and 76.6 for females, while for Hanoi the figures are 74.9 and 68.2, respectively (VGSO 2014).

4 Demographic Background

4.1 *Fertility, Life Expectancy and Mortality*

4.1.1 Fertility Rate

In the last three decades, the fertility rate in Vietnam has gradually decreased. The total fertility rate (TFR) fell sharply from 2.33 children per woman in 1999 to 2.03 in 2009 and 2.05 in 2012. The figure for 2014 is 2.09 (VGSO 2015). Since 2006, Vietnam's TFR has declined continuously to below the fertility replacement level.[4] The Vietnam Family Survey 2006 shows that the proportion of respondents who agreed that families should have many children was quite low (18.6% of people aged sixty-one or older, 6.6% of people aged 18–60 and 2.8% of adolescents), according to a report by the Ministry of Culture, Sport and Tourism (MOCST), General Statistics Office, Institute for Family and Gender Studies, & UNICEF (2008). Today's families are more interested in how to provide good parenting than in having many children. Rural residents had higher rates in terms of encouraging families to have more children than other respondents. There is a fundamental difference between urban and rural fertility rates. In 2009, the TFR was 1.81 children per woman in urban areas, much lower than the 2.14 children per woman in rural areas and in 2012, it was 1.80 compared with 2.17. The TFR difference between urban and rural areas in 2014 was 0.36 with 1.85 for urban and 2.21 for rural areas. As for the Red River Delta, the TFR has fallen from 2.11 in 2009 to around 2.05 in 2010 and 2011, thereafter increased to 2.11 in 2012 and 2013, then was very high in 2014: 2.30 (VGSO 2015).

4 The replacement fertility is the level of fertility at which a cohort of women on average is having only enough female children to replace itself in the population reproduction.

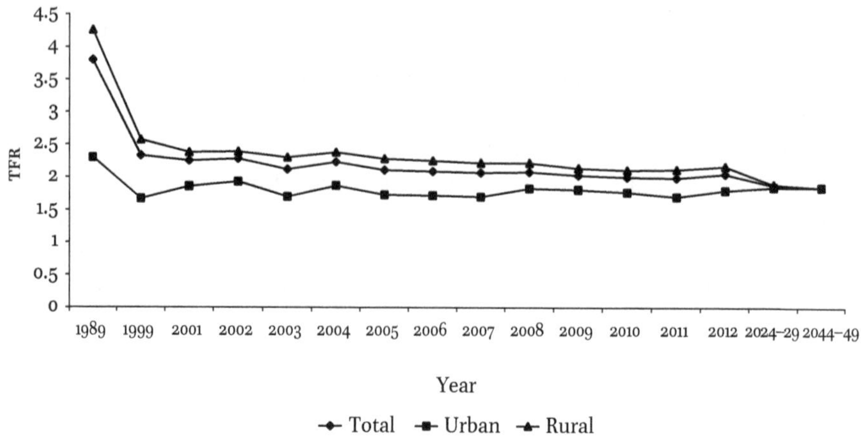

FIGURE 4.1 The total fertility rate (TFR) in Vietnam 1969–2012 and projected to 2049.
SOURCES: VGSO & UNFPA (2016). INTERCENSAL CENSUS 2014: FERTILITY IN VIETNAM: DIFFERENTIALS, TREND, AND DETERMINANTS. NEWS PUBLISHER, HANOI.

4.1.2 Sex Ratio at Birth (SRB)

The sex ratio is the ratio of males to females in a population and usually is estimated as the number of males to 100 females in the population. Sex ratio at birth is expressed by the number of resident male live births (for a specific geography such as country, state, county for a specified time period, usually a calendar year) divided by a 100 resident female live births (for the same geography and time period).

Figure 4.2 presents the sex ratio at birth in Vietnam from 2001 to 2009 (starting in 2006 the data began to be disaggregated by urban/rural residence). For the period from 2001 to 2005, data in the table indicate no apparent trend in Vietnam's sex ratio at birth and the ratio varied between 104 and 109 boys for every 100 girls born. This variation was within a range that was somewhat higher than normal levels, but could nevertheless be considered normal within the random variation that could occur when the study sample is small. However, starting in 2006 and up to the present, the sex ratio at birth in Vietnam began to show signs of substantial increase. According to the results of the Survey of Population Change in 2006, the sex ratio at birth in Vietnam was 109.8 boys for every 100 girls. In 2007 and 2008 the sex ratios at birth were 111.6 and 112.1 respectively. In 2009, the sex ratio at birth fell slightly, but remained at a high level of 110.5 boys for every 100 girls and in 2012 was 112.3, and 112.2 in 2014 (VGSO 2012, 2015). It is projected that the SRB will increase until 115 in 2020 before going down. Son preference, the one to two child policy, advanced technology

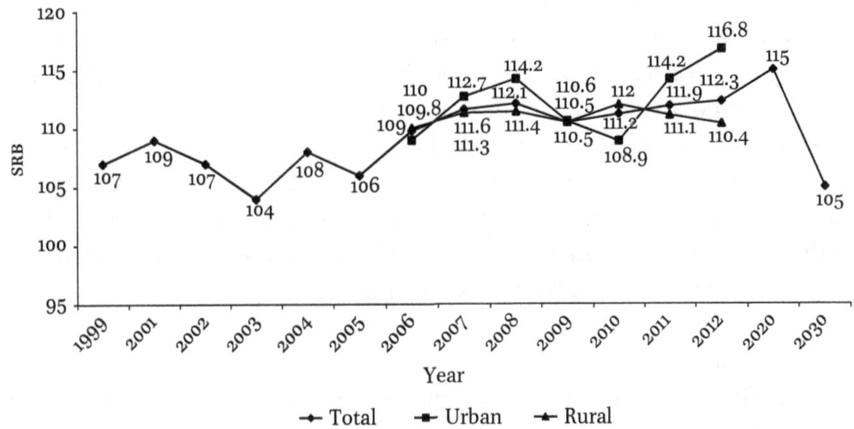

FIGURE 4.2 Sex ratio at birth by urban/rural residence for Vietnam 1999–2012 and projected to 2030.
SOURCES: VCPHCSC 2010, VGSO 2011.

that allow parent to select the sex of birth (ultrasound and abortion) as they want and poorly managed medical achievements are among the most important reason for this situation, and this will have knock-on effects in terms of the care of children and the elderly (Institute for Family and Gender Studies 2012). Increased SRB would affect marital availability of population and ability of family members to take care of elderly people later.

The Red River Delta had the highest sex ratio (115.3 in 2009, 120.9 in 2012 and 118 in 2014) in the country. Here, access to health services with modern equipment was relatively easy. Residents also had higher levels of education and economic wealth so they could afford, and were willing to pay for diagnostic services determining early foetal sex[5] (VCPHCSC 2010; VGSO 2012; VGSO 2015). This will increase pressure on the care system in the Red River Delta.

The reason for having a son was mainly "to continue the family line" (85.7%). In addition, a significant proportion of respondents said sons would offer "a refuge in their old age" (54.2%) and would "do large work, heavy work" (23.4%) (MOCST et al. 2008). Rural people identified the reason for having a son as "a refuge in their old age" more than urban residents, probably because they enjoy fewer social services and worse access to health care when they become older.

5 According to VCPHCSC (2010), in the 2009 Vietnam Population and Housing Census, Vietnam contains 6 regions: Northern Midlands and Mountains; Red River Delta, North and South Central Coast, Central Highlands, Southeast, and Mekong River Delta.

4.1.3 Crude Death Rates (CDR)

Data from the 2009 Population Census indicate that the CDR for the entire country was 6.8 deaths per 1000 population, while for urban areas it was 5.5 per 1000 population and in rural areas, 7.4 per 1000 population. The CDR in 2009 was higher than in 1999 (5.6) but lower than in 1989 (7.3). In 2012 the CDR slightly increased to 7.0, with 5.9 in urban areas and 7.5 in rural areas and in 2014 the figures were 6.9, with 6.05 in urban areas and 7.24 in rural areas. One of the reasons for the slight increase of CDR is an increase of elderly population during recent years (VCPHCSC 2010; VGSO 2012; VGSO 2015).

4.1.4 Life Expectancy

Average life expectancy in 2009 for males was 70.2 years and for females it was 75.6 years. Overall life expectancy at birth for the entire country was 72.8 years compared to 73.0 years in 2012 (70.4 for males and 75.8 for females) and 73.2 years in 2014 (70.6 for males and 76.0 for females). Average life expectancy for the whole country, male and female in 1999 was 68.2 years, 66.5 years and 70.1 years respectively. In 1989, life expectancy for males and females was 63 and 67.5. Thus there is an increasing trend of life expectancy during last few decades. Results of the 1989–2009 Censuses and 2012–2014 intercensal surveys show that average life expectancy of men is lower than that of women. Among the main reasons, men died due to traffic and labor accidents more frequently than women (VCPHCSC 2010; VGSO 2012; VGSO 1991; VGSO 2015).

4.2 *Proportion of Older People (65+) and Young Children (below 15)*

The share of the population below 15 years of age has declined from 39% in 1989 to 25% in 2009, 24% in 2012, 23.5% in 2014 and is projected to go down to 17.6% in 2049. The proportion of the population aged 65 years and older is increasing. In 1989, the proportion of the population aged 65 and older was 4.7%, while in the 2012 it had increased to 7.1%, and is projected to increase to 18% in 2049 (VCPHCSC 2010; VGSO 2012; VGSO 1991; VGSO 2015).

By 2012, the proportion of the population of working age (15–64 years) accounted for 69%, while the dependent proportion (below age 15 and 65 years and older) accounted for 31%. The figures for 2014 are 69.4% and 30.6%. Thus, Vietnam is in the period of the so-called demographic dividend, when each dependent is supported by 2 working-age people (VGSO 2012, 2015).

One of the important indicators of population ageing is the ageing index, which is the ratio of the number of people aged 60 and older per 100 people aged below 15 years. Figure 4.4 shows that the ageing index for Vietnam increased from 18% in 1989 to 24% in 1999, and reached 36% in 2009 and 42.7% in 2012, higher than the average for Southeast Asia (30%). This shows

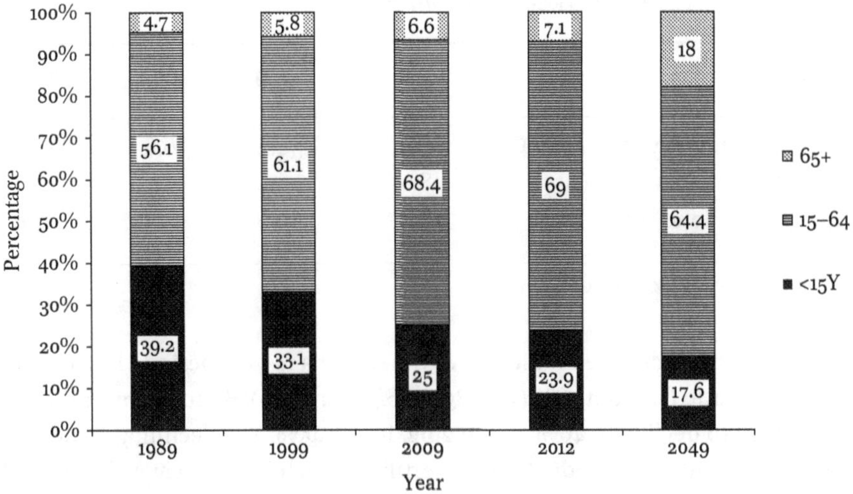

FIGURE 4.3 Proportion of population aged under 15, 15–64 and 65+ and ageing index, 1989–2012 and projected to 2049.
* PROJECTED FOR VARIANT OF MEDIUM FERTILITY LEVEL (VGSO 2011).
SOURCES: VCPHCSC 2010; VGSO 2012.

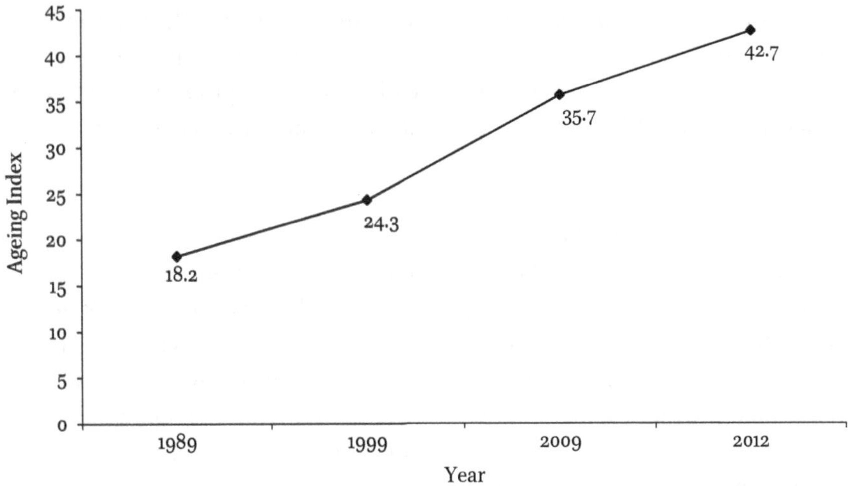

FIGURE 4.4 Ageing index (%), 1989–2012.
SOURCES: VCPHCSC 2010; VGSO 2012.

that population ageing in Vietnam was taking place very rapidly over the past three decades (VCPHCSC 2010; VGSO 2012)

The total dependency ratio represents the number of the population under age 15 (0–14) and aged 65+ per 100 people aged 15–64. The total dependency

TABLE 4.1 Dependency ratio 1989–2012 (*Unit: Percent*)

Year	1989	1999	2009	2012
Child dependency ratio (0–14)	69.8	54.2	36.6	34.6
Aged dependency ratio (65+)	8.4	9.4	9.7	10.3
Total dependency ratio	78.2	63.6	46.3	44.9

SOURCES: VCPHCSC 2010, VGSO 2012

ratio in Vietnam declined rapidly over time: over a 10-year period, the total dependency ratio fell from 78% (in 1989) to 64% (in 1999). By 2009, this ratio had continued to decline to 46% and in 2012, it was 45%. The declining trend was mainly attributable to reductions in fertility, which in turn, caused the child dependency ratios to decline. This indicates that the l burden on the working age population continued to decline (VCPHCSC 2010; VGSO 2012; VGSO 1991).

In addition, data from the Vietnam Family Survey 2006 showed that, dependency ratios are different from area to area and by group of population. The proportion of dependents in urban areas was lower than in rural areas due to smaller urban families. Low-income areas in the Northwest, Northern Central and Central Highlands had a higher proportion of dependents than average and in general, poor households had a higher proportion of dependents than well-off households, naturally increasing their economic burden (MOCST et al. 2008).

4.3 *Family Composition and Size*

Family composition[6] and size reflect different types of family, number of members and number of generations in the household. The result of the Vietnam Population and Housing Census Surveys, as well as several sample size surveys such as the Vietnam Annual Population Change Surveys or the Vietnam Household Living Standard Surveys, in recent decades demonstrates the steady reduction of family size and the nuclearization of the family (including parents and children) in Vietnam.

According to the Census results, on the 01 April, 2009, Vietnam had 22,628 thousand households, an increase of 36% compared with 1999. The average annual growth rate in households was 3.1% during the 1979–1989 period, 2.5%

6 According to the Vietnam Population and Housing Census Surveys, family composition and size refers to household composition and size. So, family composition and size in this chapter refers to the household composition and size.

during the 1989–1999 period and 3.1% during the period 1999–2009. The average number of persons per household in 2009 was 3.8 persons, compared with 4.6 persons in 1999, 4.8 persons in 1989 and 5.2 persons in 1979. The differential in household size between urban and rural areas is insubstantial, at 3.7 and 3.9 persons respectively (VCPHCSC 2010; VGSO 1991). In 2012 the average number of persons per household was 3.7, with 3.6 in urban and 3.8 in rural area. The Red River Delta had the lowest average number of persons per household, with 3.5 persons. The highest percentage of small household size (from 1 to 4 persons) also belongs to the Red River Delta: about 77.0% (VGSO 2012; VGSO 2015). Decreased family size affects the ability to take care of the elderly and children due to the fact that there are fewer people staying at home.

The VHLSS 2014 also showed that the average household size of the poorest households was higher than that of the richest households, that of mountain households was higher than plain households, and that of households in rural areas was higher than in urban areas (VGSO 2016).

At the time of 2009, among 1,749,334 households in Hanoi the household sizes were distributed as follows: 30.6% for 4 persons; 20.3% for 3 persons; and 16.1% for 2 persons. Households with 8 or more persons accounted for a small percentage (Hanoi SO 2010).

Regarding the types of family, the results of the Vietnam Family Survey 2006 show that the two-generation family pattern comprising parents and children was more common in Vietnam, accounting for 63.4% while the number of three-generation families or more, was declining. The proportion of three-generation households was higher in urban areas. This may be due to a lack of housing in urban areas and the increasing trend among young people to migrate to the city for work and then get married (MOCST et al. 2008).

The sample survey in Hanoi of 2011 also showed that, among 1,211 families, the most common type of family in Hanoi was the nuclear family with 63.0%, one generation families accounted for 6.3% and two generation families, 56.7%. Extended families accounted for 37.0%, 34.4% included only three generation families and 2.6% were four or more generation families (Nguyen 2014a).

The reduction of family size positively influenced daily life in general, and both material and mental health supports in particular. In term of material support, the average income and average expenditure per person significantly increased when the family size (i.e. number of family members) reduces (VGSO & UNICEF 2007). By contrast, there were some negative consequences in the reduction of family size, including the reduction in children's communication capacity/opportunties and increased or possible loneliness of the older adults.

In parallel with the reduction of family size and the nuclearization of the family structure, some emerging forms of family were emerging such as un-registered married couples, premarital cohabitation of college students/ workers, gay/lesbian families, and "separated" families. This meant the family where most of main laborers were absent due to working far away. For example, the result of the Vietnam Family Survey 2006 shows that the percentage of un-registered married couple accounted for 31.9% of new couples during the period 2001–2006 (i.e. after the Marriage and Family Law 2000 came into force) (MOCST et al. 2008). As regards the trial cohabitation[7] of college students, the study of the Institute for Family and Gender Studies surveying 415 participants in Ho Chi Minh in 2010 indicates that nearly 30% of respondents agreed that this form was not an abnormal pattern in the current society. The acceptance rate was greater in the younger participants and accounted for 36.2% of those from 17–25 years old and reached nearly 40% of college students. In other words, this emerging family form was acceptable to a part of the population, especially, the young, despite their unclear understanding of its negative impacts on their life later. In terms of gay or lesbian families, although it was not approved by legislation in Vietnam, the increasing number of this family pattern was emerging as an emerging phenomenon in the development of the family in Vietnam (Nguyen 2016).

In the acceleration of industrialization and modernization, the trend of migration for work, both international and internal, is increasing. From 1990 to 2009, there were about 500,000 overseas migrants working in over 40 countries and territories, of which one third was female labor (Department of Overseas Labor – cited in the report of Phan Luong Cu – Deputy Head of the National Assembly's Social Affairs Committee, 2010). This led to the geographic separation of family members in peace time (what was named "separated" family earlier). This phenomenon was common during the Vietnam Resistance war against the French or America. At that time, the separation was mainly men's absence due to going to the battlefields while most of women stayed at home to take care of the children and old parents. This phenomenon in modern families however became worse because all healthy working-age people had to migrate for work has left behind older adults and small children in many villages.

---

7 This is named "hôn nhân thử-trial marriage" in Vietnamese in which people live together temporarily in the same house as a couple, however they do not try to have children and it does not necessarily lead to a real marriage. This situation seems to be not uncommon among college students and workers in industrial zones.

4.4 *Marriage and Divorce*

Marriage in Vietnam is quite universal. The Census of 2009 indicates that 67% of men and 64% of women were currently married. The figure for 2014 is even higher: 72.2% of men and 79.7% of women. Almost all men marry at least once in their life. The proportion of ever married for each young age group 15–19 and 20–24 declined slightly for both men and women during 1989–2009.

Singulate mean age at marriage (SMAM) has shown an increasing trend for men. SMAM among men in 1989 was 24.4, in 1994 it was 25.4, in 2009, 26.2, in 2012, 26.6, and in 2014 it was 26.8, while there was no change for the SMAM among women. It has even decreased, when compared with 1989: from 23.2 in 1989 to 22.8 in 1999, 2009 and in 2012 before increasing a little bit in 2014 (22.9). For both men and women, the SMAM in urban areas was higher than in rural areas. In 2009, SMAM among urban men was higher than among rural men by 2.1 years and in 2012 by 3.5 years. However, in 2014 the difference had reduced to 1.4 years. This differential among women was 2.4 years in 2009, 4.0 years in 2012, and 2.1 years in 2014, suggesting that urban residents have a tendency to marry later than rural residents (VCPHCSC 2010; VGSO 2012; VGSO 2015).

Divorce tended to increase in Vietnam during recent decades. Comparison of data from the three population censuses in 1989, 1999, and 2009 shows an increase in divorce cases. Only 0.5% of the population aged fifteen and over was divorced in 1989, and this rate was 0.8% in 1999 and 1.0% in 2009. An upward trend was identified in both urban and rural areas and for both men and women (Nguyen 2014b).

The children stayed with the mother after most divorce cases (64.3%). In fact, serious paternal support was not always provided. This has increased the burden placed on mothers and children after divorce and adds to their disadvantages in life (MOCST et al. 2008).

The Vietnam Family Survey 2006 pointed to three main causes for divorce: lifestyle conflict (27.7% of divorcees), particularly between generations; adultery (25.9%); and economic hardship (13%) (MOCST et al. 2008). A major consequence of family breakdown was the negative impacts on children's development due to their parents' time insufficiency to care for them (Nguyen 2016).

4.5 *Living Arrangements*

According to previous surveys, patrilocal co-residence was common in Vietnam as an effective strategy of mutual intergenerational support. According to the Vietnam Family Survey 2006, eating and living together with the husband's family after marriage was common, with 64.8% of the population aged 18–60 doing so. For our Hanoi survey 2010 there were about 62% of respondents agreeing that three generations should share a house. Explaining for the reasons why they thought like that, about 72% said in order for parents and married children to provide mutual help, in addition to about 11.4% agreeing that children were capable to support parents and 5.4% agreeing that parents were capable to support married children.

However, a diversified picture could also be seen when it came to other forms of living arrangements after marriage, such as living with the husband's family but eating separately (1.3%); living and eating with the wife's family (8.4%); or living and eating completely separately (23.7%). Young couples living separately from their parents after marriage tended to be more common in urban areas. Eating and living with the wife's family were increasingly accepted by young people (MOCST et al. 2008, 68). A survey in Hanoi 2011 showed that about one fourth of respondents said that they lived separately right after marriage, among them the figures for urban, next to urban and far from urban areas are: 45.5%, 17.8% and 15.1% (Nguyen 2014a).

The family arrangements of the majority of the Vietnamese people were the result of a compromise between their ideals and particular demographic and socio-economic circumstances. Many factors affect this pattern. Empirical studies in the Red River Delta of Vietnam confirmed the role of many factors in influencing living arrangements after marriage. A later marriage age, the freedom to choose a partner for oneself, increased living standards, at least one of either the husband or wife working for the government, non-agricultural work, and an urban location, were the most important factors that act to decrease the probability of ever living with the husband's parents after marriage (Goodkind 1997b; Nguyen & Hirschman 2000; Nguyen 2009).

Regarding the distance between the parent's and their married children's houses there was a difference between urban and rural areas. In rural areas the children after leaving their parent's home could find easily a house located next to or near their parents, however this was more difficult for urban residents due to the unavailability of land before the "Doi Moi-Renovation" in 1986. However, given the introduction of the market economy since Doi Moi, there were more possibilities for urban residents to find an appropriate house that was located close by their parent's house. Therefore parents and children could more easily help each other. Our survey in Hanoi 2010 showed that about 20% of respondents had non-coresidence children living close by their house (next to or within 15 minutes of walking). This altered the paternal or maternal relationship because many daughters could live close to their parents after marriage.

5 Changes in Policy and Legislation

The Vietnamese government's and the Party's viewpoint of *seniores priores*[8] is that it is a good Vietnamese tradition, i.e. "taking care of the material and cultural life of the elderly is a national moral standard, and that affection for these is the responsibility of the whole population, the Party and authorities of all levels" (SRVG 1996). Vietnam's law and policy also emphasises the responsibilities of the family in taking care of the elderly. For example, Article 64 of the 1992 Constitution stipulates that: "Children have the responsibility of respecting and taking care of their grandparents and parents" (VNA 1992). The 2000 Ordinance of the Elderly stipulates that the elderly should be cared for by the government and society (Article 2) and specifies that it is mainly the responsibility of the family to take care of the elderly: "Taking care of the elderly is the main responsibility of families with elderly ones" (Article 3) (VNA 2000b). Decree number 30/2002/NĐ-CP issued on 26 March 2002 by the Prime Minister with stipulation and guidance on implementing some articles of the Elderly Ordinance specifies that "Those responsible for taking care of the elderly are their spouses, their own children, legally adopted children, children-in-law, nephews or nieces (nephews or nieces of parents-in-law)"[9] (SRVG 2002). Item 3, Article 37, Consititution 2013 of the Socialist Republic of Vietnam states (2013): The elderly people are respected, cared for and promoted by the state, family and society in the cause of the country's development and defence.

The 2000 Law on Marriage and Family (VNA 2000a) has specific stipulations on the care of the elderly. Item 4, Article 2 of the 2000 Law on Marriage and Family stipulates that: children have the responsibility of respecting and taking care of parents; grandchildren have the responsibility of respecting and taking care of grandparents; and family members have the responsibility of caring, looking after, and helping each other. Articles 35 and 36 stipulate that: children have the responsibility of loving, respecting, and being grateful to parents; and the right to take care of parents, especially when their parents are old, disabled or ill. Children are strictly forbidden to persecute and insult parents. Article 57 stipulates that adults who do not patrilocate with parents have the responsibility of supporting parents who lack the ability to work or providing assets for them to live. Item 2 of Article 59 stipulates that adult grandchildren who do not patrilocate with grandparents have to support grandparents if they cannot work, cannot support themselves, or if there

8 Literally "elders first".

9 SRVG (2002): Item 1, Article 2, Decree number 30/2002/NĐ-CP.

is no one else to support them. In addition, there are articles and items in the Criminal Law naming crimes related to taking care of the elderly. Article 151 of the Criminal Law (VNA 2009) stipulates: the "Crime of persecuting grandparents, parents, spouses, children, grandchildren and those who has been raising violator up" and Article 152 stipulates the "Crime of refusing or eluding responsibility for support."

The Law on the Elderly (2009) further stipulates the measures to be taken by the state and society in order to create conditions for the elderly to study, conduct research and participate in cultural, physical and sport activities, entertainment, and travel. The activities are: to provide information, materials, instructors so that the elderly can participate in study and research; to support and guide the elderly to participate in cultural, tourist, and physical activities suitable to their health and psychological state; to provide the location, tools and other material foundations suitable to the activities of the elderly; to encourage enterprises and individuals to produce and trade products and goods meeting the elderly's demands (Article 14 of the Elderly Law). At the same time, the elderly are entitled to discounts on fares, and service charges when using certain services as stipulated by the Government (Article 16 of the Law on the Elderly).

Based on the view of the Party and legal stipulations, the government has issued many kinds of policies relating to caring for and promoting the role of old people. For example, according to Decree No. 06/2011/NĐ-CP, Article 6, Item 2, all poor elderly aged 60–80 who do not have any one to take care of them, or the person responsible for providing care for such an elderly person should receive a monthly social allowance from the government of 180,000 VND[10]; all poor elderly aged 80 or older who do not have any one to take care of them or the person responsible for providing care for such an elderly person should receive a monthly social allowance from the government of 270,000 VND; all elderly aged 80 or older who do not have a salary or a monthly social insurance, should receive a monthly social allowance of 180,000VND; all elderly aged 60 or older who are being taken care of in social protection centers, should receive 360,000VND monthly; and all elderly aged 60 who qualify for provision of care in social protection centers but who are being cared for in the community, should receive 360,000VND monthly. In addition, 3,000,000VND is paid to support the funeral costs of elderly people; elderly people who are 70 or older also get gifts from government leaders and elderly associations on the occasion of their birthday; elders who are 60 years old or older receive discount price

10 01 USD is about 20,600 to 20,800VND at the time of May-July 2011.

tickets for public transportation (at least 15% discount) and for sightseeing tours of cultural or historical places or museum visits (at least 20% discount); and nursing homes for elderly people are encouraged and supported by some priorty policies; etc.

The elderly are given and granted health insurance by the state and social organizations, which helps reduce the economic burden on families taking care of elderly people when they are ill, especially for families in financial difficulties. As the results of the National Survey of the Elderly (2011) indicate, the Vietnamese elderly lacked opportunities to access health services. The proportion of the elderly using health insurance is low; 26.1% of the elderly did not have any form of health insurance. 51.1% of elderly people cannot afford medical treatment. More than 30% of them still had finance their own health treatment and medicine. The proportion covered by health insurance only accounts for 15% (Vietnam Women Union et al. 2012).

Results from the National Survey on the Elderly 2011 also showed that many elderly people had no knowledge of their rights. More than 50% of the interviewed elderly people only knew about the right to subsidies, and life expectancy grants. Understanding of other benefits such as the priority use of health services, discounts on public services, legal aid, income tax exemption, preferential loans with low interest rates remained quite modest. The reasons for this could be that, the elderly health care system in Vietnam was not yet organized into a network from the central to provincial and district levels as was true of other specialties (Giang & Bui 2012).

In summary, policies related to elderly care or family supports for the elderly were mentioned quite uniformly in the legal system and state policies. From direct support in terms of money to indirect support (policies and mechanisms of care), these policies helped most older people improve their health conditions, and reduced the economic and time pressure in the families of the elderly. However, there were many shortcomings in the implementation process as the health care system for the elderly was not expanded and remains inconvenient/ difficult to access. The level of support from health insurance remained limited, so many families did not want to use this option. Many older people and their families were unaware of the health care policies for the elderly, which also diminished, in practice, the effectiveness of the policy implementation.

After the start of economic renovation in 1986 which encouraged the development of a multi-sector commodity economy, state control over labor and land became weaker. Many rural elderly no longer received subsidies from the co-operatives, and had to work in their own fields instead. Though others did receive some levels of social security insurance, the level of support received was very low. Many people continued to work as a primary laborer in the family and many others still relied upon economic support from family members (Bui et al. 1996, 182–183; Andien Research Group 1992). Village and kinship relationships were a new opportunity to resume their previous important role in economic activities and social organisations. Rural residents restored traditional activities which support and reinforce the relationship within kinship and the village, such as holding lineage meetings, setting lineage and communal statutes, and so on (Nguyen 1991).

In urban areas, while the reform did not modify economic relationships within (and between) families as did the de-collectivisation of agriculture in rural areas, it opened a wide and diverse range of choices for income generation and consumption. Urban residents were now depending less on the state for subsidising housing and other living expenditures.

Regarding childcare, Vietnam was the first country in Asia and the second in the world to ratify its participation in the United Nations Convention on the Rights of the Child (in February 1990). Vietnam respects and has legislated on the fundamental rights of children under the Convention on the basis that they conform with the provisions of Vietnam's Constitution and laws. The basic constitutional rights of children are legally protected through a relatively complete and uniform system of stipulations seen in many laws such as the Civil Code, the Law on Marriage and Family Criminal Law, Labor Law, and others. In particular, the National Assembly approved the amended Law on Child Care and Education on 15 June 2004 to replace the 1991 Law on Child Care and Education.

Besides perfecting the system of legislation, Vietnam, step by step, built a system of policies, programmes and action plans for children and gradually integrated goals for children into socio-economic development strategies. Many national target programmes were developed and implemented. These national programmes had a positive impact on child care, education and protection. They included the National Target Programme for Poverty Reduction (1998–2000 and 2000–2006); the National Action Plan for Children (2001–2010); the Population and Family Planning Program; the National Nutrition Strategy (2001–2010); the Action Plan to prevent and combat trafficking in women and children (2004–2010); and others. Targets "Increasing communes appropriate to children" and "Increasing the cared percentages of children living in special conditions" were put into a list of national targets on socio-economic development during 2006–2010. The government implemented strategies and measures to reform health finance policy including increasing public finance resources, decreasing direct pay from patients, improving health care centers and giving them priority for health networks at the grassroots level, preventive health care, hospitals at the provincial, district and inter-commune levels. The government implemented policies that protect children from the risks of commercialization and its impact in the health care system, for example policies on free health care for children under 6, providing, without charge, health insurance cards for poor children, etc. The Solution No. 05/2005/NQ-CP dated 18/4/2005 of the Government also issued priority policies on tax relief for land used for private health care centers to develop a system of health care service provision. According to data from World Health Organization (WHO) in 2012, the number of patient beds/10,000 persons in Vietnam was the highest figure in the Southeast Asian region (MOH & Health Partner Group-HPG 2013). Improvement of the health care system, especially in rural areas, helped children to expand their health care access opportunities.

However, there were limitations in implementing policies regarding the child care system since there were gaps in policies for children's health care. For example, mental health care for children was given almost no attention. Many poor people, among them children, did not use health insurance regularly, instead they self-treated when getting sick because the service fee discount system did not work effectively (UN 2006; UNDP 2012). New policies in health care, with more participation of the private sector expanded the gap between poor and better-off children, rural and urban children, and mountainous and plain children, etc. (MOH & HPG 2013). A number of care workers did not do well to take care of children. Free health insurance cards for children under 6 were implemented for almost a decade however until 31/12/2014 the percentage of children under 6 receiving this card was only 85.6% (MOLISA 2015).

6 Care Relations

6.1 *Child Care*

For the last ten years, Vietnam's economy grew rapidly and with relative stability. This created favourable conditions for childcare services. Investment capital for the social sectors increased with a focus on poverty reduction, universal education, health care development, strengthening maternal and child health, and combating HIV/ AIDS. This investment directly affected childcare (World Bank 2008).

Besides the state budget, the Government of Vietnam implemented policies on the strengthening of child protection, care and education which attracted investment resources for children from the community. These resources may be in forms of people's contributions, revenue from the sale of government bonds, public bonds, capital sources from enterprises, various types of child support funds, and others.

The system of Funds for Children also played an important role. The Child Support Fund had a four level system and is present in 100% of provinces/ cities, 80% of districts and 70% of communes/wards in the country. Each year the Child Support Fund mobilised nearly two million USD and supports thousands of children through various programmes (CHXHCNVN 2007). There were also various forms of child support funds such as the Fund of Love, the Support Fund for Poor Children, the Young Talent Foundation, the Fund for Poor Students, and others. All these forms mobilised a significant source of investment for children, particularly disadvantaged groups of children.

Later on, childcare in Vietnam made very significant progress, particularly in the two basic fields of education and health care.

In terms of education, a national education system was gradually completed to include all educational levels and school types (public, people-founded and private). The construction of a safe and friendly learning environment was promoted at primary education and preschool education bases. Models such as flexible classes, combined classes and classes of love were used to enhance alternative forms of education for children of education age who did not enroll at primary school, children who were at risk of dropout or repetition, children with disabilities, street children, children of fishermen and others. Education quality received increasing attention via education reform programmes (CHXHCNVN 2008).

Vietnam recorded continuous progress in implementing the right of the child to education which the Constitution guarantees. In fact, according to the criteria set out by the UN Committee on Economic, Cultural and Social Rights, Vietnam is considered to be in compliance with international obligations in implementing the right of the child to education. This was because Vietnam took important steps to realise this right, including allocating adequate resources to ensure economic and material access (for example, through exemption of tuition fees for disadvantaged children). Vietnam also made strong efforts to ensure that this right is fulfilled without discrimination (UNICEF Vietnam 2008).

Child health care also made clear progress. The under-five mortality rate (U5MR) fell from 58.1 per thousand in 1990 to 25 per thousand in 2008 and 23.8 per thousand in 2010. The infant mortality rate (IMR) decreased from 44.4 per thousand to 15.5 per thousand during this time (15.8 per thousand in 2010). Over 90% of infants were immunised against six common diseases, according to Ministry of Planning and Investment (MPI 2008). The under-five child malnutrition rate decreased from 29.0% in 2002 to 24.0% in 2006 and 17.5% in 2010. From 2002 to 2005, the maternal mortality rate decreased from 100/100.000 to 80/100.000 and reached 69/100.000 in 2009 (NIN 2012). The proportion of the rural population with access to clean water increased from 52% in 2002, to 62% in 2005, and 66.4% in 2009. The proportion of families with sanitary toilet facilties was 54% in 2009 (87.8% in urban and 39.0% in rural areas). This had a great impact on health care issues for children, ensuring that children were living in an increasingly hygienic environment and preventing gastrointestinal diseases. The prevention of HIV/AIDS for children was also implemented through the National Action Plan for Children and HIV/AIDS.

Increasing attention ws given to child injury prevention through child injury prevention programmes and organisation of campaigns to raise awareness on this issue in the community. Models such as the "safe house", "safe school" and "safe community" were formed and replicated widely in society. Specifically, hundreds of communes currently implement the "safe house" model and nearly one hundred schools pilot the "safe school" model. As of 2005, five communes in Vietnam were recognised as meeting standards of "safe communities" at the international level. (CHXHCNVN 2007) Although the effectiveness of the implementation of programmes and models was limited, this start was necessary and important for the safety of children's lives.

Child protection programmes were increasingly improved, based on the needs approach, to meet the basic rights of a child. These activities overcame the consequences of violations while also focusing on developing preventative services, raising awareness among the population, and strengthening monitoring activities. The number of children in special difficulties who received support and care has increased (CHXHCNVN 2007).

Vietnam gradually set up a relatively comprehensive legal framework for child protection, care and education. *The Law on Child Protection, Care and Education* approved by the National Assembly on 15 June 2004 (from 2016 it was known as the Children's Law) prescribes the principle that "in all child-related activities of agencies, organisations, families and individuals, the interests of the child shall be of primary concern," as well as the principle of "no discrimination against children" and it clearly defines ten groups of basic rights and duties of the child.

Along with the addition and modification of laws, the Government of Vietnam issued and directed the implementation of many separate policies for children. This was shown through the programmes, strategies, plans and projects that had a direct impact on the implementation of children's rights to health care, education and protection in Vietnam and reduces inequalities among children in different regions, and children of different ethnic and social groups, in meeting these basic needs. The Government of Vietnam also attended to the integration *of the goals for children into economic and social development plans* at national and local levels. For example, indicators of sex ratio at birth, infant mortality rate, immunization rate for children, malnutrition rate for children under 5, etc. were integrated into the national statistics indicators or in the socio-economic development plans.

However, in spite of these advantages, Vietnamese children faced challenges posed by the negative impact of the processes of market economic development, involving opening up and integration into the world, which took place in Vietnam. These include, for example, poverty, unequal access to development opportunities between groups with different living standards and between areas and regions, and other social issues. According to the VHLSS 2014, the average expenditure on education per capita per month of the richest quintile was 5.4 times higher than that of the poorest quintile, and in urban areas it was 2 times higher than in rural areas. There was also a tendency among the rich household group for children to attend private schools (where they have to pay more and receive more care) which was 12.8 times higher than the poorest household group (VGSO 2016).

Regarding the relationship between parents and children, preliminary analyses from the Vietnam Family Survey 2006 show that the relationship was generally very close in Vietnamese families. Most parents were very concerned about their children's study and spiritual and emotional lives, while treating boys and girls equally. They were also concerned about their children's problems, and are aware of, and provide advice on, their friendships. For example, about 90% of parents always knew about their children's studying time at school and at home, and their study results. The proportion of parents knowing specifically about studying time and study results increases in line with their income and education. The percentages of parents in the two lowest income groups knowing about their children's studying time at school was the lowest (81–88%), compared to those of parents of the three higher income groups (92–95%). Among parents with a college or university education, 96.6% knew about their children's studying time at school. This percentages among parents with elementary school, and no education is 81% and 70.2%, respectively. In single parent families, the percentages of parents who always knew about children's study is lower. Children having both parents received more attention (89% in families with both parents compared to 76.9% in single families knowing about their children's study time in school). Children with both parents receive more attention about their studying time at home: 92.9% compared to 86.5% in single parent cases.

In general, parents knew about their children's relationships with friends. They knew more about the places their children went to than they did about their children's close friends. Parents in families with higher incomes paid more attention to their children's friendships. (Tran et al. 2011).

However, many parents did not have time to provide their children with both the material and emotional support. Data from the Vietnam Family Survey 2006 indicated how much time parents spent with their children. Regarding children aged 7–14, the percentage of fathers spending less than one hour per day taking care of their children is 29.6%. There was still a significant proportion of fathers and mothers who did not have time to take care of children aged under 15: 6.8% of the mothers and 21.5% of the fathers (Tran et al. 2011). The parent-child relationship in some family groups still faced difficulty. For example, single parent families, poor families, and families with parents with low education levels, required attention, and needed help to improve the parent-child relationship.

The parent-child relationship in a single parent family needed major attention. Children in these families suffered many disadvantages due to the inability of the parent to care for them adequately, both materially and psychologically, which had long-term effects on their personality development. Intensive studies on single parent families were required so that suitable measures and policies were put in place, and convenient environments were created to support the parent-child relationship in these families.

Social organizations in the community, including socio-political organizations (especially women's unions and youth unions), NGOs and other civil society organizations implemented roles and responsibilities for childcare. Depending on the scope of functions, each social organization had its own unique activities related to the implementation of child care. These organizations also had an active partnership with one another and support government agencies. They also established collaboration with schools and families in promoting childcare in the community. The working scope of these social organizations was very diverse, and played the most important role in spreading awareness about childcare, policies and laws related to childcare and the implementation of developmental projects related to childcare. The deployment of child care groups or organizing local playgrounds for children were initiatives which receive positive responses from families.

Regarding market involvement, in the process of industrialization today, the socialization of child care was one of many NGOs' interests. Many private childcare centers appeared. In addition, a new form of babysitter by domestic worker appeared in the family. This new form facilitated more diverse childcare, especially in urban settings, and many parents could be assured of the safety of their children when they were working dedicatedly. However, this new form of childcare support was not affordable by all families, especially poor and middle-income families[11]. In addition, the quality of baby sitters by domestic workers was controlled by the government, and most domestic workers were not trained (MOLISA et al. 2012).

6.2 *Elderly Care*

According to the Census 2009, the percentage of old people (aged 60 or older) in Vietnam's population increased from 7.1% in 1979, to 7.2% in 1989, to 8% in 1999, to nearly 9% in 2009, and 10.2% in 2012 (VCPHCSC 2010; VGSO 2012). Thus, the population of Vietnam approached the aging line (according to international convention, a country in which 10% of its population are elderly is considered to be an aging population country). According to the Vietnam Family Survey 2006, the percentage of households with members aged 60 or older was 32.6, of these 35.7% were in urban areas and 31.4% in rural areas. Also, households of 3 or more generations accounted for 26.7% with a higher percentage in urban areas (MOCST et al. 2008).

Nationally, approximately 30% of old people received pensions, early retirement pensions or other monthly benefits, and more than 70% of old people lived by working and with the support of their descendants, according to National Assembly Committee for Social Affairs (NACSA 2006). According to data from the Ministry of Labor-Invalids and Social Affairs in 2006, a third of old people were poor or close to poverty and were facing problems in their material life, especially those living in rural and mountainous areas; more than 100,000 old people had to live in temporary houses and many did not have enough warm clothes in winter; and cases of children and grandchildren mistreating or failing to take care of their parents and grandparents still existed, according to Ministry of Labor – War Invalids – Social Affairs (MOLISA 2006).

---

11 According to figures of the General Statistics Office, the average monthly income of workers working in households in 2010 was VND 2,027,000 (General Statistics Office, 2011), excluding other expenses paid by employers and was not enough to pay the rent and other daily expenses. In comparison, the average monthly wage of a simple laborer in 2010 was VND 1,748,000 (General Statistics Office, 2010) and the average income of laborers in industrial zones was VND 2,200,0000 a month (information provided by Hanoi Industrial and Processing Zones Management Board); the starting salary of civil officials with university degrees who passed probation in 2011 is VND 1,924,000 (minimum salary of 830,000 × 2.34).

A report by the Ministry of Health in 2006 reveals that about 95% of old people were suffering from a disease and that each old person had 2.69 diseases on average, mainly chronic and non-infectious ones. The percentage of old people in good health was about 5–7%, those with bad health about 23%, and the rest were in average health (NACSA 2006).

Most of the old people in Vietnam at present were born and grew up while the country was at war, and reached adulthood in the period of subsidisation. When the country shifted to a market economy mechanism, the people had to cope with many economic problems because they either did not have accumulated assets, or the assets they had accumulated were not enough to live on and to provide for their healthcare in their old age. These facts require more attention and better care of old people by the state, community and families.

During the Renovation period (or *Doi Moi* as called in Vietnamese, since 1986), the state issued many policies relating to old people in order to deal with the challenges of population aging, such as enhancing the role of the family in taking care of old people, promoting the role of old people, improving the health and happiness of old people, and ensuring a supportive environment for old people. However, the policies on old people only focused on supporting the small proportion of old people in extreme difficulties such as the lonely, poor, or helpless old people or old people without any income. They did not support all old people in the country, who were often facing difficulties due to old age, and social inequality. Most old people in Vietnam still had to live mainly from their own labor or to depend on relatives', children's or grandchildren's support.

Empirical evidence confirmed the close relationship between old people and their descendants in Vietnamese families. Old people maintain important roles and positions in families, and families were also extremely important to old people. This was expressed in the mutual support and help between grandparents, parents and children in both the material and the psychological senses, the support and care given when they were sick, the sharing of the work burden and taking care of the grandchildren. In the present conditions, Vietnamese families tried to fulfil their duties of supporting and took care of old people, and maintaining harmonious relationships between old people and their descendants. This also meant that a considerable proportion of old people who had no choice but to depend on their descendants when they could not take care of themselves any longer, or could not afford the cost of healthcare and medical services.

However, the daily life of some of their descendants had many obstacles. According to the results of the Nation-wide survey on the Vietnamese family

(2006), about one third of surveyed households having older adults was the poor, as a result, looking after old parents was a difficulty, especially, with the lack of public support policies (MOCST et al. 2008). The vast majority of the elderly received emotional care from their children. They shared their feelings either of sadness or happiness with their family members, however, a small number of them were taken care of only in terms of their material life and their spiritual needs are neglected. The main causes of this phenomenon were the children's time insufficiency, their unwillingness to listen to older adults' ideas and the lack of mutual concern (Le 2017).

Contemporary economic and social conditions also changed the structure, values, and norms of the traditional family and, thus, the ideal living environment for the elderly. In the future, the percentage of old people living with their descendants could decrease due to changes in jobs, the perceptions of the younger generations and of old people themselves in arranging their lives when they got old. It also meant that old people may encounter more difficulties in providing for themselves and taking care of their own health and may have needed more help and support from the government, communities and social organisations.

Taking care of old people and strengthening the values in the relationships between old people and their descendants, in families, depended largely on raising the awareness of individuals (children and old people) of filial piety. Therefore, the maintenance and expansion of education which aimed to introduce changes in the family relationship during industrialization process, as well as the establishment of democratic, progressive and happy family relationships, become increasingly urgent.

Adherence to a guiding view provided by the Party and state policies, at the community level many caring activities for the elderly were implemented. The movement of building a "cultural family" with criteria such as cozy, harmonic, progressive, healthy and happy, families, with a good performance of their civic obligations to build cultural families, and cultural villages; the establishment of happy family clubs, intergeneration clubs, "exemplary grandparents and parents, diligent children" clubs, family economic development clubs, women's clubs that did not have a third child; various forms of rich and practical advocacy and education, such as launching movements "exemplary grandparents and parents, diligent children", "lighting love in each family", "for a warm family without violence"; and so on, were widely held in localities, and these made great contributions to the consolidation of the family and the care of the elderly.

Community organizations such as reconciliation groups and the Elderly Association also played an important role in the elderly care. These community organizations intervened in times of family conflict to protect the rights of the elderly as well as to preserve solidarity within each family. At the same time, community organizations also had initiatives to better protect older people. In addition to the club forms, these organizations also had initiatives such as those to set up common houses for elderly people to gather together for entertainment in the day time, from where they could return home in the night time.

However, current outside interventions in the cases of conflicts, especially violence against the elderly, faced many obstacles, especially from the awareness of the community itself. Despite relatives, authorities and mass organizations such as the reconciliation team, the Fatherland Front, the Women's Union trying to encourage adult children and helping the elderly, in some cases, when the adult children did not accept recommendations, then there was no way to help the victims because they were still psychologically cautious and considered it a family affair (Le 2017). This could limit the ability of the society to assist these elderly victims.

From the market approach, the establishment of a variety of models of nursing homes for different groups of older adults was significantly important. The first private nursing home was built nearly two decades ago but this model developed quickly later on thanks to high demand and the increase in living standards. These centers were mainly located in urban areas and aimed at providing services for the better off customers. In addition to care for diet, these nursing homes offered a variety of activities for older adults including health care, spiritual activities, recovery and therapy. The advantages of these centers were that they had professional staff trained well for elderly care. However, the limitation of these kinds of elderly care was the rather high cost of care. Reports from several elderly care centers in Hanoi (such as Thien Duc, Nhan Ai) informed that the costs for elderly care in the center, range from 150 to 1,000 USD, much higher than the income of those who had a middle living standard.

In addition, similarly to childcare, domestic workers also had an important role in taking care of elderly people. There were a variety of kinds of help care workers for the elderly at home, patient care workers in hospitals, etc. An advantage of this kind of care was that the fee was lower than that of caring provided in a center. However, domestic workers usually were trained well in taking care of elderly people, according to a report by MOLISA, ILO, & Institute for Family and Gender Studies (2012).

It is noteworthy that in the context of industrialization, modernization, and especially, globalization, the value system in the current family in Vietnam substantially changed. In addition to the traditional values such as "'respecting older adults, yielding of younger persons" (kính trên, nhường dưới), "respecting older adults" (trọng xỉ), the new values, for example, respect for "individual freedom rights", "gender equality" and "child rights" were more and more accepted. This alternation, to some extent, led to decreasing harmony in grandparents-parents and children relationships and to increasing generational conflicts. For example, the results of the Nation-wide survey on the Vietnamese family (2006) showed that about 1/10 of responses from three-generation-households and above stated that there was disagreement in life styles, money management and expenditures, ways of households' economic development, and methods of teaching children (MOCST et al. 2008).

7 Conclusion

This chapter provides a broad picture on the cultural and socio-economic background of the care institution within and between families in Vietnam during the past decades The basic features of Vietnam's society were inclusive of community spirit, mutual interest of family members, filial piety and respect toward the elderly, love and care toward children. Linkage with neighbours and relatives was also a part of these features. Marriage and child bearing, especially for a son to continue the family line and took care of his elderly parents, were very important. Normally, the son was responsible for living with and taking care of his parents. Therefore, son preference played a central role in Vietnamese family life and continues to this day. The role of women in the family was very important, including care-giving for all family members, especially the elderly and children. High fertility and family-community coherence were necessary conditions to maintain Vietnam traditional member caring methods.

Socio-economic changes during recent decades created favourable conditions for family care, and at the same time raised new challenges. Education and living standards were improved, and employment expanded, which enabled families to provide better care. Industrialisation and urbanisation changed knowledge and behaviour in care-taking, for example, writing letters, e-mail and making phone calls instead of direct visits to express emotional care. Migration patterns also changed. Migration for employment helped improve people's living standards, on one hand, making care in terms of the material aspect better; but on the other hand, resulted in less direct communication which is a part of emotional life. The trend of feminisation among migrants caused those who were mostly responsible for home care to leave their home villages leaving only the elderly and children. Instead of being cared for, many of the elderly were responsible for taking care of their grandchildren. Smaller family size maybe a favourable condition for childcare, but limited the care for the elderly. Vietnamese society was in the process of population aging, in which the demand for elderly care increases while social services in this regard remained limited, and families were still key institutions in this duty.

Few years ago, state laws and policies made specific provisions to ensure care of the elderly and children. However, changes made in the nature and forms of care in Vietnam were not fully met by these policies. In the meantime, community, the family and market institutions contributed actively to the care system for elderly people and children. Their role became more and more important in elderly and children care in Vietnam.

Under the combined effects of cultural, economic, social factors and policies mentioned above, there were changes in the care system in Vietnam during this period. A comprehensive understanding of the socio-economic-cultural context and the above-mentioned policy system served as a basis for a deeper analysis of the current family caring pattern.

References

Andien Research Group. (1992). Tuoigia Andien: Mot so dac diem nhankhauxa hoi. *Tap chiXa hoi hoc, So* 2(38), 15–20. [Andien elderly: A few socio-demographic characteristics. *Sociological Review*, 2(38), 15–20].

Banister, Judith. (1993). *Vietnam population dynamics and prospects*. Berkley: Institute of East Asian Studies, University of California.

Bui, Ngoc Thanh, Huu Dung Nguyen, & Pham Do Nhat Tan (Eds.). (1996). *Nghiencuuchinhsachxa hoi nong thon Vietnam*. Ha Noi: NXB Chinh tri QuocGia. [*Studies on the implementation of social policies in rural areas in Vietnam*. Hanoi: National Political Publishing House].

CHXHCNVN. (2007). *Baocao Quoc Gia-Danhgiagiuakyviec Viet Nam thuchien van kien 'Mot The gioiphu hop voitreem'*. Ha Noi. [*National report-mid-term review of Vietnam's implementation of document "A world fit for children"*. Ha Noi: CHXHCNVN].

CHXHCNVN. (2008). *Baocaolanthu Ba vathuTu-Viet Nam thuchien* CRC *Giaidoan 2002–2007*. Ha Noi. [*The third and fourth reports- Vietnam's implementation of CRC in 2002–2007 period*. Ha Noi: CHXHCNVN].

Dinh, Gia Trinh. (1968). *So thao Lich su Nhanuocva Phapquyen Vietnam*. Ha Noi: NXB Khoa hoc xa hoi. [*Draft of Vietnam state and law*. Hanoi: Social Sciences Publishing House].

Do, Thai Dong. (1991). Giadinhtruyen thong vanhungbienthai o Nam Bo Viet Nam. Rita Liljestrom va Tuong Lai (Chu Bien), *Nhung Nghiencuu Xa hoi hoc vegia Dinh Viet Nam* (pp. 69–83). Ha Noi: NXB Khoa hoc xa hoi. [Modifications of the traditional family in the South of Vietnam. In Rita Liljestrom, & Tuong Lai (Eds.), *Sociological Studies on the Vietnamese Family* (pp. 69–83). Hanoi: Social Sciences Publishing House].

Freedman, Ronald, Arland Thornton, & Li-Shou Yang. (1994). Determinants of co-residence in extended households. In Arland Thornton, & Hui-Sheng Lin (Eds.), *Social change and the family in Taiwan* (pp. 335–358). Chicago: The University of Chicago Press.

Giang, Thanh Long, & Dai Thu Bui. (2012, May). *Viet Nam aging survey (VNAS), 2011: Key findings.* Paper presented at the Launching of the report on national survey of elderly people in Vietnam, Hanoi.

Goodkind, Daniel. (1997a). *Post-marital residence patterns amidst socialist transformations in a Northern province of Vietnam, 1948–93.* Paper presented at the annual meeting of the association for Asian studies, Chicago.

Goodkind, Daniel. (1997b). *Post-marital residence patterns amidst socialist transformations in a Northern province of Vietnam, 1948–1993.* Paper presented at the annual meeting of the association for Asian studies, Chicago 1997.

Hanoi, SO. (2010). *Hanoi annual statistics 2009.* Hanoi: Statistical Publisher.

Institute for Family and Gender Studies. (2012). *Overview of Vietnam family development during 2011–2020 period.* Unpublished Project Report, Hanoi.

Lavely, William & Xinhua Ren. (1992). Patrilocality and early marital co-residence in rural China, 1955–1985. *The China Quarterly, 130*, 378–391.

Le, Ngoc Lan. (2017). *Elderly people in Vietnamese family in the context of ageing population and social changes.* Unpublished Ph. D. Dissertation, Graduate Academy of Social Sciences, Hanoi.

Luong, Phan Cu. (2010, August). *Legal regulations on Vietnamese labors oversea and emerging issues in implementing the laws.* Paper presented at the Committee of Social Affairs, National Assembly.

Mai, Huy Bich. (2000). "Noi cu trusau hon nhan o Dong bang song Hong". *Tap chi Xa hoi hoc, so 4*(72), 33–42. [Residence patterns after marriage in the Red River Delta. *Sociological Review, 4*(72), 33–42].

Mai, Thi Tu, & Thi Nham Tuyet Le. (1978). *Women in Vietnam.* Hanoi: Foreign Languages Publishing House.

Marr, David G. (1981). *Vietnamese tradition on trial, 1920–1945.* Berkeley, California: University of California Press.

MOCST, Institute for Family and Gender Studies, & UNICEF. (2008). *Ket qua Dieu tra Gia dinh Viet Nam nam 2006.* Ha Noi. [*Result of the survey on the Vietnamese family 2006.* Hanoi].

MOH & Health Partner Group-HPG. (2013). Bộ Y tếViệt Nam vànhómđốitác y tế (2013), *Báocáotổngquanngành Y tếnăm 2013- Hướngtớibaophủchămsócsứckhỏetoàndân*, HàNội. [*The joint annual health review reports on universal coverage of health care*]. Hanoi: MOH and HPG.

MOLISA. (2006). *Baocaoviecthuchien Phaplenh Nguoicaotuoi.* tai Ky hop Thu 9, Quoc Hoi Khoa XI. [*Report on implementation of the ordinance on the elderly.* In 9th session of XI national assembly]. Unpublished report. Hanoi: MOLISA.

MOLISA. *Ten Year's Evaluation report on the law of children protection, care, and education.* (59/BC-BLDTBXH; June 15, 2015)

MOLISA, ILO, & Institute for Family and Gender Studies. (2012). *Decent work for domestic workers in Vietnam*. Hanoi: MOLISA, ILO and IFGS.

MPI. (2008). *Vietnam continues its way to implement the millennium development goals.* Ha Noi: Ministry of Planning and Investment.

NACSA. (2006). *Baocaogiam sat viecthuchiencacchinhsachvaluatvenguoicaotuoi.* Ngay 31 thang 5 nam 2006. [*Report on monitoring the implementation of policies and law on the elderly* – 31st May 2006].

National Assembly Economic Committee. (2014.) *Macroeconomic report 2014 economic institution reform: Key for restructuring.* Hanoi: the Economic Committee of the National Assembly and UNDP in Vietnam.

Nguyen, Duc Truyen. (1997a). Van hoavasukethua van hoatrongviec chia thuake o Dong bang song Hong hien nay. *Tap chi Xa hoi hoc. So 3*(59), 48–54. [Culture and the cultural heritage in the Division of inheritance in the Red River Delta at present time. *Sociological Review, 3*(59), 48–54].

Nguyen, Huu Minh. (1991). Bien doikinhte-xa hoi vakhananggiamchuanmuc so con trongcacgiadinhnongdan Bac Bo. *Tap chi Xa hoi hoc, So 4*(36), 38–47. [Socio-economic changes and the possibility for reducing number of children in the Northern Plain's peasant households. *Sociological Review, 4*(36), 38–47].

Nguyen, Huu Minh. (2000). Cacyeu to tac dong den khuonmautuoiket hon cuadan cu Dong bang song Hong. *Tap chi Xa hoi hoc, So 4*(72), 21–32. [Factors that affect the marriage age of population in the Red River Delta. *Sociological Review, 4*(72), 21–32].

Nguyen, Huu Minh. (2009). Sống chung với gia đình chồng sau khi kết hôn ở nông thôn Việt Nam và các yếu tố tác động. *Tạp chí Xã hội học, Số 4*(108), trang 3–15. Hà Nội. [Living with husband's family after marriage in the Vietnam rural areas and affecting factors. *Sociological Review, 4*(108), 3–15].

Nguyen, Huu Minh. (Ed.). (2014a). *Cultural life of Hanoi residents.* Hanoi: Social Sciences Publisher.

Nguyen, Huu Minh. (2014b). Changes in socio-demographic characteristics of the Vietnamese family. In Zsombor Rajkai (Ed.), *Family and social change in socialist and post-socialist societies – Change and continuity in Eastern Europe and East Asia.* (pp. 359–412). Leiden: Brill Publisher

Nguyen, Huu Minh. (2016). Vietnam family after 30 years of renovation. *Vietnam Social Sciences, 1*(171). 50–59.

Nguyen, Huu Minh, & Charles Hirschman. (2000). Mo hinh song chungvoigiadinhchongsaukhiket hon o Dong bang Bac Bo vacacnhan to tac dong. *Tap chi Xa hoi hoc. So 1*(69), 41–54. [Patrilocal co-residence after marriage in the Red River Delta and its determinants. *Sociological Review, 1*(69), 41–54].

Nguyen, Huu Minh, & Thi Hong Tran. (2011). Thai do cuathanhthieunien Viet Nam ve hon nhanvagiadinh. *Tap chi Nghien cuu Gia dinh va Gioi, 4*(21), 3–14. [Vietnam youth attitudes toward marriage and family issues. *Journal of Family and Gender Studies, 4*(21), 3–14].

Nguyen, Ngoc Huy, & Van Tai Ta. (1987). *The Le Code: Law in traditional Vietnam: A comparative Sino-Vietnamese legal study with historical-juridical analysis and annotations.* Athens, Ohio: Ohio University Press.

Nguyen, Tai Thu. (Ed.). (1997b). *Anhhuongcuacac he tutuongva ton giaodoivoi con nguoi Viet Nam hien nay.* Hanoi: NXB Chinh Tri QuocGia. [*The impacts of ideologies and religion on Vietnamese people at present time.* Hanoi: National Political Publishing House.]

Nguyen, Thanh Liem, & Huu Minh Nguyen. (2011). *Migration and urbanization in Viet Nam: patterns, trends and differentials.* Hanoi: UNFPA and GSO.

Nguyen, Tu Chi. (1993). The Traditional Viet Village in Bac Bo: Its organizational structure and problems. In Phan Huy Le, Nguyen Tu Chi, Nguyen Duc Nghinh, Nguyen Dinh Dau & Nguyen Khac Tung (Eds.), *The traditional billage in Vietnam* (pp. 44–142). Hanoi: The Gioi Publishers.

Nguyen, Van. (2017, April 19). Towards health care coverage for all people in 2025. Retrieved from http://suckhoedoisong.vn/huong-toi-bao-phu-y-te-toan-dan-toi-nam-2025-n130581.html

NIN. (2012). *Major findings from general survey introducing national strategy of nutrition 2011–2020 period.* Hanoi: National Institute of Nutrition.

Rydstrom, Helle, & Lisa Drummond. (2004). Introduction. In Lisa Drummond, & Helle Rydstrom (Eds.), *Gender practices in contemporary Vietnam* (pp. 1–26). Singapore: Singapore University Press.

SRVG. (1996). *Huongdanthuchien Chi thi So 117/CP cua Thu TuongChinhphuve 'Cham socnguoicaotuoiva ho trocachoat dong cho Hoi Nguoicaotuoi Viet Nam'.* [Instruction 117/CP of the Prime Minister: *Elderly care and support for activities of the Vietnam elderly association*]. Hanoi: SRVG.

SRVG. (2002). *Nghi dinh Chinh phu so 30/2002/ND-CP.* [*Decree 30/2002/NĐ-CP,* Item 1, Article 2]. Hanoi: SRVG internal circulation.

SRVG. (2011). *Baocaocua Thu Tuong Chinhphutruoc Quoc hoi vetinhhinhkinhte-xa hoi nam 2011, Kehoach phat trienkinhte-xa hoi nam 2012 va 5 nam 2011–2015.* [*Prime*

Minister's report to the NA on the socio-economic situation in 2011, on plan to develop socio-economic in 2012 and the five years 2011–2015]. Hanoi: SRVG internal circulation.

Taylor, Keith. W. (1983). *The birth of Vietnam*. Berkeley, CA: University of California Press.

Tong, Cuc Chinh Tri. (1993). *Mot so hieubietve ton giao, ton giao o Viet Nam*. Ha Noi: NXB Quandoi Nhandan. [*Some knowledge about religion, and religion in Vietnam*. Hanoi: People's Army Publishing House].

Tran, Dinh Huou. (1991). Vegiadinhtruyen thong Viet Nam voianhhuong Nhogiao. Rita Liljestrom va Tuong Lai (Chu Bien). *Nhungnghiencuu Xa hoi hoc vegiadinh Viet Nam* (pp. 25–46). Ha Noi: NXB Khoa hoc xa hoi. [About Vietnamese family tradition under the influence of confucianism. In Rita Liljestrom, & Tuong Lai (Eds.), *Sociological Studies on the Vietnamese Family* (pp. 25–46). Hanoi: Social Sciences Publishing House].

Tran, Thi Van Anh, Huu Minh Nguyen, & Thi Minh Khuong Ha. (2011). Relationship between parents and juveniles. In Ministry of Culture, Sports and Tourism, Institute for Family and Gender Studies & UNICEF (Eds.), *Intra-family relationships of the Vietnamese families: Key findings from in-depth analyses of the Vietnam family survey* (pp. 7–30). Hanoi: Social Sciences Publishing House.

United Nation. *General comment no. 7, implementing child rights in early childhood, committee on the right of the child.* (CRC/C/GC/7/Rev.1; September 20, 2006).

UNDP. (2012). *Social services for human development: Vietnam human development report 2011*. Hanoi: UNDP

UNICEF Vietnam. (2008). *Analysis based on the rights of the child.* Hanoi: UNICEF Vietnam.

VCP. (2011). Van Kien Dai hoi Dang toanquoclanthu 11. Hanoi: NXB Chinh tri QuocGia. [*11th national congress of the Vietnam communist party documents*. Hanoi: Political Publishing House].

VCPHCSC. (2000). *1999 Vietnam population and housing census: Sample results*. Hanoi: Statistical Publishing House, Vietnam Central Population and Housing Census Steering Committee.

VCPHCSC. (2010). *The 2009 Vietnam population and housing census: Major findings*. Hanoi: Statistical Publishing House.

VGSO. (1991). *Detailed analysis of sample results: 1989 census*. Hanoi: Statistical Publishing House.

VGSO. (2001). *Results of survey on economics and life of households 1999–2000*. Hanoi: Statistical Publishing House.

VGSO. (2008). *Statistic yearbook 2007*. Hanoi: Statistical Publishing House.

VGSO. (2011). *Population projections for Vietnam 2009–2049*. Hanoi: Statistical Publishing House.

VGSO. (2012). *Dieutra Kehoachhoagiadinhvabiendoidan so: Nhungket qua chuyeu*. Hanoi: NXB Thong ke. [*Population and family planning change survey at the time April 01, 2012: Major findings*. Hanoi: Statistical Publishing House].

VGSO. (2014). *Report of survey on labor-job, 4th quarter 2014*. Hanoi: Statistical Publishing House

VGSO. (2015). *Dieutra Dan so va Nha o giuakythoi diem 1/4/2014: Cacket qua chuyeu*. Hanoi. NXB Thong ke, 9/2015. [*Intercensal population and housing survey 1/4/2014: Major findings*. Hanoi. Statistical Publishing House].

VGSO. (2016). *Result of the Vietnam household living standard survey 2014*. Hanoi: Statistical Publishing House.

VGSO & UNFPA. (2016). *Intercensal census 2014: Migration and urbanization in Vietnam*. Hanoi: News Publisher.

Vien, Su Hoc. (1991). *Quoc Trieu Hinh Luat: Luat Hinh Trieu Le*. Ha Noi: NXB Phaply. [*The penal code of the national: The penal code of the Le Dynasty*. Hanoi: Legal Publisher.]

Vietnam Women Union, Vietnam Elderly Association, Institute of Medical-Sociology, & Dongduong Research and Consultation Company. (2012). *Report on national survey of elderly people in Vietnam 2011*. Hanoi: VWU, VEA, IMS and IMRD.

VNA. (1992). *Hienphapnuoc Cong Hoa Xa Hoi Chu Nghia Viet Nam-1992*. [*Vietnamese constitution* 1992]. (n.d.; April 15, 1992)

VNA. (2000a). *Luat Hon Nhanva Gia Dinh*. [*Law on marriage and family*]. (22/2000/QH10; June 9, 2000)

VNA. (2000b). *Phaplenhvenguoicaotuoi*. [*Ordinance of the elderly*]. (23/2000/PL-UBT-VQH10; August 28, 2000)

VNA. (2009). *Luat nguoi cao tuoi*. [*Law of elderly people*]. (39/2009/QH12; November 23, 2009)

Vu, Tuan Anh. (1995). Economic reforms and socio-economic problems of development'. In Tuan Anh Vu (Ed.), *Economic reforms and development in Vietnam* (pp. 13–94). Hanoi: Social Science Publishing House.

Vu, Tu Lap, Trung Phuong Dam, Duc Thinh Ngo, Ngoc Thanh To, & Thi Hoang Uyen Dinh. (1991). *Van hoava cu dan Dong bang song Hong*. Ha Noi: NXB Khoa hoc xa hoi. [*Culture and people in the Red River Delta*. Hanoi: Social Sciences Publishing House].

Weinstein, Maxine, Te-Hsiung Sun, Ming-Cheng Chang, & Ronald Freedman. (1994). Co-residence and other ties linking couples and their parents. In Arland Thornton & Hui-Sheng Lin (Eds.), *Social change and the family in Taiwan* (pp. 305–334). Chicago: University of Chicago Press.

World Bank. (2008). *Vietnam development report 2009: The capital problems*. Washington, DC: World Bank.

PART 2

Attitudes and Practices in Care

CHAPTER 5

Care Relations within the Family

Jo-Pei Tan and Rahimah Ibrahim

1 Introduction

In Part 1, the depiction of elderly and child care across three Southeast Asian countries reflects a scenario in which familial care networks were in transition with filial norms and expectation among these traditional societies being challenged by the varying speed of socio-economic development, demographic changes and diverse social conditions across each country. On one hand, fundamentally, filial norms prevailed as part of the cultural heritage on the provision of support among families there during the period of investigation. On the other hand, historical background, country specific population policies, socio-demographic characteristics and economic development led to varying effects on intergenerational support for the young and old generations across these countries.

While the discussion in Part 1 focused on the broader perspective and national level development, Part 2 comprises three chapters which utilises survey data at a specific area-level to examine the attitudes and practices in care across the three Southeast Asian societies along the hypotheses presented in chapter 1. Looking at the key notions raised in chapters 2, 3 and 4, the three middle income societies in Southeast Asia – Malaysia, Thailand and Vietnam – were facing unique and country specific challenges in care provision for the young and old generations. In the case of Malaysia, despite the rapid economic development, strong cultural notions and religious values of familial care, the increasing economic pressure on families, demands for female/family friendly policies and the ageing of the population revealed a demand for more integrated policies to address inequalities across social groups and, redistribution of care provision from the family to other sectors that included community, the public and private sectors. Care relations in ageing Thailand showed a picture of diversification of care providers, gender-free child-preference, changing living arrangements and an increase in state policies to strengthen family relations and support for older persons. Yet, there were concerns regarding whether the intergenerational family solidarity among Thai society would continue or change when the country matures into an aged society. Vietnam, the

© KONINKLIJKE BRILL NV, LEIDEN, 2019 | DOI:10.1163/9789004384330_006 most traditional country among the three, characterised by strong son preference, feminisation of care provision within the family network, limited support in social care services, was challenged by the migration for employment among women, increasing demand for elderly care and the struggle of families, as the key sector for care provision, to cope, especially within the urban areas. Broadly speaking, this provided a landscape of the role of family, state, market and community in the context of care provision for old and young generations across these Southeast Asia societies.

We argued that families in Thailand, Malaysia and Vietnam may have shared similarities in family culture and norms such as filial obligation and family as the main source of care, and welfare systems that were characterised by modest social protection coverage, less developed public policies and social care services for the elderly. However, the different phases of transition in the demographic, policy development and socio-economic terms may eventually lead to varying effects on intergenerational patterns and support provision across these countries. For example, in terms of the population's structure, Malaysia was relatively young while Thailand and Vietnam were ageing. Importantly, each of these societies were in transition and differed in terms of socio-economic development. This led to a variation in the practice of filial obligation. At the national level, intergeneration contribution and exchange could be expected to vary across age cohort and between rural and urban areas across countries. However, evidence of changing family systems and societal norms was emerging where there was a consistent decline in coresidence with parent, and changing attitudes and expectations for filial responsibilities among younger and older generations (Xie 2010; Park, Phua, McNally & Sun 2005).

Thus, the present chapter examines and compares the patterns of care practices between adult children and parents while exploring the changes, continuity and development of care relations across Bangkok Metropolis, Hanoi and Kuala Lumpur, which serve as case studies. The detailed analysis of the survey data aims to provide a comprehensive understanding of how care relations and support provision relate to the family, state, the market and community. Specifically, in terms of living arrangements, the chapter explores the filial norms and patterns of intergenerational support within coresident families[1] with the aims of highlighting the effect of situational factors such as the characteristics of adult children (i.e. age, education, marital status and gender) and parents (i.e. health, marital status, old age) that may have made

1 Coresident family refers to individuals who were living in the same household.

cross-generation support and care unique for the three Southeast Asian societies during the survey period, i.e. 2010–2011. The findings from our surveys need to be considered within a certain context, which is that the data is only drawn from specific areas or at a societal level, namely the Bangkok Metropolis, Hanoi and Kuala Lumpur. Therefore, in this chapter, it is our aim to explain and interpret the area-specific findings based on secondary information from the national level information as discussed in Part 1. Caution needs to be used in data interpretation as there may be a distinction between the scenarios at the national level and specific area level. For example, it is acknowledged that, Hanoi includes both urban and rural areas, is relatively more traditional compared to a more urbanized city, such as Ho Chi Minh.

In terms of the theoretical framework, the present chapter adapts Bengston and Schrader's Intergenerational Solidarity Framework (1982) to explore the norms and practice of intergenerational support across the three Southeast Asia societies. This framework provides an understanding of care transactions between generations by examining the various elements of solidarity that include affectual, functional, normative and associational solidarity (Bengtson & Schrader 1982). More importantly, findings from this chapter aim to address three hypotheses presented in chapter 1: (1) strong family relationships led to care provision by family; (2) Southeast Asian families were patriarchal in the context of care relations and; (3) care transactions within Southeast Asian families were more attributable to the parent's characteristics than the children's characteristics.

For the present study, based on the discussion in chapter 1, 'support and care within families' refers to any provision of support and care from adult children to parents/parents-in-law or vice versa who were living in the same household during the survey period. As explained in chapter 1, the basic questionnaire was adapted from the EASS project with 841 samples in Bangkok Metropolis, 889 samples in Hanoi and 1113 samples in Kuala Lumpur. A *coresident family* subsample was created where only households with adult children who co-resided with at least one of their parents/parents-in-law (PIL) (referred to as a coresident household) were included in the analysis (n=1197, 29.6%); while households of adult children who did not reside with parents (referred to as a non-coresident household) were analysed separately to reflect 'support and care between families' (n=2843, 70.4%) (See chapter 6 for details). For the data analysis, this chapter focuses on the practice and attitudes of support and care in the normative dimensions of family solidarity. They include: filial attitudes and familial responsibilities; types of support that comprised affectual, functional and associational; flow of support between generations (i.e. upward and downward). It also looks at the moderating effect of adult children and parental characteristics. (Details of comparison between living arrangements are discussed in Part 3 of this volume)[2].

2 Sample Profile

2.1 *Characteristics of Coresident Families*

Table 5.1 presents the demographic profile of intergenerational *coresident families* (referred to as coresident households) from samples of Bangkok Metropolis, Kuala Lumpur and Hanoi. It can be seen that the age distribution differed across the three societies[3]. The Kuala Lumpur sample reported the lowest average age of 27 years old with 75.5% in the young age group compared to older samples in Hanoi and Bangkok Metropolis with the average of 35 years old and a smaller percentage (40%) in the young age group. Adult children in Kuala Lumpur reported a larger family size with a mean of 4.54 as compared to those in Hanoi (mean=4.30) and Bangkok Metropolis (mean=3.48). In terms of marital status, the sample in Kuala Lumpur reported a significant proportion of unmarried adult children of 73.5; while Hanoi and Bangkok Metropolis reported greater numbers of married respondents with 70.1% and 54.4% respectively.

In terms of education attainment, a relatively significant proportion (22.8%) of the sample had obtained a tertiary education: Bangkok Metropolis reported the highest proportion of 27.1%, followed by 26.7% in Hanoi and 19% in Kuala Lumpur. It can be argued that a substantial proportion of the samples was educated. Data on socio-economic status were only available for Kuala Lumpur and Hanoi. The majority, or 60% of the sample perceived themselves to be in the middle-income group. Country discrepancy in self-perceived socio-economic status was detected among low and high-income groups. Kuala Lumpur reported two thirds or 35.8% of the sample in the low-income group and Hanoi reported almost 25% of the sample was in the high-income group. While these three Southeast Asia societies shared similarities

2 It is assumed that during the period of investigation support and care within families was to be provided by other family members living in the same household and in most instances, support was presumed to be unpaid. However, the researchers do not rule out the possibility that some family carers may have received some financial support from other family members. Nevertheless, information on financial support from other family members was not available in the current survey.

3 The age groups are divided into old (Baby boomers or older), middle (Generation x) and young (Generation Y and Z). According to UNJSPF (2009), the Traditionalists are those born between 1925 and 1945, the Baby Boomers born between 1946 and 1964, generation X born between 1965 and 1980, generation Y – also known as the Millennial, or generation Me – born between 1981 and 2000, and generation Z born after 2000.

TABLE 5.1 Sample characteristics

Variables	Bangkok Metropolis	Hanoi	Kuala Lumpur
Age cohort (Generation)			
Young	43.1%	46.1%	75.5%
Middle	33.9%	27.0%	18.8%
Old	23.1%	27.0%	5.7%
Gender and marital status			
Married sons	19.6%	31.1%	12.5%
Married daughters	34.8%	39.0%	14.0%
Unmarried sons	22.6%	17.0%	39.1%
Unmarried daughters	23.0%	12.9%	34.4%
Living standards			
High		24.5%	7.0%
Middle		66.4%	57.2%
Low		9.1%	35.8%
Number of Siblings	3.48	4.30	4.54
Education level			
Low (Secondary and lower)	72.9%	73.3%	81.0%
High (Tertiary)	27.1%	26.7%	19.0%
Provision of care to family members (Yes)	–	36.7%	20.4%
Types of care			
Spouse	–	8.3%	1.6%
Parent	–	63.6%	84.1%
Parent In-Law	–	24.8%	10.3%
Children	–	3.3%	4.0%
Health demand			
All healthy/ healthy+ deceased	72.2%	57.0%	89.0%
Either ONE unhealthy	27.8%	43.0%	11.0%
Current Family household Size (Mean)	5.11	5.21	5.58
Living arrangement			
2 generation	42.1%	28.5%	71.4%
3 generation	39.7%	60.6%	27.5%
4 & 5 generation	9.7%	10.6%	0.6%
Skip-generation	8.5%	0.3%	0.5%

within sample characteristics, the relative differences need to be taken into account when examining the nature and dynamics of support and care in the following sections.

2.2 *Selected Demographic Characteristics*

In order to analyse the varying contribution of the sample characteristics, the practice and attitudes towards support and care within co-resident families are examined based on a set of adult children and parent characteristics. *Adult children characteristics* included in the analysis are: agein years, education level which is categorised into three levels, namely Low for 'No education or primary school,' Middle for 'Secondary school' and High for 'Tertiary education or higher,' gender, and marital status, with '1' coded as Married and '0' coded as Unmarried.

Parent's characteristics, as demand of care indicators, includes health status, marital status and age. *Parental health status* is also considered as one of the proxy indicators of the burden of caring for parents, specifically health-demands. Higher scores indicate higher degrees of poor health among living parents (this also includes parents-in-law). Parental health demands are then categorised into: (1) low demand when both parents were healthy or, one was healthy and one deceased and; (2) high demand when at least one parent was in poor health.

Parental marital status is categorised into two, where parents or parents-in-law who were currently married are labelled as 'has spouse'; while those who were widowed or divorced are categorised as 'without spouse.' *Old age of parents* was recorded as the percentage of those reported as having at least one parent above 65 years old at the time of the study. Other indicators for the burden of caring and support include the *number of children in household* and if they had *young children aged 7 and below* living in the same household.

The analyses also include other country specific variables. They are: *locality* which is divided into urban and rural; *living standard/Socio-economic status* which refers to the high or low socio-economic status of the sample; and finally *ethnicity* which is categorised as Malay, Chinese and Indian ethnic background. Ethnicity is only available in the Kuala Lumpur sample.

2.3 *Data Analysis Strategy*

First, the practice in care in relation to the extent and types of support, and demographic characteristics of adult children and parents were analysed with descriptive statistics that include percentage and frequency. The distribution of care attitude variables was related to associational solidarity. Normative elements such as family relationships, filial attitudes and expectations for familial responsibilities were also explored, followed by a further comparison with selected demographic characteristics. Specifically, a comparative analysis that includes t-test and analysis of variance (ANOVA) was then conducted to examine the variation across age groups, education levels, gender, marital status and interaction of marital status and gender, and health status among parents. Finally, aseries of multiple regression models were carried out to determine the unique contribution of each selected factor/predictor for intergenerational support amongst sample from Bangkok Metropolis, Hanoi and Kuala Lumpur.

3 Practice and Attitudes Towards Intergenerational Support across Three Societies

3.1 *Practice in Care: Types and Flow of Care Provisions*

Empirical findings in this section help us to understand and explore the types and flow of care provision in three Southeast Asian societies, namely Bangkok Metropolis, Hanoi and Kuala Lumpur. Guided by the Intergenerational Solidarity framework, the dimensions or elements of solidarity examined include, emotional support and functional support (i.e. financial assistance and household chores) to reflect upon the transaction of care within intergenerational co-resident households in the three societies. It should be noted that the focus of the present study is on the different possible patterns of within-family care, rather than how intergenerational care relations in coresident households differed from that of non-coresident households. The comparison between the two types of living arrangement will be integrated and discussed in chapter 8, which revisits the key empirical findings of the present chapter up to chapter 7 to addresses the hypotheses, which were discussed in the chapter 1.

3.1.1 Emotional Support

Emotional support which refers to the sharing of feelings, affectional bonding and listening to problems, has received increasing attention in the studies on care provision and quality of care. This type of support tends to be less emphasised as compared to tangible or instrumental support among families in the more traditional Southeast Asian societies. In general, this study found the exchange of emotional support to be more upward from adult children to parents than downward from parents to adult children. Results also showed that on average, during the survey period there was a regular exchange of emotional support between parents and adult children, where they 'sometimes' or 'often' listened to each other's personal problems. This pattern was in accordance with past studies which noted that the upward flow of support from adult children to parents in Southeast Asia societies were more regular than children receiving assistance from parents (Chan 2005). In addition, coresident living arrangements may have also encouraged greater provision of emotional care, in terms of companionship, listening and problem sharing, for parents who were living within the same household. Results from the ANOVA comparative analysis also noted significant differences in intergenerational emotional support across societies, $F_{AC\ to\ Parent}=3.08$ and $F_{Parent\ to\ AC}=3.18$ (see Table 5.2). In comparison, the upward flow of emotional care from adult children to parents was found to be more intense in Bangkok Metropolis; while downward flow was stronger in Hanoi and Kuala Lumpur. In comparison to their own parents, exchange of emotional support between adult children and parents-in-law was relatively lower, especially in Bangkok Metropolis and Kuala Lumpur. Country comparison notes that Hanoi reported more regular emotional support between adult children and parents-in-law than Bangkok Metropolis or Kuala Lumpur.

3.1.2 Functional Support

Intergenerational exchange of functional or tangible support was often found to be intense among many Southeast Asian societies such as Thailand, the Philippines, Singapore and Vietnam (Biddlecom, Chayovan & Ofsteadal 2002; Anh, Bui, Goodkind & Knodel 1997). Overall, the flow of financial support tended to be upward from adult children to parents and the least regular flow of support was downward from parent-in-law to adult children (See Table 5.2). This pattern confirmed findings from past studies in various Southeast Asian societies which consistently showed that the flow of financial support is often greater from adult children to parents than vice versa (Chan 2005; Lin & Yi 2013; Biddlecom et al. 2002; Anh et al. 1997).

Results from ANOVA indicated significant differences in the transaction of financial support across countries, $F_{AC\ to\ Parent}=24.28$ and $F_{Parent\ to\ AC}=19.97$ (see Table 5.2). Based on the 5-point scale, the flow of upward support was strongest in Bangkok Metropolis with a mean of 3.27 while downward support was more apparent among families in Kuala Lumpur with a mean equalling 2.62. In terms of domestic tasks, a similar upward flow of support was found where adult children reported they provided more support to their parents in terms of cleaning, meal preparation, running errands and other domestic tasks in their coresident household. ANOVA comparative analysis revealed that there were significant differences in household support between the three societies, $F_{AC\ to\ Parent}=19.06$ and $F_{Parent\ to\ AC}=23.68$ with Hanoi reporting the lowest mean score for household support from adult children to their own parents but highest mean for support from adult children to parents-in-law among the three societies, $F_{AC\ to\ PIL}=19.06$ and $F_{PIL\ to\ AC}=23.68$ (see Table 5.2).

TABLE 5.2 Types and flow of support among co-resident families: Emotional, functional, associational and normative

Intergenerational Support	Mean		
	Bangkok Metropolis	Hanoi	Kuala Lumpur
Provided support to parents			
Financial support	3.27	2.47	2.69
Emotional support	3.45	3.31	3.25
Household chores support	3.38	2.74	3.06
Received support from parents			
Financial support	2.05	2.16	2.62
Emotional support	2.93	3.14	3.14
Household chores support	2.66	2.27	2.90
Provided support to parents-in-law (PIL)			
Financial support	2.47	2.55	2.38
Emotional support	2.51	3.00	2.55
Household chores support	2.39	3.01	2.56
Received support from parents-in-law (PIL)			
Financial support	1.46	1.57	1.41
Emotional support	2.05	2.84	2.17
Household chores support	1.68	1.61	1.96
Family relationship			
Frequency of supper together	6.11	6.90	6.43
Frequency of activities together	4.86	2.01	4.22
Filial attitudes			
Feeling grateful	6.65	6.84	6.10
Support parents' livelihood	6.60	5.75	5.87
Familial responsibilities			
Financial support from:			
Unmarried adult man to own parents	6.16	5.34	5.98
Unmarried adult woman to own parents	6.16	4.93	5.95
Married adult man to own parents	5.88	5.50	5.92
Married adult woman to own parents	5.86	3.73	5.85
Married man to parents-in-law	5.57	2.96	5.57
Married woman to parents-in-law	5.46	5.13	5.49

3.1.3 Comparison between Emotional and Functional Support

As shown in Table 5.2, the extent of emotional and functional support between adult children and their own parents and parents-in-law across the three societies was diverse. It was found that emotional support was the most frequently exchanged support between generations in co-resident households, followed by domestic tasks and financial support. Country discrepancy was detected with the frequency of exchange between types of support less apparent in Bangkok Metropolis compared to Hanoi and Kuala Lumpur, particularly in terms of downward support from adult children to their own parents. The higher level of downward emotional support was not a surprise, especially among adult children who are in co-residence with their parents. Past research has documented that coresidence has been viewed as a form of financial assistance to elderly parents (Jones 2007). This may explain the smaller amount of financial exchange compared to emotional and practical support between generations in coresident households. Having said that, the discrepancies across countries in relation to the exchange of emotional, financial and practical support shed lights on underlying socio-cultural and demographic differences among the three countries. For example, the exchange of emotional and functional support between adult children and parents-in-law was found to be more regular among the sample in traditional and patriarchal Hanoi.

3.2 *Norms and Familistic Values*

Guided by the intergenerational solidarity framework, this section examines associational (i.e. the frequency of family interaction, activities) and normative elements which include filial norms and familistic values to reflect upon perceptions and attitudes towards care responsibilities within intergenerational *coresident households* in the three societies. In addition, family relationships and norms related to filial and familial obligations are considered significant underlying factors accounting for the various dimensions of support between generations and further delineate the various patterns of intergenerational relations in Bangkok Metropolis, Hanoi and Kuala Lumpur. More importantly, while the previous section examined the practice of intergenerational support, this section looks into the attitudes towards care through the individual's expectation of familial responsibilities on the provision of support to one's own parents and parents-in-law, which was strongly prescribed by the patriarchal family system and societal norms.

3.2.1 Associational Solidarity and Normative Elements

Results showed that bonding and relationships between families in coresident households were close. Specifically, there was a high frequency of having a meal with the family; on average, they tended to have supper together 'several times a week' as part of the regular family bonding activities. Country differences were reported where this family practice tends to be least regular in Bangkok Metropolis and most frequent in Hanoi, $F=50.96$, $p<0.001$ (See Table 5.2). In addition, on average, Hanoi families reported the least family outings, reporting engaging in family leisure activities once a year or less, with an average score of 2; while those in Kuala Lumpur had an average score of 4.22 and Bangkok Metropolis, with an average score of 4.86, tended to have them once a month, $F=308.97$, $p<0.001$.

The overall pattern shows that respondents expressed strong feeling of gratitude towards their parents' efforts in their up-bringing and clearly indicated their intention to contribute and support their parent's livelihood (average scores ranged between 'somewhat agree' and 'agree') (see Table 5.2). However, some discrepancies across three samples were detected with Kuala Lumpur tending to report the highest means scores for feeling grateful to parents, $F=137.65$, $p<0.001$. While it was found that Hanoi reported the highest score for feeling grateful to parents, they also revealed the lowest mean score for provision of support to parents, $F=61.74$, $p<0.001$.

Based on these findings, it can be seen that the families in all three samples had strong family values about filial responsibility towards parents' well-being, with a more consistent pattern being observed across gender and marital status of adult children, especially in the case of Bangkok Metropolis and Kuala Lumpur. Specifically, it was found that unmarried adult children, both men and women, in Bangkok Metropolis and Kuala Lumpur were perceived to have greater responsibility towards their own parents, while, in Hanoi, men irrespective of their marital status were expected to support their own parents financially. It is also obvious that in Hanoi, daughters, especially married daughters, were also least expected to contribute to their own parent's financial well-being while married women or daughters-in-law tended to have greater responsibility for supporting their parents-in-law than married sons. In addition, the sample in Hanoi also perceived that married sons have the least responsibility to contribute financially to parents-in-law compared to those in Bangkok Metropolis and Kuala Lumpur.

In other words, while there was a consistent pattern of filial norms towards married men and unmarried children in which married sons and, unmarried sons and daughters were expected to provide financial support to their own parents. This evidence supports the notion on filial responsibility of sons in the provision of parental support in Southeast Asian families. However, the greater expectations on married daughters than on married sons to perform filial responsibilities to parents-in-law reflected a stronger patriarchal norm among families in Hanoi compared to Kuala Lumpur and Bangkok Metropolis. Date (2015) suggested that the differentiation of expectation of familial responsibilities based on gender and marital status will be useful to explore the diversity of filial norms and family systems in Asian societies, including Malaysia, Thailand and Vietnam. Thus, these findings will be discussed in relation to the patriarchal family norm across the three societies in the following discussion section.

3.3 *Characteristics of Adult Children and Intergenerational Support*

3.3.1 Age

Literature showed that the provision of support tended to follow different age trajectories. In co-resident households, the flow of support may vary according to children's age/marital cycle: Transition in the direction of support may be more likely to follow the path of satisfying adult children's needs at the early stage of adult children's marriage and at the late stage may function to satisfy elderly parents' needs (Chen 2005; Zhang 2004). In addition, the role and attitudes towards intergenerational support showed different patterns across age groups. Adult children of the younger cohort, especially dual-career couples, were found to provide greater financial support in exchange for childcare (Parker & Patten 2013); while older children who may experience numerous stresses in their careers, marriages, and bringing up of off-spring, and were less agreeable to multigenerational living arrangements than younger ones (Hsu, Lew-Ting & Wu 2001).

In this section we focused on age group differences pertaining to the transaction of emotional, financial and domestic chores assistance between age groups in the three Southeast Asia societies. Specifically, samples were divided into three age groups, namely young, middle and old for ANOVA comparison analysis (See Table 5.3). There were some similarities in the patterns of intergenerational support across age groups in Bangkok Metropolis, Hanoi and Kuala Lumpur. In the first instance, the transaction of financial, domestic tasks, and emotional support was greater from one's own parents to adult children among those in the young age group than those in the old age group across these three societies, with emotional support being the most regular, followed by domestic tasks and financial support. As expected, upward support from adult children to parents was more regular among the middle and old generations. The transaction between adult children and parents-in-law (PIL) was more regular among younger generations. Age difference in intergenerational transactions was found to be more obvious between adult children and their own parents compared to PIL, especially in relation to upward support from parents to adult children.

TABLE 5.3 Age differences in the intergenerational relations in Bangkok Metropolis, Hanoi and Kuala Lumpur

Intergenerational Support	Bangkok Metropolis, Mean				Hanoi, Mean				Kuala Lumpur, Mean			
	Y	M	Old	F-value	Y	M	Old	F-value	Y	M	Old	F-value
Support to parents												
Financial support	2.82	3.50	3.84	11.47***	2.17	2.86	2.62	7.93***	2.53	3.33	2.86	58.75***
Emotional support	3.48	3.39	3.48	–	3.35	3.35	3.20	–	3.23	3.38	3.02	–
Household chores support	3.28	3.40	3.58	–	2.31	3.14	3.31	18.78***	3.00	3.33	3.00	4.01*
Support from parents												
Financial support	2.62	1.71	1.36	20.84***	2.90	1.57	1.30	57.68***	2.93	1.66	1.28	64.89***
Emotional support	3.46	2.85	1.94	25.07***	3.34	3.10	2.76	8.99***	3.29	2.76	2.24	24.21***
Household chores support	3.26	2.85	1.94	21.44***	3.11	1.65	1.26	93.92***	3.11	2.28	1.97	33.76***
Support to PIL												
Financial support	2.18	2.53	2.80	–	2.52	2.66	2.44	–	2.38	2.36	2.44	–
Emotional support	2.24	2.81	2.36	–	2.98	3.04	2.99	–	2.69	2.46	2.38	–
Household chores support	2.16	2.47	2.60	–	2.97	2.94	3.15	–	2.72	2.48	2.31	–
Support from PIL												
Financial support	1.58	1.43	1.36	–	2.11	1.44	1.24	20.01***	1.66	1.26	1.13	4.35*
Emotional support	1.92	2.13	2.12	–	2.90	2.89	2.72	–	2.26	2.11	2.06	–
Household chores support	1.95	1.45	1.72	2.05	2.24	1.41	1.25	22.22***	2.22	1.77	1.69	3.44*

TABLE 5.3 Age differences in the intergenerational relations in Bangkok Metropolis, Hanoi and Kuala Lumpur (*cont.*)

Intergenerational Support	Bangkok Metropolis, Mean				Hanoi, Mean				Kuala Lumpur, Mean			
	Y	M	Old	F-value	Y	M	Old	F-value	Y	M	Old	F-value
Provided financial support from:												
Unmarried adult man to own parents	6.30	5.88	6.29	4.73*	5.61	5.42	4.82	6.35**	5.96	6.05	6.00	–
Unmarried adult woman to own parents	6.33	5.84	6.33	7.07**	5.24	4.91	4.43	5.94**	5.95	5.96	6.00	–
Married adult man to own parents	6.06	5.68	5.54	–	5.68	5.74	4.97	9.71***	5.91	5.92	6.00	–
Married adult woman to own parents	6.04	5.67	5.83	–	3.91	3.80	3.36	–	5.24	5.87	5.94	–
Married man to parents-in-law	5.74	5.38	5.52	–	3.10	3.02	2.66	4.36*	5.55	5.58	5.86	–
Married woman to parents-in-law	5.68	5.38	5.52	5.14**	5.24	5.27	4.81	–	5.47	5.50	5.71	–

Note: p*<.05; p**<.01; p***<.001 ; Age group: Y=Young, M=Middle, Old=Old

Comparing the three countries, a different pattern of exchange was found among respondents in the Hanoi and Kuala Lumpur samples. While children in the youngest age group received more support from their parents than other age groups, those in the middle age group in Hanoi and Kuala Lumpur were found to provide more financial support to their own parents. In addition, downward support from PIL to adult children was also significantly more regular in the youngest age group for those societies. Age difference in upward and downward support between adult children to parents-in-law was not detected among Bangkok families.

In terms of familial responsibilities as the indicator for filial and patriarchal norms, no age difference was detected in Kuala Lumpur. It is interesting to note that a similar pattern was reported across age groups in Hanoi, which implied strong expectation of financial responsibility on sons to support their own parents than married daughters, and married daughters bear greater responsibility to support PIL. Age comparison also revealed that the youngest age group in Hanoi expressed a significantly stronger opinion on the financial responsibility of unmarried children and married sons to support their own parents. In Bangkok Metropolis, young adult children perceived that married women have the greatest responsibility to support PIL; while those in the middle age group showed the strongest agreement with the notion that unmarried children (both male and female) should support their own parents financially. This finding implied that the middle age group in Bangkok Metropolis, who were often 'sandwiched' between demands from their career, upbringing of children, and support to their parents, expected their unmarried children to share more responsibility on the provision of support to their own parents.

3.3.2 Education Level

Results in Table 5.4 showed that intergenerational support tended to be differentiated by educational levels. In accordance with expectations, adult children who were less educated tend to receive less support from their parents, particularly financial support. Similar patterns were detected in all three societies. Cross-country differences were detected in downward intergenerational support across education levels. It was revealed that in Kuala Lumpur, those who are less educated were significantly more likely to support parents with financial and household chores assistance, while in Hanoi, more educated adult children provided significantly greater emotional support to their own parents. A different pattern of support from PIL was also revealed in the case of Hanoi where less educated adult children received significantly less household chore support from PIL. However, they were compensated with significantly more regular financial support from PIL as compared to those with a higher education attainment.

TABLE 5.4 Education level differences in the intergenerational relations in Bangkok Metropolis, Hanoi and Kuala Lumpur

Intergenerational Support	Bangkok Metropolis, Mean			Hanoi, Mean			Kuala Lumpur, Mean		
	Low	High	t-value sig	Low	High	t-value sig	Low	High	t-value sig
Support to parents									
Financial support	3.43	3.09	–	2.56	2.30	–	2.82	2.57	2.27**
Emotional support	3.33	3.58	–	3.25	3.49	2.03*	3.28	3.22	–
Household chores	3.38	3.39	–	2.76	2.68	–	3.16	2.95	2.51**
Support from parents									
Financial support	1.73	2.38	-3.79***	1.87	2.91	-6.11***	2.39	2.86	-4.31***
Emotional support	2.62	3.27	-3.79***	3.08	3.28	–	3.02	3.27	-2.96***
Household chores	2.41	2.93	-2.79***	2.00	2.99	-6.05***	2.81	2.99	–
Support to PIL									
Financial support	2.37	2.62	–	2.51	2.76	0.78	2.30	2.55	–
Emotional support	2.37	2.71	–	3.01	2.96	-1.06	2.48	2.68	–
Household chores support	2.42	2.36	–	3.00	3.09	0.23	2.54	2.61	–
Support from PIL									
Financial support	1.35	1.62	–	1.62	1.33	2.03**	1.45	1.34	–
Emotional support	1.95	2.20	–	2.84	2.82	–	2.08	2.36	–
Household chores support	1.62	1.78	–	2.00	2.99	-2.01*	1.89	2.09	–
Provided financial support from:									
Unmarried adult man to own parents	6.00	6.33	-2.53*	5.27	5.53	–	5.94	6.04	–
Unmarried adult woman to own parents	6.02	6.33	-2.46*	4.82	5.23	–	5.92	5.98	–
Married adult man to own parents	5.74	6.03	-2.18*	5.43	5.76	–	5.88	5.96	–
Married adult woman to own parents	5.75	5.99	–	3.57	4.16	-2.56**	5.81	5.90	–
Married man to parents-in-law	5.47	5.42	–	2.77	3.49	4.36*	5.55	5.60	–
Married woman to parents-in-law	5.42	5.51	–	5.17	5.05	–	5.43	5.55	–

Note: p*<.05; p**<.01; p***<.001

In terms of filial responsibilities, differences in intergenerational support across education levels were only detected between families in Bangkok Metropolis and Hanoi. In Bangkok Metropolis, adult children who were more educated perceive greater financial responsibility lies with unmarried children (irrespective of gender) and married men to their own parents than those who were less educated. While in Hanoi, a different pattern of expectations on filial responsibilities was revealed. Adult children with higher education attainment expected married daughters/women to provide greater financial assistance to their own parents and similarly, they also had a significantly greater expectation for married men to provide greater financial assistance towards PIL compared to those who were less educated. These findings reflect differences in patriarchal family norms according to education level in Hanoi, and variations in filial expectations for unmarried children and married sons according to education level, in Bangkok Metropolis.

3.4 *Gender and Marital Status*

3.4.1 Gender

Women played a key role in support provision to parents and more so in terms of emotional and functional than financial support. The following section presents evidence on the gendered divisions of support and the implications of marital status on intergenerational support across the three societies. The results in Table 5.5 show the significant effects of gender on intergenerational support among the three societies. Gender differences were found in all types of support in the Kuala Lumpur sample, in which sons tended to provide more financial support but daughters seemed to offer more emotional and functional support in the form of household chores. Within the Bangkok Metropolis sample, gender differences only appeared for functional support, in that daughters tended to provide more support for household chores for their parents. The results seemed to tie in well with the gender roles and male breadwinner model. In contrast, the only exception to this gendered intergenerational support provision was in Hanoi. Specifically, sons tended to provide more financial and functional support than daughters among the sample in Hanoi.

In relations to the types of support received from parents, country differences were detected. In Bangkok Metropolis, sons were significantly more likely to receive financial support from parents compared to daughters. In contrast, daughters in the Kuala Lumpur sample tended to receive greater financial support from their parents than sons. Interestingly, parents in the Bangkok Metropolis sample also tended to provide sons with significantly more household chores support compared to daughters. The results demonstrated the

TABLE 5.5 Gender differences in the intergenerational relations in Bangkok Metropolis, Hanoi and Kuala Lumpur

Intergenerational Support	Bangkok Metropolis, Mean			Hanoi, Mean			Kuala Lumpur, Mean		
	Son	Daughter	t-test	Son	Daughter	t-test	Son	Daughter	t-test
Provided support to parents									
Financial support	3.21	3.31	–	2.85	2.08	5.08***	2.84	2.54	2.77**
Emotional support	3.31	3.55	–	3.25	3.38	–	3.17	3.34	−2.08*
Household chores support	3.10	3.58	−2.56*	2.99	2.49	3.54***	2.94	3.19	−2.79**
Received support from parents									
Financial support	2.30	1.88	2.35*	2.16	2.15	–	2.50	2.74	−2.17*
Emotional support	2.96	2.92	–	3.07	3.20	–	3.09	3.19	–
Household chores support	2.92	2.49	2.25*	2.25	2.30	–	2.87	2.93	–
Provided support to parents-in-law									
Financial support	2.61	2.40	–	2.12	2.84	−4.30***	2.67	2.13	2.85**
Emotional support	2.29	2.63	–	2.60	3.28	−5.29***	2.56	2.54	–
Household chores support	2.21	2.49	–	2.29	3.50	−7.78***	2.44	2.67	–
Received support from parents-in-law									
Financial support	1.47	1.46	–	1.32	1.74	−3.69***	1.32	1.50	–
Emotional support	1.92	2.13	–	2.46	3.10	−4.78***	2.16	2.18	–
Household chores support	1.74	1.65	–	1.39	1.76	−3.06**	1.95	1.96	–
Provided financial support from:									
Unmarried adult man to own parents	6.15	6.16	–	5.24	5.43	–	5.93	6.03	–

TABLE 5.5 Gender differences in the intergenerational relations in Bangkok Metropolis, Hanoi and Kuala Lumpur (*cont.*)

Intergenerational Support	Bangkok Metropolis, Mean			Hanoi, Mean			Kuala Lumpur, Mean		
	Son	Daughter	t-test	Son	Daughter	t-test	Son	Daughter	t-test
Unmarried adult woman to own parents	6.09	6.22	–	4.72	5.11	–	5.90	6.01	–
Married adult man to own parents	5.95	5.83	–	5.51	5.49	–	5.82	6.02	−2.38*
Married adult woman to own parents	5.91	5.83	–	3.64	3.81	–	5.73	5.97	−2.78**
Married man to parents-in-law	5.56	5.57	–	2.97	2.95	–	5.53	5.62	–
Married woman to parents-in-law	5.40	5.51	–	5.08	5.18	–	5.47	5.51	–

Note: p*<.05; p**<.01; p***<.001

importance of sons in Bangkok Metropolis, whereas in Kuala Lumpur, the patriarchal norms in relations to support given by parents were less obvious. This finding showed a dependency of sons on parents for financial support amongst the Bangkok Metropolis sample. This may also reflect a lengthening of parental investment to include adult children, especially sons (Croll 2006) with the spread of investment to include financial assistance during marriage preparation, and, early stage of career and parenthood (Chen 2005; Zhang 2004). In addition, it could also be a reflection of the preference for sons among the urbanised sample of Bangkok Metropolis. The parental support of providing household chores assistance for sons may also indicate a change in the relationship between parents and daughters among families in Bangkok Metropolis. Past studies, in the 1980s, documented a no-sex bias in child preference (See chapter 3 Kamnuansilpa, Chamratrithirong & Knodel 1982; Wongboonsin & Ruffolo 1995) as compared to a clear son preference in the 1970s among the urban population in Thailand (Prachuabmoh & Knodel 1977 – See chapter 3, Section 1.3). While, the census did not gather information on race or ethnicity, many people were of Thai ethnicity, others were of full or partial Chinese,

Indian and other ancestries. Thakur (1990) reported strong son preference among Indians in Bangkok; however, the son preference tended to be stronger among the less educated and more financially constrained group. Thus, due to the lack of recent data, this calls for further investigation on the dynamic and quality of parent-children relationships among the current population of Thailand, especially between parents and daughters.

While no significant gender difference was found in upward and downward intergenerational support for PIL in the Bangkok Metropolis and Kuala Lumpur samples, a different pattern was observed in Hanoi. The Hanoi sample presented a unique case in which daughters provided and received significantly more support than sons from PIL for all three types of support. The only exception was the provision of financial support in the Kuala Lumpur sample wherein PIL provide significantly more regular support for sons than daughters. Thus, it is interesting to note the salience of children's gender in the support provider role for PIL in the Hanoi sample, which reflected the apparent influence of patriarchal norms among families in the Hanoi sample that led to daughters providing more support for PIL within co-resident living arrangements. It can also be argued that the change of PIL-daughter relationship in which daughters received more support from PIL may be due to co-resident living arrangements which increased the odds of support from the PIL. It may suggest that PIL's support was intended for the sons, which indirectly contributed to the support for daughters-in-law in the Hanoi sample.

In terms of norms, Table 5.6 demonstrated that the significant effect of gender in the expectation of financial support was only found in the Kuala Lumpur sample. Within this sample, daughters incoresident households had higher expectations for married adult men/sons and women/daughters to provide financial support to their own parents compared to sons. The expectation for married adult women/daughters was not in accordance with the notion of patriarchal family norms in which married women were often least expected to provide financially for their own parents. This may imply changes in familial norms among females in the Kuala Lumpur sample. As half of the Kuala Lumpur sample comprised Malays, previous studies noted that among Malay families, females were expected to contribute more in the care-giving of parents (See chapter 2). Also, in Kuala Lumpur, since married women were found to be more likely to work (Kenayathulla 2013), the burden of financial support also falls on them. Again, this reflected the active contribution in care provision and old-age support from married daughters. There were no significant differences across and within countries in terms of expectations of support for parents-in-law.

TABLE 5.6 Marital status difference in the intergenerational relations in Bangkok Metropolis, Hanoi and Kuala Lumpur

Intergenerational support	**Bangkok Metropolis, Mean**			**Hanoi, Mean**			**Kuala Lumpur, Mean**		
	Married	**Unmarried**	**t-test**	**Married**	**Unmarried**	**t-test**	**Married**	**Unmarried**	**t-test**
Provided support to parents									
Financial support	3.53	3.00	2.839**	2.57	2.26	–	3.29	2.49	7.27***
Emotional support	3.51	3.35	–	3.29	3.43	–	3.28	3.24	–
Household chores support	3.34	3.29	–	3.01	2.14	5.75***	3.23	3.01	2.42*
Received support from parents									
Financial support	1.69	2.48	–4.30***	1.65	3.35	–10.13***	1.66	2.96	–12.30***
Emotional support	2.72	3.16	–2.37*	3.06	3.42	–3.00**	2.64	3.31	–6.51***
Household chores support	2.14	3.25	–6.00***	1.72	3.51	–13.41***	2.23	3.15	–8.45***
Provided financial support from:									
Unmarried adult man to own parents	6.07	6.27	–	5.11	5.86	–4.15***	6.00	5.97	–
Unmarried adult woman to own parents	6.06	6.28	–	4.68	5.47	–4.09***	5.93	5.96	–
Married adult man to own parents	5.78	6.03	–	5.41	5.75	–2.02*	5.96	5.91	–
Married adult woman to own parents	5.79	5.94	–	3.54	4.16	–2.84**	5.90	5.83	–
Married man to parents-in-law	5.46	5.69	–	2.83	3.32	–2.17*	5.61	5.56	–
Married woman to parents-in-law	5.41	5.54	–	5.07	5.29	–	5.53	5.47	–

Note: p*<.05; p**<.01; p***<.001

3.4.2 Marital Status

Marital status also entailed expanded intergenerational exchanges and differences in expectations of intergenerational support. Results across the three societies showed that being unmarried entailed greater support from parents in all three types of support. High coresidence and lower financial stability of early career adults may offer some insight as to why the unmarried received higher support for financial, emotional, and household chores when compared to married adults.

In terms of upward support, Table 5.6 shows that being married entailed significantly higher financial and household chores support to parents, particularly in the Kuala Lumpur sample. However, for the Bangkok Metropolis sample, the provision of financial support was higher whereas for Hanoi, household chores support was higher. Data also showed that the majority of male spouses (95.5%) were working whereas nearly two thirds (57.1%) of female spouses were working. Thus, the repercussions of marital status – and the likelihood of married women being employed – on intergenerational support could be supported by the present study.

As seen in Table 5.7, comparison across societies showed that significant differences in the expectations for financial support provision to parents and parents-in-law between married and unmarried adults were only observed in the Hanoi sample. There were significantly greater expectations for financial support provision to one's own parents by unmarried adults compared to married adults. Similarly, the unmarried sample in Hanoi not only perceived that married men should have a greater responsibility to support PIL, they also had higher expectations of married women to support their own parents than of married men. Patriarchy favoured the male lineage and thus, parental support expectations are greatest on males regardless of their marital status. Nonetheless, when it came to their own parents, there were greater expectations of married women to provide financial support.

3.4.3 Interaction of Marital Status and Gendered Provision of Support

Results from multi-country data analysis in Table 5.7 show that there were differences in intergenerational support to parents according to gender and marital status in terms of financial, emotional and household chores support. We argued that not only gender, but also the marital status of children, had different implications for intergenerational support to and from parents, as well as the expectations of support to parents and parents-in-law.

In general, upward flow of support among married sons and daughters was more in the form of monetary and domestic task support but less in the form of time and energy spent in listening to parents' problems. Specifically, financial

TABLE 5.7 Marital status and gender differences in the intergenerational relations in Bangkok Metropolis, Hanoi and Kuala Lumpur

Intergenerational support	Bangkok Metropolis, Mean					Hanoi, Mean					Kuala Lumpur, Mean				
	MM	MW	UM	UW	F	MM	MW	UM	UW	F	MM	MW	UM	UW	F
Provided support to parents															
Financial support	3.83	3.38	2.67	3.32	5.70**	3.15	2.05	2.31	2.18	13.47***	3.54	3.08	2.64	2.31	18.19***
Emotional support	3.60	3.46	3.04	3.66	–	3.26	3.31	3.26	3.66	–	3.22	3.33	3.15	3.34	–
Household chores support	3.30	3.36	2.88	3.68	2.81*	3.48	2.58	2.04	2.27	23.54***	3.21	3.26	2.86	3.18	4.66**
Received support from parents															
Financial support	1.68	1.70	2.75	2.21	7.94***	1.60	1.69	3.24	3.49	45.82***	1.43	1.87	2.82	3.13	44.41***
Emotional support	2.53	2.83	3.33	3.00	2.80*	2.94	3.17	3.41	3.44	3.95**	2.41	2.85	3.30	3.32	18.30***
Household chores support	2.15	2.13	3.50	3.00	13.24***	1.56	1.86	3.50	3.51	61.65***	2.06	2.38	3.11	2.92	25.00***
Provided financial support from:															
Unmarried adult man to own parents	6.02	6.10	6.27	6.26	–	4.97	5.22	5.69	6.10	5.48**	6.01	5.99	5.89	6.06	–
Unmarried adult woman to own parents	5.96	6.11	6.21	6.34	–	4.41	4.89	5.20	5.83	7.06***	5.92	5.94	5.88	6.04	–
Married adult man to own parents	5.84	5.74	6.08	5.98	–	5.37	5.44	5.81	5.66	–	5.93	5.99	5.78	6.05	–
Married adult woman to own parents	5.78	5.80	6.06	5.83	–	3.48	3.58	3.96	4.41	3.10*	5.88	5.93	5.68	6.00	3.44*
Married man to parents-in-law	5.51	5.44	5.65	5.72	–	2.86	2.81	3.19	3.49	–	5.71	5.52	5.46	5.67	–
Married woman to parents-in-law	5.42	5.40	5.44	5.64	–	5.02	5.11	5.19	5.44	–	5.73	5.35	5.38	5.58	–

Note: MM= Married man; MW= Married women; UM= Unmarried man; UW= Unmarried women
$p^{*}<.05$; $p^{**}<.01$; $p^{***}<.001$

provision remained highest for married sons and similar results were reported in all three societies (see Table 5.7). Country comparison also showed that gender and marital status have different implications on household chores support according to countries. In Hanoi and Kuala Lumpur, domestic task support to parents was more likely provided by married sons and daughters. However, in Bangkok Metropolis, this type of support was more provided by daughters, irrespective of their marital status, than sons.

In terms of the downward provision of intergenerational support, Table 5.7 also demonstrated the significance of children's marital status and gender in the types of support provided by parents. All three types of support from parents significantly differed by marital status and gender with country specific variations. It is notable that financial and emotional support from parents were mostly provided to unmarried daughters in Hanoi and Kuala Lumpur. Meanwhile, unmarried sons in Bangkok Metropolis tended to reap the highest financial support from parents. The discrepancy among the country samples was also observed for functional support in which unmarried sons tended to be given most of these two kinds of support by their parents in both Bangkok Metropolis and Kuala Lumpur; while parents in Hanoi tended to support unmarried daughters in their domestic chores.

Interestingly, cross countries differences were observed in cross countries comparisons. Married daughters in Bangkok Metropolis reported the highest mean of 3.38 in financial support to parents in comparison to their counterparts in Kuala Lumpur and Hanoi, with a mean of 3.08 and 2.05 respectively. It is important to note that married women in Bangkok Metropolis and Kuala Lumpur were the second highest financial support providers after married men. In Hanoi, married women have the lowest mean of 2.05 in providing financial support to parents, which is slightly below the mean of 2.18 for unmarried women.

In terms of who were expected to provide financial support for parents, significant differences by marital status and gender was only observed in the Hanoi sample. Unmarried daughters have the highest expectations for all types of providers, including for married women's support to their own parents. This means that with respect to financial support expectations towards parents, marital status afforded lower expectations for females but higher expectations for males. In Hanoi, unmarried daughters tended to expect more from other family providers. This may also be attributable to the fact that, in reality, unmarried daughters were increasingly supplying parental support in the steadily-increasing multigenerational family; therefore, their expectations of others to chip in some financial support also increased.

3.5 *Characteristics of Parents and Intergenerational Support*

In accordance with the depiction presented in Part 1 of this volume, data from the current study indicate that family support in caring for other family members was evident among co-resident families in the three Southeast Asian societies, especially care for parents. Data showed that 26.1% had provided care and support to another family member such as a spouse, parent, parent-in-law or children at some point in their life. Among those who had provided care for other family members, a majority or 74% provided care to their parents, followed by 17.4% parents-in-law,5% spouse and 3.6% children. While a similar pattern of care provision was reported in Kuala Lumpur and Hanoi, the proportion was greater in Hanoi (36.7%) as compared to Kuala Lumpur (20.4%). The larger proportion in Hanoi may be attributable to its older age cohort where the older sample also meant they were more likely to have older parents or parents-in-law who needed more assistance. There was no data available on provision of care for other family members for Bangkok Metropolis.

In this section, the characteristics of parents are examined in terms of parental health status, marital status, old age, and living arrangements. These variables are also used as indicators of the demand and need of care for dependent family members, especially parents (See Table 5.8). It is assumed that the demand for care tended to be stronger among those who had: a living parent with poor health status, in old age (above 65 years old); parents with no spouse; and also among those who stayed in the same household with parents and their own children, irrespective of their health status.

In relation to the *marital status of parents,* two categories were created where parents or parents-in-law who were married during the survey period were labelled as 'has spouse' and those who are widowed or divorced were categorised as 'without spouse.' Countries difference was detected with Kuala Lumpur reporting the highest number of parents with 'no spouse' (75.8%), followed by 70.8% in Hanoi and 51.8% in Bangkok Metropolis. As for the *age of parents*, the percentage of those reported to have at least one parent above 65 years old at the time of the study ranged from 24.2% in Kuala Lumpur to over 50% in Hanoi and Bangkok Metropolis. However, our data on *parental marital status* and *old age* do not specifically differentiate between elderly parents who were coresiding or not coresiding with adult children in the current household. Thus, this may not provide a comprehensive picture of the burden of care and support for parents within the same household but the literature still considered parent's marital status and old age as robust indicators on the burden of caring for elderly parents (Teh, Ng, Tey & Siti-Norlasiah 2013; Silverstein, Gan & Yang 2006).

TABLE 5.8 Indicators for demand of care

	Bangkok Metropolis	Hanoi	Kuala Lumpur
Parental Marital Status			
Both parent & PIL (No spouse)	9.2%	20.0%	8.4%
Parent only (No spouse)	33.4%	37.2%	60.8%
PIL only (No spouse)	9.2 %	13.3%	6.6%
Both parent & PIL (Has spouse)	48.2%	29.5%	24.2%
Parental Age			
At least one parent above 65 years old	50.1%	54.2%	26.1%
Adult children with:			
At least 1 child age 7 or below	22.7%	35.4%	15.9%
Number of children in household (mean)	0.86	1.22	0.58
0	52.3%	32.1%	75.3%
1	38.6%	24.8%	6.8%
2	19.5%	33.9%	8.6%
3–6	9.1%	9.2%	9.3%

Note: PIL=Parents in law

Another indicator for the burden of caring and support included is the *number of children in household* and if they had *young children aged 7 and below* living in the same household. Discrepancies across societies provide information to support socio-demographic variation across Bangkok Metropolis, Hanoi and Kuala Lumpur. In Hanoi, 70% of the intergenerational households were with children of such age; while only one third, and almost half of those in Kuala Lumpur and Bangkok Metropolis, respectively, reported having children aged 7 or below in their household. While only 22.2% of the total co-resident households had young children below 7 years old, differences were revealed across countries; the highest number or 35.4% were reported among families in Hanoi, followed by 22.7% in Bangkok Metropolis and 15.9% in Kuala Lumpur. This may imply a significant amount of childcare provision among these co-resident families.

Parental health status is used as one of the proxy indicators of burden of caring for parents with health problems. Higher scores indicate a higher degree of poor health among living parents (including parents-in-law). Overall, it can be seen that co-resident families in Hanoi tended to experience greater demand for care due to the parent's poorer health status compared to their counterparts in Bangkok Metropolis and Kuala Lumpur, F=69.89, p<.001. Results showed that more than 40% of the sample in Hanoi reported they had at least one unhealthy parent as compared to only 27.8% in Bangkok Metropolis and 11% in Kuala Lumpur.

Table 5.9 presented findings on intergenerational support exchange based on parental health status in Bangkok Metropolis, Hanoi and Kuala Lumpur. Findings from t-tests showed that parental health status was closely related to provision of support from parents to adult children.

Interestingly, data showed that *parental health status* was more positively related to *downward support* from parents to adult children than upward support from adult children to parents, especially in Bangkok Metropolis and Hanoi. Among Hanoi families, better health status among parents was only significantly related to greater downward support of finance, emotional and household chore assistance from parents to adult children. In the Bangkok Metropolis sample, parents with better health provided more domestic assistance for adult children. In contrast, the flow and transaction support according to parental health status was most obvious in Kuala Lumpur. Adult children tended to receive a greater extent of financial support and help in domestic tasks from parents who were in good health. In return, adult children were also found to provide more regular financial and emotional support to parents who were unhealthy.

Findings showed that the transaction of care provision between adult children and PIL was not significantly related to health status, with the exception of Hanoi. PIL who had better health provided significantly more regular financial and household chore support to adult children in Hanoi while parents having worse health did not significantly correlate to more support from adult children. The current findings are different from past studies that showed that the health condition of elderly parents was an important indicator in children's provision of support (or upward support) in Western (Silverstein et al. 2006), East Asian (Lin & Yi 2013) and Southeast Asian societies (Chan 2005; Biddlecom et al. 2002; Anh et al. 1997).

4 Factors Affecting Intergenerational Care Relations

Table 5.10 presents the results of the multiple regression models that were carried out to determine the unique predictors for intergenerational support amongst the sample from Bangkok Metropolis, Hanoi and Kaula Lumpur. Specifically, predictors that include characteristics of adult children and parents, filial norms, family interaction, and support from parent(s) to adult

TABLE 5.9 Intergenerational support and parental health status in Bangkok Metropolis, Hanoi and Kuala Lumpur

Intergenerational support	Bangkok Metropolis			Hanoi			Kuala Lumpur		
	Healthy	Unhealthy	t-test	Healthy	Unhealthy	t-test	Healthy	Unhealthy	t-test
Support to parents									
Financial support	3.22	3.37	–	2.46	2.48	–	2.64	3.17	-3.59^{**}
Emotional support	3.45	3.44	–	3.38	3.23	–	3.22	3.54	-2.39^{*}
Household chores support	3.38	3.32	–	2.63	2.88	–	3.05	3.27	–
Support from parents									
Financial support	2.08	1.94	–	2.40	1.83	3.71^{***}	2.68	2.19	3.00^{**}
Emotional support	2.91	2.89	–	3.24	2.99	2.18^{*}	3.16	2.98	–
Household chores support	2.79	2.27	2.35^{*}	2.65	1.77	6.12^{***}	2.94	2.59	2.22^{*}
Financial assistance	1.61	1.51	–	2.10	1.98	–	1.03	1.15	–
Support to PIL									
Financial support	2.59	2.53	–	2.58	2.52	–	2.43	2.17	–
Emotional support	2.64	2.59	–	3.09	2.93	–	2.55	2.43	–
Household chores support	2.53	2.41	–	3.04	2.99	–	2.50	2.78	–
Support from PIL									
Financial support	1.37	1.71	–	1.82	1.35	3.85^{***}	1.41	1.35	–
Emotional support	2.19	2.12	–	2.89	2.79	–	2.22	1.87	–
Household chores support	1.73	1.76	–	1.91	1.34	4.57^{***}	1.93	1.91	–
Financial assistance	1.45	1.49	–	1.95	2.01	–	1.04	1.00	–

Note: $p^{*}<.05$; $p^{**}<.01$; $p^{***}<.001$; PIL = Parents in law

TABLE 5.10 Multiple regression on parents for predicting support from adult children to parents among coresident families in Bangkok Metropolis, Hanoi and Kuala Lumpur

Predictors	Unstandardised Beta, Unβ		
	Bangkok Metropolis	Hanoi	KualaLumpur
Adult children characteristics			
Status (ref: Married Son)			
Married Daughter	0.61	-0.22	-1.45**
Unmarried Son	-5.18***	-6.31***	-6.08***
Unmarried Daughter	-2.20*	-5.97***	-6.00***
Age cohort (ref: Young)			
Older generation	1.75*	2.00**	-0.01
Middle generation	0.62	0.93	-2.64**
AC Education level	-0.29	-0.86	-0.67
Children below 7 (at least 1)	0.26	-0.32	0.93
Parental characteristics			
Age 65 or > (at least 1)	1.52*	0.89	0.96*
High health demand	0.61	-0.44	0.48
No spouse	-.11	0.22	.97**
Filial norm	1.25***	0.19	0.00
Family interaction	0.32**	0.56***	0.06
Support from Parents to AC	0.43***	0.52***	.28***
Others predictors			
Urban		-44	-0.30
Living standard		-.13	-0.54**
Ethnicity (ref: Malay)			
Chinese			-0.38
Indian			-0.25
Adjusted R-squared	**0.50**	**0.61**	**0.51**
F	17.63***	33.74***	37.21***

Note: * p<0.05; **p<0.01; *** p<0.001
Support: Composite of Financial, Emotional and Care support from both Parents & PIL
Children age 7 or below: Adult children with at least one child age 7 or below (1=Yes, 0=No)
Age 65 or >: At least one parent age 65 or more (1=Yes, 0=No)
High health demand: 1=Yes, 0=No
Living standard: 1=High, 2=Medium, 3=Low/poor

children, were included in the models for predicting upward support from adult children to parents. In addition, country specific variables that include locality, living standards and ethnicity were also included but only for the Hanoi and Kuala Lumpur regression analysis. The main objective of this series of regression analyses is to examine and identify the unique predictors that determine the extent of care provision from adult children to parents, after taking into account variations of all the selected factors.

Overall, these models were all found to be significant ($p<0.01$) and the predictors entered into the final regression models explained a substantial portion of the variance in predicting upward support from adult children to parents among coresident families in Bangkok Metropolis (49% of variance), Hanoi (61% of variance) and Kuala Lumpur (51% of variance). In other words, the characteristics of adult children, parents, filial norms, family interaction and support from parents made a significant contribution in determining the extent of adult children providing support to their parents in all three societies.

4.1.1 Bangkok Metropolis

In the Bangkok Metropolis model, factors that made a significant contribution to upward intergenerational support includedgender, marital status, age, parent's age, norms, family relationships and reciprocal support from parents, with gender and marital status indicating the strongest contributionin the provision of support from adult children. Among those who coreside with their parents in Bangkok Metropolis, it was found that unmarried sons ($\beta=-5.18$) and daughters ($\beta=-2.20$) tended to be less likely to provide support to their parents compared to married sons.

Additionally, adult children in the old age group also reported greater support for parents ($\beta=1.75$). Adult children who reported having at least one parent above the age of 65 were also more likely to provide more support to their parents ($\beta=1.52$). Similarly, the extent of support provision to parents was also greater among adult children who endorsed filial norms ($\beta=1.25$), reported stronger family interaction ($\beta=0.32$), and received more regular support from parents ($\beta=0.43$) in terms of financial, emotional and domestic tasks.

4.1.2 Hanoi

Results for the Hanoi sample demonstrated that gender, marital status, age, education level, family relationships and support from parents predicted the extent of upward support from adult children to parents. Similar to Bangkok, marital status and gender were the strongest predictors in determining the support from adult children in the Hanoi sample. In particular, married sons had a stronger role in providing support to elderly parents than unmarried children, irrespective of their gender (β_{son}=–6.31; $\beta_{daughter}$=–5.97). Adult children who were older (β=2.00), reported more frequent family interaction (β=0.56) and support from parents (β=0.52),were more likely to provide higher levels of downward support to their parents. The results failed to show any significant contribution of locality and living standard in predicting the provision of support from adult children to parents among coresidentfamilies in Hanoi.

4.1.3 Kuala Lumpur

The intergeneration care provided by adult children to parents within the Kuala Lumpur sample was determined by a diverse group of variables;adult children's characteristics (i.e. marital status and gender) were the strongest predictors, with modest contributions from parental age, marital status and support provision as well as country-specific variable – living standards. Results from the regression analysis demonstrated that married sons were more likely to provide support to their parents compared to married daughters (β=–1.48) and unmarried children, irrespecive of gender (β_{son}=–6.08; $\beta_{daughter}$=–6.00) in the Kuala Lumpur sample. They also indicated that adult children in the middle age group (β=–2.64) were less likely to support their parents compared to those in young age groups. The characteristics of parents were also linked to downward support of parents in the sample. Adult children with at least one elderly parent over the age of 65 (β=0.90) and no spouse (β=0.97) were found to provide more support to their parents.

Evidence of mutual support between generations was also detected where parents who provided a greater extentof support to children (β=0.28) were more likely to receive more support from adult children in these coresident households. The addition of country specific variables made a significant contribution in explaining the variance of downward support from adult children to parents. It was found that controlling for the preceding predictors, adult children who reported poor living standards (β=–0.54) were less likely to provide more support to their parents than those with better living standards. However, the results failed to show any significant contribution of ethnicity and locality in predicting provision of support from adult children to parents among coresident families in Kuala Lumpur. In other words, the provision of support to parents wasnot significantly different between ethnic groups and between urban and rural areas.

5 Conclusion

Based on the Intergenerational Solidarity Framework, the findings highlight the significance of filial norms and practice of intergenerational support within these *co-resident families*, as well as the contribution of adult children and parent characteristics and, other family related factors that may make cross-generation care unique for these three Southeast Asian societies. These empirical findings on coresident households also pave the way to address the hypotheses for this volume, as discussed in chapter 1 and set the scene for a more integrated discussion about the provision of care across different living arrangements between these three Southeast Asian societies in chapter 8. Some of the key findings related to care and support within families of co-resident households are as follows:

The findings highlighted both similarities and differences in the practice and attitudes towards care provision within coresident households across the three Southeast Asian societies. The present findings demonstrated a *support-receiving pattern among parents* in multi-generational coresident households across Bangkok Metropolis, Hanoi and Kuala Lumpur. With no surprises and in line with the current literature, intergenerational support across Southeast Asia families tended to report more intense upward support from adult children to parents as compared to downward support from parents to children (Lin & Yi 2013; Chan 2005).

In terms of the types of support, the *exchange of emotional support* was more regular than financial and practical support between adult children and parents or parents-in-law across all three societies. On one hand, this finding is unexpected as instrumental support such as monetary and practical care was reported as the most intense intergenerational transfer, especially among traditional Asian societies (Lin & Yi 2013), which often lacked well-developed public old-age support systems (Parker & Patten 2013) and adequate financial security due to low SES among parents. On the other hand, in Southeast Asian families, coresidence itself may be considered as a type of informal support where companionship, financial, practical and emotional care was directly available for parents in this type of living arrangement; and for adult children, such arrangements helped both parties to share costs and domestic tasks (Jones 2007; Chan 2007; Teh et al. 2013). Therefore, it may be plausible that the nature of and the 'invisible' support within coresident households led to the under report of financial and practical exchange between generations.

While, some studies argued that the transaction of non-instrumental care was often taken for granted in the coresident household, others asserted that the dynamic of coresidence also varied from one country to another. For example, the 2015 Malaysia Population and Family Survey (MPFS) reported that 70% of older persons were living with others. It was found that Malaysian grandparents were not passive recipients but assumed different roles within the families that include culture/value socialisation agent, religious teachers, family 'watch dog' and, childcare provider especially during times of family adversity (Yusuf 2014). As for Hanoi, the role of parents within coresident households tended to change according to the family life cycle. Parents assumed the role of care provider to the family during the early stage of coresidence; and the role was reversed to that of care recipient within the household at a later stage (Le 2017). Knodel & colleagues (2013) noted an upward support flow within coresidence among Thai households. Specifically, daughters were the main care provider for parents and, also the most preferred family member for daily activities assistance (see literature in Part 1, chapter 3, Figure 3.11). Therefore, direct support within intergenerational coresidence was often taken for granted and, care transactions may not necessarily be financially related within coresident households in Southeast Asian societies.

Key findings from the regression analysis clearly show that the characteristics of adult children had a stronger contribution than parents' characteristics in predicting the upward support from adult children to parents among *coresident households* of the three samples. In other words, this highlights that it was the adult children who determined the provision of intergenerational support to parents and, the flow of upward support was less related to parents' characteristics and other familial factors.

First, the findings suggest that not only gender, but also the marital status of children, had different implications on intergenerational support to and from parents as well as the expectations of support to parents and parents-in-law across the three societies. Parents from all three samples tended to put greater emphasis on unmarried sons than unmarried daughters for upward support. Thus, a gendered division of support was observed, and demands of support were unevenly distributed between married couples. Even when married, adult daughters continued to provide for older parents or parents-in-law. This was also in line with the increasing number of dual earner families and expanded opportunities in education and work for females (Chiam 2008; Horton 2002; Nakavachara 2010; Therborn 2014); and therefore, women during the survey period had to balance the demands arising from within the family as well as from the workplace. The role of women was becoming more salient in the provision of parental support, particularly in caregiving roles espoused by gender stereotypes, that are more warm and nurturing. Given the fact that women also had to jump on the bandwagon of providing financial support, the finding also challenges the 'male breadwinner model' because women may not have earned as much as men due to the gender disparity in earnings. As argued by Pyke & Johnson (2003), the reproduction of subordinate feminine qualities, which affected the role of women in Asian cultures, sponsored internalised oppression and shaped the workings of Asian ethnic identities. Nonetheless, with rapid population ageing, married daughters have had to hastily take on the role of sons in providing support to parents.

However, there were diversities across the three societies. Intergenerational financial support was higher in Bangkok and Kuala Lumpur; while household chore support was higher among married children in Hanoi. This may be explained by their different SES status and, financial and time affordability between the three societies. Married children in Hanoi may have limited financial resources to support their parents due to their lower socio-economic standing and thus, they provided more regular household chores as a type of alternative support to parents. In comparison, samples in both Bangkok Metropolis and Kuala Lumpur showed that children could afford to contribute financial resources to support parents due to the more progressive economic development in Thailand and Malaysia. Interestingly, data from coresident households in Bangkok indicated sons' dependency on parents for financial support, while daughters experienced less household chore support from their parents. In Hanoi, a continuity of son dependency was observed which contributed indirectly to the stronger parental support for daughters-in-laws. The higher expectation of daughters, irrespective of marital status, on care provision to the parents continued to be relevant amongst the sample in Kuala Lumpur. This highlighted changes as well as continuity in the relationships between parents and adult children, especially the relationship between daughters and parents within coresident household in these societies.

Secondly, among coresident families, the findings also demonstrate significant differences in intergenerational support according to the *age* and *education attainment* of adult children across the three societies. Intergenerational support was in the expected direction whereby parents were more likely to provide greater support to the younger cohort; while older children engage more in the provision of support to parents. From the exchange perspective, financial transfer from parents to adult children in their early adulthood often was perceived as a type of investment for old-age security (Xie & Zhu 2009). Among Southeast Asian families, downward support from parents has the probability to extend into adulthood/pre-marriage and tends to be overwhelming (Lillard & Willis 1997; Frankenberg, Cheng, Birditt & Zarit 2002; Yaacob 2004). In addition, children may have played different roles in intergenerational support depending on their stage of life whether it is early, middle or late adulthood. The better financial standing of older children enabled them to provide monetary support, while the middle age group may struggle with the demands of an early career and having young families. These circumstances could lead to lack of time and resources (Hsu et al. 2001), thus, they would swap financial and practical support for emotional care for parents. While, it can be seen that the younger generation were the beneficiaries of upward care transaction, the country variation in age structures also had implications on intergenerational care relations according to age, whereby elderly parents in Bangkok Metropolis and Hanoi were being supported by an older cohort that reflected the population age structure in the two countries compared to Kuala Lumpur. It is also interesting to note that the middle age group in the Kuala Lumpur sample were less likely than other age groups to care for parents within the coresident household. This finding may reflect the struggle of the middle or sandwich generation in the urban areas of Kuala Lumpur to cope with the demands of care from both children and elderly parents.

Education levels of adult children demonstrated a positive relationship with downward care transaction from parents whereby more educated children received a greater extent of care from parents across all three societies. This may be due to better socio-economic standing among these parents who can provide more regular care to adult children and, these investments were extended to adulthood (Lillard & Willis 1997; Frankenberg, Lillard & Willis 2002). This may also have been motivated by the expectation of 'repayment' from children at a later stage of life as old-age support (Lin & Yi 2013; Silverstein et al. 2006). Nonetheless, the association between adult children's education level and upward care transaction provided to parents was not clear across the three societies. Among coresident households in Kuala Lumpur, a lower education level was related to providing more financial and household chores support to parents. As a low education level was often a proxy of socio-economic standing, this finding may reflect the need of care for parents especially among those from low SES families in the Kuala Lumpur sample. As for intergenerational support from PIL, in Hanoi, a lower education level was related to less household chore support but more regular financial support from PIL as compared to those with higher education attainment. This suggests the importance of the children-PIL relationship in Hanoi and, demonstrated that PIL tend to step-in during the time of financial need especially for adult children with low education levels (which are considered a proxy for low SES status).

Thirdly, the *health status of parents* was found to have diverse relationships with intergenerational support among adult children in the three samples. Specifically, health demands and the care burden among adult children were found to vary across societies. Adult children in Hanoi experience higher degrees of care burden as reflected in their greater parental health demands, more intense self-reported care provision to other family members, a larger proportion of parents in old age, a higher likelihood to live in a household with three or more generations, and more likely to have young children in families than those in Bangkok Metropolis and Kuala Lumpur. Past studies documented a consistent financial transfer from adult children to elderly parents when parents were old, in poor health and economically constrained (Silverstein et al. 2006). This relationship was not confirmed with our current findings in ANOVA, with the exception of Kuala Lumpur. Poor health status among parents was not linked to greater support from adult children in coresident households. However, healthy parents provided significantly more support to adult children. In fact, regression analysis noted that the old age of parents was related to greater support from adult children. This may imply that the health demands of parents had a more reciprocal relationship with the provision of support among families in Kuala Lumpur compared to the other two societies. As noted by Teh & colleagues (2013), the increased need in parents for care, caused by declining health and mobility from either parents or losing of their spouse, may evoke filial obligations that convert into support from adult children in Malaysia.

Finally, country variation in norms related to care for parents and parents-in-law based on gender and marital status reflects the diversity of filial norms across the three Southeast Asian societies. These variations also imply a distinction in the family system within these Southeast Asian samples and thus challenge the hypothesis of the *patriarchal family model among Southeast Asian families led to greater care provision* as presented in the chapter 1. Findings across the three samples noted filial norms on feelings of gratitude towards parental investment and devotion to support parent's livelihood was confirmed, with the exception of Hanoi. These results conform to the filial obligations and cultural expectations in Asian societies (Yi & Lin 2009) and thus, deviate from intergenerational patterns in Western societies, in which women, especially daughters, were more involved in support for older parents or parents-in-law (Chesley & Poppie 2009; Parker & Patten 2013) and, priority was given to caring for the wife's parents rather than the husband's parents (Shuey & Hardy 2003). Interestingly, findings also reveal significant differences in filial expectations across three societies especially for the Hanoi sample. The argument for the patriarchal family model for Southeast Asian families was complex, embedded within a cultural context and thus, varied across the region as shaped by the historical and political development of each society. As proposed by Date (2015), the different expectations of financial support for sons and daughters towards their own parents and parents-in-law were useful indicators for filial piety norms under patriarchal, patrilineal culture. It was suggested that the 'mountain-shaped' distribution for sons and 'valley-shaped' distribution for daughters denote patriarchal, patrilineal culture; while the flat distribution which indicated no differences between sex and marital status, denoted a non-patriarchal or bilateral culture. Thus, the 'strong mountain-valley shape' for sons and daughters reflected a stronger inclination towards patriarchal family systems in the Hanoi sample; while the 'flat' distribution revealed an inclination towards non-patriarchal or bilateral family culture in the Kuala Lumpur and Bangkok Metropolis samples.

To recapitulate, the interesting findings across and within the countries in relation to intergenerational support among coresident households seemed to stem from cultural factors such as patriarchy and family-focused norms that are common in the three societies studied. The main themes behind this chapter are how Southeast Asian families were uniquely challenged by the significant demographic trends traversing their societies, each at varying speeds and with repercussions on the stability of the informal support provided by the family. Given that there were limited alternatives for social protective mechanisms for support and care for older persons, the security of older persons is also contingent upon the strength of cultural values in supporting older parents. On one hand, it is a welcomed insight that families still thrived on reproduced norms and values but with the weakening effect of filial norms, due to the lower number of children and with that, the potential support from male providers and the struggles of middle generation. On the other hand, the increasing role of women in intergenerational care provision may have led to work-family conflict for women, especially among those who have to be responsible to both their children and ageing parents. Nevertheless, older parents in coresident households were also providing important types of care to children, especially married women, due to the limited social care services in the three societies. While the findings evidenced the uniqueness of family-focused Asian societies in bracing themselves through emerging challenges, akin to the bamboo plant that despite its vulnerable condition, became more resilient due to its suppleness and clustered growth, which represents flexibility and solidarity within the family.[4] With the variation in care provision for parents across different groups and countries, it also raised concerns regarding the capacity and ability of adult children and families to continuously be the main provider for old-age support within Southeast Asian societies, especially among lower income groups, the middle age generation and families with health care demands.

---

4 The limitations of the available dataset need to be taken into account in that it did not capture the indirect transaction of support between generations. For example, the contribution of parents and adult children in sharing the household such as cost-sharing of household expenses, financial support from other family members (as token of support for parental care) and child care services provided by parents (if there were) was undocumented or underreported. Additional information on the indirect support across-generations could provide a more comprehensive and clearer picture of intergenerational support within co-resident families. Thus, cautions need to be exercised during the interpretation of the findings.

References

Anh, Truong Si, The Cuong Bui, Daniel Goodkind, & John Knodel. (1997). Living arrangements, patrilineality and sources of support among elderly Vietnamese. *Asia-Pacific Population Journal, 12*, 69–88.

Bengtson, Vern.L., & Sandi S. Schrader. (1982). Parent-Child Relations. In D.J. Mangen & W.A. Peterson (Eds.), *Research Instruments in Social Gerontology, Vol. 2* (pp. 115–128). Minneapolis: University of Minnesota Press.

Biddlecom, Ann, Napaporn Chayovan, & Mary Beth Ofstedal. (2002). Intergenerational support and transfers. In A.I. Hermalin (Ed.), *The Well-Being of the Elderly in Asia: A Four-Country Comparative Study* (pp. 185–229). Ann Arbor: The University of Michigan Press.

Chan, Angelique. (2005). *Formal and informal intergenerational support transfers in South-Eastern Asia.* Proceedings of the United Nations expert group meeting on social and economic implications of changing population age structures.

Chan, Angelique. (2007). Economic well-being of older adults in Southeast Asia: Individual, family and state support. In Gabriele Sinigoj, Gavin Jones, Katsuiku Hirokawa, & Sepp Linhart (Eds.), *The Impact of ageing: A common challenge for Europe and Asia* (pp. 185–195). Berlin: lit Verlag.

Chen, Feinian. (2005), Residential patterns of parents and their married children in contemporary China: A life course approach. *Population Research and Policy Review, 24*, 125–148.

Chesley, Noelle, & Kyle Poppie. (2009). Assisting parents and in-laws: Gender, type of assistance, and couples' employment. *Journal of Marriage and Family, 71*(2), 247–262.

Chiam, Heng Keng. (2008). Child care in Malaysia: Then and now. *International Journal of Child Care and Education Policy, 2*(2), 31–41.

Croll, Elisabeth. (2006). The intergenerational contract in the changing Asian family. *Oxford Development Studies, 34*(4), 473–491.

Date, Heiwa. (2015). Variety of filial piety norm and its changes: A descriptive analysis among 9 societies using comparative Asian family survey data. Paper presented at the *7th next generation global workshop: Care and gender*, 7th-8th December, University of Kyoto, Japan.

Frankenberg, Elizabeth, Lee Lillard, & Robert Willis. (2002). Patterns of intergenerational transfers in Southeast Asia. *Journal of Marriage and Family, 64*(3), 627–641.

Hsu, Hui-Chuan, Chin-Yin Lew-Ting, & Shwu-Chong Wu. (2001). Age, period, and cohort effects on the attitude toward supporting parents in Taiwan. *Gerontologist, 41*(6), 742–750.

Horton, Susan (Ed.). (2002). *Women and Industrialization in Asia.* New York: Taylor & Francis.

Jones, Gavin. (2007). Challenges of ageing in East and Southeast Asia: Living arrangements of older persons, social security trends and retirement options. In Hrsg. Gabriele Sinigoj, Gavin Jones, Katsuiku Hirokawa, & Sepp Linhart (Eds.), *The impact of ageing: A common challenge for Europe and Asia* (pp. 79–95). Berlin: LIT Verlag.

Kamnuansilpa, Peerasit, Apichat Chamratrithirong, & John Knodel. (1982). Thailand's reproductive revolution: An update. *International Family Planning Perspectives, 8*(2), 51–56.

Kenayathulla, Husaina Banu. (2013). Higher levels of education for higher private returns: New evidence from Malaysia. *International Journal of Educational Development, 33*(4), 380–393. doi:10.1016/j.ijedudev.2012.05.008

Knodel, John, Vipan Prachuabmoh, & Napaporn Chayovan. (2013). *The changing well-being of the Thai elderly: An Update from the 2011 survey of older persons in Thailand.* Ann Arbor: Population Studies Center, University of Michigan, June.

Le, Ngoc Lan. (2017). *Elderly people in Vietnamese family in the context of ageing population and social changes.* Unpublished doctoral dissertation, Graduate Academy of Social Sciences, Hanoi.

Lillard, Lee, & Robert Willis. (1997). Motives for intergenerational transfers: Evidence from Malaysia. *Demography, 34*(1), 115–134.

Lin, Ju-Ping, & Chin-Chun Yi. (2013). A comparative analysis of intergenerational relations in East Asia. *International Sociology, 28*(3), 297–315.

Nakavachara, Voraprapa. (2010). Superior female education: Explaining the gender earnings gap trend in Thailand. *Journal of Asian Economics, 21*(2),198–218.

Park, Keong-Suk, Voonchin Phua, James McNally, & Rongjun Sun. (2005). Diversity and structure of intergenerational relationships: Elderly parent-adult child relations in Korea. *Journal of Cross-Cultural Gerontology, 20,* 285–305.

Parker, Kim, & Eileen Patten. (2013). *The sandwich generation: Rising financial burdens for middle-aged Americans.* Washington, D.C.: Pew Research Center, Social & Demographic Trends Project.

Prachuabmoh, Visid, & John Knodel. (1977). *Preferences for sex of children in Thailand: Result from the second round of a national survey.* Bangkok: Institute of Population Studies, Chulalongkorn University.

Pyke, Karen, & Denise Johnson. (2003). Asian American women and racialized femininities: "Doing" gender across cultural worlds. *Gender & Society, 17*(1), 33–53.

Shuey, Kim, & Melissa Hardy. (2003). Assistance to aging parents and parents-in-law: Does lineage affect family allocation decisions?. *Journal of Marriage and Family, 65*(2), 418–431.

Silverstein, Merril, Daphna Gan, & Frances Yang. (2006). Intergenerational support to aging parents: The role of norms and needs. *Journal of Family Issues, 27*(8), 1068–1084.

Teh, Jane Kimm Lii, Sor Tho Ng, Nai Peng Tey, & Ismail Siti-Norlasiah. (2013). Ethnicity and support for parents in Malaysia. *Asian Women, 29*(4), 51–72.

Thakur, Vikram Chandra. (1990). Indus Tsangpo suture zone in Ladakh – its tectonostratigraphy and tectonics. *Proc. Indian Acad. Sci. (Earth Planet Sci.), 99*(2), 169–185.

Therborn, Goran. (2014). Family systems of the world: Are they converging?. In Judith Treas, Jacqueline Scott, & Martin Richards (Eds.), *The Wiley-Blackwell companion to the sociology of families* (pp. 3–19). Chichester, UK: John Wiley & Sons, Ltd.

Wongboonsin, Kua, & Vipan Prachuabmoh Ruffolo. (1995). Sex preference for children in Thailand and some other South-East Asian countries. *Asia Pacific Population Journal, 10*(3), 43–62.

Xie, Gu Hung (2010, April 7). *Residence pattern, behavior of providing support for parents, and well-being of the elderly.* Retrieved from http://www.sspress.cn/news/7588.htm.

Xie, Yu, & Haiyan Zhu. (2009). Do sons or daughters give more money to parents in urban China?. *Journal of Marriage and Family, 71*(1), 174–186.

Yaacob, Harun. (2004). *Malaysia: Papers on Society and Culture.* Wellington: Victoria University of Wellington, New Zealand.

Yi, Chin-Chun, & Ju-Ping Lin. (2009). Types of relations between adult children and elderly parents in Taiwan: Mechanisms accounting for various relational types. *Journal of Comparative Family Studies, 40,* 305–324.

Yusuf, A. Muri. (2014). *Metodologi Penelitian Kuantitatif, Kualitatif & Penelitan. Gabungan.* Jakarta: Prenadamedia Group.

Zhang, Qian Forrest. (2004). Economic transition and new patterns of parent-adult child coresidence in urban China. *Journal of Marriage and Family, 66,* 1231–1245.

CHAPTER 6

Care Relations among Non-coresident Families

Nguyen Huu Minh, Tran Thi Minh Thi, Patcharawalai Wongboonsin, Jo-Pei Tan and Rahimah Ibrahim

1 Introduction

During the past decades demographic and cultural changes significantly altered the nature of intergenerational ties as reflected in, amongst others, the decline in multigenerational coresidence. Initially, these transformations raised concerns about the level of intergenerational support left within families. A shift in emphasis was envisioned from instrumental support to emotional bonds. Residential proximity was no longer considered a prerequisite for strong emotional bonds.

Chapter 5 discussed in detail the relationship between elderly parents and adult children who were living in the same household and how this related to the exchange of functional and emotional support. However, not living together did not mean that there was no exchange of support between parents and children. Cultural values such as filial norms and the benefits of mutual help in terms of functional and emotional support contributed to close relationships between elderly parents and adult children after their leaving the parents' house.

There was a common denominator of significance for the care and support between parents and adult children who were living separately. However, this was varied depending on the socio-economic environment and culture (Heylen, Morterlmans, Hermans & Boudiny 2012; Grundy & Henretta 2004; Hagestad 2001). For example, as reflected in chapter 5, Vietnamese traditional culture prefers sons to daughters, and affects the practice of patrilocal living arrangement. Therefore, the extent of mutual support between adult sons and elderly parents was probably higher than between elderly parents and adult daughters in Vietnam, while it may be different in Malaysia and Thailand, as already noted in chapters 2 and 3.

This chapter focuses on mutual support and care between parents/parents-in-law and children who were not living in the same household, in terms of the following three types of support and care: financial support, emotional support (i.e. listening to personal problems), and household chores support (i.e. providing care and doing daily house work). As with chapter 5, this chapter will

 | DOI:10.1163/9789004384330_007

firstly present the broad picture of support and care by each society, namely Bangkok Metropolis, Hanoi and Kuala Lumpur, and then it will identify the differences and similarities within and amongst these three societies, and finally, multiple regression models will be used to determine the factors that were uniquely related to the provision of intergenerational support and care between parents and children.

This chapter applies the definition of support and care as adopted in chapter 5. Accordingly, 'support and care between families' refers to any provision of support and care from adult children who were not living in the same household to parents/parents-in-law or vice versa. For this purpose, a subsample of 2843 *non-coresident families* (or 70.4% of the total sample) was created where only households with adult children who did not coreside with any of their elderly parents/parents-in-law were included in the analysis. Similarly to the findings described in chapter 5, the perception on and provision of support and care were only examined in terms of the normative dimension that includes: filial attitudes and familial responsibilities; types of support that include affectual, functional and associational; the flow of support between generations; and the moderating effect of adult children's and parents' characteristics on intergenerational support among non-coresident families. Detailed description of these variables was presented in chapter 5.

For the analysis strategy, the study relied upon descriptive statistics and multivariate regression models. Specifically, the pattern of support exchange between elderly parents and parents-in-law with adult children by age groups, education level, gender, marital status and parents' characteristics were described using univariate statistics such as frequencies, the mean and comparative t-test and an analysis of variance (ANOVA). In addition, multivariate regression was also used to test the relationship between the provision of support and selected variables and to predict intergenerational support for parents and parents-in-law respectively.

2 Sample Profile

Similarly to that for coresident families in chapter 5, the data source for non-coresident families in this chapter was derived from the three surveys in Bangkok Metropolis, Hanoi and Kuala Lumpur conducted in 2010–2011. The description of the data and the questionnaire used in this study were presented in chapter 1.

In this chapter, variables representing a sample demographic profile were divided into individual level (i.e. sex, age cohort, gender, education), family level (i.e. parental health status, parental marital status, availability of young children at home, geographical proximity, locality) and country level variables, namely, socio-economic status/living standard, locality and ethnicity. Meanwhile, dependent variables included in the analysis were different types of support: (1) functional exchange which comprised financial and domestic tasks and (2) emotional exchange that parents and children experience in their daily lives.

The distribution of indicators used in the descriptive analysis is presented in Table 6.1. The findings revealed that there were some differences between societies on several indicators. For example, the sample distribution according

TABLE 6.1 Description of indicators for the non-coresident sample

Indicator	Bangkok Metropolis	Hanoi	Kuala Lumpur
Sex of respondent			
Male	34.7%	45.4%	48.3%
Female	65.3%	54.6%	51.7%
Age cohort (years)			
Young	10.5%	6.7%	14.6%
Middle	29.8%	25.0%	26.1%
Old	59.7%	68.3%	59.4%
Education			
Primary school or less	57.9%	10.9%	34.2%
Secondary school	32.5%	70.4%	50.5%
College, Tertiary or higher	9.6%	18.7%	15.3%
Gender and Marital Status			
Married man	32.1%	48.3%	47.9%
Married woman	52.9%	48.7%	40.9%
Unmarried man	6.0%	0.7%	6.1%
Unmarried woman	9.0%	2.2%	5.1%
Socioeconomic Status			
High	–	18.2%	6.4%
Middle	–	71.5%	52.6%
Low	–	10.4%	41.0%
Parent health demand			
All healthy/Healthy + deceased	65.4%	50.7%	83.8%
Either one unhealthy	34.6%	49.3%	16.2%

TABLE 6.1 Description of indicators for the non-coresident sample (*cont.*)

Indicator	Bangkok Metropolis	Hanoi	Kuala Lumpur
Parent marital status			
Both/either parents and PIL has spouse	27.5%	34.3%	50.9%
Both parents and PIL with no spouse	72.5%	65.7%	49.1%
Adult children with least one child less than 7 years old			
No	87.8%	83.1%	73.8%
Yes, at least have one	12.2%	16.9%	26.2%
Geographical distance to parent			
Next door	17.8%	32.8%	6.4%
Within 15 min by walk	2.8%	28.8%	3.2%
15–30 min by car	4.5%	17.8%	13.3%
30 min-1 hour by car	7.1%	4.9%	17.2%
An hour to 3 hour sby car	17.1%	9.0%	26.9%
More than 3 hours by car	50.7%	6.7%	33.1%
Geographical distance to PIL			
Next door	10.3%	39.3%	5.1%
Within 15 min by walk	6.3%	25.3%	3.7%
15–30 min by car	5.3%	19.8%	11.7%
30 min–1 hour by car	9.6%	4.3%	20.9%
An hour to 3 hours by car	21.6%	7.0%	28.4%
More than 3 hours by car	46.8%	4.3%	30.2%
Residential area			
Rural		64.6%	67.7%
Urban		35.4%	32.3%
Ethnicity (Kuala Lumpur)			
Malay			66.5%
Chinese			19.5%
Indian			13.9%

Note: PIL = Parents-in-law

to sex of adult children was more equal in Hanoi and Kuala Lumpur than in Bangkok Metropolis. In comparison, the age structure of the Hanoi sample was older in which almost 70% of the sample was in old age group compared to the other two samples (59.7% in Bangkok Metropolis and 59.4% in Kuala Lumpur). In terms of education levels, the percentage of adult children who completed secondary school or higher qualifications in Hanoi (18.7%) was significantly higher than in Kuala Lumpur (15.3%) and Bangkok Metropolis (9.6%). Similarly, the percentage of married adult children in Kuala Lumpur (Men=47.9%; Women=40.9%) was much lower than that in Hanoi (Married men=48.3%; Married women=48.7%) and Bangkok Metropolis (Married men=32.1%; Married women=52.9%).

Findings on the geographical distance between adult children's residence and their parents' or parents-in-law's revealed that the percentage of the Hanoi sample who lived close to their parents was higher, in which 32.8% lived next door and 28.8% within 15 minutes as compared to Bangkok Metropolis (17.8% living next door and 2.8% within 15 minutes) and Kuala Lumpur (6.4% living next door and 3.2% within 15 minutes). This may reflect a higher urbanisation level in Bangkok Metropolis and Kuala Lumpur compared to Hanoi. Socio-economic status of the samples, which reflected the living standard of households in Hanoi and Kuala Lumpur was also different, in which Kuala Lumpur (41%) reported a greater percentage of families in the low SES group than Hanoi (10.4%). In addition, the percentages of those in high and middle levels of SES in Hanoi (High: 18.2%; Middle: 71.5%) were much higher than in Kuala Lumpur (High: 6.4%; Middle: 52.6%). These differences between the three samples were taken into account during the analysis and interpretation of the findings.

3 Care Practice and Attitudes across Generations of Non-coresident Families

3.1 *Practice in Care: Types and Flow of Support*

Intergenerational solidarity is best understood within the context of shared expectations and obligations between individuals as they age and the succession of generations. This section describes the pattern and flow of support and care between parents and children who were living in different households across three Southeast Asian societies in terms of emotional and functional support (i.e. financial assistance and household chores).

3.1.1 Emotional Support

Results showed that respondents perceived that the exchange of emotional support tended to be more upward from adult children to parents than downward from parents to adult children among *non-coresident families* (Table 6.2). This pattern was in accordance with several past studies on the upward flow of support from adult children to parents in Southeast Asian societies (Chan 2005; Lee, Parish & Willis 1994). The exchange of emotional support tended

TABLE 6.2 Types and flow of support among non-coresident families

Intergenerational support	Mean		
	Bangkok Metropolis	Hanoi	Kuala Lumpur
Provided support to parents			
Financial support	2.98	2.39	3.02
Emotional support	2.70	3.19	2.92
Household chores support	1.93	2.69	2.66
Received support from parents			
Financial support	1.39	1.37	1.58
Emotional support	2.17	2.85	2.54
Household chores support	1.38	1.47	1.89
Provided support to PIL			
Financial support	2.51	2.18	2.31
Emotional support	2.05	2.76	2.39
Household chores support	1.73	2.46	2.16
Received support from PIL			
Financial support	1.31	1.23	1.31
Emotional support	1.78	2.47	2.06
Household chores support	1.33	1.37	1.57
Filial attitudes			
Feeling grateful	6.58	6.83	6.08
Support parent's livelihood	6.50	5.52	5.89
Familial responsibilities			
Financial support from:			
Unmarried adult man to own parents	5.93	5.06	5.90
Unmarried adult woman to own parents	5.92	4.74	5.86
Married adult man to own parents	5.68	5.22	5.82
Married adult woman to own parents	5.69	3.78	5.73
Married man to parents-in-law	5.39	3.11	5.49
Married woman to parents-in-law	5.38	4.91	5.40

to be more often from adult children to their own parents than to parents-in-law (PIL). In particular, adult children in Hanoi were most likely to provide emotional support to their parents (mean=3.19) and PIL (mean=2.76), while adult children in Bangkok Metropolis were least likely to do so (parents=2.70; PIL=2.05).

3.1.2 Functional Support

Functional support in this study referred to support in helping the older parents in household chores and provision of financial support. The possibility of a financial exchange between adult children and parents was relatively high. As with emotional support, financial support tended to be more upward from adult children to parents than downward from parents to adult children as showed in Table 6.2. In addition, the provision of financial support from adult children to the parents tended to be higher than to PIL in the three societies. The PIL were also found to provide less financial support to adult children than their parents. Specifically, based on the 5-point scale, the level of financial assistance to parents from adult children in Kuala Lumpur was the highest with a mean score of 3.02, while Bangkok Metropolis children provided the greatest financial assistance to PIL with a mean score of 2.51. The adult children in Hanoi reported a lower level of financial assistance to their parents on both two sides (mean: Parent=2.39; PIL=2.18) compared to those in Bangkok Metropolis (mean: Parent=2.98; PIL=1.39) and Kuala Lumpur (mean: Parent=3.02; PIL=1.58).

Household chores support included help with housework such as going to the market, cooking, washing, repairing something, caring for elderly and sick family members, and other tasks. Unlike financial support that could be carried out through bank transactions or online services, and which were not affected by geographical distance, support for household chores depended very much on the distance between respondents and their parents. Findings showed that support of household chores was mostly from adult children to parents. This type of support was not frequently provided by elderly parents to their own children who were in employment. In the three societies, adult children in Hanoi were found to be most likely to provide household chores support to parents with a mean score of 2.69, while adult children in Kuala Lumpur tended to receive more care support from PIL with a mean score of 1.57. The extent of household chores exchanged between adult children and parents (mean: support to parent=1.93; support from parent=1.38) and PIL (mean: support to PIL=1.73. support from PIL=1.33) in Bangkok Metropolis was relatively low, in comparison to other societies, namely Hanoi and Kuala Lumpur.

3.1.3 Comparison between Emotional and Functional Support

It is interesting that mutual care and support of non-coresident family members differed significantly across the three societies. Adult children in Bangkok Metropolis and Kuala Lumpur provided financial support to parents and PIL more than emotional support, while adult children in Hanoi provided emotional support at a higher level in comparison to financial assistance. The discrepancies across countries in relation to the exchange of emotional, financial and practical support shed lights on underlying socio-cultural and demographic differences among the three societies. The flow of support from parents and PIL to adult children tended to focus on emotional and household chores support rather than financial assistance.

3.2 *Norms and Familistic Values*

Substantial evidence from Southeast Asia showed that financial transfers within families served as insurance for family members (Frankenberg, Lillard & Willis 2002; Bengtson & Roberts 1991; Emerson 1976). The results also suggested that money was exchanged for time between parents and children. Additionally, there is some evidence that is consistent with the idea that parents provided financial support to pay for the education of their children and that this was perceived partly as a loan, which was later repaid in old-age support provision (Frankenberg, Lillard & Willis 2002; Bengtson & Roberts 1991). Modernization forced the traditional views of filial piety to be socially reconstructed. The idea that adult children were responsible for the care of their elders became less viable because of the vast increases in economic development, greater access to education, and job mobility for young adults (Tran 2016).

The above notion seem to support the exchange theory, which suggests that the extent of intergenerational transfers contains an element of insurance because the investments are made early in life in order to receive support when problems arise during old age. The theory assumes that giving support is a cost for the giver, and receiving support is a benefit for the receiver. Given this, the theory argues that intergenerational relations can be seen as exchange relations. The delayed exchange occurs as parents give first and children return the gift later in their life course, which means children 'pay back' their parents by providing them support and care at a later stage of life. In addition, the exchange in which children provide support to elderly parents in order to receive money or property when their parents die, is called a prospective exchange. The most common form of exchange is direct exchange. This occurs when parents and children exchange different goods more or less at the same time, such as care support, financial exchange, emotional exchange, and social support. For example, parents might take care of the grandchildren in exchange for the visits and attention they obtain from their children. Parents can give money to their children when they are old in order to receive more household help or more attention from their children.

In societies influenced by the Confucian ideology of filial piety, the family relationship, in particular, the familial obligation and performance of intergenerational exchanges would be beyond the regular norms of exchanges and altruism resulting from cultural and ideological influences. In most developing countries, the literature notes that families are the primary source of support for aging individuals. Families as a source of old age support have received particular attention in Asia, where populations are aging rapidly (Knodel, Friedman, Anh & Cuong 2000; Frankenberg, Lillard & Willis 2002). For example, in Vietnamese culture, there is a saying that children are *saving property* "con cai la cua de danh", which conveys a very similar meaning to the spirit of the exchange theory in terms of parents investing in children in order to receive a pay back when they are old.

3.2.1 Associational Solidarity and Normative Elements

Normative elements were assessed through respondent's perceptions of filial values, toward attitudes of filial piety, and the provision of parental support and expectation of familial responsibilities. As shown in Table 6.2, the overall pattern indicated that respondents expressed strong feeling of gratitude towards their parents' efforts in their up-bringing and clearly indicated their intention to contribute and support their parents' livelihood (see Table 6.2). However, some discrepancies across the three samples were detected with the highest mean scores of 6.83 in Hanoi for feeling grateful to parents. This probably highlighted the strong social norms influenced by Confucian ideology when the society was developing. However, it was interesting to note that non-coresident adult children in Hanoi reported the lowest mean score of 5.52 for the provision of economic support to their parents, with those in Bangkok Metropolis having the strongest sense of filial obligation to provide support to their parents, with a mean of 6.50. One reason is probably that many of the Bangkok Metropolis sample were migrants. They accordingly found financial support as the most viable and affordable option to maintain family relationships as they could not physically take care of their parents by going back home very often. Meanwhile, the non-coresident sample in Hanoi were mostly in the rural areas, they lived close by their parents and regularly visited to give housework and emotional support on a face-to-face basis. Given that they also did not get much income, they did not prioritize financial support. In addition, the literature shows that, for elders in rural Vietnam, the most important source of living was income from the agricultural sector, followed by child support and pensions. For those aged under 69, they tended to rely on income from self-employment, the state pension and child support. The older they were, the more important was child support. In addition, they could not enjoy a good pension, since they were mainly in the informal sector of the economy due to their low education attainment (Trinh & Tran 2017).

In terms of expectations of familial responsibility, the present study operationalized it as the respondents' degree of agreement on the obligation to provide financial support to parents and PIL. As shown in Table 6.2, adult children in *non-coresident families* were required to indicate the expected obligation of unmarried adult men, unmarried adult women, married adult men and married adult women to provide financial support to parents and PIL. The data revealed a very strong family value about filial responsibility towards parents' well-being in the three societies with average score ranging above 3, based on a 6-point scale (see Table 6.2). *Non-coresident* adult children in Bangkok Metropolis and Kuala Lumpur showed a strong pattern of filial responsibility toward their parents, especially care of unmarried children for their own parents. A more consistent pattern was observed across gender regarding obligation towards parents and PIL especially in the cases of Bangkok Metropolis and Kuala Lumpur, too. At the same time, children in Hanoi were less expected to provide financial support to parents than in Bangkok Metropolis and Kuala Lumpur. It is noted that, the norm of the patriarchy pattern in Hanoi remained strong, as filial responsibility of married men and married women to their own parents and parents-in-law tended to be different (See Table 6.2). More discussion about the differences between the groups of respondents will be presented in the next section.

3.3 *Characteristics of Adult Children and Intergenerational Support among Non-coresident Households Age*

As for the age groups, it was considered that people from different age cohorts, growing up at different points in historical time, were products of the different life experiences which defined their life-span development stage. Therefore, they may have had different perceptions on and expectations for intergenerational support. However, data from the present study showed that there was no clear pattern on the impact of age on intergenerational support among those who did not coreside with parents or parents-in-law. Results in Table 6.3 showed that the adult children in the middle age group were the most active in providing financial care to parents in general, especially children in Hanoi, $F=4.76$, $p<.001$. A plausible explanation for this was that the middle age group could be considered the most active working group, with the strongest ability to earn economically which enabled them to engage more in the provision of financial support to parents or PIL.

Note: * $p<0.05$; ** $p<0.01$; *** $p<0.001$In addition, as shown in Table 6.3, ANOVA comparative analysis also demonstrated that age group had a close linkage with financial support from parents towards their children. Especially, the older the children were, the less frequently they received financial support from their parents. Finding also showed that adult children of younger age tend to need financial support from the parents when they were at the beginning of their career and experience less stable economic conditions. This relationship was found to be consistent across all three societies, $F_{Bangkok}=8.65$, $p<.001$; $F_{Hanoi}=44.04$, $p<.001$; $F_{KL}=38.70$, $p<.001$.

Regarding providing financial support to PIL, the results in Table 6.3 also showed that there was no significant difference between age groups. However, as for receiving financial support from PIL, the pattern was similar to those receiving financial support from parents in which adult children in the younger age group were more likely to receive financial support from their PIL. This relationship was also detected across all three societies, $F_{Bangkok}=3.70$, $p<.05$; $F_{Hanoi}=33.70$, $p<.001$; $F_{KL}=9.61$, $p<.001$.

'Sharing and listening to other's problem' between parents and adult children was another aspect which reflects the exchange of emotional support between generations. The current data failed to demonstrate a clear association between age group and frequency of emotional support to parents in the three societies. However, in all three societies, adult children in the young age group tended to receive more emotional support from their parents. There was also no clear association between emotional support and age group amongst adult children and PIL pair.

Helping parents with household chores was common among children from all three societies in which there was no significant difference in household chore support from children across age groups in Bangkok Metropolis, Hanoi and Kuala Lumpur. In terms of parents helping children with household chores, comparative analysis reported significant differences across age groups in Hanoi, $F=44.26$, $p<.001$ and Kuala Lumpur, $F=2.29$, $p<.001$. It was highest among the young age cohort with those in Hanoi receiving the greatest support from parents. This finding corresponds well with a previous study on the role of old parents in helping young married children, especially with child care (Tran 2014).

Age of children in Hanoi is a significant predictor of the level of filial responsibilities to parents and parents-in-law (see Table 6.3). The younger the children, the greater the filial responsibility toward parents was perceived to be. In addition, the patriarchal norms of filial piety to the husband's parents rather than to the wife's parents, were consistent with the above discussion.

TABLE 6.3 Types and flow of support by age groups

Intergenerational support	Bangkok				Hanoi				Kuala Lumpur			
	Young	Middle	Old	Sig.	Young	Middle	Old	Sig.	Young	Middle	Old	Sig.
Provided support to parents												
Financial support	2.80	3.08	2.93		2.00	2.52	2.38	4.76***	2.97	3.15	2.89	
Emotional support	2.81	2.69	2.64		3.22	3.17	3.21		2.94	2.99	2.81	
Household chores support	1.96	2.88	1.97		2.55	2.65	2.76		2.76	2.66	2.55	
Received support from parents												
Financial support	1.74	1.30	1.33	8.65***	2.19	1.37	1.15	44.04***	2.07	1.47	1.27	**38.70*** **
Emotional support	2.61	2.11	2.01	5.90**	3.19	2.89	2.72	4.56**	2.85	2.50	2.29	**11.57*** **
Household chores support	1.49	1.42	1.28		2.33	1.48	1.24	44.26***	2.43	1.79	1.50	**2.29*** **
Provided support to PIL												
Financial support	2.63	2.55	2.43		2.21	2.21	2.16		2.21	2.40	2.24	
Emotional support	1.96	2.06	2.09		2.96	2.71	2.75		2.49	2.45	2.27	
Household chores support	1.80	1.65	1.80		2.47	2.47	2.44		2.22	2.19	2.10	
Received support from PIL												
Financial support	1.56	1.30	1.22	3.70*	1.79	1.27	1.09	33.70***	1.42	1.40	1.14	**9.61*** **
Emotional support	1.83	1.87	1.66		2.60	2.51	2.42		2.24	2.06	1.99	
Household chores support	1.46	1.33	1.28		1.94	1.46	1.17	27.10***	1.82	1.62	1.39	**10.31*** **
Filial attitudes												
Feeling grateful	6.59	6.60	6.57		6.90	6.81	6.83		6.16	6.06	6.07	
Support parent's livelihood	6.54	6.43	6.52		5.72	5.59	5.47		5.93	5.90	5.88	

Intergenerational support	Bangkok				Hanoi				Kuala Lumpur			
	Young	Middle	Old	Sig.	Young	Middle	Old	Sig.	Young	Middle	Old	Sig.
Familial responsibilities												
Financial support from:												
Unmarried adult man to own parents	6.07	5.92	5.91		5.28	5.33	4.93	4.18*	5.97	5.96	5.86	
Unmarried adult woman to own parents	6.06	5.92	5.89		5.22	4.92	4.63	3.74*	5.88	5.94	5.81	
Married adult man to own parents	5.85	5.70	5.64		5.70	5.42	5.11	6.79**	5.88	5.89	5.77	
Married adult woman to own parents	5.87	5.69	5.66		4.18	4.05	3.63	5.69**	5.74	5.83	5.67	
Married man to PIL	5.59	5.35	5.37		3.32	3.30	3.01		5.44	5.62	5.44	
Married woman to PIL	5.63	5.33	5.35		5.32	5.14	4.79	5.23**	5.35	5.49	5.38	

Note: * $p<0.05$; ** $p<0.01$; *** $p<0.001$

3.3.1 Education Attainment

Findings shown in Table 6.4 indicate that adult children with higher education provided greater financial support to their parents and PIL and this was most clear in the case of Kuala Lumpur, $F_{Parents}$=6.03, p<.001; F_{PIL}=2.18, p<.05. It is possible that adult children with higher educational attainment often have better jobs and therefore better financial resources (Table 6.4).

Data also showed that among non-coresident families, educational level also was closely related to the frequency of financial support from parents and parents-in-law, however the pattern is clearer in Bangkok Metropolis, $F_{Parents}$=4.29, p<.001; F_{PIL}=2.10, p<.05 and Kuala Lumpur, $F_{Parents}$=3.42, p<.001. Regarding financial support from parents or parents-in-law, it is hypothesised that parents were more likely to give more to children with lower education attainment because a lower education level is often associated with lower socio-economic status. It is also considered that adult children with fewer resources would benefit more from this type of financial support than the adult children who are rich in economic resources and so they were perceived as more deprived by an altruistic parent. However, in this study, it is interesting that children with higher education levels received more financial support from parents and parents-in-law. A plausible explanation for this would be that adult children with higher education levels tend to come from well-off families with parents who were capable of providing financial assistance to adult children.

The association between education and frequency of emotional support via listening to parents' problems was strong for those in non-coresident families. Specifically, those with higher education levels provided a greater degree of emotional support to their parents and also received more regular emotional care from their parents. This result corresponds to the findings from previous studies which emphasized the important role of education in increasing the frequency of caring for the emotional needs of one's parents (Bengtson & Schrader 1982; Cooksey & Craig 1998). It was also found that the relationship between education level and emotional support tended to be the strongest among Kuala Lumpur respondents, F=3.23, p<.01, followed by those in Bangkok Metropolis, F=2.49, p<.05 and was the weakest in the Hanoi sample, n.s.

In addition, non-coresident adult children with higher education attainment reported higher percentages of providing domestic support for their parents. This may suggest that those with higher education levels might have a greater awareness of their responsibility to support their parents. Interestingly, those with higher levels of education also received more regular care support from their parents than those with a lower education attainment. The result is similar across all three societies, although at different levels. In terms of upward exchange, the pattern of association between household chores

TABLE 6.4 Types and flow of support by education levels

Types of support	Bangkok			Hanoi			Kuala Lumpur		
	High	Low	T-test sig	High	Low	T-test sig	High	Low	T-test sig
Provided support to parents									
Financial support	2.99	2.96	–	2.40	2.32	–	3.13	2.31	**6.03*****
Emotional support	2.84	2.52	2.49*	3.21	3.02	–	2.98	2.56	**3.23****
Household chores support	1.93	1.93	–	2.73	2.34	2.67***	2.69	2.44	**1.97***
Received support from parents									
Financial support	1.54	1.21	4.29***	1.38	1.30	–	1.63	1.24	**3.42*****
Emotional support	2.31	1.99	2.51*	2.84	2.90	–	2.63	1.90	**5.57*****
Household chores support	1.48	1.27	2.68**	1.48	1.36	–	1.93	1.61	**2.65****
Provided support to PIL									
Financial support	2.64	2.36	–	2.19	2.09	–	2.36	2.05	**2.18***
Emotional support	2.17	1.93	–	2.78	2.55	–	2.43	2.13	**2.26***
Household chores support	1.78	1.67	–	2.45	2.50	–	2.20	1.94	**2.10***
Received support from PIL									
Financial support	1.40	1.22	2.10*	1.24	1.18	–	1.33	1.19	–
Emotional support	1.89	1.65	1.98*	2.49	2.36	–	2.09	1.90	–
Household chores support	1.38	1.28		1.37	1.32	–	1.59	1.41	–
Filial attitudes									
Feeling grateful	6.66	6.52	2.56**	6.83	6.82	–	6.08	6.07	–

TABLE 6.4 Types and flow of support by education levels (*cont.*)

Types of support	Bangkok			Hanoi			Kuala Lumpur		
	High	Low	T-test sig	High	Low	T-test sig	High	Low	T-test sig
Support parent's livelihood	6.51	6.49	–	5.48	5.71	–	5.87	5.94	–
Familial responsibilities									
Financial support from:									
Unmarried adult man to own parents	5.97	5.89	–	5.06	5.00	–	5.94	5.83	–
Unmarried adult woman to own parents	5.94	5.90	–	4.74	4.77	–	5.90	5.78	–
Married adult man to own parents	5.75	5.62	–	5.21	5.28	–	5.85	5.76	–
Married adult woman to own parents	5.78	5.63	–	3.75	3.91	–	5.76	5.66	–
Married man to parents-in-law	5.46	5.34	–	3.11	3.06	–	5.52	5.43	–
Married woman to parents-in-law	5.42	5.34	–	4.90	5.00	–	5.43	5.35	–

Note: * $p<0.05$; ** $p<0.01$; *** $p<0.001$

support and education is more clearly visible in Hanoi, $F_{parent}=2.67$, $p<.001$ and then Kuala Lumpur, $F_{parent}=1.97$, $p<.05$; $F_{PIL}=2.10$, $p<.05$. For the downward exchange, the pattern is clear in Kuala Lumpur, $F_{parent}=2.65$, $p<.01$ and Bangkok Metropolis, $F_{parent}=2.68$, $p<.01$ (Table 6.4).

Data also showed that there was a difference in perception on the role of education on filial attitudes across the three societies. Specifically, it was found that 'the higher the educational attainment of children, the stronger the feeling of gratitude to parents', was only detected among Bangkok Metropolis respondents, $F=2.56$, $p<.01$. This observation was not found in the case of Hanoi or Kuala Lumpur.

3.4 *Gender and Marital Status*

3.4.1 Gender

Table 6.5 showed the types and flow of support according to the gender of adult children in Bangkok Metropolis, Hanoi and Kuala Lumpur. In this study, the females in Bangkok Metropolis provide financial support to parents more frequently than their male counterparts; while males or sons in Hanoi and Kuala Lumpur are significantly more engaged in their parents' financial well-being than females or daughters, $F_{Hanoi}= 26.83$, $p<.001$; $F_{KL}= 10.49$, $p<.001$. In addition, sons in Hanoi played a more important role in providing household chores support for their parents, $F=5.74$, $p<.05$. It is understandable that in a society with high patriarchal norms such as Hanoi, sons are expected to be the main care providers to their parents both financially and functionally (i.e. household chores support). It can be noted that household chores that sons referred to in this study may have combined help from his (the son's) family members. The current findings reflect Bangkok Metropolis less patriarchal than Hanoi.

Support to parents-in-law is another dimension of intergenerational solidarity among non-coresident family members. The role of daughters-in-law and sons-in-law in the household was very important in explaining care transactions between parents and children. In such a society influenced strongly by patriarchal values, married children tended to live with the husband's family. Therefore, daughters-in-law were expected to provide care for their parents-in-law. Traditionally daughters-in-law were considered by parents-in-law, as their own children since they lived with the husband's family throughout their life, while sons-in-law were considered to be guests of the family (*dau con re khach*). Such a traditional notion may have affected the pattern of care to parents in Hanoi. However, in Bangkok Metropolis, it was acceptable for married children to live with the wife's family. As a result, financial support was observed to be the highest in Bangkok Metropolis with sons-in-law playing more important

TABLE 6.5 Types and flow of support by gender

Intergenerational support	Bangkok			Hanoi			Kuala Lumpur		
	Son	Daughter	t-test sig	Son	Daughter	t-test sig	Son	Daughter	t-test sig
Provided support to parents									
Financial support	2.85	3.05	–	2.73	2.18	26.83***	3.18	2.88	10.49***
Emotional support	2.40	2.87	12.49***	3.20	3.19	–	2.82	3.02	5.34*
Household chores support	1.80	2.00	–	2.83	2.60	5.74*	2.58	2.73	–
Received support from parents									
Financial support	1.43	1.37	–	1.35	1.38	–	1.64	1.53	–
Emotional support	2.04	2.25	–	2.74	2.92	–	2.46	2.61	–
Household chores support	1.33	1.41	–	1.52	1.44	–	1.84	1.93	–
Provided support to PIL									
Financial support	2.68	2.40	–	1.96	2.40	20.28***	2.35	2.27	–
Emotional support	2.11	2.02	–	2.65	2.87	5.61*	2.33	2.46	–
Household chores support	1.79	1.69	–	2.26	2.65	18.15***	2.06	2.29	5.99**
Received support from PIL									
Financial support	1.32	1.31	–	1.25	1.22	–	1.31	1.31	–
Emotional support	1.84	1.74	–	2.40	2.54	–	2.02	2.12	–
Household chores support	1.40	1.29	–	1.37	1.36	–	1.50	1.65	5.04*

Intergenerational support	Bangkok			Hanoi			Kuala Lumpur		
	Son	Daughter	t-test sig	Son	Daughter	t-test sig	Son	Daughter	t-test sig
Filial attitudes									
Feeling grateful	6.63	6.55	–	6.83	6.83	–	6.08	6.08	–
Support parent's livelihood	6.51	6.49	–	5.43	5.59	–	5.90	5.89	–
Familial responsibilities									
Financial support from:									
Unmarried adult man to own parents	5.91	5.94	–	4.75	5.31	–	5.86	5.94	–
Unmarried adult woman to own parents	5.86	5.94	–	4.44	4.99	–	5.82	5.89	–
Married adult man to own parents	5.71	5.66	–	5.13	5.30	–	5.79	5.85	–
Married adult woman to own parents	5.71	5.68	–	3.59	3.93	–	5.70	5.75	–
Married man to parents-in-law	5.42	5.37	–	2.99	3.20	–	5.43	5.54	–
Married woman to parents-in-law	5.42	5.35	–	4.75	5.05	–	5.37	5.43	–

roles than daughters-in-law in providing financial support to parents. In contrast, in Hanoi, sons-in-law perceived that they had the least responsibility in the provision of the three types of care to parents-in-law, while daughters-in-law performed a significant amount of the care for the husband's parents, $F_{Financial}=20.28$, $p<.001$; $F_{Emotion}=5.61$, $p<.05$; $F_{Household}=18.15$, $p<.001$. Among those in Kuala Lumpur, daughters-in-law also played a substantial role in providing household chores support for the husband's parents compared to sons-in-law for his wife's parents, $F=5.99$, $p<.01$. In relation to the emotional support of the spouse's parents, there was a gender difference in which, female respondents reported higher proportions of listening to the problems of parents-in-law than male respondents, but this pattern applied for only Hanoi, $F=5.61$, $p<.05$.

In developed countries, intergenerational solidarity tended to be downward toward children, as people tended to be richer when they become older. This trend was also contributed to by low fertility. In Southeast Asia, financial provision from parents and parents-in-law was low, especially in Hanoi. Parents were found to pay more attention to providing emotional care for their children and children-in-law. This pattern was particularly consistent and obvious in Hanoi with a mean score for sons of 2.74 and daughters, 2.92, as well as for sons-in-law 2.40 and daughters-in–law, 2.54. Parents in Kuala Lumpur demonstrated the highest sense of responsibility for helping children with household chores than the other two societies whereby daughters-in-law tend to receive more household chores support from parents-in-law than sons-in-law.

3.4.2 Marital Status

Marital status was closely related to intergenerational support of non-coresident family members, especially in Hanoi and Kuala Lumpur (Table 6.6). As an explanation, married adult children tended to provide financial support more frequently to their parents compared to those who were unmarried and at the same time, they also received less financial support from their parents. This pattern was consistent across the three societies – 'support to parents': $F_{Bangkok}=2.80$,$p<.01$; $F_{Hanoi}=2.30$,$p<.05$; $F_{KL}=2.30$,$p<.05$; 'support from parents': $F_{Bangkok}=-2.40$,$p<.05$; $F_{Hanoi}=-7.80$,$p<.001$; $F_{KL}=-7.80$,$p<.001$. Data revealed no significant difference between married and unmarried adult children in terms of emotional support to their parents. However, unmarried adult children received more frequent emotional support from their parents than those who are married. This however, was only applicable to cases in Hanoi, $F=-2.40$, $p<.05$ and Kuala Lumpur, $F=-3.7$,$p<.001$.

Among *non-coresident families*, married adult children in Hanoi were found to provide more frequent household chores support to parents than unmarried respondents, $F=2.30$, $p<.05$. However, that pattern was not found in the Bangkok

TABLE 6.6 Marital status difference in the intergenerational relations in Bangkok Metropolis, Hanoi and Kuala Lumpur

Intergenerational support	Bangkok Metropolis, mean			Hanoi, mean			Kuala Lumpur, mean		
	Married	Unmarried	t-test	Married	Unmarried	t-test	Married	Unmarried	t-test
Provided support to parents									
Financial support	3.06	2.54	2.8**	2.43	1.69	2.3*	3.10	2.80	2.3*
Emotional support	2.69	2.90	–	3.19	3.38	–	2.94	2.90	–
Household chores support	1.95	1.76	–	2.71	2.08	2.3*	2.65	2.81	–
Received support from parents									
Financial support	1.37	1.68	−2.4*	1.32	3.00	−7.8***	1.48	2.30	−7.8***
Emotional support	2.16	2.44	–	2.82	3.54	−2.4*	2.48	2.95	−3.7***
Household chores support	1.40	1.34	–	1.44	2.69	−5.3***	1.77	2.66	−3.7***
Provided financial support from:									
Unmarried adult man to own parents	5.95	5.95	–	5.03	5.04	–	5.95	5.90	–
Unmarried adult woman to own parents	5.94	5.95	–	4.71	4.91	–	5.90	5.90	–
Married adult man to own parents	5.70	5.85	–	5.23	5.54	–	5.85	5.83	–
Married adult woman to own parents	5.70	5.90	–	3.74	4.54	−2.1*	5.76	5.75	–
Married man to parents-in-law	5.42	5.54	–	3.10	3.96	−2.4*	5.53	5.50	–
Married woman to parents-in-law	5.41	5.50	–	4.91	5.20	–	5.43	5.42	–

Note: p*<.05; p**<.01; p***<.001

Metropolis or Kuala Lumpur samples. Data from the present study also showed that unmarried adult children in Hanoi, $F=-5.3$, $p<.001$ and Kuala Lumpur, $F=-3.70$, $p<.001$ received household chores support more frequently than the married ones. However, differences between married and unmarried adult children in giving and receiving household chores support from parents was not clearly shown in the Bangkok Metropolis non-coresident sample.

In relation to filial norms, the results showed a clear difference in the expectation of financial obligation for a "married adult woman to her own parents" and a "married man to his parents-in-law" between married and unmarried adult children in Hanoi. It was found that unmarried adult children in *non-coresident* families showed a more gender-balanced expectation compared of those who were married where those who were unmarried tend to have higher expectations of a "married adult woman to provide financial support to her own parents" (mean=4.54) and a "married man to provide financial support to his parents-in-law" (mean=3.96) compared to married respondents, $M_{MAWtoParents}=3.74$ and $M_{MMtoPIL}=3.10$.

3.4.3 Interaction of Marital Status and Gender in Provision of Support

As discussed in Section 5.2, the different expectations for married daughters and married sons to perform filial responsibility to parents and parents-in-law suggested an interaction between gender and marital status. This interaction effect of marital status and gender was important in explaining the diversity of filial norms in Southeast Asian societies. Thus, this part analysed the types and flow of support by marital status and gender among *non-coresident* families (Table 6.7).

Marital status was statistically related to intergenerational support of non-coresident family members. As shown in Table 6.7, there was a consistent relationship across all three societies whereby married men and married women perceived greater responsibility of financial support to their parents than their unmarried counterparts. In particular, the degree of financial support provided by adult children in Hanoi was relatively lower than that of children in Bangkok Metropolis and Kuala Lumpur.

The results regarding downward financial support from parents to unmarried men and unmarried women also revealed a similar pattern across the three societies. It can be seen that among *non-coresident families*, parents often provided support to unmarried children rather than married ones. This was especially obvious among unmarried daughters and sons in Hanoi and Kuala Lumpur. In comparison, the extent of financial support to unmarried adult children in Bangkok Metropolis was relatively low.

As for emotional support, in the Bangkok Metropolis *non-coresident* sample, women regardless of whether they were married or unmarried provided

TABLE 6.7 Types and flow of support by marital status and gender

Intergenerational support	Bangkok					Hanoi					Kuala Lumpur				
	MM	MW	UM	UW	Sig.	MM	MW	UM	UW	Sig.	MM	MW	UM	UW	Sig.
Provided support to parents															
Financial support	2.98	3.10	2.00	2.93	5.12**	2.76	2.21	1.80	1.63	10.25***	3.25	2.96	2.96	2.60	5.26***
Emotional support	2.45	2.84	2.25	3.38	5.86***	3.20	3.18	3.40	3.38	–	2.85	3.03	2.76	3.09	–
Household chores support	1.83	2.03	1.55	1.90	–	2.84	2.62	2.20	2.00	3.71**	2.54	2.74	2.87	2.74	–
Received support from parents															
Financial support	1.36	1.37	1.95	1.52	3.16*	1.31	1.33	2.80	3.13	20.46***	1.50	1.45	2.33	2.26	20.43***
Emotional support	2.05	2.22	2.10	2.72	–	2.71	2.89	3.60	3.50	2.86*	2.37	2.58	2.93	2.97	6.04***
Household chores support	1.33	1.45	1.40	1.31	–	1.47	1.42	3.20	2.38	10.54***	1.66	1.87	2.73	2.57	24.80***
Filial attitudes															
Feeling grateful	6.65	6.56	6.61	6.65	–	6.83	6.84	7.00	6.94	–	6.06	6.10	6.19	6.08	–
Support parent's livelihood	6.51	6.48	6.63	6.61	–	5.43	5.56	6.00	6.17	–	5.89	5.91	6.02	5.92	–
Familial responsibilities															
Financial support from:															
Unmarried adult man to own parents	5.99	5.93	5.59	6.18	–	4.77	5.30	3.83	5.44	6.25***	5.88	6.04	5.95	5.83	–
Unmarried adult woman to own parents	5.94	5.94	5.59	6.18	–	4.45	4.96	3.83	5.28	5.27***	5.83	5.98	5.93	5.77	–

TABLE 6.7 Types and flow of support by marital status and gender (*cont.*)

Intergenerational support	Bangkok					Hanoi					Kuala Lumpur				
	MM	**MW**	**UM**	**UW**	**Sig.**	**MM**	**MW**	**UM**	**UW**	**Sig.**	**MM**	**MW**	**UM**	**UW**	**Sig.**
Married adult man to own parents	5.73	5.65	5.68	5.94	–	5.14	5.32	5.50	5.56	–	5.79	5.91	5.88	5.77	–
Married adult woman to own parents	5.74	5.67	5.68	6.03	–	3.60	3.88	4.50	4.56	2.86*	5.71	5.81	5.82	5.67	–
Married man to parents-in-law	5.49	5.37	5.27	5.71	–	2.99	3.17	3.67	4.10	2.53*	5.44	5.63	5.42	5.58	–
Married woman to parents-in-law	5.50	5.36	5.22	5.66	–	4.75	5.08	5.00	5.22	2.56*	5.37	5.51	5.42	5.42	–

Note: MM = Married man; MW = Married women; UM = Unmarried man; UW = Unmarried women

* $p<0.05$; ** $p<0.01$; *** $p<0.001$

greater support to their parents compared to men, while the difference between the interaction of marital status and gender is not clear in Hanoi and Kuala Lumpur. In addition, results also showed that unmarried adult children in Hanoi and Kuala Lumpur received more emotional support from their parents than married ones; however, there was no clear difference of this kind of support in Bangkok Metropolis.

In provision of household chores to parents, married men and married women in the *non-coresident* sample of Hanoi showed greater support as compared to those who were unmarried; while there were no significant differences in Bangkok Metropolis and Kuala Lumpur. In terms of downward support, parents in Hanoi and Kuala Lumpur demonstrated greater support in assisting unmarried men and unmarried women with household chores, especially unmarried sons (Table 6.7).

In terms of the perception of familial responsibilities, there was no significant difference between marital status and gender in Bangkok Metropolis and Kuala Lumpur. Data only revealed significant differences between some groups in the Hanoi sample. Specifically, a higher degree of agreement was found among women for nearly all statements as compared to men. A comparison of marital status showed that in general, there was stronger support among unmarried respondents regarding the statements that a "married adult woman [needs to provide financial support] to [their] own parents", a "married man [needs to provide financial support] to [his] parents-in-law", a "married woman [needs to provide financial support] to [her] parents-in-law" compared to those who were married.

3.5 *Characteristics of Parents and Intergenerational Support*

Parental characteristics such as parental health status, marital status and old age are used as independent variables to predict changes in the caring level of children to parents. These characteristics can be considered as indicators of the demand and needs of caring for parents (A description of these indicators is shown in Table 6.1).

We can see that there was a high percentage of respondents having both parents and PIL with no spouse, with about 70% reported in Bangkok Metropolis and 50% in Hanoi and Kuala Lumpur. At the same time, there was a high percentage of respondents having at least one parent above 65 years old with 61.7% in Bangkok Metropolis, 75.3% in Hanoi and 51.9% in Kuala Lumpur. In relation to 'health condition', while the percentage of either parent being unhealthy was lower than the two above mentioned indicators, it was still considered high, where there were almost 50% in Hanoi, 75% in Bangkok Metropolis and, the least, 16.2% in Kuala Lumpur. It was assumed that the demand for caring would be stronger among those who had a living parent with a poor health status, in old age (above 65 years old), and with a parent with no spouse. Thus, the data imply that there was a high demand of parental support from children in *non-coresident families* across all three societies. In this part, we will analyse in more detail the relationship between parental marital status and parental health regarding intergenerational support.

The *marital status of* [*a*] *parent* can be considered as a determining factor in a strong relationship between elderly parents and adult children[1]. It is noted that on one hand, elderly parents without a spouse may need more support both financially and practically from their children. On the other hand, spouseless parents may also provide support to children in order to gain the feeling of solidarity through family attachment and to ameliorate the feeling of loneliness from losing or not having a spouse. They may have wanted to provide support to children and grandchildren in order to secure a 'pay back' in other words, as a means of securing emotional and financial security from their children at a later stage of life. Data in Hanoi showed that parents without a spouse needed more financial support from their children than parents with a spouse (Table 6.8). In addition, parents who were living with their spouse in Hanoi and Kuala Lumpur provided greater support to their children in terms of emotional and household chores support. It can be seen that the marital status of parents was an important indicator of intergenerational exchanges in Hanoi and Kuala Lumpur societies.

In terms of familial responsibilities, the difference between adult children having both parents living and only one living parent was clear in the case of Kuala Lumpur and to some extent for Hanoi. However, the difference between these two groups was not very pronounced. In Hanoi, the mean score of respondents with both parents living was much higher (mean=5.47) for the statement a "married adult man [needs to provide financial support] to [his] own parents" than those with only one living parent (mean=5.15).

Previous research emphasised that, changes in a parent's health may have consequences for the lives of their adult children (Kaufman & Uhlenberg 1998). However, the results from the present study showed that there was no clear association between the provision of financial support by non-coresident children and the health status of parents or parents-in-law. In addition, a similar pattern was observed for the upward exchange of emotional care and household chores assistance to parents and parents-in-law in all three societies. The

1 Sex differentiation of the "parent" is an interesting point to look at in terms of the relationship between parents and children. However, here we just focused on the situation of parents who were alive or not to reflect the general demand of help from of parents.

TABLE 6.8 Types and flow of support by parent marital status

Intergenerational support	Bangkok			Hanoi			Kuala Lumpur		
	No spouse	With spouse	T-test Sig	No spouse	With spouse	T-test Sig	No spouse	With spouse	T-test Sig
Provided support to parents									
Financial support	2.93	3.05	–	2.50	2.26	2.3*	3.03	3.02	–
Emotional support	2.62	2.81	–	3.17	3.22	–	2.88	2.97	–
Household chores support	1.92	1.94	–	2.71	2.66	–	2.63	2.69	–
Received support from parents									
Financial support	1.35	1.46	–	1.16	1.63	−6.4***	1.35	1.81	−6.1***
Emotional support	2.08	2.31	–	2.71	3.02	−3.1**	2.44	2.63	−2.2*
Household chores support	1.31	1.50	−2.4*	1.24	1.76	−7.0***	1.67	2.11	−5.6***
Filial attitudes									
Feeling grateful	6.56	6.64	–	6.83	6.83	–	6.07	6.11	–
Support parent's livelihood	6.50	6.47	–	5.52	5.52	–	5.89	5.90	–
Familial responsibilities									
Financial support from:									
Unmarried adult man to own parents	5.90	6.05	–	5.04	5.10	–	5.86	6.03	−2.4*
Unmarried adult woman to own parents	5.89	6.03	–	4.70	4.86	–	5.82	5.97	−2.2*

TABLE 6.8 Types and flow of support by parent marital status (*cont.*)

Intergenerational support	Bangkok			Hanoi			Kuala Lumpur		
	No spouse	With spouse	T-test Sig	No spouse	With spouse	T-test Sig	No spouse	With spouse	T-test Sig
Married adult man to own parents	5.65	5.79	–	5.15	5.47	−2.7**	5.78	5.93	–
Married adult woman to own parents	5.67	5.79	–	3.73	3.91	–	5.68	5.85	−2.2*
Married man to parents-in-law	5.36	5.51	–	3.08	3.18	–	5.45	5.62	−2.1*
Married woman to parents-in-law	5.34	5.52	–	4.85	5.13	−2.1*	5.36	5.52	–

Note: * $p<0.05$; ** $p<0.01$; *** $p<0.001$

only significant association between parents' health status and upward emotional support was found among *non-coresident* respondents in Kuala Lumpur where healthy parents received a greater degree of emotional support from their non-coresident adult children.

Within non-coresident families, downward support from parents to children revealed a clear difference between two groups of parents. Data revealed that in the cases of Bangkok Metropolis and Hanoi, parents tended to provide more financial support to non-coresident children when the parents were healthy, $F_{Bangkok}=-2.38$, $p<.05$; $F_{Hanoi}=-2.63$, $p<.01$; while downward support between parents-in-law and children was only obvious in Hanoi, $F=-2.22$, $p<.05$. Thus, the different trends in financial exchange between non-coresident parents and children reflected diversity across societies in terms of the cultural norms and provision of social and health care services. By comparison, in Hanoi, it was revealed that downward emotional support among non-coresident families was weaker among unhealthy parents, $F=-3.35$, $p<.001$; while in the Kuala Lumpur sample, the relationship was inversed, $F=2.59$, $p<.01$. It was also found that there were no differences in emotional exchanges between parents and children in non-coresident households in Bangkok Metropolis regardless of the health status of parents.

In addition, the results also indicated that the extent of household-chores support from parents to non-coresident children changed significantly according to the parents' health status. In Hanoi and Kuala Lumpur, it was demonstrated that healthy parents would provide greater household chores support to non-coresident children compared to parents who were unhealthy, $F=-4.05$, $p<.001$. Similarly, parents-in-laws in the Hanoi sample strongly perceived the need to provide greater household support when their health condition was good, $F=-3.89$, $p<.001$. This may have reflected a strong family attachment among the non-coresident families where healthy parents tended to support their children and in return, they expected to rely on their children for old-age security as a 'pay back' for supporting their children with housework (Table 6.9).

In relation to the expectations regarding filial obligation, non-coresident respondents with parents in good health tended to endorse the statement that an "unmarried adult man/woman [needs to provide financial support] to [his/her] own parents"; and this was especially clear in Hanoi. Similar results were reported in the non-coresident sample of Kuala Lumpur in which those with healthy parents tended to express a higher degree of agreement for statement that a "married man/woman [needs to provide financial support] to parents-in-law" compared to those with parents with poor health.

TABLE 6.9 Types and flow of support by parents' health demand

Intergenerational support	Bangkok			Hanoi			Kuala Lumpur		
	Unhealthy	Healthy	T-test Sig	Unhealthy	Healthy	T-test Sig	Unhealthy	Healthy	T-test Sig
Provided support to parents									
Financial support	3.05	2.96	–	2.38	2.40	–	2.89	3.05	–
Emotional support	2.67	2.69	–	3.14	3.24	–	3.27	2.88	**3.15****
Household chores support	1.91	1.94	–	2.71	2.66	–	2.66	2.67	–
Received support from parents									
Financial support	1.26	1.48	2.38*	1.27	1.47	2.63**	1.62	1.58	–
Emotional support	2.18	2.15	–	2.68	3.01	3.35***	2.82	2.49	**2.59****
Household chores support	1.33	1.43	–	1.31	1.62	4.05***	1.65	1.94	**2.52***
Provided support to PIL									
Financial support	2.57	2.63	–	2.17	2.19	–	2.42	2.31	–
Emotional support	1.98	2.09	–	2.66	2.86	–	2.60	2.36	–
Household chores support	1.68	1.81	–	2.42	2.49	–	2.23	2.17	–
Received support from PIL									
Financial support	1.34	1.30	–	1.17	1.29	2.22*	1.38	1.30	–
Emotional support	1.82	1.77	–	2.36	2.59	2.26*	2.27	2.03	**2.06****
Household chores support	1.28	1.38	–	1.23	1.49	3.89***	1.49	1.59	–
Filial attitudes									
Feeling grateful	6.64	6.64	–	6.82	6.85	–	6.17	6.10	–

Intergenerational support	Bangkok			Hanoi			Kuala Lumpur		
	Unhealthy	Healthy	T-test Sig	Unhealthy	Healthy	T-test Sig	Unhealthy	Healthy	T-test Sig
Support parent's livelihood	6.45	6.48	–	5.44	5.61	–	5.84	5.93	–
Familial responsibilities									
Financial support from:									
Unmarried adult man to own parents	5.97	6.06	–	4.94	5.33	2.62**	5.81	5.99	–
Unmarried adult woman to own parents	5.99	6.03	–	4.55	4.98	2.71**	5.79	5.93	–
Married adult man to own parents	5.80	5.78	–	5.18	5.33	–	5.70	5.90	–
Married adult woman to own parents	5.46	5.79	–	3.62	3.76	–	5.67	5.80	–
Married man to parents-in-law	5.56	5.51	–	3.06	3.13	–	5.32	5.57	**2.04***
Married woman to parents-in-law		5.51	–	5.05	4.96	–	5.16	5.49	**2.54***

Note: Unhealthy = At least one unhealthy parent; Healthy = All healthy/one healthy and one deceased

* $p<0.05$; ** $p<0.01$; *** $p<0.001$

4 Factors Affecting Intergenerational Support among Non-coresident Families

The results of the multivariate analysis of predictors for intergenerational support amongst non-coresident families in Bangkok Metropolis, Hanoi and Kuala Lumpur are presented in Table 6.10. The dependent variable is the extent of intergenerational support from children to parents and parents-in-law in the three societies. In the final model, predictors included the characteristics of adult children and parents, filial norms, family interaction, support from parents to adult children, and geographical distance from parents. These factors were included in the models for predicting upward support from adult children to parents. In addition, country specific variables that included locality, living standard and ethnicity were also included for the Hanoi and Kuala Lumpur regression analysis. Specifically, it was noted that these selected predictors explained a substantial amount of the variance in downward support among non-coresident families across the three societies, ranging from 16% to 38%. The regression models for predicting intergenerational support from adult children to parents and parents-in-law among non-coresident families are presented separately in Table 6.10 and 6.11, respectively.

4.1.1 Bangkok Metropolis

In the non-coresident sample of Bangkok Metropolis, married daughters were more likely to support their parents than married sons (β=0.60). Meanwhile, unmarried sons reported providing less support to non-coresident parents (β=−1.47). The farther the geographical distance from parents, the less likely adult children provided support to their parents (β=−0.15). In addition, the more support non-coresident adult children received from their parents, the more likely that parents received support from non-coresident (β=0.36). Thus, a mutual relationship wass clearly expressed in this situation. For the intergenerational exchange between children and parents-in-law living in different households, only mutual help had an important role in explaining the findings of upward support (β=0.60). The findings revealed that the more support non-coresident children receive from their parents-in-law the more the parents-in-law support non-coresident children.

4.1.2 Hanoi

The findings revealed that the interaction of marital status and gender, endorsement of filial norms, support from parents to adult children, locality and living standard were all significant predictors of intergenerational support from children to parents among non-coresident families in Hanoi. The result

TABLE 6.10 Factors predicting support from respondent to parents in non-coresident families

Predictors	Unstandardised Beta, Unβ		
	Bangkok Metropolis	Hanoi	Kuala Lumpur
Adult children characteristics			
Status (ref. Married Son)			
Married Daughter	0.60*	−0.75**	−0.06
Unmarried Son	−1.47*	2.90**	−0.45
Unmarried Daughter	0.60	−4.00***	−1.01+
Age Cohort (ref. Young)			
Middle generation	0.62	0.59	0.21
Old generation	0.59	0.46	0.39
Education level	0.72	0.82**	0.30
With children below 7 (at least 1)	−0.06	−0.27	−0.24
Parental characteristics			
Health demands	−0.05	−0.25	0.24
No spouse	0.44	−0.38	−0.11
Filial norm	0.02	0.30**	−0.04*
Support from Parents to AC	0.36***	0.27***	−0.08
Distance from parent residence	−0.15*	−0.84	0.37***
Other predictors			
Urban residence		0.98***	−0.06
Low living standard		−0.74***	−1.22***
Ethnicity (ref. Malay)			
Chinese			−0.58+
Indian			−0.28
Adjusted R-squared	0.16	0.20	0.22
F	6.76***	9.04***	9.68***

Note: +p<0.10; * p<0.05; **p<0.01; *** p<0.001
Children age 7 or below: Adult children with at least one child age 7 or below (1 = Yes, 0 = No)
High health demand: 1 = Yes, 0 = No
Living standard: 1 = High, 2 = Medium, 3 = Low/poor

TABLE 6.11 Factors predicting support from respondent to parents-in-law in non-coresident families

Predictors	**Unstandardised Beta, Unβ**		
	Bangkok Metropolis	**Hanoi**	**Kuala Lumpur**
Adult children characteristics			
Status (ref. Married Son)			
Married Daughter	0.11	1.08***	0.08
Age Cohort (ref. Young)			
Middle generation	0.41	−0.10	0.47
Old generation	0.77	0.31	0.13
Education level	0.65	0.27	0.20
With children below 7 (at least 1) (0,1)	−0.30	−0.49	−0.45+
Parental characteristics			
Health demands (1,2)	0.51	−0.17	−0.27
No spouse	0.29	−0.28	−0.41*
Filial norm	−0.00	0.34***	0.14
Support from Parents to AC	0.60***	0.50***	0.75***
Distance from parent residence	0.06	−0.02	0.15*
Other predictors			
Urban residence		0.40	0.11
Low living standard		−0.95***	−0.64***
Ethnicity (ref. Malay)			
Chinese			−0.43
Indian			−0.54
Adjusted R-squared	**0.23**	**0.26**	**0.38**
F	**8.50*** **	**12.38*** **	**19.71*** **

Note: * $p<0.05$; ** $p<0.01$; *** $p<0.001$

Children age 7 or below: Adult children with at least one child age 7 or below (1 = Yes, 0 = No)

Age 65 or >: At least one parent age 65 or more (1 = Yes, 0 = No)

High health demand: 1 = Yes, 0 = No

Living standard: 1 = High, 2 = Medium, 3 = Low/poor

from regression models showed that, in general, married children provide more support to parents than unmarried children ($\beta_{\text{Married daughters}}$=–0.75; $\beta_{\text{Unmarried son}}$=–2.90; $\beta_{\text{Unmarried daughters}}$=–4.00) and married sons specifically reported the greatest support to parents who do not share a household with them. Those with higher educational levels were also found to provide more support to their own parents (β=0.82). The extent of support provision to parents was also greater among adult children who endorsed filial norms, and who received more regular support from their parents in terms of financial, emotional and domestic tasks (β=0.27). The condition of economic development in societies may have also influenced the expectation and extent of support from children to parents and vice versa. When children were poor, they tended to provide less financial assistance to their parents. After taking into account locality and the living standard of adult children, the results demonstrated that urban residence strengthens the support from children to parents who are not-coresiding with their children (β=0.98), and as expected, children with lower socio-economic status provided less support to their parents (β=–0.74).

Regarding support from non-coresident children to parents-in-law, more regular support was found amongst married daughters (β=1.08), children who endorsed filial norms (β=0.34), those who received support from parents (β=0.50), and those from families with a better living standard (β=–0.95).

4.1.3 Kuala Lumpur

Regression models for Kuala Lumpur demonstrated that the endorsement of filial norms (β=–0.04), support from parents to adult children (β=0.37), and living standard (β=–1.22) were significant predictors of intergenerational support from children to parents among *non-coresident* families. It was found that the extent of support provision to parents was smaller among adult children who endorsed filial norms, however this relationship was not very strong. Adult children who received less regular support from their parents in terms of financial, emotional and domestic tasks tended to provide less support for their parents. Results from the regression analysis showed that poor non-coresident children are more likely to provide less support to their parents.

As for support from non-coresident children to parents-in-law, geographical distance from parents-in-law had a significant effect in which, the farther adult children lived from their parents-in-law the more support they provided to them(β=0.15). Adult children with lower living standards were also less likely to provide support for their parents-in-law living in a different household (β=–0.64). In addition, among the Kuala Lumpur non-coresident sample, the characteristics of parents-in-law had an important role in determining the provision of support for the parents. It was found that among non-coresident households, parents-in-law with no spouse were less likely to receive support from children compared to those with a spouse (β=−0.41).

In summary, the model showed strong patriarchal norms in the context of care relations. The patriarchal pattern was especially strong in Hanoi; married children are more likely to provide support to their parents than unmarried children among non-coresident families. Also, when children endorsed filial norms, they are more prone to support and care for their parents, especially in Hanoi. In contrast, the opposite direction was observed among non-coresident families in Kuala Lumpur.

The pattern of gender neutrality was clear for non-coresident families in the Bangkok Metropolis and Kuala Lumpur cases. There was an obvious mutual relationship in intergenerational support whereby among those who live away from their parents and parents-in law, provision of support from parents to adult children tends to lead to more regular support from adult children to parents. It was universal among the three societies that the characteristics of parents had less significant influence on the extent of support from children compared to other predictors for adult children who do not share a household with their parents or parents-in-law.

5 Discussion

The mutually supportive relationship in the non-coresident families in this chapter was analysed from two aspects: care and support from non-coresident children to parents and parents-in-law; care and support from parents and parents-in-law to non-coresident children. Support levels were measured by the frequency of support. Although the survey data did not analyse each type of support separately, analyses from these two aspects provided a broad picture about the mutual support relationship between parents and non-coresident children in the three cities and the factors associated with this relationship.

In general, intergenerational support between parents and non-coresident children in all three survey areas was quite powerful. Regarding the three main dimensions inclusive of financial assistance, care support (including care for aging parents, children, and the sick) and emotional support (listening to problems, sharing thoughts of life aspects), the data reflect that there remained strong support relationships in most non-coresident families, especially in terms of financial and emotional support.

In terms of the reciprocity of support between parents and non-coresident adult children, the downward flow from ageing parents to non-coresident adult children was lower than the upward flow. There were some possible explanations for this finding. One plausible explanation was that the parents wanted to conserve their money for their own support later in life, given the limited scope of coverage social pensions in Vietnam (Tran 2009; Tran 2017). Another reason could be that there were more children as compared to the number of parents, so support flow from parents to children was less to each child than the support from children to parents. Among non-coresident families, support from children to parents and parents-in-law was expressed more clearly in financial and housework assistance than in emotional support. That may have been related to a generation gap regarding the perception of support where young people perceived that providing monetary assistance, gifts and helping parents directly in other ways, were enough, while the parents considered listening or sharing concerns and affection as more important (Le 2017).

Regarding the downward flow among non-coresident families, as shown in other studies, this relationship was also very strong. Supporting descendants by contributing to income generation and listening to their problems confirmed the social status of elderly people in families; on the other hand, it was a way to express their responsibility to help their children. More importantly providing support enabled the elderly people to feel helpful in their old age which could tighten the relationships between generations, and improved their status and position in the non-coresident family. These mutual relationships helped old people maintain power, status, reputation and an association with their non-coresident descendants. This was considered a rational choice because with this help the elderly people expected to receive care from their children when they faced difficulty, as stated in previous research (Cohen & Wills 1985; Le, Nguyen & Tran 2011; Emerson 1976).

The relationship between children and their spouses' parents was basically similar to the trend of children-parents' relationship. This was the case although the support of children to their spouses' parents was generally lower than that to their own parents, except in Hanoi where the daughter's financial support and care work for her parents was lower than that for her parents-in-law. Both traditional culture and distance from each other may have contributed to this situation because in Hanoi, upon marriage, daughter-in-law are expected to live with or live near the husband's family These results confirm findings from other studies in Southeast Asia on the intergenerational support among non-coresident members of extended families (Lee, Parish & Willis. et al. 1994; Knodel, Friedman, Anh, & Cuong 2000).

Yet, there were significant differences among the three sites on intergenerational support patterns. In particular, Hanoi and Kuala Lumpur shared attitudes of son preference and putting men in the position of family leaders as influenced by the norms of male chauvinism, while Bangkok Metropolis emphasised the role of women and mother-side relationships. The level of emotional and care support was higher in Hanoi families compared to Bangkok

Metropolis and Kuala Lumpur. In contrast, regarding financial assistance, a higher level was recorded in Bangkok Metropolis and Kuala Lumpur. These differences were expressed clearly in both directions, from children to parents and vice versa, which may reflect that societies with higher economic development can better provide financial support to parents than those in a lower economic setting. In other words, despite these societies all being influenced by filial piety emphasizing the care responsibility of children toward parents, the different patterns of practice may have been a result of the complexity in the interaction between the different pace of socio-economic development and the family systems which still prevailed in the societies.

Financial support for parents-in-law was expressed more clearly in Bangkok Metropolis and Kuala Lumpur than in Hanoi. However, care work and emotional support were recorded better in Hanoi. Data also show that differences in support provision to the husband's parents and wife's parents were clearly expressed in Hanoi compared to Bangkok Metropolis and Kuala Lumpur which had a trend of providing more for the husband's parents.

In general, the three cities shared a pattern of mutual support. This means that the level of children's support to parents was closely associated with support from parents to children as noted by Gibson (1992) and that caregiving was normally conceptualised as a two-way relationship. This practice fitted very well with the ideal that the family should function as a mutual help network in which the adult child takes care of the parents without eliciting any feelings of low self-esteem, dependency or humiliation on the part of the parents. This practice was probably also a reflection of the sign of psychological feeling as described by equity theory (Walster, Walster & Berscheid 1978) where receiving more support than one gave led to distress and guilt, whereas receiving less support than one gave was a source of distress because people feel exploited and unfairly treated.

Mutual support was a social construction that was affected by social values as well as individual characteristics. Individual, family and community factors had different roles in explaining the mutual relationship between parents and children in all the three cities. At the society level, there were filial norms from children to parents, and different roles of sons or daughters that were specified in the society. If the value of son were more highly evaluated then mutual support between parents and sons would be stronger than with daughters and vice versa.

In reality, a combination of sex and marital status (to make clear the role of married and unmarried people) was one of the important variables explaining intergenerational relationships among non-coresident family members. Based on the cultural traditions of each country, it was assumed that there was a fundamental difference between the flow from sons or daughters to parents, and vice versa, under which, the flow to and from daughters was more frequent in Bangkok Metropolis, but the flow to and from sons was more frequent in Kuala Lumpur and Hanoi. However, initial results suggest that this assumption is confirmed convincingly only in Bangkok Metropolis and Hanoi. Support from married daughters to parents was stronger than that of married sons in Bangkok Metropolis and weaker than married sons in Hanoi. Meanwhile, in Hanoi, support from married daughters to her husband's parents was stronger than support from married sons to his wife's parents. Differences for the Kuala Lumpur cases was not significant. This could be related to the structure of ethnic composition in the Kuala Lumpur sample where the bilateral Malays account for 50% of the sample while patriarchal Chinese and Indian account for the other 50%. Obviously, traditional understanding of gender roles in support and care should be reconsidered in the new context. In the period of industrialisation, urbanisation and globalisation, the differentiation of sons or daughters in the care sector could be gradually reduced in some aspects of life.

Children's education had a medium effect on the support level to their parents. The higher education the children received, the higher support they provided in return. One reason which has probably caused this, was that residents with higher education could have been more aware of the importance of support to parents in their life. However, in a more advanced society, more highly educated people were also associated with living farther from their parents, and were more likely to break the traditional patterns including helping with domestic chores and housework. Modernization also imparted values, aspirations and skills which encouraged and facilitated women's modern roles, and tended to produce a stronger orientation towards the labor market and a career (Subbarao & Raney 1995). By exposing women to non-traditional roles and providing them with the means to establish viable alternatives to motherhood, education expanded their life choices. Higher education helps women who used to be responsible mainly for care work in the family to have more opportunities outside of their homes.

Normative solidarity, i.e. the expectations regarding filial obligations and parental obligations as well as norms of the importance of familistic values, was considered as an important dimension in measuring intergenerational solidarity (Bengtson & Schrader 1982; Bengtson, Giarrusso, Silverstein, & Wang 2000). It was supposed that those with higher evaluation of filial norms would provide more support to their parents and parents-in-law. However, this assumption was confirmed only for the Hanoi case. This is probably attributable to the fact that Hanoi was less developed compared to Bangkok Metropolis and Kuala Lumpur. For this reason, the impact of traditional norms was relatively strong in Hanoi.

Usually, one may expect unhealthy parents to be in need of more help compared to those who are healthy. However, findings from the three sites showed that regardless of parents' characteristics such as their health demands or marital status, the support of children t was revealed. This was also the case for parents-in-law.

Among other factors, the distance from the parents' home had a medium significance in affecting the support of children to parents and spouses' parents in Bangkok Metropolis and Kuala Lumpur, but in different directions. Normally a closer distance would make support easier. However, in this study, for the support from children and parents, it was shown significantly only for Bangkok Metropolis that the farther the distance, the lesser the support. As for the relationship between children and their spouses' parents, the significance of distance was only shown for Kuala Lumpur but in the opposite direction: the farther the distance, the higher the support. One reason is that parents were living in rural areas so the children needed to provide more support for their parents.

The role of residence in urban or rural area was analysed only for Hanoi and Kuala Lumpur. It is indicated that living in an urban area increased support to parents in Hanoi, but not in Kuala Lumpur. Similar finding also applied to support for spouses' parents. A reason may be that Kuala Lumpur is more urbanised than Hanoi, therefore the urban factor was not important in Kuala Lumpur.

Living standards had an important role in explaining the support from children to parents as well as spouses' parents, which was applicable to both Hanoi and Kuala Lumpur. Better living standards increased the ability of the children to provide support to their parents and parents-in-law. This result was completely reasonable and conformed to previous findings on this issue. Although the role of this factor was not examined in Bangkok Metropolis, it is suggested that living standards could contribute to explain support patterns in Bangkok Metropolis as well.

There was a difference between people's attitude and behaviour on intergenerational support. Frequency of support in practice was lower than the level of attitude support, probably because support behaviour would depend more on different contextual factors. Almost all respondents, regardless of whether they were sons or daughters, from all the three sites, expressed the highest support for the attitude of filial norms to their parents (there was a lower level in Kuala Lumpur compared to Hanoi and Bangkok Metropolis). However, the attitude to financial support for parents and parents-in-law was varied between the three sites. The attitude level to financial support of the

Hanoi residents was lower than that of Bangkok Metropolis and Kuala Lumpur residents, as it was in behaviour support. It is worth noting that in Hanoi, the attitude to support of the female respondents was higher than of male respondents regardless of whether this was to parents or parents-in-law. Confucian ideas in Hanoi was also expressed clearly with the belief that there should be higher financial support to the grooms' parents than to the brides' parents. The findings show a pattern of diversification and transformation in those Southeast Asian families.

References

Bengtson, Vern, & Robert Roberts. (1991). Intergenerational solidarity in aging families – an example of formal theory construction. *Journal of Marriage and the Family, 53*(4), 856–870.

Bengtson, Vern, & Sandi Schrader. (1982). Parent-child relations. In D. Mangen, & W. Peterson (Eds.), *Handbook of research instruments in social gerontology* (pp. 115–185). Minneapolis: University of Minnesota Press.

Bengtson, Vern, Roseann Giarrusso, Merril Silverstein, & Haitao Wang. (2000). Families and intergenerational relationships in ageing societies. *Hallym International Journal of Ageing, 2*(1), 3–10.

Chan, Angelique. (2005). *Formal and informal intergenerational support transfers in South-Eastern Asia.* Paper presented at the United Nations expert group meeting on social and economic iImplications of changing population age structures, Population Division, Department of Economic and Social, Affairs United Nations Secretariat, Mexico City.

Cohen, Sheldon, & Thomas Wills. (1985). Stress, social support, and the buffering hypothesis. *Psychological Bulletin, 98*(2), 310–357. doi:10.1037/0033-2909.98.2.310.

Cooksey, Elizabeth, & Patricia Craig. (1998). Parenting from a distance: The effects of paternal characteristics on contact between nonresidential fathers and their children. *Demography, 35*(2): 187–200.

Emerson, Richard. (1976). Social exchange theory. *Annual Review of Sociology, 2*(1), 335–362. doi:10.1146/annurev.so.02.080176.002003.

Frankenberg, Elizabeth, Lee Lillard, & Robert Willis. (2002). Patterns of Intergenerational transfers in Southeast Asia. *Journal of Marriage and the Family, 64*(3), 627–641.

Gibson, Charyl. (1992). A revised conceptualization of social support. *Journal of Clinical Nursing, 1*(3): 147–152.

Grundy, Emily, & John Henretta. (2004, November 19–23). *Intergenerational exchanges in families with three generations: A comparative analysis.* Paper presented at the annual meeting of the gerontological society of America, Washington, D.C.

Hagestad, Gunhild. (2001). Adult intergenerational relationships. *Gender and generation programme: Exploring future research and data collection options* (pp. 125–143). New York and Geneva: UNECE and United Nations Population Fund.

Heylen, Leen, Dimitri Morterlmans, Maarten Hermans, & Kim Boudiny. (2012). The intermediate effect of geographic proximity on intergenerational support: A comparison of France and Bulgaria. *Demographic Research, 27*(17), 455–486.

Kaufman, Gayle, & Peter Uhlenberg. (1998). Effect of life course transition on the quality of relationship between adult children and their parents. *Journal of Marriage and the Family,* 60, 924–938.

Knodel, John, Jed Friedman, Truong Si Anh, & Bui The Cuong. (2000). Intergenerational exchanges in Vietnam: Family size, sex composition, and the location of children. *Population Studies: A Journal of Demography, 54*(1), 89–104. doi:10.1080/713779067.

Le, Ngoc Lan. (2017). *Elderly people in Vietnamese family in the context of ageing population and social changes.* Unpublished Ph.D. Dissertation. Graduate Academy of Social Sciences, Hanoi.

Le, Ngoc Lan, Huu Minh Nguyen, & Quy Long Tran. (2011). Relationship between the elderly and their offspring. In Ministry of Culture, Sports and Tourism, & Institute for Family and Gender Studies (Eds.), *Intra-family relationships of the Vietnamese families: Key findings from in-depth analyses of the Vietnam family survey* (pp. 31–56). Ha Noi: Social Sciences Publishing House.

Lee, Yean-Ju, William L. Parish, & Robert J. Willis. (1994). Sons, daughters, and intergenerational support in Taiwan. *American Journal of Sociology, 99*(4), 1010–1041.

Subbarao, Kalanidhi, & Laura Raney. (1995), Social gains from female education: A cross-national study, *economic development and cultural change, 44*(1), 105–128.

Tran, Thi Minh Thi. (2014). "Chinhsachchamsoctreem: Kinhnghiemcuacacnuoc Dong Au vathuctien o Viet Nam". *Tap chi Khoa hoc xa hoi Viet Nam,* So 12, 62–72. [Child care in Eastern Europe and implications to Viet Nam. *Viet Nam Journal of Social Sciences, 12*, 62–72].

Tran, Thi Minh Thi. (2016). Mô hình sắp xếp nơi ở của NCT hiện nay và những yếu tố ảnh hưởng. Tạp chí Nghiên cứu Gia đình và Giới. 5, 1–24. [Living arrangement of the elder and determinants. *Journal of Family and Gender Studies. 5*, 1–24].

Tran, Thi Minh Thi. (2017, February 28). *Sharing responses on the ground – Aging society and the surrounding challenges in Asia: Elderly care in aging society of Vietnam.* Paper presented at the Toyota foundation public symposium in Seoul, Korea.

Tran, Van Son. (2009). Experiences of social pension in Viet Nam (2001–2009). Paper presented at the OECD/IOPS global forum on private pensions, designing adequate DC pensions: Global experience and lessons from Asia Pacific, Australia, Sydney.

Walster, Elaine, William Walster, & Ellen Berscheid. (1978). *Equity: Theory and research.* Boston: Allyn and Unwin.

CHAPTER 7

Main Elderly and Child Care Provider: Who Is and Who Should Be?

Patcharawalai Wongboonsin and Pataporn Sukontamarn

1 Introduction

In intergenerational family relations, care can be downward and upward. Previous studies focused on the provision of elderly care with an objective to enhance well-being of elders and their family caregivers (see Lowenstein & Ogg 2003, among others). Some other studies focused on intergenerational childcare from the perspectives of intergenerational solidarity and child welfare (Barranti 1985; Schultz 1988; Bengtson & Robertson 1985; Bengtson 2001; Blau 1995).

The welfare-triangle model developed by Esping-Andersen (1990) and Esping-Andersen Gallie, Hemerijck & Myles (2002) includes three sectors of care provision: State, market and family. Meanwhile, Evers et al. (1994) incorporate in their welfare diamond these four sectors: State, market, family, and a heterogeneous cluster of community, voluntary, non-market or non-profit care providers. For intense care needs, Razavi (2007, 21) includes four institutions in her care diamond model: family/household; markets; public sector; and not-for-profit sector, including voluntary and community provision. Those three models share the notion that familial care is provided on an informal and unpaid basis while the care market provides care in return for earnings or fees. On the other hand, the non-profit/ not-for-profit care is of a relatively voluntary or charity basis. According to Razavi & Staab (2008), the not-for-profit care sector includes different types of care provision, by charities, NGOs, or through voluntary and "community" provision. Both the care market and the non-profit/ not-for-profit care include formal, informal, home-based or center-based services. In the meantime, the care provision by the state or the public sector is formal and may be directly in the form of publicly organized or financed center-based services and/or indirectly by subsidizing the family/household, market, or non-profit providers to do so. Regulating those non-state care providers is also part of the state's role in the realm of care.

As one may see in renowned family sociology and demography literatures (Murdock 1949; Parson 1968; Bourdieu 1984; Bronfenbrenner 1979), family was

 | DOI:10.1163/9789004384330_008

considered a social institution at the primary and fundamental level, with natural rights in reproductive, supportive, and parenthood function. This social institution was ideally expected to contribute caring people, male and female, with human capital, social capital, and cultural capital to the societies. Meanwhile, state government was considered a political institution with a broad and far reaching social contract to contribute to the well-being of its people through law and political order, policies and programs. They were ideally expected to regulate social interactions to the best interest of the society, even though they may in practice carry a negative impact on certain parts of the society. This was based on notions raised by political philosophers (See, interpretation and criticism in Baumrin 1969 and Wraight 2008). Given the burden of care shouldered by family members, particularly those in the working age, the process of defamilization was revealing in modern societies, against the background of demographic shift, especially through public responsibility. Among others, the role of the state as the welfare provider became noticeable, besides paid care services, not only in western countries, but also in Southeast Asia, albeit in a different degree, scope and feature.

Based on the perspective of intergenerational family relations, this chapter set out to investigate the prevalent practices in and attitudes towards care provision in Southeast Asian modernizing societies, while also examining if diversity existed during 2010–2011. Those of the people in Kuala Lumpur in Malaysia, Bangkok Metropolis in Thailand, and Hanoi in Vietnam served as the case study, based on the surveys in the respective societies during that time, as mentioned in the introductory chapter. It focused on two major groups of care recipients. They were the elderly and the children.

To explore the prevalent practices in elderly and child care, this chapter adapted the models developed by Esping-Andersen (1990), Esping-Andersen, Gallie, Hemerijck & Myles (2002), Evers, Pilj & Ungerson (1994), and Razavi (2007) to identify the sectors in which care services were provided in those modern societies during the period of investigation. This was based on the notions of the most responsible care provider and individuals or institutions taking part in care provision for the elderly and the children. This included both informal and formal care. For the attitudes towards care provision, this chapter focused on the family-state balance of responsibility in different aspects of elderly and child care. This was based, on the one hand, on the notion of shared responsibility between the family and the state raised in Daatland & Herlofson (2003) in modern welfare states. As revealed in chapters 5 and 6, in the selected societies of Malaysia, Thailand, and Vietnam during the period of investigation, the term "family" likely encompassed those belonging to the "family network" as well. The term "family" for these societies probably included those beyond the immediate family. Therefore, in this chapter we used the term "family" to mean "family network" or "family and kin".

Based on the findings in the previous chapters of this volume, it was evident that all the three societies of Malaysia, Thailand and Vietnam placed great value on the family. Familism was, quite clearly, a cultural value in these societies. However, this chapter argues that even in societies which placed great value on the family, there could be demand for the role of the state in the provision of care, both elderly care and child care. One question which arises was: how could we know if people in these societies would like the state to provide support for elderly care and child care, and if so, to what extent? An investigation into the attitude of individuals towards care provision for the elderly and the children can contribute to a better understanding if familialism prevailed in practice across the three societies or defamilizing care can be instead expected. This could lead to changes in policies regarding the provision of elderly care and child care by the state in these societies.

This chapter is divided into five sections. After the introduction, data and methodology employed in this study is presented. Section 2 provides a descriptive analysis of the practices and attitudes towards elderly and child care. The analysis on the practices covers five different sectors involved in care provision – family, state, market, not-for-profit, and others, while the analysis on the attitudes is based on the family-state balance perspective for different types of elderly and child care. Specifically speaking, it focuses on descriptive analyses of attitudes towards who should take responsibility for elder's medical treatment and nursing care, elder's livelihood, child rearing and child care work. Section 4 provides ordered-probit analyses of attitudes towards those four different types of elderly and child care in Kuala Lumpur, Bangkok Metropolis, and Hanoi. The concluding remarks in the final section comparatively discuss the main findings on elderly and child care across all societies under investigation.

2 Data and Methodology

As mentioned earlier, the study relied on the merged data of three most recent family surveys carried out in Kuala Lumpur, Bangkok Metropolis, and Hanoi during 2010–2011. Please see chapter 1 for the description of the data.

In order to investigate the attitudes towards the provision of elderly care and child care of respondents from the three Southeast Asian societies, the study analyzedthe opinions of respondents whether it should be the responsibility of the family or the government in elderly care and child care.

Specifically, the study usedthe following question from the cross-society data.

"Who do you think should be responsible for the following?

a. Elderly's medical treatment and nursing care
b. Elderly's livelihood
c. Children's rearing and care work
d. Children's education cost"

For each type of family care, there were 5 choices for the respondents to choose. They are: Always family, mostly family, equally between family and government, mostly government, and always government.

The four criteria were chosen as they represented two major dimensions of elderly care (healthcare and livelihood) and two major dimensions of childcare (child rearing and education). The questionnaires for all three societies contained exactly the same questions, so that comparison across societies was possible.

These four types of family care were the dependent variables in the statistical analysis in this chapter. The independent variables included comparable demographic and socio-economic characteristics of the respondents and those in terms of intergenerational family relations commonly used in demographic and sociological studies in family studies.

Descriptive statistics of the variables used in the regression analysis are presented in Table 7.1. From the demographic and socio-economic perspective, the age distribution appeared similar between Bangkok Metropolis and Hanoi, while Kuala Lumpur respondents consisted of a larger proportion of young generation.[1] For Bangkok Metropolis, the proportion of females (60.9%) was higher compared to Hanoi and Kuala Lumpur. This was possibly due to the fact that many male household members were not available for interview and were thus replaced by female household members. With regards to marital status, almost 90% of respondents from Hanoi were married, compared to 77% and 65% for Bangkok Metropolis and Kuala Lumpur, respectively. Bangkok Metropolis had the largest proportion of respondents

1 This study was of the notion that the current societies across the globe make up of different cohorts or generations of people, and that there were different values between generations. As in previous chapters, this study relied upon UNJSPF (2009), which categorizes the Traditionalists as those born between 1925 and 1945, the Baby Boomers born between 1946 and 1964, the generation X born between 1965 and 1978, the generation Y – also known as the Millennial, or generation Me – born between 1979 and 2000, and the generation Z born after 2000. In this study we used the term "Old Generation" to represent the Baby Boomers and older generations, "Middle Generation" to represent generation X, and "Young Generation" to represent generation Y.

TABLE 7.1 Descriptive statistics: Percentage of individuals in each category

		Bangkok Metropolis (n = 910)	Hanoi (n = 1118)	Kuala Lumpur (n = 1523)
Age	Young	20.8	1t9.0	40.3
	Middle	33.4	26.8	25.6
	Old	45.8	54.2	34.1
Gender	Female	60.9	51.2	47.0
Marital status	Married	77.3	89.0	64.5
Education	Primary or lower	45.4	7.0	17.7
	Some secondary	39.2	71.1	56.4
	Tertiary or higher	15.4	21.9	25.7
Living standard	Low	–	8.6	36.8
	Medium	–	70.5	55.6
	High	–	20.8	7.1
Living arrangement	Single person/1-generation households	16.4	8.2	9.7
	2-generation households	45.6	52.3	60.2
	3-gen, 4-gen, 5-gen, other types of households	38.0	39.4	30.1
Living with parents	Live with/nearby to at least one parent	28.9	33.2	37.3
Living with parents-in- law	Live with/nearby to at least one parents-in-law	8.2	25.6	7.6
Living with adult child	Live with adult child	58.2	41.3	17.8
Living with adult child*Married daughter	Living with at least one married daughter	6.15	2.50	1.90
Face to face contact with parents	At least weekly	35.5	52.7	49.6
Face to face contact with parents-in-law	At least weekly	14.1	41.9	23.9
Ethnicity	Malay			65.3
	Chinese			19.1
	Indian			15.6
(Mean values) Number of children	Average number of children	1.492	2.353	2.003

with primary education or lower (45.4%), while Hanoi had the largest proportion of respondents with tertiary education or higher (21.9%). For living standard, the majority of respondents from both Hanoi and Kuala Lumpur reported themselves as being middle class. Compared to Hanoi, a larger proportion of respondents from Kuala Lumpur reported themselves as having low living standard.

From the perspective of intergenerational family relations, the majority of households in all three countries appeared to be 2-generation households. Bangkok Metropolis had the largest proportion of respondents living in single person/1-generation households (16.4%). Kuala Lumpur had the largest proportion of respondents who lived with their parents (37.3%), while Hanoi had the largest proportion of respondents who lived with their parents-in-law (25.6%). Kuala Lumpur had the smallest proportion of respondents who lived with an adult child (17.8%), compared to Bangkok Metropolis and Hanoi (58.2% and 41.3%, respectively). Bangkok Metropolis had the largest proportion of respondents who lived with at least one married daughter (6.15%), followed by Hanoi and Kuala Lumpur (2.5% and 1.9%, respectively). Hanoi had the largest proportion of respondents who had face-to-face contact with their parents at least weekly (52.7%), as well as the largest proportion of respondents who had face-to-face contact with their parents-in-law at least weekly (41.9%). It appeared that for Bangkok Metropolis and Kuala Lumpur, it was common for parents and parents-in-law to provide financial assistance to their children after their children get married. However, this appeared less common in the case of Hanoi. For Hanoi, 29% reported that they did not receive any financial assistance from their parents since married, compared to 2.8% and 0.8% for Bangkok Metropolis and Kuala Lumpur, respectively. A similar pattern holds for the case of financial assistance from parents-in-law. As expected, for the sample from Kuala Lumpur, Malays made up the largest ethnic group. The average number of children was smallest in the case of Bangkok Metropolis, followed by Kuala Lumpur and Hanoi (1.49, 2.0, and 2.35, respectively).

3 Elderly Care: Descriptive Analysis

3.1 *Practice of Elderly Care*

This section discusses the practice of elderly care in Kuala Lumpur, Bangkok Metropolis, and Hanoi. Figure 7.1 presents the overall picture of the different sectors that were involved in elderly care. Two types of involvement are

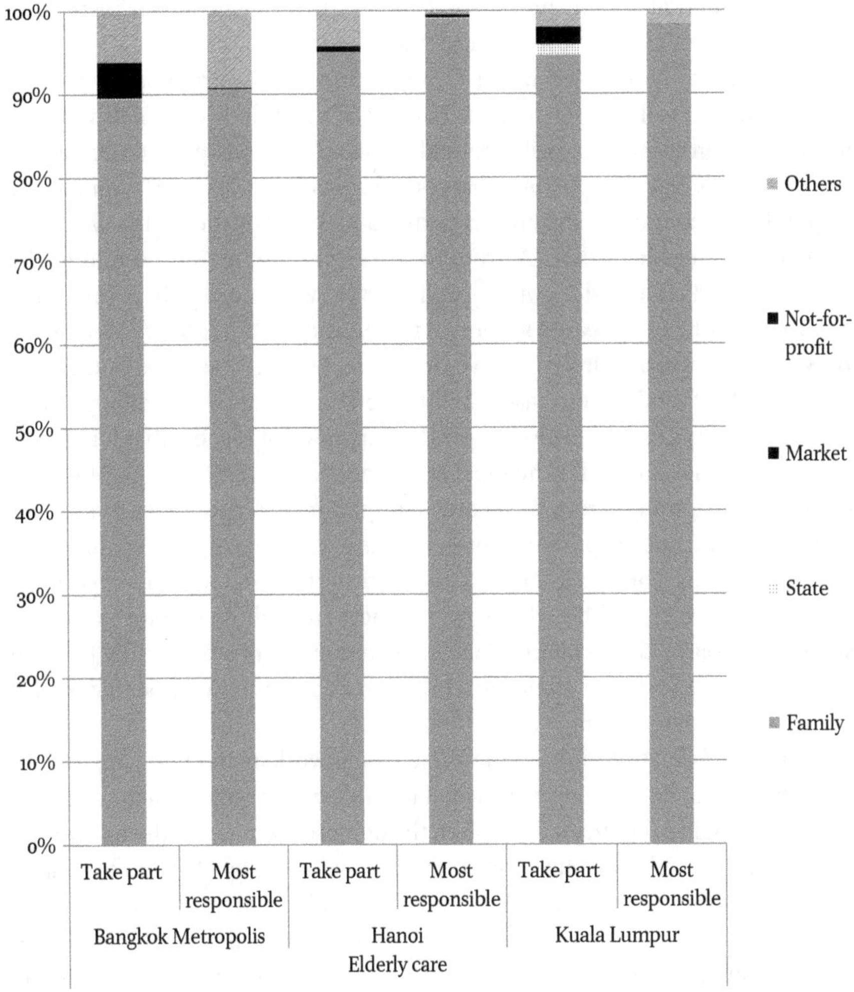

FIGURE 7.1 Practice of elderly care by sector.
SOURCE: AUTHORS' CALCULATION.

discussed here: whether the sector took part in elderly care, and whether the sector was most responsible for elderly care. The five sectors discussed are: the family, the state, the market, the not-for-profit sector, and others. Here the family included all children of the elderly as well as relatives. The state involvement was in the form of governmental nursing homes. The market included domestic workers and trained caretakers or nurses. The not-for-profit sector included neighbors, friends, staff of community-based care center, and non-governmental nursing home. Here, "others" meant any person/institution other than those in the above four sectors.[2]

As Figure 7.1 shows, for Kuala Lumpur, Bangkok Metropolis, as well as Hanoi, the family played the most prominent role in elderly care. This was true for "the person most responsible for elderly care," and "the person taking part in elderly care." For "the person most responsible for elderly care," over 90% of respondents in all three societies reported a member of the family was most responsible for elderly care. As can be seen from the figure, the role of the state, the market, and the not-for-profit sectors were negligible in this case. The role of "others" appeared second in importance in the case of elderly care. However, due to data limitation we do not know which sectors/institutions constituted "others" in this case. For "the person taking part in elderly care," the picture was similar to the case of "the person most responsible for elderly care." The family was by far the most important sector. For Bangkok Metropolis, the not-for-profit sector was second in importance. A closer look at the data reveals that the not-for-profit sector in this case was made up mainly of neighbors and friends. For Kuala Lumpur, the state and the market appeared to be of equal importance, although the role of the state and the market was much smaller compared to the family. For Kula Lumpur, the market mainly referred to domestic workers. The domestic workers in Kuala Lumpur appeared to play a small role in elderly care.

Further information on the role of domestic workers in child care and elderly care in Kuala Lumpur is provided in Table 7.2, based on the question in the questionnaire relating to how often the domestic worker do the followings: looking after elderly parents; looking after baby; escorting children to school; helping children with homework; and household chores. The data reflect clearly that the domestic workers in Kuala Lumpur played a small role in both child care and elderly care, although the role in child care seemed to be slightly

2 Some data limitations should be noted here. Due to differences in the way some of the questions were asked in each country, the overall picture was aggregated in slightly different ways for each country. For Kuala Lumpur, the person most responsible for elderly care meant the person most responsible for respondents' parents. For Bangkok and Hanoi, the person most responsible for elderly care meant the person most responsible for respondents' parents as well as spouse's parents. For the person who took part in elderly care, for all three countries the elderly meant both respondent's parents and spouse's parents. For Kuala Lumpur, the question asked was "Who are taking care of the following family members who needed care?" (multiple answers possible) whereas for Bangkok and Hanoi, the question asked was "Who are taking care of your own parents?" and "Who are taking care of your spouse's parents?" (multiple answers possible). These differences should therefore be taken into account when making comparison of the data from each country.

TABLE 7.2 Role of domestic workers in Kuala Lumpur: How often does the domestic worker do the following?

	Almost every day	Several times a week	About once a week	About once a month	Several times a year	About once a year	Never	Not applicable
Elderly care:								
Look after elderly parents	0.39% (6)	0.07% (1)	0.07% (1)	0.07% (1)	0% (0)	0.07% (1)	2.95% (45)	96.39% (1468)
Child care:								
Look after baby	0.72% (11)	0.07% (1)	0% (0)	0% (0)	0% (0)	0.07% (1)	2.76% (42)	96.39% (1468)
Escort children to school	0.20% (3)	0.20% (3)	0% (0)	0% (0)	0% (0)	0% (0)	3.22% (49)	96.39% (1468)
Help children with homework	0.07% (1)	0.13% (2)	0.07% (1)	0.07% (1)	0% (0)	0% (0)	3.28% (50)	96.39% (1468)

Note: From 1523 individuals, only 55 people (3.6%) report having a domestic worker
Source: Authors' calculation

larger. However, it appeared that the major role of the domestic workers in Kuala Lumpur was to help with household chores.

3.2 *Attitudes towards Elderly Care*

3.2.1 Overall Picture: Society Comparison

Based on the questionnaires comparable across the three societies, respondents were asked to choose whose responsibility they thought each type of elderly care should be: always government's responsibility (coded 1); usually or mostly government's responsibility (coded 2); equal responsibility between government and family (coded 3); usually or mostly family's responsibility (coded 4); or always family's responsibility (coded 5).

Figures 7.2 and 7.3 presents the opinions regarding who should take responsibility for elderly care. Figure 7.2 presents the opinions of respondents from Bangkok Metropolis, Hanoi, and Kuala Lumpur regarding who should take responsibility for elder's medical treatment and nursing care. The majority of Thai respondents chose mode 3, i.e. equal responsibility between government and family. On the other hand, the majority of the respondents in Hanoi as well as those in Kuala Lumpur chose mode 4, i.e. usually or mostly family's

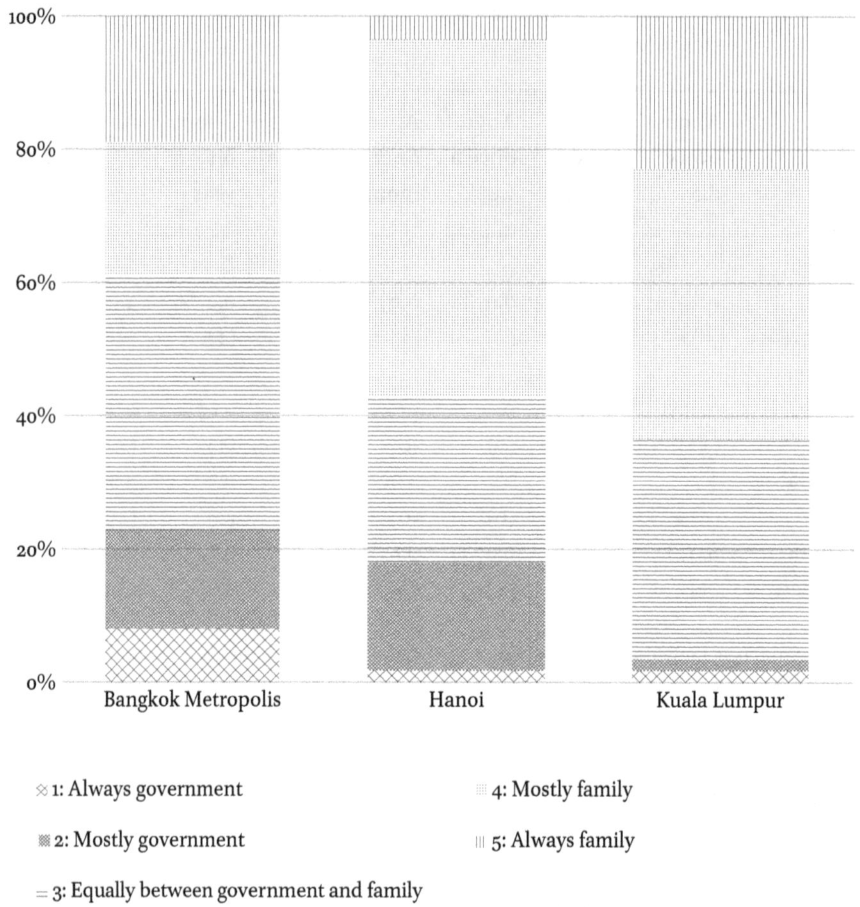

FIGURE 7.2 Percentage distribution of the attitudes regarding who should be responsible for elder's medical treatment and nursing care.
SOURCE: AUTHORS' CALCULATION.

responsibility. It appeared that Thai respondents leaned more towards the role of government in elder's medical treatment and nursing care compared to those in Hanoi and Kuala Lumpur.

The opinions regarding who should take responsibility for the general livelihood of the elderly had a very similar pattern as in the case of elder's medical treatment and nursing care, as can be seen in Figure 7.3. Compared to the case of elder's medical treatment and nursing care (Figure 7.2), it appeared that respondents from Bangkok Metropolis and Hanoi placed more importance on the role of the family in taking care of the general livelihood of the elderly.

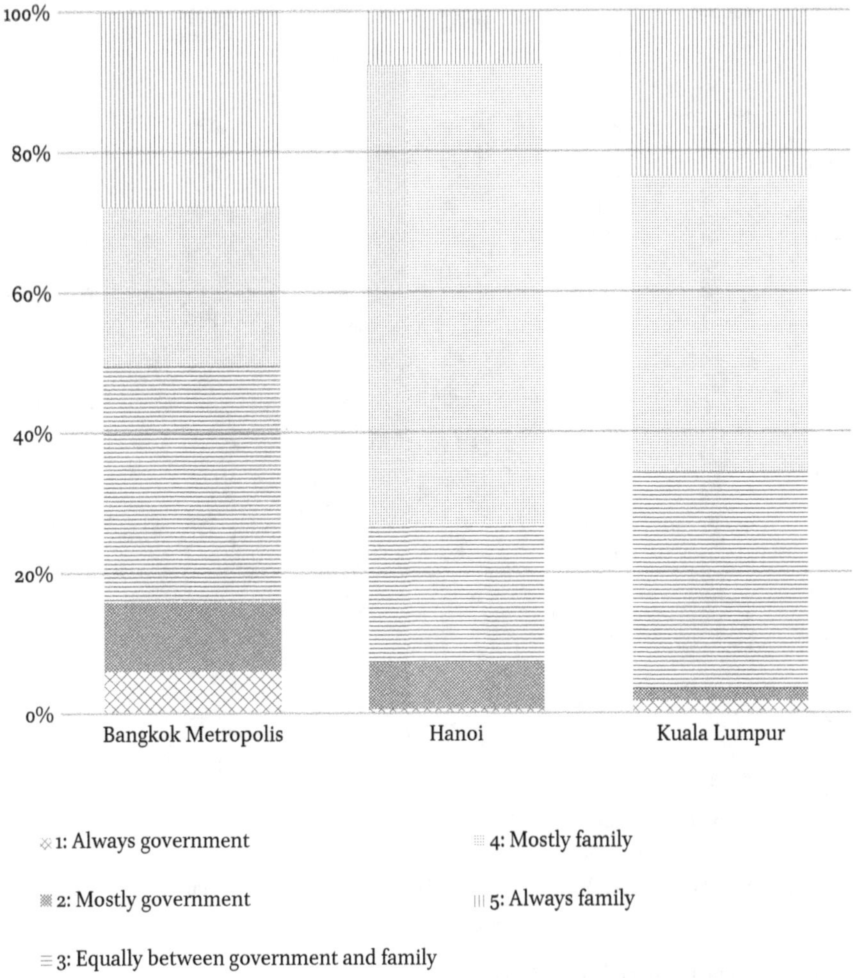

FIGURE 7.3 Percentage distribution of the attitudes regarding who should be responsible for elder's livelihood.
SOURCE: AUTHORS' CALCULATION.

4 Child Care: Descriptive Analysis

4.1 *Practice of Child Care*

Figure 7.4 presents the overall picture of the different sectors involved in the practice of child care in Bangkok Metropolis, Hanoi, and Kuala Lumpur. Similar to the case of elderly care, two types of involvement are discussed: whether the sector took part in child care, and whether the sector was most responsible

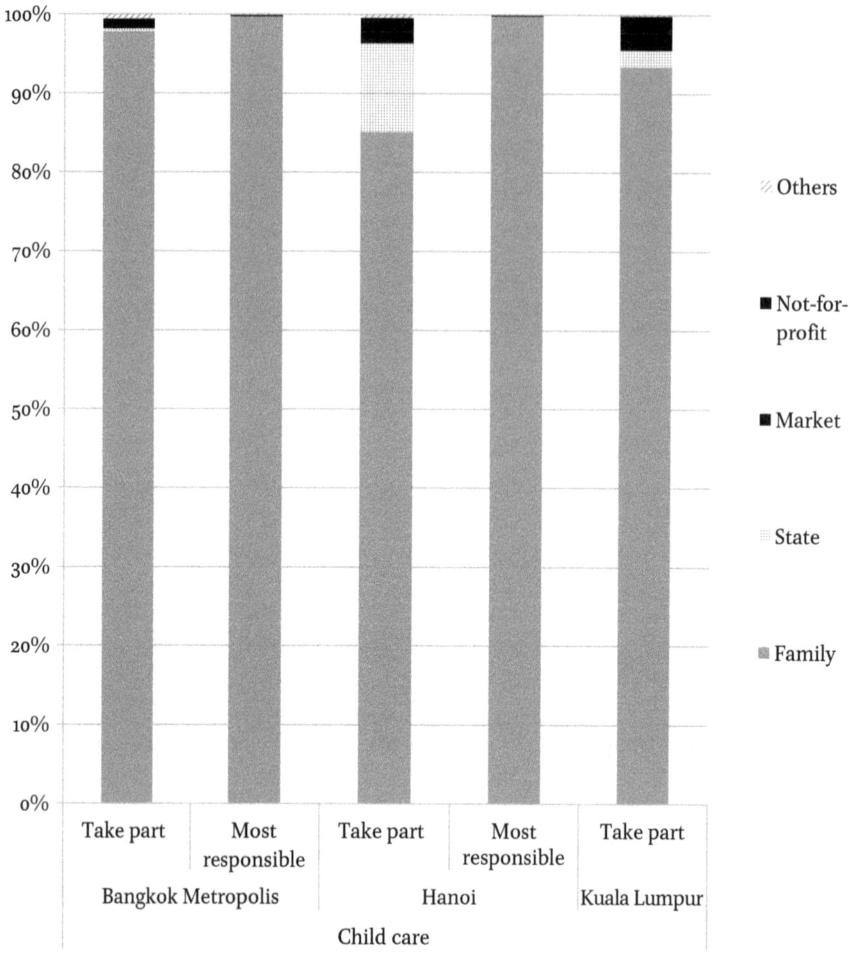

FIGURE 7.4 Practice of child care by sector.
SOURCE: AUTHORS' CALCULATION.

for child care. The five sectors were: the family, the state, the market, the not-for-profit sector, and others. The family included the father, the mother, the grandparents, elderly brother/sister, as well as relatives. The state involvement here meant governmental childcare center, while the market meant domestic workers and trained caretakers or nurses. The not-for-profit sector included neighbors, friends, staff of community-based care center, and non-governmental childcare center. Others included any other person/institution not categorized as one of the four sectors just mentioned.[3]

3 As in the case of elderly care, some data limitations should be noted here. For Malaysia, the question on who the respondent thought to be the most important person for child care was

As Figure 7.4 shows, for the person most responsible for child care, for both Bangkok Metropolis and Hanoi, over 99% of the respondents reported a member of the family. The result here suggests that the family was the only one most important sector for child care for Bangkok Metropolis and Hanoi. For the person taking part in childcare, the family still dominated all other sectors. Comparing Bangkok Metropolis and Hanoi (the questions asked were the same for Bangkok Metropolis and Hanoi, therefore direct comparison was possible), it appeared that the role of the government was much more prominent in the case of Hanoi. Government child care centers appeared to be taking part in child care for a considerable proportion of respondents. This was part of the socialist policy in Vietnam. In the case of Bangkok Metropolis, it appeared that the roles of the government, the market, and the not-for-profit sectors in taking part in child care were very small. The main sector taking part in child care remained the family. For Kuala Lumpur, there was a small role for the state, the market, and the not-for-profit sectors. For Kuala Lumpur, further information on the role of domestic workers in child care is provided in Table 7.2.

4.2 *Attitudes towards Child Care*

4.2.1 Overall Picture: Society Comparison

The opinions regarding who should take responsibility for child care are investigated in Figure 7.5, and Figure 7.6 Similar to the case of elderly care, the questionnaire asked the respondents to choose whose responsibility they thought each type of elderly care and child care should be: always government's responsibility (1); usually or mostly government's responsibility (2); equal responsibility between government and family (3); usually or mostly family's responsibility (4); or always family's responsibility (5). Figure 7.5 presents the opinions of respondents in Bangkok Metropolis, Hanoi, and Kuala Lumpur regarding who should take responsibility for children's rearing and care work. For respondents in Hanoi and Kuala Lumpur, mode 4, i.e. usually or mostly family's responsibility, was chosen by the largest number of respondents. For respondents in Hanoi in particular, the proportion of respondents choosing mode 4 was as large as 72%. For respondents in Hanoi and Kuala Lumpur, the preferences appeared similar to the case of elderly care. For Bangkok Metropolis, however, the opinions regarding children's rearing and care work appeared

not asked. Therefore, for Kuala Lumpur, we only have information on who took part in child care. For Bangkok and Hanoi, the question regarding the person taking part in child care asked "Who are taking part in child care?" (multiple answers possible). For Kuala Lumpur, the question asked was "Who are taking care of the following family members who needed care?", and we chose the answers for "non-schooling children (aged 5 or younger)" and "schooling children (aged 6–12)" to mean child care. These differences should be taking into account when interpreting the findings regarding child care.

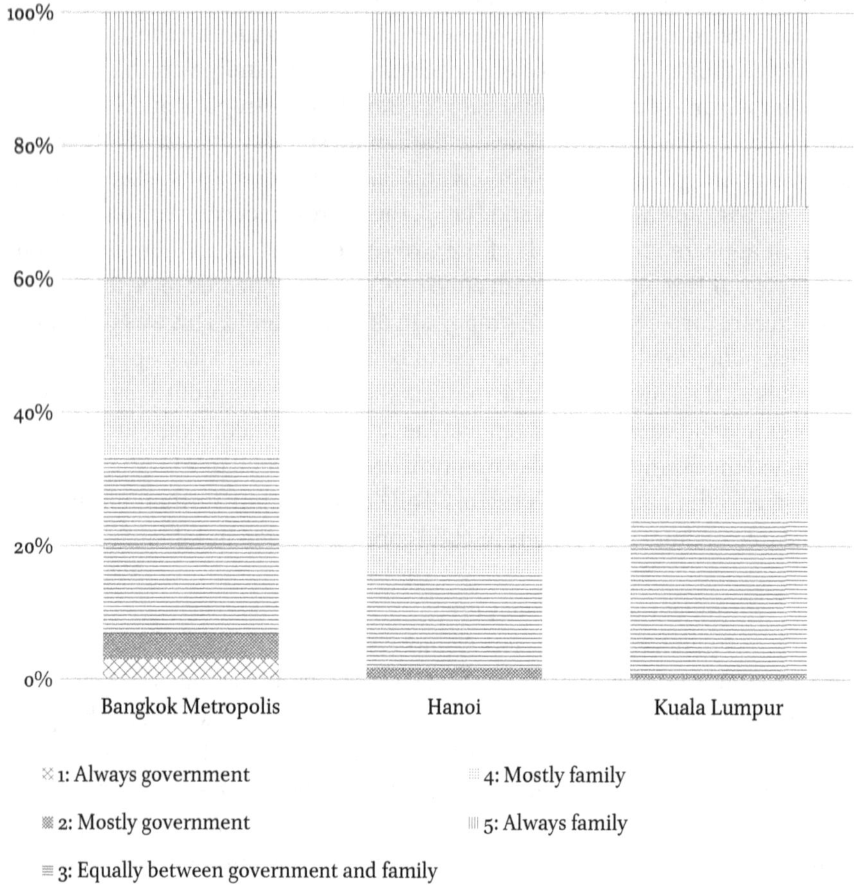

FIGURE 7.5 Percentage distribution of the attitudes regarding who should be responsible for children's rearing and care work.
SOURCE: AUTHORS' CALCULATION.

very different from the case of elderly care. Here mode 5, i.e. always the responsibility of family, had the largest number of respondents among all modes. It thus appeared that Thais tend to prioritize the role of family in child rearing.

Once we consider children's educational cost, however, respondents from Bangkok Metropolis placed more importance on the role of government, as can be seen in Figure 7.6. Here mode 3, i.e. equal responsibility between government and family, was chosen by the largest number of respondents from Bangkok Metropolis. For Hanoi and Kuala Lumpur, the preferences still had a similar pattern to the case of children's rearing and care work, i.e. mode 4 was chosen by the largest number of respondents. For children's educational cost, respondents from Bangkok Metropolis led towards the role of the government

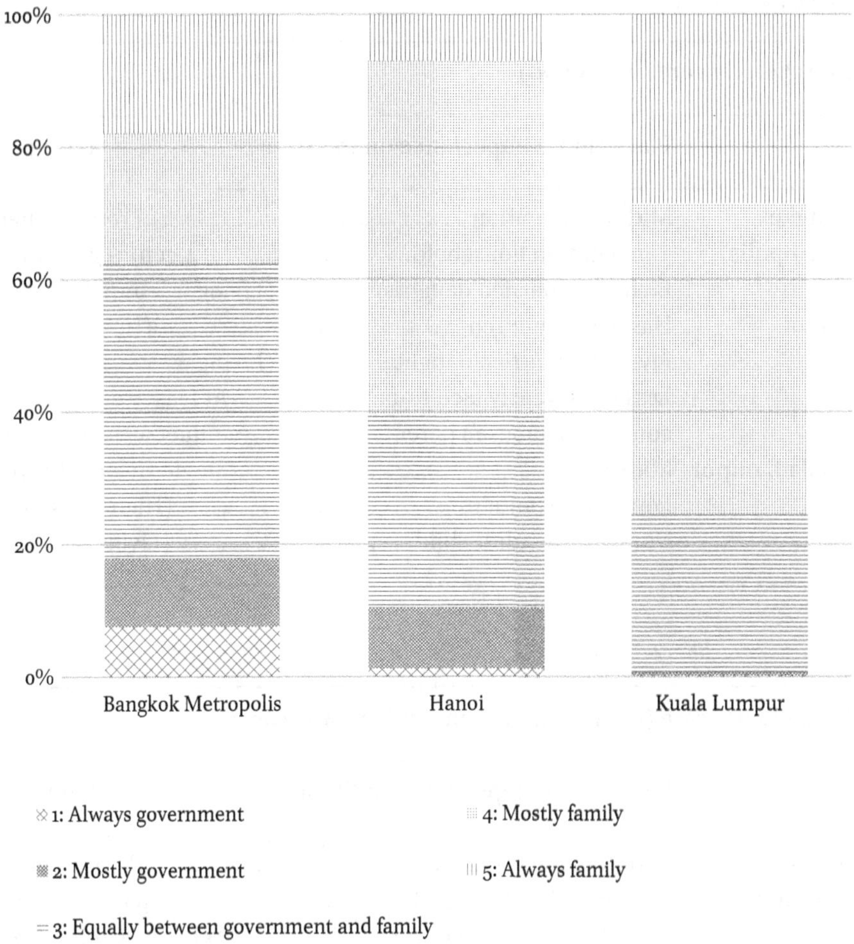

FIGURE 7.6 Percentage distribution of the attitudes regarding who should be responsible for children's educational cost.
SOURCE: AUTHORS' CALCULATION.

compared to respondents from Hanoi and Kuala Lumpur. Respondents from Kuala Lumpur placed more importance on the role of family in children's educational cost compared to respondents from the other two societies.

5 Family or State Responsibility: Elderly and Child Care?

This section presents statistical analysis of the factors which are correlated with attitudes towards elderly and child care along the family-state balance

TABLE 7.3 Summary of main results

EC1: Elderly care (livelihood)

	Places more importance on the state	(compared to)
Bangkok Metropolis	Middle generation	(Young generation)
	1-generation household	(2-gen/3+gen household)
	Living w/ married daughter	(Living w/ son/single daughter)
Hanoi	Has fewer children	(Has more children)
	Living w/ married daughter	(Living w/ son/single daughter)
	Less than weekly face-to-face contact w/ spouse's parents	(At least weekly face-to-face contact w/ spouse's parents)
Kuala Lumpur	Married	(Single/divorced/separated)
	Low living standard	(High living standard)
	Not living w/adult child	(Living w/adult child)

EC2: Elderly care (medical treatment and nursing care)

	Places more importance on the state	(compared to)
Bangkok Metropolis	Middle generation	(Young generation)
	1-generation household	(2-generation household)
	Less than weekly face-to-face contact w/ parents	(At least weekly face-to-face contact w/ parents)
Hanoi	Young generation	(Old generation)
	Has fewer children	(Has more children)
Kuala Lumpur	Young generation	(Middle generation)
	Married	(Single/divorced/separated)
	Low living standard	(High living standard)
	1-generation household	(2-generation household)

CC1: Child care (children's rearing and care work)		
	Places more importance on the state	**(compared to)**
Bangkok Metropolis	Middle generation	(Young generation)
	Female	(Male)
	1-generation household	(3+gen household)
Hanoi	1-generation household	(3+gen household)
	Living w/ married daughter	(Living w/ son/single daughter)
Kuala Lumpur	Female	(Male)
	Low living standard	(High living standard)
	Chinese	(Malay)

CC2: Child care (educational cost)		
	Places more importance on the state	**(compared to)**
Bangkok Metropolis	(*None of the characteristics used can explain the preference regarding who should be responsible for children's educational cost*)	
Hanoi	Tertiary education or higher	(Primary education or lower)
	Not living w/adult child	(Living w/ son/single daughter)
	Living w/ married daughter	(Living w/ son/single daughter)
Kuala Lumpur	Female	(Male)
	Low living standard	(High living standard)
	Chinese	(Malay)

responsibility perspective using ordered-probit regressions. Here, the dependent variable represents the opinions of respondents regarding who should take responsibility for each type of elderly care and child care. Specifically, the dependent variable is the opinion of individuals regarding who should take responsibility for: (1) elder's medical treatment and nursing care, (2) elder's general livelihood, (3) children's rearing and care work, and (4) children's educational cost. Each dependent variable ranges from 1 to 5, as discussed above. The regressions are run separately for Bangkok Metropolis, Hanoi, and Kuala Lumpur. The explanatory variables include personal characteristics, living arrangement, and family characteristics. For respondents from Kuala Lumpur, variables indicating ethnicity are also included in the regressions.

Appendixes A1, A2, A3, A4 in the Appendix present the results from the ordered-probit analysis. The summary of the main results from Appendixes A1, A2, A3, A4 is presented in Table 7.3 Table 7.3 is divided into 4 sections. Parts EC1 and EC2 provide the summary of the results regarding elderly care in terms of general livelihood, and medical treatment and nursing care, respectively. Parts CC1 and CC2 present the summary of the results regarding children's rearing and care work, and children's educational cost, respectively.

5.1 *Elderly Care*

The results on the preferences regarding who should be responsible for elder's general livelihood are reported in Part EC1 in Table 7.3 In the case of Bangkok Metropolis, the results show that middle generation placed greater importance on the role of government in the provision of support for elderly's general livelihood compared to young generation. It was possible that middle generation was burdened with both the responsibility of elderly care and child care, as well as their own career, and therefore would like the support of the government regarding elder's general livelihood. Living arrangement appeared to be correlated with preferences in this aspect. Those living in 2-generation households and those living in 3-generation, 4-generation, 5-generation, and other types of households placed more importance on the role of family in the provision of care for elder's general livelihood compared to people living alone or in 1-generation households. Those living alone or in 1-generation households were likely to need the government's support in old age more than other groups, so it was not surprising that they placed more importance on the role of government in elder's general livelihood. The results also show that those living with at least one married daughter placed greater importance on the role of government in the provision of support for elderly's general livelihood compared to those living with sons or single daughters. As Table 7.4 shows, patriarchal family system is not observed in the case of Bangkok Metropolis.

TABLE 7.4 Living arrangements of elderly (60 years and older)

	All elderly respondents			Elderly with both son(s) and daughter(s)		
Living arrangements of elderly	**Bangkok Metropolis (n = 205)**	**Hanoi (n = 227)**	**Kuala Lumpur (n =415)**	**Bangkok Metropolis (n = 104)**	**Hanoi (n = 153)**	**Kuala Lumpur (n = 273)**
	(1)	(2)	(3)	(4)	(5)	(6)
Not living with children	26.8%	28.6%	30.8%	21.1%	25.5%	26.0%
Living with son(s) only	27.3%	53.3%	30.8%	23.1%	56.9%	28.6%
Living with daughter(s) only	23.4%	9.7%	23.6%	18.3%	5.2%	23.1%
Living with both son(s) and daughter(s)	22.4%	8.4%	14.7%	37.5%	12.4%	22.3%
Total	100%	100%	100%	100%	100%	100%

As discussed in Ofstedal, Knodel & Chayovan (1999), Thailand had a bilateral family system. Therefore, the explanation for the preference for government support for elderly's general livelihood among those living with married daughters could be because married daughters living with their parents were likely to have many responsibilities, including child care, elderly care, household chores, and possibly their own career. Those living with married daughters possibly understand this, and therefore would like to have more government support for elderly's general livelihood.

In the case of Hanoi, people who had more children tend to place more importance on the role of family in elder's general livelihood. This was possibly that respondents with a large family (i.e. having many children) placed value on the role of family in the provision of care. Also, those who had face-to-face contact with spouse's parents more than once a week also tended to place more importance on the role of family in elder's general livelihood. For respondents in Hanoi, those who lived with at least one married daughter placed more importance on the role of government in elder's general livelihood compared to those who live with sons or single daughters. In the case of Vietnam, patriarchy appeared to be the norm. As Table 7.4 shows, a strong patriarchal family system can be clearly observed in the case of Hanoi. For all elderly respondents from Hanoi, 53.3% lived with their sons only (without their daughters). This was in contrast with the 9.7% who lived with their daughters only (without their sons). Once we limit our analysis to elderly who had both sons and daughters, the figures showed an even larger difference: while 56.9% lived with their sons only, a mere 5.2% lived with their daughters only. As discussed in Guilmoto (2012), in Vietnam, especially in the North, sons in traditional family settings had an essential role in family support. Therefore, those who lived with at least one married daughter were likely to be the group who do not follow the traditional norm. This may be due to certain family circumstances, or certain attitudes and preferences. These characteristics may have made them more open to the idea that the government provides more support for elder's general livelihood.

For Kuala Lumpur, those who were married appeared to place more importance on the role of government regarding elder's livelihood compared to those who were not married. It was possible that the married had many responsibilities and therefore would like the government to provide support and played a role in elder's general livelihood. Those with high living standard placed more importance on the role of family compared to those with low living standard. It thus appeared that those with low living standard would like more assistance from the state in this area. Living arrangement was also correlated with preference in this aspect; those who lived with adult children placed more importance on the role of family compared to those who didn't.

Table 7.3 Part EC2 presents the main results of the analysis of the opinion regarding who should be responsible for elder's medical treatment and nursing care. For Bangkok Metropolis, similar to the case of elder's livelihood, middle generation placed more importance on the role of government in the provision of support for elder's medical treatment and nursing care compared to young generation. Also, those living in 2-generation households tended to place more importance on the role of family compared to those living alone or in 1-generation households. It was possible that those living alone or in 1-generation households had (or expect to have) more need for the government to provide support in the area of elder's medical treatment and nursing care. Moreover, those had face-to-face contact with their parents more than once a week also tended to place more importance on the role of family compared to those who had face-to-face contact with their parents less often. This was not surprising, as those who saw their parents often were those with strong intergenerational ties, and therefore were more likely to place more importance on the role of family in caring for the elderly who were unwell.

The results for Hanoi show that old generation placed more importance on the role of family in elder's medical treatment and nursing care, compared to young generation. This possibly reflected the shift in values and attitudes of different generations. The differences between generations could be due to age and experience. It is also possible that the young generation may change their attitudes as they grow older.

For those living in Hanoi, people who had more children place more importance on the role of family in elder's medical treatment and nursing care compared with those who had fewer children. It is possible that those with fewer children expected to rely more on the government in elder's medical treatment and nursing care.

For Kuala Lumpur, middle generation placed more importance on the role of family in the area of medical treatment and nursing care compared to young generation. Similar to the case of Hanoi, there was possibly a shift in the attitudes of generations regarding who should be responsible for elderly care, where young generation placed more importance on the role of government compared to older generations. Marital status was also correlated with preference in this regard; those who were married placed more importance on the role of government in elder's medical treatment and nursing care compared to those who were unmarried. It was possible that those who were married had many responsibilities, including child care, and therefore had a preference for the government's support in the area of elder's medical treatment and nursing care. Moreover, those who had high living standard and middle living standard also placed more importance on the role of family in elder's medical treatment and nursing care compared to those with low living standard.

5.2 *Child Care*

Part EC1 in Table 7.3 shows the main results on the preferences regarding who should be responsible for children's rearing and care work. For Bangkok Metropolis, those who were middle generation placed more importance on the role of government compared to young generation. This result was similar to the case of elderly care. Females also placed more importance on the role of government in children's rearing and care work, compared to males. It appeared that the groups with more responsibilities (i.e. middle generation and females) had a preference for the government's support in children's rearing and care work. The results also show that those living in 3-generation, 4-generation, 5-generation, and other types of households placed more importance on the role of family in children's rearing and care work compared to those living alone or in 1-generation households. The result was similar to the case of elderly care. Those living in households with two or more generations appeared to place value on the role of family in the provision of care, both for elderly and children.

For Hanoi, those living in 3-generation, 4-generation, 5-generation, and other types of households placed more importance on the role of family in children's rearing and care work compared to those living alone or in 1-generation households. This result was similar to the case of Bangkok Metropolis. Moreover, for Hanoi, those living with at least one married daughter placed more importance on the role of government in children's rearing and care work compared to those living with sons or single daughters. This result was similar to the case of elder's general livelihood.

For Kuala Lumpur, those with high living standard placed more importance on the role of family compared to those with low living standard. The result was similar to the case of elderly care. It appeared that those with high living standard placed value on the role of family in the provision of care for both the old and the young. Females placed more importance on the role of government in children's rearing and care work compared to males. The results also show that those of Chinese ethnicity preferred the government to play more role on child rearing and care work as compared to those of Malay ethnicity.

The preferences regarding who should be responsible for children's educational cost are reported in Part CC2 in Table 7.3. In the case of Bangkok Metropolis, as reported in Table 7.A4, none of the variables are statistically significant at the 10% level. This suggests that the personal, household, and socio-economic factors employed in the model do not explain the preference regarding who should be responsible for children's educational cost.

For Hanoi, those with at least tertiary education placed more importance on the role of government in children's educational cost compared to those with primary education or lower. Those with higher education appeared to prefer the support of government in children's educational cost. Compared to those living with sons or single daughters, the study found those not living with adult children prioritized the role of government in children's educational cost. Moreover, those living with at least one married daughter also preferred the role of government in children's educational cost compared to those who lived with sons or single daughters. As patriarchal family system prevailed in Vietnam, those who lived with married daughters were not following traditional norms. As discussed earlier, this may be due to certain family circumstances, or certain attitudes and preferences. These characteristics may make them more open to the idea of government support in the area of child care.

For Kuala Lumpur, the results were quite similar to the case of children's rearing and care work. Those with high living standard preferred the role of family compared to those with low living standard. On the other hand, females looked for the government to play more role on children's educational cost as compared to males. Moreover, those of Chinese ethnicity expected more active role of government in children's educational cost, as compared to those of Malay ethnicity.

6 Concluding Remarks

This chapter finds famililism to prevail in the practice of both elderly and child care in Bangkok Metropolis, Hanoi, and Kuala Lumpur. Informal support systems were mainly relied upon in those societies. As assumed by Razavi (2007, 21) in her notion of care provision in developing countries, this chapter finds the role of non-familial care institutions to have been supplementary to that of the family in Kuala Lumpur, Bangkok Metropolis and Hanoi during the period when the surveys were carried out. This study also finds reliance on non-familial care services to be only minimal in practice in those three societies.

With regards to elderly care, for Bangkok, the not-for-profit sector (in this case mainly neighbors and friends) played the second most important role in taking part in elderly care. For Kuala Lumpur, the second most important role went to the market. For Hanoi, other sectors besides the family played a small and negligible role in elderly care. For all three cases, the family was by far the one most important sector in the practice elderly care.

With regards to child care, for Bangkok and Kuala Lumpur, the not-for-profit sector and the market played a small role in taking part in child care (the role is very small compared to the family). For Hanoi, the government played the second most important role in taking part in child care, in the form of government child care centre/kindergarten. In Vietnam, the government appeared to play quite an important role in taking part in child care, while for Thailand and Malaysia, the role of the government in this area was still quite limited.

Besides the practice of elderly care and child care, this chapter investigates the preferences of respondents in the three societies regarding the role of family versus government in the provision of care. Overall, the findings point to the differences between the three societies. Respondents from Kuala Lumpur placed more importance on the role of family in elderly care and child care compared to respondents from Bangkok Metropolis and Hanoi, where the redistribution of responsibility appeared relatively revealing in terms of burden sharing. In other words, it was not that the family was to be substituted by the state nor that the family was to be the sole responsible unit of the society.

For both elderly care and child care, time and money appeared to be the two main resources required for the provision of care, while knowledge, experience, and other factors played a supporting role. Elderly care in terms of general livelihood, and child care in terms of children's rearing and care work, could be viewed as time-intensive. On the other hand, medical treatment and nursing care for the elderly, and children's educational cost, mainly required financial resources.

Viewing care in terms of the resources required, we can interpret the results in Table 7.3 as follows. The ability to provide care (i.e. the availability of time and financial resources), together with culture, were the main factors shaping the preferences of the respondents in the three societies. Overall, respondents from all three societies placed great importance on the role of family. This was especially true for those who had the resources required for the provision of care.

For the residents of Bangkok Metropolis, the most burdened groups in terms of time expressed demand for government support in time-intensive elderly care and child care. The results show that middle generation placed greater importance on the role of government in the provision support for elderly's general livelihood and children's rearing and care work, as compared to young generation. Middle generation, sometimes referred to as sandwich generation, were likely to be heavily burdened with elderly care and child care. Many had to balance elderly care and child care with their career.

Moreover, for the residents of Bangkok Metropolitan, the findings that young generation placed more importance on the role of family in elderly care and children's rearing and care work, compared to middle generation, was evidence that the attitudes of the younger respondents in the survey were in line with the 2nd National Plan on the Elderly (2002–2021), which emphasized the role of family and community for elderly care (Bureau of Empowerment for Older Persons, 2009). Given the preference of the young generation in Bangkok Metropolis, this National Plan was likely to be feasible and successful.

Females in Bangkok Metropolis placed greater importance on the role of government in children's rearing and care work, compared to males. Females were likely to be more time-constrained compared to males. In the Thai society, as Figure 7.7 shows, female labor force participation rate was quite high (ranging between 64% and 65% during 2009–2012). However, in most cases females were still the main caretaker of young children in the family. It was not surprising that females (who had to shoulder both the responsibility of work and child care) demanded more government support in children's rearing and care work.

Those living in multi-generational households placed more importance on the role of family in the provision of both types of elderly care and children's rearing and care work. The availability of other household members to help

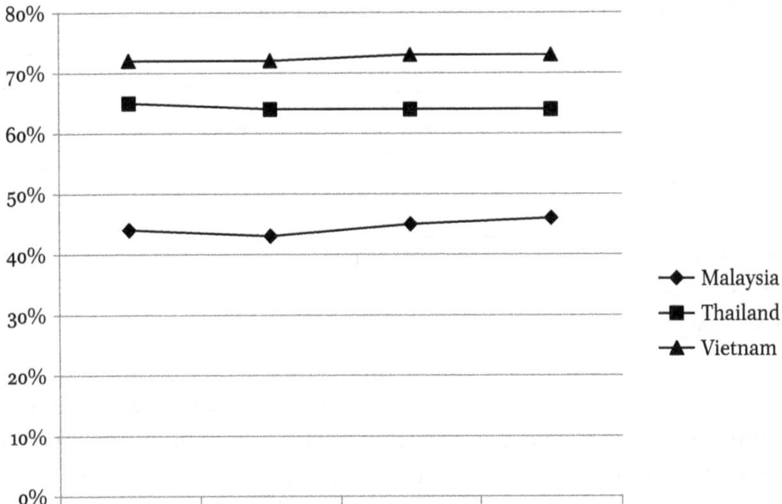

	2009	2010	2011	2012
Malaysia	44%	43%	45%	46%
Thailand	65%	64%	64%	64%
Vietnam	72%	72%	73%	73%

FIGURE 7.7 Female labor force participation rate (% of female population aged 15+): Thailand, Vietnam, and Malaysia.
SOURCE: WORLD BANK. 2014B.

with the provision of care increased the resources (in terms of time and perhaps financial resources) available in the household.

The residents of Bangkok Metropolis who lived with their married daughters placed more importance on the role of government in the provision of elderly care in the area of general livelihood. This was possibly because married females were time-constrained due to child care, elderly care, and work. Those living with their married daughters perhaps understood their daughters' situations and therefore expressed more demand for government support in elderly care.

With regards to the educational cost, none of the characteristics employed in the study could explain the preference of the residents of Bangkok Metropolis regarding who should be responsible for children's educational cost. This was possibly because the Thai government was already providing public education to all children. Therefore there was no particular demand in this area from certain groups.

In the case of the residents of Hanoi, the results show that the educated group, and the young generation, expressed demand for the government to provide more support in financial resource intensive areas of elderly care and

TABLE 7.5 GDP per capita and Gini coefficients for Thailand, Vietnam, and Malaysia

	Thailand	Vietnam	Malaysia
GDP per capita (USD)*	5,779	1,911	10,514
Gini coefficient**	40	35.6	46.2

Note: * = GDP figures are for 2013; ** = Gini coefficient figures are for year 2009 for Thailand and Malaysia, and year 2008 for Vietnam
SOURCES: WORLD BANK (2014a) AND UNITED NATIONS (N.D.)

child care. In particular, the educated group wanted the government to provide more support for children's educational cost. The young generation placed more importance on the role of government in the provision of elderly's medical treatment and nursing care, compared to the old generation.

For Vietnam, as Table 7.5 shows, the level of GDP per capita was lowest among the three economies, and the level of inequality is also lowest. As Vietnam was an emerging economy, there were changes in the values and traditions of the people. The results suggest that education, tradition, and culture all played an important role in shaping people's preferences regarding who should be responsible for elderly care and child care in Vietnam. It appeared that those with higher education placed importance on the provision of education for the younger generation, and they were of the view that children's educational cost should be, at least partly, the government's responsibility. One possible explanation could be because those with tertiary education were exposed to ideas regarding the role of the government, and therefore felt that the government should take responsibility in children's educational cost.

The young generation placed more importance on the role of the government in the provision of elderly care. The old generation, perhaps due to culture and traditional values, still placed importance on the role of family.

Moreover, those who had at least weekly face-to-face-contact with their spouse's parents, placed more importance on the role of family for time-intensive elderly care, compared to those who had less than weekly face-to-face contact with their spouse's parents. It appeared that culture and tradition could be one explanation here. Those who had frequent contact with their spouse's parents were likely to be following traditional values and cultures, compared to those who have less frequent contact. They therefore placed more importance on the role of family in elderly care and child care.

The role of culture and tradition in Vietnam was also evident in the findings that those who lived with their married daughters placed more importance on the role of government in both elderly care and child care. As Table 7.4 shows, the majority of elderly in Vietnam lived with their sons. In particular, for those who had both sons and daughters, around 56% lived with their sons only (and not their daughters) while around 5.2% lived with their daughters only (and not their sons). Those who lived with their sons were more likely to be following traditional values and cultures, compared to those who lived with their daughters. Those who lived with their daughters were probably less traditional and more open to the idea that the government played a role in family care. This could be one explanation for the finding that those who lived with their married daughters placed more importance on the role of government in elderly care and child care, compared to those living with their sons or single daughters.

Overall, for Hanoi, the young and the educated were likely the driving force for the country's shift towards more role of the government in the provision of care. It also appeared that the role of traditional values and cultures was still quite prominent in Hanoi.

For the residents of Kuala Lumpur, the group with high living standard clearly placed more importance on the role of family in all four areas of elderly care and child care, compared to those with low living standard. Viewing this in terms of resources required for the provision of care, it appeared that those who had the financial resources available placed greater importance on the role of family in the provision of care.

The findings that economic situations shape people's preferences in Kuala Lumpur had important implications. As Table 7.5 shows, while Malaysia had the highest GDP per capita, compared to Thailand and Vietnam, it also had the highest level of inequality among the three economies, based on the Gini coefficient. The high level of inequality was possibly one factor leading to the least well-off group to demand more support from the government in the area of elderly care and child care. Based on the statistics, it appeared that the least well-to-do group would like more redistribution in the form of government's role in the provision of elderly care and child care. For the case of Kuala Lumpur, government policies regarding elderly care and child care therefore should carefully consider the situations of the least well-off group in particular, as they were the group that expressed more demand for government support in these areas.

For respondents from Kuala Lumpur, middle generation placed more importance on the role of family in elder's medical treatment and nursing care compared to young generation. As noted by Sim & Hamid (2010), Malaysia was facing the challenges of pension system, particularly in terms of the limited scope of coverage, benefits level, sustainability of the scheme and adequacy for the well-being of the pensioners. While the elderly seemed to expect familial support, the Malaysia survey did reflect concerns among the younger generation about such challenges. Culture and tradition, which differed by ethnic groups, also appeared to shape people's preferences regarding child care. The Chinese expressed more demand for government support in the areas of children's rearing and care work, as well as children's educational cost, compared to Malays.

One aspect that Bangkok Metropolis shared a similarity with Kuala Lumpur was the difference between males and females in the preferences regarding child care. For both Bangkok Metropolis and Kuala Lumpur, females placed more importance on the role of government in child care, as compared to males. As shown in Figure 7.7, Malaysia hadby then relatively low rate of female labor force participation, compared to Thailand and Vietnam. Malaysian women at the working age, particularly young working mothers, suffered the lack of family-friendly facilities and flexible work policies at most workplaces in Malaysia. It was the case despite certain enterprises, such as CIMB Bank, IBM Malaysia and BASF Asia-Pacific Service Centre SdnBhd, were implementing a work-life balance policy (Boo 2014). In the case of Kuala Lumpur, it was possible that the women who would like to join the labor force but are unable to do so, possibly because of lack of flexible work policies, demand more support from the government in the area of child care. Viewed in terms of women's empowerment, defined as the process by which those who were denied the ability to make strategic life choices acquired such an ability (Kabeer, 1999), the findings that females expressed a preference for more support from the government in child care could be seen as part of the process of women's empowerment. It appeared that females in Bangkok Metropolis and Kuala Lumpur would like more support from the government in child care, in order to free up their time for employment or other activities.

In sum, the results in this chapter point to the main differences in the preferences of residents in the three societies in transition regarding the role of government in the provision of elderly care and child care. Overall, the availability of the resources required for the provision of care (time and financial resources), together with culture and tradition, appeared to be the main forces driving people's preferences. For Bangkok Metropolis, the results suggest that the most burdened group in terms of time (the middle generation and females) wanted the government to provide more support for elderly care and child care. For residents of Hanoi, the educated, as well as the younger generation, appeared to place more importance on the role of government. In the case of Kuala Lumpur, the most financially constrained group (the least well-off) wanted the government to provide more support for elderly care and child care. The findings suggest that the respective government should have taken into account these preferences when designing policies regarding elderly care and child care.

References

Barranti, Chrys. (1985). The grandparent/grandchild relationship: Family resource in an era of voluntary bonds. *Family Relations*, *34*(3), 343–352.

Baumrin, Bernard Herbert (Ed.). (1969). *Hobbes's leviathan – Interpretation and criticism*. Belmont, CA: Wadsworth.

Bengtson, Vern L. (2001). Beyond the nuclear family: The increasing importance of multigenerational bonds. *Journal of Marriage and the Family*, *63*, 1–16.

Bengtson, Vern L., & Joan F. Robertson (Eds.). (1985). *Grandparenthood*. Beverly Hills, CA: Sage.

Blau, David M. (Ed.). (1995). *The economics of child care*. New York: Russell Sage Foundation.

Boo, Su-Lyn. (2014, July 1). Malaysia's missing women workers. *The Malay mail online*. Retrieved from http://www.themalaymailonline.com/malaysia/article/malaysias-missing-women-workers.

Bourdieu, Pierre. (1984). *Distinction: A social critique of the judgment of taste*. Translated by R. Nice. Cambridge, MA: Harvard University Press.

Bronfenbrenner, Urie. (1979). *The ecology of human development: Experiments by nature and design*. Cambridge, MA: Harvard University Press.

Bureau of Empowerment for Older Persons. (2009). the 2nd National Plan on the Elderly (2002–2021). Retrieved from http://www.dop.go.th/download/laws/law_th_20161107091458_1.pdf.

Daatland, Svein Olaf, & Katharina Herlofson. (2003). Norms and ideals about elder care. In Ariela Lowenstein & Jim Ogg (Eds.), *Old age and autonomy: The role of service systems and intergenerational family solidarity* (pp. 125–163). Haifa: Center for Research and Study of Aging, The University of Haifa, Israel.

Esping-Andersen, Gøsta. (1990). *The three worlds of welfare capitalism*. Princeton, NJ: Princeton University Press.

Esping-Andersen, Gøsta, Duncan Gallie, Anton Hemerijck, & John Myles. (2002). *Why we need a new welfare state*. New York: Oxford University Press.

Evers, Adelbert, Marja Pilj, & Clare Ungerson. (Eds.). (1994). *Payments for Care*. Aldershot, UK: Avebury.

Guilmoto, Christophe Z. (2012). Son preference, sex selection, and kinship in Vietnam. *Population and Development Review*, *38*(1), 31–54.

Kabeer, Naila. (1999). Resources, agencies, achievements: Reflections on the measurement of women's empowerment. *Development and Change*, *30*, 435–464.

Lowenstein, Ariela, & Jim Ogg (Eds.). (2003). *Old age and autonomy: The role of service systems and intergenerational family solidarity*. Haifa: Center for Research and Study of Aging, The University of Haifa, Israel.

Murdock, George Peter. (1949). *Social structure*. New York: The MacMillan Company.

Ofstedal, Mary B., John Knodel, & Napaporn Chayovan. (1999). Intergenerational support and gender: A comparison of four Asian countries. *Asian Journal of Social Science*, *27*(2), 21–41.

Parsons, Talcott (Ed.). (1968). *Knowledge and society – American sociology*. New York: Basic Books.

Razavi, Shahra. (2007). *The political and social economy of care in a development context: Conceptual issues, research questions and policy options*. Geneva: United Nations Research Institute for Social Development, June.

Razavi, Shahra, & Silke Staab. (2008, September 19). *The social and political economy of care: Contesting gender and class inequalities*. Paper presented at the equal sharing of responsibilities between women and men, including care-giving in the context of HIV/AIDS, the United Nations Division for the Advancement of Women.

Schultz, James H. (1988). *The economics of aging*. Belmont, California: Wadsworth.

Sim, Ong Fon, & Tengku Aizan Hamid. (2010). Social protection in Malaysia – Current state and challenges towards practical and sustainable social protection East Asia: A compassionate community. In Mukul G. Asher, Sothea Oum, & Friska Parulian (Eds.), *Social protection in East Asia – Current state and challenges* (pp. 182–219). Jakarta: ERIA.

United Nations. (n.d.). *Data*. Retrieved from https://data.undp.org/dataset/Income-Gini-coefficient/36ku-rvrj.

UNJSPF. (2009). *Overcoming generational gap in the workplace*. New York: Secretariat Headquarters, United Nations Joint Staff Pension Fund.

World Bank. (2014a). *Data*. Retrieved from http://data.worldbank.org/indicator/NY.GDP.PCAP.CD.

World Bank. (2014b). *Data*. Retrieved from http://data.worldbank.org/indicator/SL.TLF.CACT.FE.ZS.

Wraight, Christopher D. (2008). *Rousseau's the social contract: A reader's guide*. London: Continuum Books.

PART 3

Synopsis and Way Forward

CHAPTER 8

Convergence versus Divergence: Care Relations across Three Societies

Jo-Pei Tan, Ki Soo Eun, Patcharalawai Wongboonsin, Kua Wongboonsin, Rahimah Ibrahim and Nguyen Huu Minh

1 Introduction

Based on the findings in chapters 5, 6 and 7, this chapter examines and discusses key points of similarity and difference in family relations, values and care provision amongst co-resident and non-coresident families in Bangkok Metropolis, Hanoi and Kuala Lumpur. A critical analysis of the findings follows the hypotheses presented in chapter 1; and its discussion is presented in three separate sections. The first section discusses family relationships and care provision depicting findings that reflect strong family relationships and their relationship to care provision provided by family members within the three societies. It also discusses attitudes and practices for intergenerational care across the three societies. The second section focuses on patriarchal values and their relationship with care relation within families in the three Southeast Asian societies. The final section discusses the contribution of adult children and parental characteristics in predicting the provision care between adult children and parents as well as parents-in-law among coresident and non-coresident families in the three societies.

2 Family Relationship and Care Provision

Consistent with the literature on care provision and intergenerational support in Asian societies, evidence from the current surveys in Bangkok Metropolis, Hanoi and Kuala Lumpur support the notion that family in Southeast Asian societies had a crucial role in care provision to other family members. Specifically, it supports the hypothesis presented that *there were strong family relationships which led to care provision by the family.* There was a considerable proportion of the samples in the three cities who provided care and support to other family members that included their own parents, parents-in-law and children. These findings reflect that 'family' within Southeast Asian society comprised

 | DOI:10.1163/9789004384330_009

members beyond the immediate family. Family in the Southeast Asian region can be seen as a network of family members that included extended family members who were all expected to contribute to the provision of care and support. This network of social relationships formed by spouses, parents-children, siblings and the wider extended family constitutes a dynamic and evolving social system, the family system (Whitchurch & Constantine 1993). This network of relationships depicted a situation where the social actors in the provision of familial care were not restricted to the immediate family. Similarly, there was evidence of reciprocity of support provision between adult children and parents/parents-in-law in both coresident and non-coresident families. These findings reflect the substantial role of the family as the main source of support and care for the old and young populations in these Southeast Asian societies (Knodel 2009; Teh, Ng, Tey & Siti-Norlasiah 2013). For example, the 2010 survey in Ho Chi Minh City showed that family members were the only care-takers of the elderly when they are sick (89.9%), in which the children take care of them most frequently (65.1%) and followed by spouse (24.8%) (Institute for Family and Gender Studies 2010). More recent data in Thailand also reflected the substantial role of the family in care-taking (NSO 2015) and also elderly preferences for family members as the main care-giver, especially daughters (Knodel, Teerawichitchainan & Pothisiri 2016). The contribution of the wider family network in care provision was also evident in Malaysia. Recent national surveys reported that care of young children was provided by family members, namely: grandparents (60.4%), other relatives (22.5%), and older siblings (17.1%) (NPFDB 2014) and this was similar for the care for the elderly in the Malaysian society (Teh, Lii, Tho, Peng, & Siti-Norlasiah 2013).

Upward intergenerational support was clear where adult children were more likely to provide support to their parents than receive assistance from the parents within the three societies in both types of living arrangement. While these findings confirm past research in Southeast Asian societies, which included Thailand, Philippines, Vietnam, Singapore (Chan 2005a, 2005b) and Malaysia (Lillard & Willis 1994), and support the existence of these traditional familial norms across three societies: a sense of filial piety and patriarchal norms (Huou 2013); notions of gratitude, merit and demerit (Wongsith 1990); and religious obligation as well as indebtedness to parents (Yaacob 2004) that entailed the obligation of children to their parents. It is also important to note that variation in types of care was detected between coresident and non-coresident families.

The greater emotional exchange between parents and adult children among co-resident households may be explained by the notion that coresidence itself may be perceived as a type of care for parents, in which the readily available care and resources exchange was often invisible and under-reported (Jones 2007; Teh et al. 2013). Co-residence was not an uncommon living arrangement among Southeast Asian societies families. It was perceived not only as an expression of filial piety but also as a type of support in terms of providing care for older people and children. The exchange of instrumental care especially financial assistance may be reduced in this type of living arrangement as co-residence may itself be perceived as a form of instrumental care to parents. In contrast, financial assistance was more substantial from adult children who lived separately from their parents than those in the same residence (Xie & Zhu 2009). It can be expected that adult children who were not co-residing with elderly parents were 'substituting' their unavailability to provide care in the form of monetary support. Thus, it is not surprising that among non-coresident families, adult children were more likely to provide financial support to parents and in return, receive emotional support from them.

The different socio-economic development between the three societies may have led to country variation in intergeneration support among non-coresident families. Adult children in Bangkok Metropolis and Kuala Lumpur were more likely to provide monetary and emotional support to their parents/parents-in-law while, in Hanoi, emotional support to parents/parents-in-law tended to be more visible. The higher GDP per capita in Malaysia and Thailand compared to Vietnam may be the explanation for the greater financial contribution to parents/parents-in-law among co-resident households in Kuala Lumpur and Bangkok samples. While the 2006 Vietnamese Family Survey shows that elderly persons tend to rely on monetary support from children (40%) as their main source of income, followed by their own labor (30%), pension/benefits (25.9%) and savings (1.6%) (Ministry of Culture, Sports and Tourism, 2008 as cited in Lan 2013), Vietnam also reported the lowest GDP per capita among the three economies which may suggest the lack of financial resources among co-resident households in Hanoi and thus, led to the greater provision of emotional support to parents/parents-in-law. For the case of Hanoi, this also may reflect a lack of financial assistance for elderly persons who did not share residence with adult children.

Analysis of the elderly care and child care provision within the three societies revealed general patterns and country variations that were recognisable. In terms of similarities, it can be clearly seen that elderly and child care provision heavily relied upon an informal support system, namely the family sector, while other non-familial sectors played a minor role in supplementing the provision of care within the three societies irrespective of the living arrangements. This supported the notion of familism in the practice of both elderly and child care in Bangkok Metropolis, Hanoi and Kuala Lumpur.

Guided by a notion of care provision in developing countries (Razavi 2007), the findings also revealed that the supportive and minimal role of non-familial sectors tended to vary among families in the three societies. The contribution of the not-for-profit sector, market and state in both elder and child care provision showed unique societal preferences, In addition to culture, the availability of policy, time and financial resources are the shaping forces of the distinctive attitudes and practice for intergenerational support in the three societies. Bangkok Metropolis perceived that the role of the non-profit sector, which mainly included neighbours and friends, mostly in elderly care provision, was not to be neglected. This redistribution of care support to the community that included neighbours and friends in Bangkok Metropolis may likely to be a response to the policy development at national level in Thailand. For example, the Thai government has rolled out various programmes and interventions based on the 2nd National Plan on the Elderly (2002–2021) that emphasizes the role of family and community for elderly care (Bureau of Empowerment for Older persons 2009). In comparison, without a clear policy supporting the role of the not-for-profit sector in elderly care in Malaysia, Kuala Lumpur perceived the market sector, which mainly referred to domestic workers, as an important source in both elderly and child care provisions. In the last two decades, there was a trend of hiring foreign domestic workers to substitute the caregiving role of families in Malaysia (Tan & Gibson 2013) and in 2010 the Department of Statistics (2010) reported a total of 2.4 million international immigrants or 8% of total population in the country. In addition, declining coresidence with parents and increasing employment opportunities for women (Knodel 2009; Wongbonsin & Entz 1996) have created push factors for utilising other non-familial sectors to supplement the demands of elderly and child care provision.

In Hanoi, the supplementary role of the state in elderly and child care provision was more apparent than other sectors. One possible explanation is under its socialist welfare regime, care-taking of the elderly was regulated by the state law and, child care centres and kindergartens are set up by the state government in Vietnam. In addition, the strong culture and norms in Vietnam that emphasize care within the family also explain their heavy preference for family as the main care provider instead of other non-familial care provision (i.e. market), these tended be expensive, affordable only by those in the high socio-economic group, their availability was limited and based in rural areas (Nguyen 2017). Thus, it can be seen that the government in Vietnam tended to be more involved in care provision compared to the limited governmental role in Malaysia and Thailand. Thus, based on the Care Diamonds welfare model, the practice of care services for elder and child care among these three societies was largely dependent on family with minor complementary support from community, market and state, which supported the familism notion on the importance of family role in care provision within developing countries (Razavi 2007; Ochiai 2009).

The present study also hypothesises that *there was a difference between attitude and practice for intergenerational support within Southeast Asian families.* The discrepancy between practice and attitudes towards care provision across generations highlighted the increasing expectation on government to contribute and support elderly and child care provision in the three societies, especially among married children, daughters and the middle generation. While we acknowledge that care practice was heavily skewed towards family, the attitudes towards the responsibility of care, shed lights on the expectation on other sectors to contribute and share the demands of care with the family sector. This is an indication of the redistribution of the care burden to the state and other sectors.

This shifting trend towards shared-responsibility and supplementary roles was also noted in recent studies. Wongsith (1990) noted that Thai people expect the government to play a more active role in the welfare of elderly, despite the majority endorsing women's obligation to please and take care of the needs of their parents and parents-in-law. In addition, the 2nd National Plan on the Elderly (2002–2021) which promoted the role of the community, is perceived as feasible and successful in shifting the preference of the young generation in Bangkok Metropolis. In addition, community ties and support from non-family members was found to positively relate to the well-being of the elderly and, when included as complementary effort to promote intergenerational solidarity, it could decrease dependency on family member and reduce the feeling of dependency among elderly persons (Herberholz, Suwanrada & Tangitootham 2013). A study by Ibrahim & colleagues (2015) also noted that young generations in Malaysia were not ignorant of the socio-demographic changes in families and their effects on the capacity of families to provide care (Abu Bakar & Abdullah 2013). This could be an explanation for the shifting trend in expectation on care provision among the current generation due to the diminishing support from family in their old age and the pressing need for burden sharing with other sectors. It is important to note that the expectation of shared-responsibility between family and government was relevant to the ability to provide care in terms of time and financial recourses, which shaped the preferences of the three societies.

The variation in attitudes towards care relations shed lights on the experience of the burden and ability to care between gender, age groups and education level across the three urban societies and this shaped the main differences in their preferences for the role of government. Middle generation or the sandwich generation, female and lower income groups were perceived as the most affected by care and work demands and, often heavily burdened with elderly and childcare. In Bangkok, the middle generation and females who were pressed with limited time and financial resources, demanded more supplementary support from government in the provision of elder and childcare. Nonetheless, the emphasis of the middle generation and females in Kuala Lumpur on the role of the family for elderly and child care provision revealed a different experience of care provision in this urban society. With a weak pension system and a lack of family-friendly work-life balance policies (Ong & Hamid 2010), the time-poor and resource-limited families in Malaysia replied upon the family for support for child rearing and elder care work. In Malaysia, it was also clear that lower educated groups who are also the most financially constrained group demanded more support from other sectors, especially the state, in caring for their dependent family members, with ethnic group variations.

In Vietnam, older generations and less educated groups were more likely to rely on family for support and treatment when frail and at times of illness. The 2006 Vietnamese Family Survey reported a high proportion of co-residence between elderly persons and their children (Ministry of Culture, Sports and Tourism Vietnam 2008) and, this may explain the expectation of elderly person of family members for care-taking and support. Past studies in Vietnam also showed that a low education level is one of the major obstacles for the access of the elderly to social services in Vietnam (Lan & Long 2009). The lack of awareness and limited accessibility to health care initiatives for the elderly in rural and deprived areas not only failed to meet the demand of the elderly, but also led to the dependency on family for elderly care (Khue 2007; Institute for Family and Gender Studies Vietnam 2010; Lan 2013). However, it was those with better education who demanded redistribution of this dependency in the form of government's playing a role in elderly and child care provision.

These findings imply an impending shift in expectations in terms of support in old age in these three urban societies as a result of the growing burden among adult children and families with limited financial and time resources and, weak public policies for social security and facilities of community care, against the backdrop of changing patterns of fertility and mortality, increasing female employment opportunities and soaring work demands in these three developing countries (as presented in Part 1 of this volume). The availability of the resources required for the provision of care, together with culture and tradition, appeared to be the main forces driving the propensity of family caregivers and preference towards redistribution to the government in providing care and support for elderly and children. It is thus, crucial to recognize the discrepancies *between attitude and practice for intergenerational support within Southeast Asian societies* and take into consideration the people's preferences and demands in the development of policies for elderly and childcare provision for the three societies.

3 Patriarchal Family Values across Three Societies

As shown in chapter 1, this volume hypothesises that *Southeast Asian Families were patriarchal*. Overall, findings from the surveys in Kuala Lumpur, Bangkok Metropolis and Hanoi in 2010–2011 demonstrated variation in norms and expectations of intergenerational support. The variation implied distinctions in the family system of the three societies during the period of investigation. Thus, this challenges such a hypothesis. As discussed in chapter 1, the elements of patriarchy were examined from four domains which described four dimensions of the phenomenon, namely gender domination, which related to the domination of men over women; generational domination, which described the domination of the older generation over the younger generation; the extent of patrilocality, and the preference for sons (Szoltysek, Klüsener, Poniat & Gruber 2017). Examination of the data showed that patriarchal family elements and values were only found among families in Hanoi while Kuala Lumpur and Bangkok were less inclined towards patriarchal family values.

The practice of patriarchal values within families in Hanoi was evident through the strong filial expectation of married sons to provide financial support to their parents. More importantly, married daughters were regularly expected to provide financial support to their parents-in-law while, married sons were least expected to support their parents-in-law. The contribution of married daughters in providing support for parent-in-laws was also observed in non-coresident households and they were the least expected to provide support to their parents in non-coresident households. These findings could be explained by the strong influence of Confucianism in Vietnamese culture, which highly valued patriarchal norms, lineage, patrilocal residence, filial piety, parental care and worship of ancestors (Huou 2013). For example, patrilocal coresidence was common and reflects the expectation of children, at least one son, to care for elderly parents and, daughters-in-laws were expected to meet the expectations of her parents-in-law in Vietnamese society (Ngo 2004; Minh 2011). Endorsement of these traditional values was also apparent in Hanoi, the Northern region which had a rich history of central planning and an old socialist model, while being under the process of shifting to market economy. Also, the region still had hallmarks of official policy regarding modernisation and family life compared to the central and Southern region (Luan 2011). Specifically, the findings support the patriarchy elements of male domination over female and son preferences in the context of intergenerational support in Hanoi, with strong expectation of married son to be the primary care provider of old age support. These findings depicted the active exchange between sons and parents, and between daughters-in-law and parents as well as the significance of understanding the dynamics of these relationships in care provision within the Vietnamese cultural context.

In comparison, family values among families in Bangkok and Kuala Lumpur were more bilateral with a less defined gender division in filial norms. The non-patriarchal norms reported in the Bangkok sample may be explained by the practice of Buddhism and the matrilocal structure among Thai families. While the Chinese and Indian families in Malaysia endorsed the patriarchal system, valued seniority and fathers or males as the head of the household, the majority of Malay families in the Kuala Lumpur sample were characterised by a bilateral family system with a less defined role for mothers in the family, both as the affectionate figure and the disciplinarian figure (Djamour 1959) and, there were equal expectations for the son's and daughter's family to take care of elderly parents (Yaacob 2004). Thus, the multi-ethnic composition of the Kuala Lumpur sample may have contributed to the non-patriarchal norms with a less obvious gender role division for intergenerational support.

In addition to filial norms, the intergenerational practice of patriarchal norms was also examined. Evidence indicated that filial norms and practice were differentiated by gender role and marital status. In relation to living arrangements, evidence of patriarchal family values was observed in both coresident and non-coresident families in Hanoi. A surprising result was observed in the practice of patriarchal family values among *coresident families* in Hanoi in which no significant difference was detected in the intergenerational support to parents between married sons and daughters. In contrast, a coherent pattern between patriarchal norms and practice in intergenerational support was demonstrated among *non-coresident families* in Hanoi. This indicates that patriarchal norms failed to be translated into actual practice among families who co-resided with parents/parents-in-law in Hanoi. This may be due the notion that co-residence was considered a form of support from children and, patrilocality was a normative practice among Hanoi community especially among married sons or at least in the early stages of their marriage before they set-up their own household. This 'invisible' support may be lead to a picture of equal support of married sons and daughters among those residing in the same household. However, it may also be plausible that the discrepancy between norms/expectation and actual intergenerational support reflects the reality of care provision for elderly parents among adult children in Hanoi. The adult children in Hanoi, irrespective of gender, were shouldering a more equal share in the practice of care provision for elderly parents as a result of pressing financial burdens and time constraints, together with a lack of government policy on elderly care in terms of adequate social security and facilities of community care in urban communities.

Additionally, among both types of living arrangement, it is also clear that married children in Hanoi contributed more than unmarried children, irrespective of gender. Similarly, married children living in *coresident families* in Bangkok and Kuala Lumpur were more likely to provide support to their parents compared to unmarried children. While a change in marital status or getting married may have signaled a shift in social status in the Asian cultural context, it was also associated with greater responsibility towards family as a husband/wife or towards parents and, this may have explained the more regular contribution to elderly parents among children who were married as compared to those who were single or unmarried. For example, traditionally, married sons and their wives were responsible for taking care of the sons' parents, while married daughters served their husbands' families (Li, Feldman & Jin 2004). In Wong's (2000) study on children as primary caregivers in Hong Kong, it was reported that married men who provided care were more likely to received assistance from their wives, therefore the role of primary caregivers was extended to the daughters-in-law. This suggests that married women were involved in the actual care-giving to assist their husbands who, in turn, seemed to have been designated the caregiver role by default.

Evidence of difference in family systems among the samples from Bangkok Metropolis and Kuala Lumpur cities was clearly observed in terms of intergenerational support among *non-coresident families*. Among the non-coresident families in the city of Kuala Lumpur, a bilateral family system was detected whereby there was no significant difference in intergenerational support by marital status or gender. Again, this non-significant finding may due to the multi-ethnic composition of the co-resident dataset which comprised two-thirds bilateral Malay and the remaining 30% were Chinese and Indians who adhered to patriarchal norms. As for non-coresident families in Bangkok Metropolis, married daughters were found to provide a more significant contribution to their own parents compared to married sons and this practice confirms the reduced prevalence of patriarchal norms on the expectations of financial contribution from married adult children to their own parents and parents-in-law. These findings imply a matriarchal family system among those who were not sharing a household with parents in Bangkok Metropolis. Historically, the importance of women and their relatives was recorded in the family's practice of matrilocality among the Thai peasant community in which women were in charge of the family and central in decision making because everything basically belonged to her and her family especially the land (Ramitanot 1999 as cited in Wongyannava 2011). In addition, daughters were found to be more reliable in providing financial support for the family than sons and therefore, parents preferred to send their daughters to work and earn money for the family (Santisombat 1992 as cited in Pattaravanich, Williams, Lyson & Archavanitkul 2005), and this may be a plausible explanation for the greater contribution of daughters in providing support to their parents than sons.

Figure 8.1 illustrates a summary of the norms and practice of patriarchal/non-patriarchal family systems among coresident and non-coresident families in Bangkok, Kuala Lumpur and Hanoi.

4 Care Transaction: The Contribution of Children and Parents' Characteristics

4.1 *Comparison across Three Societies*

This research proposes that *care transactions within Southeast Asian families were more attributable to the parent's characteristics than children's characteristics*. As shown in Figure 8.1, comparison across the three societies indicated that the extent of the contribution from each predictor tends to be different for each society. Overall, the results demonstrated that there was a stronger contribution of the characteristics of parents on predicting intergenerational support from adult children to parents compared to the characteristics of adult children, and the unique contribution tends to be different according to living arrangements and between parents and parents-in-law. Other factors determining intergenerational care provision included filial norms, reciprocal support and geographical distance. (The detailed results of the multiple regression analysis are presented in Table 8.1).

Data from the three societies consistently showed that characteristics of adult children were the driving forces in predicting intergenerational support to parents with mixed results on the contribution of parental characteristics as well as familial and country specific factors. The results revealed a different picture on how parent's characteristics predict intergenerational support from adult children. It was found that adult children's characteristics, namely age and interaction of gender and marital status, were the strongest predictors for intergenerational support in co-resident and non-coresident families in the three societies. What followed was a discussion of the main findings of the regression analysis according to living arrangement and between parents and

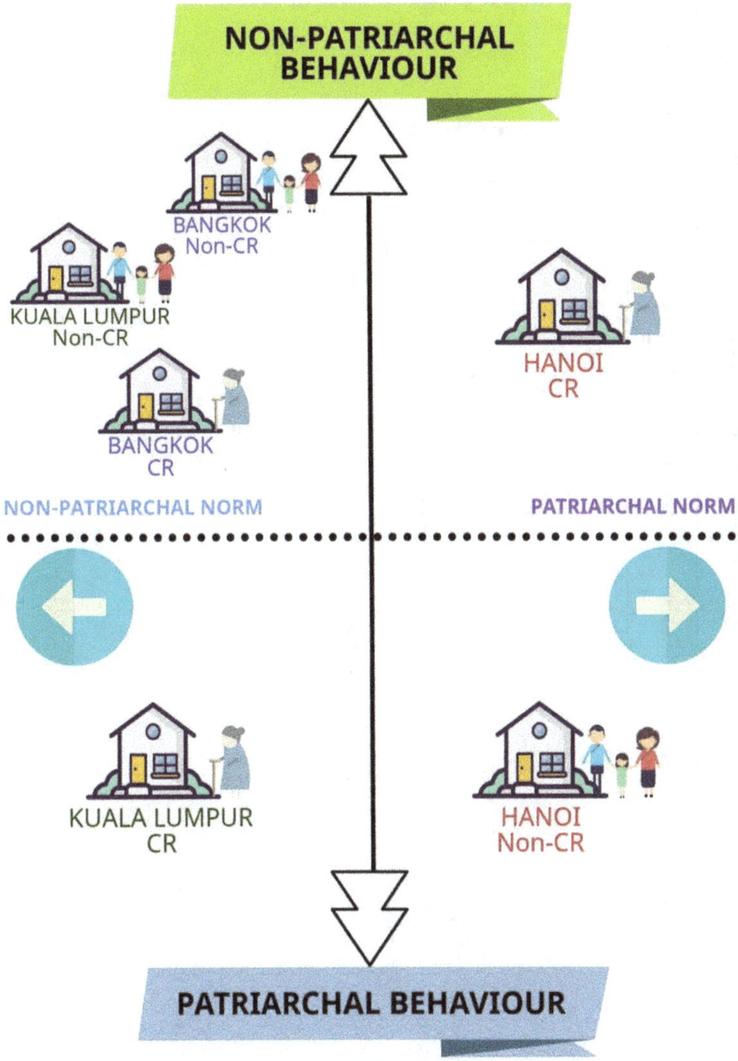

FIGURE 8.1 Summary of norms and practice for patriarchal/non-patriarchal family system among coresident and non-coresident families in Bangkok Metropolis, Kuala Lumpur and Hanoi.
Note: CR = Coresident; Non-CR = Non coresident.
SOURCE: AUTHORS.

parents-in-law. The findings for the interaction of gender and marital status of the adult children have been discussed in Section 2 of this chapter and thus, it will not be included in this section.

Age cohort: Significant difference across age groups on intergenerational support from adult children to parents was detected only in coresident families

TABLE 8.1 Summary of Multiple regression analysis for intergenerational support among both resident and non-resident families for Bangkok, Hanoi and Kuala Lumpur (UnBeta)

Predictor	Coresident, Unβ			Non-Coresident (Parents), Unβ			Non-Coresident (PIL), Unβ		
	BKK	Hanoi	KL	BKK	Hanoi	KL	BKK	Hanoi	KL
Adult children characteristics									
Gender x									
Marital status									
Married daughter	–	–	−1.45**	.60*	−.75**	–	–	1.08***	–
Unmarried son	−5.18***	−6.31***	−6.08***	−1.47*	−2.90**	–	–	–	–
Unmarried daughter	−2.20*	−5.97***	−6.00***	–	−4.00***	−1.01+	–	–	–
Older generation	1.75*	2.00**	–	–	–	–	–	–	–
Middle generation	–	–	−2.64**	0.59+	–	–	–	–	–
AC Education level	–	–	–	–	0.82**	–	–	–	–
Children below 7	–	–	–	–	–	–	–	–	−0.45+
(Min 1) (0,1)									
Parental characteristics									
Age 65 or >	1.52*	–	.96*	–	–	–	–	–	–
(at least 1) (0,1)									
High health needs (0,1)	–	–	–	–	–	–	–	–	–
No spouse		–	.97**	–	–	–	–	–	−0.41*
Familial factors									
Filial norm	1.25***	–	–	–	.30**	−.04*	–	.34***	–

Predictor	Coresident, Unβ			Non-Coresident (Parents), Unβ			Non-Coresident (PIL), Unβ		
	BKK	Hanoi	KL	BKK	Hanoi	KL	BKK	Hanoi	KL
Family interaction	.32**	.56***	–	–	–	–	–	–	–
Support from parents to AC	.43***	.52***	.28***	.36***	.27***	.37***	.60***	.50***	.75***
Distance	–	–		−.15*	–	–	–	–	.15*
Other demographic									
Urban		–	–		0.98***	–		–	–
Living standard		–	−.54**		−0.74***	−1.22***		−.95***	−.64***
Ethnicity (ref: Malay)									
Chinese			–			−0.58+			–
Indian			–			–			–
Adjusted R-squared	**0.50**	**0.61**	**0.51**	**0.16**	**0.20**	**0.22**	**0.23**	**0.26**	**0.38**
F	**17.63*****	**33.73*****	**37.21*****	**6.76*****	**9.04*****	**9.68*****	**8.50*****	**12.38*****	**19.71*****

Note: Support: Composite of Financial, Emotional and Care support from both Parents and PIL; P=Parent; PIL=Parents-in-law; AC=Adult children; Living standard: 1=High, 2=Middle, 3=Low; p<.10+, p<.05*, p<.01**, p<.001***

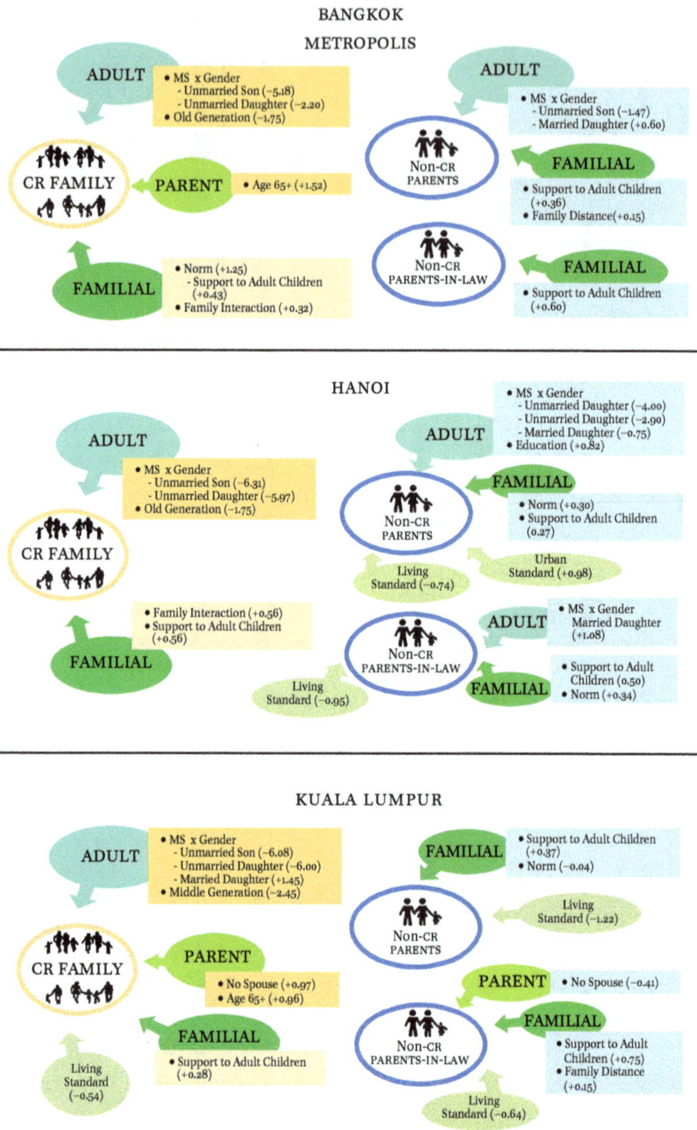

FIGURE 8.2 Factors predicting for intergenerational support in coresident and non-coresident families in Bangkok Metropolis, Hanoi and Kuala Lumpur.
Note: CR = Coresident; Non-CR = Non coresident; MS = Marital Status.
SOURCE: AUTHORS.

in all three societies. In terms of country variation, older generations in Hanoi and Bangkok were found to provide greater support to their parents/parents-in-law compared to those in the younger age group. One of the possible explanations was that the old-generation in these two societies adhered to more traditional norms and perceived stronger filial responsibilities towards their parent's old-age support than the young generation. Co-residing with parents or parents-in-law was also an indication of traditional norms and practice as compared to those who do not co-reside with parents or parents-in-law. Thus, co-resident households tended to have more significance for old generations as compared to the young generation who do not share the same sentiment about co-residence with parents.

In the case of Bangkok, the greater contribution among the old generation may be promoted by the notions of 'gratitude' whereby paying gratitude to elderly parents who contributed to the well-being of adult children was a traditional and core cultural value in Thai society (Wongsith 1990). Thai parents were expected to take care of their young children and in return, to be supported by the latter in old age (Knodel, Chayovan & Siriboon 1996; Wongboonsin & Entz 1991). This notion of reciprocity or paying gratitude to the elderly may still hold a strong place in the familial practice amongst the old generation and led to more regular intergenerational support, especially among those who co-reside with parents and parents-in-law as compared to the young generation in the Bangkok sample.

Similarly, in Hanoi, the old generation may be more influenced by the traditional filial piety notion in Vietnamese culture whereby there was an expectation of adult children to take care of their parents when they were old and frail as a form of repayment for their parents' efforts in upbringing them up (Huou 2013). Literature on co-residency in Vietnamese society noted that there is a mutual understanding between parents and adult children in relation to the exchange of support, especially among young married couples (Minh 2011). Parents in coresident families were prepared to support young adult children until they were financially capable of setting up their own household; while in return, young adults were expected to take care of their elderly parents or parents-in-law and provide support to the family (Hoa 2011), a reflection of intergenerational reciprocity. Thus, this may explain why the old-generation in Hanoi provided more regular support to their parents but also more likely to co-reside with elderly parents at a later stage in their life course. In societies in transition like Hanoi, housing constraints may have promoted co-residency between elderly parents and the old generation adult children. In other words, the old generation shouldered the burden of care provision for elderly parents and parents-in-law in both Bangkok and Hanoi.

In contrast, the middle generation who co-resided with their parents in Kuala Lumpur was found to be less likely to support their parents than the younger generation. This age cohort was found to make the strongest contribution in the Kuala Lumpur sample. Firstly, this might be explained by the double burden in care provision experienced by the middle generation. In fact, the middle generation was also known as the 'sandwich generation' and considered to be the working age population who were often pressured by both elderly and childcare responsibilities (Parker & Patten 2013). Thus, these dual-care responsibilities together with demands from their career and having a young family had an effect on their capacity to provide care to their parents in terms of companionship, time and monetary support. Results from chapter 7 also noted that the middle generation in Kuala Lumpur placed a greater demand on the role of family in elderly care provision, which reflected their heavy burden in providing old age support to their parents. More importantly, sharing a residence itself may be considered a type of support to parents, whereby children in the household provided 'invisible' emotional support, companionship or practical assistance to elderly parents through sharing the same living space. This notion of coresidence as a form of support possibly explained the lower intergenerational support from the middle generation. Given the cost of housing being high, sharing a residence may be economically motivated for the time-poor and financially struggling middle generation. It was this generation of people who needed assistance from parents who were probably perceived as the most reliable person to help with childcare, cooking, laundry and many other household duties. There was a popular saying in Southeast Asia: 'Having an elderly at home is like possessing a treasure'. The lack of support from adult children may also be attributable to the fact that the middle generation children were experiencing active downward support from their parents. Again, this may shed light on the importance of co-residence for both practical and financial reasons among the middle generation, and was thus a plausible explanation for age as a significance factor only among those in co-resident families.

Overall, these findings implied that across the three societies, provision of care and support to parents tended to differ according to age cohort and living arrangement. For example, care and support for elderly parents were often shouldered by the old generation adult children, who were motivated by stronger traditions and norms. While, those in the middle generation were feeling the time and financial strain from both child care and elderly care responsibilities, together with their notion of residence as a form of support, which led to a low engagement in terms of care provision to parents.

Parents' characteristics: The age of parents modestly contributed to greater intergenerational support among *coresident families* with a stronger significance in the sample of Bangkok Metropolis than Kuala Lumpur. In accordance with past research, there was a consistent financial transfer from adult children to elderly parents and a greater likelihood of shared-living arrangements when parents were old, widowed, or in poor health and economically constrained (Johar, Maruyama & Nakamura 2014; Silverstein, Gan & Yang 2006; Takagaki & Silverstein 2011). These findings indicate that elderly parents relied upon adult children in case of trouble or illness, and that co-residence with adult children was a form of support for old age. In terms of living arrangements, the significant contribution of parent's/parents' age in predicting intergeneration support from adult children to parents was only found in co-resident households, and it may imply that co-residing with family was a feasible solution for the provision of old age support among elderly parents in both Bangkok and Kuala Lumpur. This is in line with findings in chapter 7, which reported a high reliance or expectation on the family to bear the responsibility for elderly care among those in Bangkok and Kuala Lumpur.

However, parental needs associated with ill-health and losing a spouse were not found to provoke greater support from adult children in these Southeast Asian societies, except for Kuala Lumpur. Nonetheless, this phenomenon raised concerns regarding the capacity of familial support since downward support to parents was not significantly associated with the health and support needs of the parents. In other words, the support from adult children for elderly parents who were no longer capable of taking care of themselves in old age due to illness, deteriorating health and functionality or losing a spouse was limited and these parental needs did not provoke a greater extent of downward support from adult children. Thus, these findings highlighted the unmet health, social and emotional needs of older persons who were physically unfit due to ill health or at risk of social isolation and weak social support as a result of widowhood. In addition, the findings also implied that family who is perceived as the main care provider was not responding to the needs of this vulnerable group. This may be due to the family's lack of ability in terms of time, financial resources or knowledge to provide care to their old, frail and needy parents.

Parental characteristics, namely age and no spouse status, were not significant predictors for non-coresident families in Hanoi. The current survey showed that almost half of the non-coresiding adult children stayed nearby their parents (i.e. 15 minutes away/within same district). The short distance between households enabled adult children to provide support to their parents who were old and living alone while enabling parents to have easy access to their children for practical assistance or companionship.

Filial norm: Intergenerational support among Southeast Asian societies needed to be examined within the context of filial responsibility, socio-cultural norm and religious duty (Hamid & Chai 2013; Huou 2013; Knodel 2009; Yaacob 2004). It was found that the contribution of filial norms on intergenerational support varied across the three societies and, types of living arrangements. These results reflected the distinct family values and attitudes towards filial responsibilities across the three societies in South East Asia. Among *coresident families*, adult children who endorsed filial norms were found to provide more support to their parents/parents-in-law. Nonetheless, the significant contribution of filial norms on the upward flow of intergenerational support was only detected among coresident families in Bangkok city. The sharing of a residence with parents can be perceived as a manifestation of the cultural ideal of filial piety. Thus, adult children in Bangkok who co-resided with parents or parents-in-law may be more committed towards traditional filial responsibilities of providing care and support to their parents than those who did not share a residence with their parents.

In contrast, the significant contribution of filial norms in predicting a stronger upward flow of intergenerational support to parents and parents-in-law was detected among *non-coresident families* in Hanoi, in which a higher support for filial norms was related to more support to own parents and parents-in-law. This finding reflects the stronger influence of Confucianism on intergenerational relations within non-coresident families in Hanoi whereby they endorsed the notion of filial piety and recognised children's obligations in obeying, taking care of and manifesting gratitude to their superior and elderly persons (Huou 2013). The more significant contribution of filial norms among non-coresident families may be because adult children were compensating with more regular care provision to parents or parents-in-laws who were not living with them.

However, an unexpected finding was reported among *non-coresident* families in Kuala Lumpur whereby it was demonstrated that adult children who provide greater support to parents were found to express lower emphasis on filial norms than those who provided less support. It should be noted that this negative relationship between filial norms and the upward flow of intergenerational support was very weak in comparison to other significant predictors included in the regression models. One plausible explanation may be related to the concept of filial norms used in the study whereby it was operationalised to signify the degree of agreement on the obligations to provide material support and contribute to the livelihood of parents and parents-in-law, while intergenerational support used in the model is a composite score of financial, emotional and domestic support that adult children provide to their parents/parents-in-law. Further analysis of the different types of support may yield different results regarding filial norms. Besides that, half of the samples in Kuala Lumpur were Malays and it was noted that Malay parents did not have clear-cut expectations regarding the obligations of children to provide financial or material support or to feel indebted for their upbringing as was emphasized by the Chinese and Indian parents. Malays viewed the parent-child relationship in terms of more diffuse obligations, engendered by gifts, and the long term return from children was expressed more subtly (Li 1989). Thus, the notion of filial norms which were heavily based on financial obligations may contradict the notion of filial obligation and parental expectation of children among the Malay society. In other words, it is important to take into account the ethnic group variation when examining care transactions between generations within the Kuala Lumpur sample.

Support from parents: Reciprocity was evident in both coresident and non-coresident families across all three societies. It was clearly shown that a greater extent of support from parents was associated with more support to parents and parents-in-law. The findings reflected a dynamic and bi-directional mechanism in intergenerational support in these Southeast Asian societies which may be motivated by and negotiated on the basis of support needs and relative resources (Choi 2003; Johar et al. 2014; Takagaki & Silverstein 2011). For example, the instrumental support needs of older adults and childcare needs of dual-earner families may motivate greater exchange across generations. In other words, these findings reflected the active role of elderly parents in promoting the functionality and economic well-being of their families, irrespective of the living arrangements. Parents in Southeast Asian societies were not passive recipient of support: Two-thirds of older parents in the Philippines and more than half in Thailand provided monetary and material support to their adult children, followed by almost 40% in Vietnam (Chan 2005a, 2005b). As Chan (2005a) asserted, older persons should not always be viewed as dependent on other family members; their important contribution/support to adult children was not only crucial for enhancing the older adult's well-being, but also in improving the overall family's financial standing. In addition, the findings also reflected the demand of adult children in these three societies for regular support from parents and parents-in-law, especially among those who were not sharing a residence with them. Among co-resident families in Asian communities, parents were reported to be heavily involved in childcare, cooking, laundry, and other household duties (Lee, Lee, Yu, Sun & Liu 2000). Thus, knowing that family was the main provider for elderly and childcare in these three urban societies, with the lack of effective public policy to ease their burden, adult children have to rely on parents as the most reliable person to support the demands of their daily lives and, in return, provide financial or practical assistance to parents for their support.

Strata and living standard: Intergenerational support was found to be differentiated according to country specific characteristics, namely strata and living standard in Hanoi and Kuala Lumpur. In the case of Kuala Lumpur, intergenerational support for parents and parents-in-law was more regular among adult children with low living standards or poor economic status than those with high living standards or better economic status. This flow of upward intergenerational transfer was similar across co-resident and non-coresident families. These findings imply that among economically constrained families, the support and care for elderly parents was still very much provided by adult children whether they were co-residing or not co-residing with their elderly parents. This revealed the burden of poor families in providing care for the elderly in both groups of coresident and non-coresident in Kuala Lumpur. More importantly, this resonates with the findings in chapter 7 on the increasing expectation from the most financially constrained group in Kuala Lumpur for the government to provide more support for elderly care and childcare.

As for Hanoi, country specific factors appeared to have more significance on intergenerational transfer among non-coresident families. As coresidence, especially patrilocality was considered a common practice in Vietnamese society, it was not surprising that to compensate for their lack of physical availability and unmet parental expectation, substantial intergenerational support to elderly parents was detected among non-coresident adult children. Past literature also reported that the support from non-coresident adult children to parents often came in terms of financial or material aid (Luo 2012; Yi & Lin 2009). It may also be the case where non-coresiding adult children are migrants from outside Hanoi, and who earn a better income, were enabled to provide more support to their parents living in the more rural areas in Vietnam. As shown in the recent data, during 2009–2014, the migrant population in Hanoi accelerated with the arrival of more than 220,000 migrants from other provinces which ranked as the third largest migrant population in the country (VGSO 2015). Nonetheless, the significant difference between urban and rural areas in Hanoi implied a greater burden of elderly care among adult children in urban areas when they did not co-reside with parents. While urban location had a negative relationship with coresidence (Goodkind 1997), coresident or multi-generational households in urban areas could serve as a strategy to ease the burden of providing elderly care in the urban city of Hanoi. Thus, it is important to consider the country variations, group preferences and the contribution of different factors according to living arrangements when designing policies to address issues on care provision, especially elderly care.

5 Summary

In summary, the evidence presented highlights the main burden of care giving for old and young population in these Southeast Asian societies remained within the family with a substantial contribution from the wider family network. The diverse historical background and socio-cultural development across these three societies also led to variations in the family system, which challenged the notion of a similar patriarchal family system among those living in the city of Bangkok Metropolis, Hanoi and Kuala Lumpur. The diversity and similarity in norms lent blasts of colour to the Asian landscape reflecting a rich ethnic and religious mosaic which extended beyond patriarchal norms. The different family systems, which included patriarchal, bilateral and matriarchal systems, had implications on the differentiated expectation of sons and daughters as well as of married and unmarried children in care provision across the three Southeast Asian societies.

The degree of active role of elderly parents in supporting the needs of adult children and intergenerational exchange between parent and children was also subject to the type of living arrangement among these Southeast Asian societies. The burden of care provision for elderly parents was profound among poor families, those in urban areas, and among non-coresident families. In addition, the upward flow of intergenerational support to parents was negotiated and based on situational factors such as proximity/location and SES, and parents' capacity to fulfil the needs of their adult children.

More importantly, the intergenerational support from adult children to elderly parents was mainly determined by the characteristics of adult children supported by reciprocity from parents and cultural norms; there was a weak contribution from parental factors that include health status and widowhood. The findings raised concerns regarding the inability of adult children to meet the need for care and support of their elderly parents, during their time of need, sickness and widowhood, despite the parents' active role in supporting the needs of adult children. Thus, there was also a gap in the role of family in supporting the needs of parents especially in relation to health care and the psychological needs of the elder.

While care provision was mainly based within the informal family network, there was an emerging shift in expectation of parental care from more active engagement from non-familial sectors such as government, community and market, and there were variations in group preferences, according to age cohort, gender and economical status across all three societies. For example, the discrepancy between practice and attitudes towards care provision across the old, middle and young generations was an indication of the need for the redistribution of the care burden to other sectors, specifically to the state due to the diminishing family capacity in care provision for elderly. Thus, it is important to take into consideration the specific target groups when designing programmes and public policy regarding the provision of care for elderly and children.

References

Abu Bakar, Noor Rahamah, & Abdullah Mohd Yusof. (2013). The sustainability of dual earner at the workplace in Malaysia. *Asian Social Science*, *9*(7), 192–199.

Chan, Angelique. (2005a). *Formal and informal intergenerational support transfers in South-Eastern Asia.* Paper presented at the United Nations expert group meeting on social and economic implications of changing population age structures, Mexico City, Mexico.

Chan, Angelique. (2005b). Aging in southeast and East Asia: Issues and policy directions. *Journal of Cross-Cultural Gerontology*, *20*(4), 269–284.

Choi, Namkee. (2003). Coresidence between unmarried aging parents and their adult children: Who moved in with whom and why?. *Research on Aging*, *25*(4), 384–404. doi: 10.1177/0164027503025004003.

Department of Statistics Malaysia. (2010). *Population and housing census Of Malaysia: preliminary count report.* Putrajaya: DOSM.

Djamour, Judith. (1959). *Malay kinship and marriage in Singapore.* London: The Athione.

Goodkind, Daniel. (1997). The Vietnamese double marriage squeeze. *International Migration Review*, 108–127.

Hamid, Tengku Aizan, & Chai Sen Tyng. (2013). Meeting the needs of older Malaysians: expansion, diversification and multi-sector collaboration. *Malaysian Journal of Economic Studies*, *50*(2), 157–174.

Herberholz, Chantal, Worawet Suwanrada, & Nantarat Tangitootham. (2013). Family relations, social support, community ties and well-being in rural Thailand. *Journal of Demography*, *28*(2), 22–36.

Hoa, Dang Thi. (2011). Habitation and relationships between parents and adult children in rural areas. In Trinh Duy Luan, Helle Rydstrorm, & Wil Burghoorn (Eds.), *Rural families in Doi Moi Vietnam* (pp. 17–37). Hanoi: Social Sciences Publishing House.

Huou, Tran Dinh. (2013). *Traditional families in Vietnam and the influence of confucianism*. Unpublished Report from Institute for Family and Gender Studies, Hanoi: Vietnam.

Ibrahim, Rahimah, Tengku Aizan Hamid, Chai Sen Tyng, & Siti Suhailah Abdullah. (2015). Expectations of elderly care: Perspectives of female undergraduate in Malaysia and Japan. *Women's Studies, 36*, 47–62.

Institute for Family and Gender Studies. (2010). *Results from the survey on the elderly in Ho Chi Minh City*. Hanoi: Institute for Family and Gender Studies.

Johar, Meliyanni, Shiko Maruyama, & Sayaka Nakamura. (2014). Reciprocity in the formation of intergenerational coresidence. *Journal of Family and Economic Issues*, 1–18. doi: 10.1007/s10834-013-9387-7.

Jones, Gavin. (2007). Challenges of ageing in East and Southeast Asia: Living arrangements of older persons, social security trends and retirement options. In Gabriele Sinigoj, Gavin Jones, Katsuiku Hirokawa, & Sepp Linhart (Eds.), *The impact of ageing: A common challenge for Europe and Asia* (pp. 79–95). Berlin: LIT Verlag.

Khue, Luong Ngoc. (2007). Management of Vietnamese medical examination and treatment for Vietnamese elderly. *Journal of the Elderly, 7*(2009), 9–13.

Knodel, John. (2009). Is intergenerational solidarity really on the decline? Cautionary evidence from Thailand. In UNFPA (Ed.), *Family support networks and population ageing* (pp. 29–31). New York: United Nations.

Knodel, John, Bussarawan Puk Teerawichitchainan, & Wiraporn Pothisiri. (2016). *Caring for Thai older persons with long-term care needs*. Michigan: University of Michigan.

Knodel, John, Chayovan, Napaporn, & Siriwan Siriboon. (1996). Familial support and the life course of Thai elderly and their children. In Tamara Hareven (Ed.), *Aging and generational relations over the life course: A historical and cross-cultural perspective* (pp. 438–461). Berlin: Walter de Gruyter.

Lan, Le Ngoc. (2013). *Elderly care in Vietnam: Some issues concerned*. Unpublished Report from Institute for Family and Gender Studies, Hanoi: Vietnam.

Lan, Le Ngoc, & Long, Tran Quy. (2009). *Report on analysis of figures from housing survey 2006: Relationship between the elderly and generations in family*. Hanoi: Institute for Family and Gender Studies.

Lee, Rance P.L., Jik-Joen Lee, Elena S.H. Yu, Shong-Gong Sun, & William T. Liu. (2000). Living arrangement and elderly care: The case of Hong Kong. In W.T. Liu & Hal Kendig (Eds.), *Who should care for the elderly?: An East-West value divide* (pp. 269–296). Singapore: Singapore University Press and World Scientific Publishing.

Li, Tania. (1989). *Malays in Singapore: Culture, economy, and ideology*. Oxford University Press, USA.

Li, Shuzhuo, Marcus W. Feldman, & Xiaoyi Jin. (2004). Children, marriage form, and family support for the elderly in contemporary rural China. *Research on Aging, 26*, 352–384.

Lillard, Lee, & Robert Willis. (1994). Intergenerational educational mobility: Effects of family and state in Malaysia. *Journal of Human Resources*, 1126–1166.

Luan, Duy Trinh. (2011). Modernization and rural families in transitional Vietnam. In Trinh Duy Luan, Helle Rydstrorm, & Wil Burghoorn (Eds.), *Rural families in Doi Moi Vietnam* (pp 17–37). Hanoi: Social Sciences Publishing House.

Luo, Guifen. (2012). China's family support system: Impact of rural–urban female labor migration. In Sheying Chen, & Jason Powell (Eds.), *Aging in China* (pp. 99–126). New York, NY: Springer.

Minh, Nguyen Huu. (2011). Post-marital living arrangement in rural Vietnam. In Trinh Duy Luan, Helle Rydstrorm, & Wil Burghoorn (Eds.), *Rural families in Doi Moi Vietnam* (pp. 58–88). Hanoi: Social Sciences Publishing House.

Ministry of Culture – Sports and Tourism Vietnam. (2008). *Results from Vietnamese family survey 2006*. Hanoi: Institute for Family and Gender Studies, General Statistics Office for UNICEF.

Ngo, Thi Ngan Binh. (2004). The confucian four feminine virtues. In Drummond, & Rydstrom (Eds.), *Gender practices in contemporary Vietnam* (pp 47–73). Singapore: Singapore University Press.

Nguyen, Ha Dong. (2017). *Marketisation of nursing homes for the elderly in Vietnam: barriers and enablers*, Care in modern family: Perspective of older and younger generations in two major cities in Vietnam and the UK Conference, October 2017, Manchester, United Kingdom. Unpublished conference paper.

NPFDB. (2014). Report on key findings fifth Malaysian population and family survey (MPFS-5). Kuala Lumpur: Population and Family Research Sector National Population and Family Development Board.

NSO. (2015). *Rayngan pol beungton sumruad prachakon sungayu nai prathetthai po so 2557*. krungthepsamnakngan sathitihaengchat [*Preliminary report, survey of older persons in Thailand 2014*, Bangkok, National Statistical Office].

Ochiai, Emiko. (2009). Care diamonds and welfare regimes in East and South-East Asian societies: Bridging family and welfare sociology. *International Journal of Japanese Sociology*, *18*(1), 60–78.

Ong, Fong Sim, & Tengku Aizan Hamid. (2010). Social protection in Malaysia – Current state and challenges towards practical and sustainable social protection in East Asia: A compassionate community. In Mukul Asher, Sothea Oumand, & Friska

Parulian (Eds.), *Social protection in East Asia – Current state and challenges*. ERIA Research Project Report 2009–9 (pp. 182–219). Jakarta: ERIA.

Parker, Kim, & Eileen Patten. (2013). *The sandwich generation: Rising financial burdens for middle-aged Americans*. Social & demographic trends project. Washington, D.C.: Pew Research Center.

Pattaravanich, Umaporn, Lindy B. Williams, Thomas A. Lyson, & Kritaya Archavanitkul. (2005). Inequality and educational investment in Thai children. *Rural Sociology, 70*(4), 561–583.

Razavi, Shahra. (2007). *The Political and Social Economy of Care in a Development Context.* Conceptual Issues, Research Questions and Policy Options, Gender and Development Programme. Paper No. 3, UNSRID, Geneva.

Silverstein, Merril, Daphna Gan, & Yang Frances. (2006). Intergenerational support to aging parents: The role of norms and needs. *Journal of Family Issues, 27*(8), 1068–1084.

Szołtysek, Mikołaj, Sebastian Klüsener, Radosław Poniat, & Siegfried Gruber. (2017). The patriarchy index: A new measure of gender and generational inequalities in the past. *Cross-Cultural Research, 51*(3), 228–262.

Takagi, Emiko, & Merril Silverstein. (2011). Purchasing piety? coresidence of married children with their older parents in Japan. *Demography, 48*(4), 1559–1579.

Tan, Peck-Leong, & John Gibson. (2013). Impact of foreign maids on female labor force participation in Malaysia. *Asian Economic Journal, 27*(2), 163–183.

Teh, Jane Kimm Lii, Ng Sor Tho, Tey Nai Peng, & Ismail Siti-Norlasiah. (2013). Ethnicity and support for parents in Malaysia. *Asian Women, 29*(4), 51–71.

VGSO. (2015). *Dieu tra Dan so va Nha o giua ky thoi diem 1/4/2014: Cac ket qua chu yeu*. Hanoi. NXB Thong ke, 9/2015. [*Intercensal population and housing survey 1/4/2014: Major findings*. Hanoi. Statistical Publishing House, 9/2015]. *Điều tra Dân số và Nhà ở giữa kỳ thời điểm 1/4/2014: Các kết quả chủ yếu*. Hà Nội. NXB Thống kê, 9/2015.

Whitchurch, Gail G., & Larry L. Constantine. (1993). Systems theory. In Pauline Boss, William J. Doherty, Ralph LaRossa, Walter R. Schumm, & Suzanne K. Steinmetz (Eds.), *Sourcebook of family theories and methods: A contextual approach* (pp. 325–352). New York: Plenum.

Wong, Odalia M.H. (2000). Children and children-in-law as primary care givers: Issues and perspectives. In W.T. Liu, & Hal Kendig (Eds.), *Who should care for the elderly?: An East-West value divide* (pp. 267–321). Singapore: Singapore University Press and World Scientific Publishing.

Wongboonsin, Kua, & Anchara Entz. (1991). *Women's work and the need for child care among prekindergarten children in Bangkok Metropolitan Area*. Bangkok: Institute of Population Studies, Chulalongkorn University, Thailand.

Wongboonsin, Kua, & Anchara Entz. (1996). *Child care among children aged 3–5 in urban and rural of Thailand.* Bangkok: College of Population Studies, Chulalongkorn University.

Wongsith, Malinee. (1990). Attitudes towards family values in Thai society. Bangkok: Institute of Population Studies, Chulalongkorn University, Thailand.

Wongyannava, Thanes. (2011). The sound of sirens in social research on the Intimate Sphere in Thailand and its discontents, *Journal of Intimate and Public Spheres*, *1*(1), 36–54.

Xie, Yu, & Zhu Haiyan. (2009). Do sons or daughters give more money to parents in urban China?. *Journal of Marriage and Family*, *71*(1), 174–186.

Yaacob, Harun. (2004). *Malaysia: Papers on society and culture.* Wellington: Victoria University of Wellington.

Yi, Chin-Chun, & Ju–Ping Lin. (2009). Types of relations between adult children and elderly parents in Taiwan: Mechanisms accounting for various relational types. *Journal of Comparative Family Studies*, *40*, 305–324.

CHAPTER 9

Synopsis and Way Forward

Patcharawalai Wongboonsin, Rahimah Ibrahim, Jo Pei Tan and Tengku Aizan Hamid

1 Introduction

As the final chapter of this volume, this chapter focuses on ways to contribute to better caring societies in Southeast Asia while at the same time advancing their economies. The focus of this chapter is limited to three Southeast Asian countries, which are purposively selected as case studies of societies experiencing rapid demographic and socio-economic transitions. They are the Federation of Malaysia, the Kingdom of Thailand, and the Socialist Republic of Vietnam. From here onward, the terms Malaysia, Thailand, and Vietnam will be used to refer to these countries respectively. They exemplify societies at the crossroads due to a series of prominent changes in the cultural, socio-economic, and demographic landscape.

The discussion is divided into three sections: looking back, looking forward, and policy recommendations for moving forward. In the looking back section, this chapter firstly highlights major points identified in the previous chapters from a synopsis perspective of a nexus of different perspectives – cultural, demographic and socio-economic development – that are intertwined with care relations. It evaluates, from an across-societies' perspective, the issues of continuity and changes at the national level that were raised in chapters 2–4 on the cultural, demographic and socio-economic background, care relations, and relevant policy regimes during the past decades up to 2017. Care relations experienced at the national level, identified in chapters 2–4, amidst such ongoing and changing contexts are discussed together with key findings from chapters 5 to 8 which are a snap shot taken during 2010–2011 of care relations at the specific-area level. The latter refers to Kuala Lumpur, Bangkok Metropolis, and Hanoi, as case studies.

Section one of this chapter argues that the three Southeast Asian countries belonged to an intergenerational family network-based welfare system that was intertwined with the cultural value of filial piety. The differences in the family system of age and gender hierarchies resulted in their different patterns of care relations, particulary between adult children and elderly parents. Meanwhile, the economic, demographic and socio-cultural transition produced a complex

 | DOI:10.1163/9789004384330_010

dimension of care that made it difficult for the adult children to sustain familial care for the elderly over the long-term. This was also the case with childcare. The family network was expected to cope with these vicissitudes, amidst a cultural lag in providing a responsive legal framework and policy approaches. Care services provided by profit and non-profit oriented providers in the public and private sectors were limited to a supporting role and were in practice still minimal. The case studies of Kuala Lumpur, Bangkok Metropolis, and Hanoi during 2010–2011 confirmed these notions. The state was expected to play a more active role in face of the diminishing capacity of the family network.

Current snapshots and demographic projections show that one cannot expect the family to continue to play the same role as effectively in the future. The above notions lead to the second section, which looks forward to further challenging structural transitions. It argues that the context of care will change more dynamically in the decades to come in Malaysia, Thailand and Vietnam. While they all long for the economy to advance further, these societies will continue to age, further diminishing the capacity of the family network. The sustainability of the existing welfare system and the prospect for further economic development are major concerns for Malaysia, Thailand and Vietnam as they move forward. Policy recommendations are accordingly provided in the third section of this chapter.

2 Looking Back: A Synopsis

2.1 *Ageing and Young Middle-income Economies*

During the past decades, dramatic economic and demographic transitions characterized all three Southeast Asian countries under investigation. Malaysia and Thailand transformed from resource-based economies dependent on agriculture and primary commodities to high-middle income economies through industrialisation and urbanisation. Meanwhile, *Doi Moi* shifted Vietnam from one of poorest economies to a low-to-average middle-income socialist-oriented market economy through social transformation and modernisation.

Yet, getting old before getting rich had already characterized Thailand and Vietnam by 2017. In the process of modernization, there was a significant drop in fertility from 6 children to the below-replacement level of 1.6 in just three decades, accompanied by a lengthening of period of vulnerabilities over the lifecycle to other temporal social changes. There was, accordingly, a drastic shift in the population age-structure, with a steady reduction in the size of young and working-age population and a parallel increase in that of the elderly. Thailand became one of the world's most rapidly aging societies, followed by

Vietnam. Despite Malaysia's being relatively young, there was an increasing proportion of the elderly, those aged 60 or over from 5.2% in 1970 to 8% of the total population in 2010. Therefore, getting old before getting rich was also a concern in Malaysia.

2.2 *Age-structured and Gender Structured Societies*

Based on an analysis of chapters 2 to 4, this chapter maintains that despite Malaysia, Thailand, and Vietnam being multicultural, the Malays (and Bumiputera), the Thai people and the Vietnamese made up the majority in those respective societies during the period of investigation.

Age hierarchies and gender inequality were key prominent features shared among them in both the public and private spheres during the period of investigation. Filial piety was a long tradition and an important ideology there despite their varied kinship systems. When compared with Malaysia and Thailand, son preference was relatively strong in Vietnam, particularly in rural areas. Women continued to bear primary responsibility for unpaid work, particularly domestic and care giving work, particularly in Malaysia and Vietnam. This was the case despite improvements in the role and status of women in society and their participation in labor market due to improved education.

In Malaysia, the female workforce in the middle-income group, aged between 25 to 45 years, were likely to be the sandwiched generation overwhelmed with responsibilities for their own family and their elderly parents. Delayed marriage and motherhood, declining family size and an increasing trend of one-generation households were particularly revealed in Malaysia and Thailand. The pattern of 'Double Income No Kid (DINK)' was on the rise in Malaysia and Thailand, while the latter was on its way to a further shift of an increasing trend of a Single Income No Kid (SINK) lifestyle. The family size in Vietnam was also declining, while delayed marriage and motherhood were the trend in urban areas.

2.3 *Care Relations Amidst Insidious Socio-cultural Transitions*

Chapter 2 took note of the erosion of filial obligations and a decline in elderly care within the family system in Malaysia. This was mainly attributable to a structural shift from the prevalence of the traditional extended family towards a nuclear family, and increasing female participation in the formal labor market. The capacity of the family as the main provider of informal care to the children and the elderly was consequently diminishing. Even though childcare by parents was considered preferable, working parents were heavily dependent on family networks, neighbors, and to a lesser extent on foreign domestic workers. Otherwise, the alternative was unlicensed, rather than licensed childcare centres. Foreign domestic workers also played a supporting role to family members in elderly care. Institutional care for the elderly was not an option, regardless of ethnicity and religious practices in Malaysia.

On the other hand, the authors of chapter 3 argued that given a strong sense of filial piety, previous studies found both men and women remained single and were willing to leave the labor market to take care of their frail or elderly parents in Thailand. Yet, the proportion of women to have done so was higher than that of men there. At the same time, availability and usage of private and public day-care centres of quality for the elderly were on the rise. Diversification in childcare providers was also the case in Thailand. However, the number of quality childcare centres was relatively limited.

Chapter 4 maintained that, in Vietnam, the relatively stable and rapidly growing economy during the past decade was creating favourable conditions for childcare services. In addition to the state budget, there has been a socialisation of child protection, care and education, as reflected in a pooling of investment resources from the community, public bonds, enterprises and individual contributions. Changes in economic and social conditions resulted in the shifting structure, values, and norms of the traditional family as well as in their living arrangements. While family and kin played the main role in elderly and childcare, they looked for domestic workers for support rather than institutional care.

The case study of familial care relations in Kuala Lumpur, Bangkok Metropolis and Hanoi revealed that the main burden of elderly and childcare remained within a coresident family with substantial support from the wider family network. Such a family-network based welfare system relied upon an intergenerational exchange approach and shared responsibility among adult children, which extended to children-in-law. Yet, their different family systems spilled into different patterns of practice and expectation on the role of adult children as care providers as well as the support their elderly parents provided them. The characteristics of the adult children and the elderly parents also affected such diversity. Filial norms were less defined by gender in Kuala Lumpur and Bangkok Metropolis than in Hanoi. Emotional support was found to outweigh financial support and support with household chores. While coresidence was considered a form of filial piety, financial support served as an alternative solution among adult children who lived far away from their elderly parents. The situation was revealed to apply more in Bangkok Metropolis and Kuala Lumpur than in Hanoi where the adult children couldn't afford financial support. The case study of Kuala Lumpur, Bangkok Metropolis and Hanoi also revealed that the older the elderly, the greater degree of support from adult children was provided in both financial and non-financial terms. However, this was the case among the old rather the younger adult children. This probably reflected the interaction between affordability and a stronger notion of filial piety among the old children than the younger ones. The contribution of elderly parents was relatively weak when compared to that of the adult children provided to them. Explanations included their health status, widowhood, and a limited income, especially from work, savings, social pension or old-age allowance.

An impending shift towards further defamilialisation of care provision for both the elderly and the children was revealed in the case study of Kuala Lumpur, Bangkok Metropolis and Hanoi. According to chapter 7, while families there continued to practice family care giving, some family members were also looking at possible avenues for shared responsibility in care. This was particularly among those with limitations in terms of finances, time, and human resources. The notion further supports findings at the national level in Part 1 of this volume that the shifting demographic and socio-economic conditions had an impact on the balance of the individual's quality of life and work-family responsibilities among females. Families and female workers needed help; but they received almost nothing in the existing welfare regime to support them. Due to the limited coverage of social protection and lack of affordable quality care, family caregivers, particularly females, faced the triple burden of taking care of their children and older parents, while maintaining productivity at work.

With the increased demand for old-age support and affordable care for children and frail older persons, the commodification of care was revealed. This development was more pervasive in Malaysia and Vietnam due to the emphasis on economic liberalization and privatization, compared to Thailand that had started a policy emphasis on community-based solutions to address social problems. Furthermore, given the ineffective control and enforcement of the burgeoning care industry by the government, reliance on market solutions contributed to the increasing inequalities between the rich and the poor by segregating those who were recipients of social welfare and those who could afford to purchase care.

One may note from chapter 7 that the expectation was more for shared responsibility rather than a substitute for familial care.

2.4 *Existing Efforts at the National Policy Level*

During the past few years up to 2017, Malaysia, Thailand and Vietnam were still middle-income societies experiencing changes in the context of care, as shown from chapters 2 to 4. The study of the relevant national policy regimes in Malaysia, Thailand and Vietnam then revealed that the customary reliance of the state on family caregivers to take on most of the responsibility for care was a common strategy. It reflected the continuity of what was found in previous studies (Jittapunkul, Chavoyan, & Kespichayawattaya, 2002; Mohd, 2012).

In other words, policies in the three countries tend to strengthen and institutionalize traditional family values on the provision of care based on the assumptions of traditional family functions. Public expenditure on welfare in the three countries relied on a means test that targeted those who were severely deprived and without family support. Other vulnerable segments of the population, namely the unemployed, the sick and the frail elderly, turned to their families for assistance. The three countries shared this key approach to lower the burden of heavy welfare expenditure which enabled these governments to redirect public investments for economic growth.

Through the increase of privatisation and liberalisation, economic policies helped these three Southeast Asian countries achieve a middle-income status, but not without the social consequences of growing inequalities and increased vulnerability of the working population. On one hand, economic reforms instigated an increase in the productivity of capital along with other national resources to preserve economic competitiveness. On the other hand, social development strategies often resulted in the inefficient allocation of resources to ensure the sustainability of economic development. The activities of providing and receiving care, which are indispensable at different points during an individual's lifetime, accordingly remained largely invisible within the private sphere of the family.

A key policy emphasis was based on the efficient provision of care, which refers to quality care that costs less. Nevertheless, public expenditure in the three countries points to the fact that the provision of care was inefficient and costly. The case study of Malaysia, Thailand and Vietnam reflects that the over-reliance of policies based on traditional family care giving negatively resulted in opportunity costs shouldered by the providers and the recipients of care, as well as by the national economy.

Firstly, care providers from the working age population, particularly females, were expected to care for both young children and the elderly, which left very little room for their own quality of life and provision of old age security. Secondly, the recipients of care also faced opportunity costs from being subjected to low quality care purchased from the market and provided by low skilled domestic workers. Under these conditions, children lose the opportunity to grow up and to become part of a quality workforce and the elderly may not be able to contribute to the economy. Through strengthening education, policy-makers tried to rectify this problem, but the underlying cause was the inefficient care provision prevailing in all three societies. Thirdly, the economy was also burdened by this inefficiency, as these countries remained trapped in the middle-income status of economic development.

Nevertheless, given that they were at different levels of economic development as well as in the process of demographic shift, their policy concerns varied to some extent. It is important to note that with a higher gross national income, such upper middle-income countries as Thailand and Malaysia had more diversified policies and measures to address the needs of an ageing population, compared to Vietnam, a lower-middle income country.

Thailand is relatively advanced in terms of preparing the nation to transition from an ageing to an aged society. The shift in the boundaries of care was commensurate with growing concerns in the public arena on issues, such as, who should bear the responsibility of care, how policies promoted a positive balance between family care and work roles, and how public institutions would cope with the unprecedented demographic and social transformations combined with increasing economic pressures. Despite the fact that the Malaysian population was relatively young, the government recognised the potential threat of the financial burden of supporting an increasing older population and was in the process of mainstreaming ageing into their development policies. This was also designed to address the impact of the policy caveat noted above, which was highly visible in Malaysia which had the lowest female laborforce participation rate. However, policy development in Vietnam, which was turning into an aging society more quickly than Malaysia, was relatively slow to respond to demographic and societal changes.

3 Looking Forward: Further Challenging Structural Transition and Socio-economic Impacts

3.1 *Towards Aging, Aged and Super-aged Societies*

As indicated in Figure 9.1 which shows a demographic shift by broad age groups in Malaysia, Thailand, and Vietnam from 2015 to 2040, Thailand is about to transform from an ageing into an aged and super-aged society by 2030 and 2040, respectively. The Thai population aged 65 years and above will increase from 10% of the total population in 2015 to 13–19% during 2020–2030, and 25% in 2040. During 2030–2040, Vietnam will turn into an aged society with the population aged 65 and above growing to 14% of the total population. Malaysia will be one of the speediest countries to become an aging society by 2035 and will be on their way towards an aged society soon after 2040 (Wongboonsin & Wongboonsin 2015).

More people will be living longer, particularly females. As shown in Figure 9.2, Malaysian life expectancy at age 60 will increase to 22.6 years for the female and 18.6 years for the male population during 2025–2030 from 19.4 years and 16.9 years during 2000–2005. Meanwhile, female and male life expectancy at

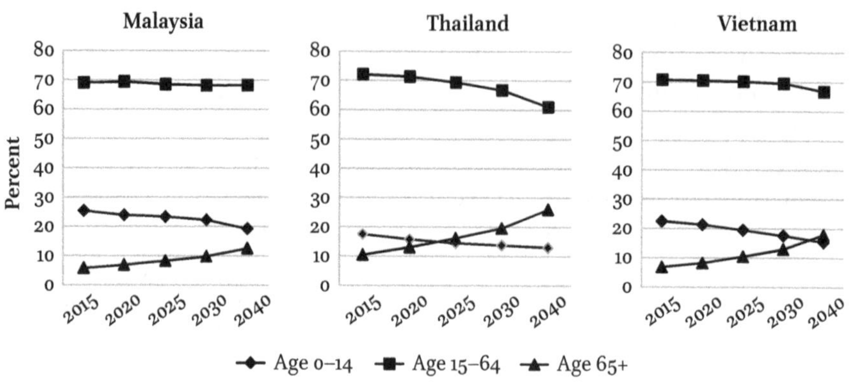

FIGURE 9.1 Demographic shift in Malaysia, Thailand, and Vietnam, 2015–2040 (medium variant).
SOURCE: WONGBOONSIN AND WONGBOONSIN (2015), BASED ON DATA FROM UNITED NATIONS, DEPARTMENT OF ECONOMIC AND SOCIAL AFFAIRS, POPULATION DIVISION (2013).

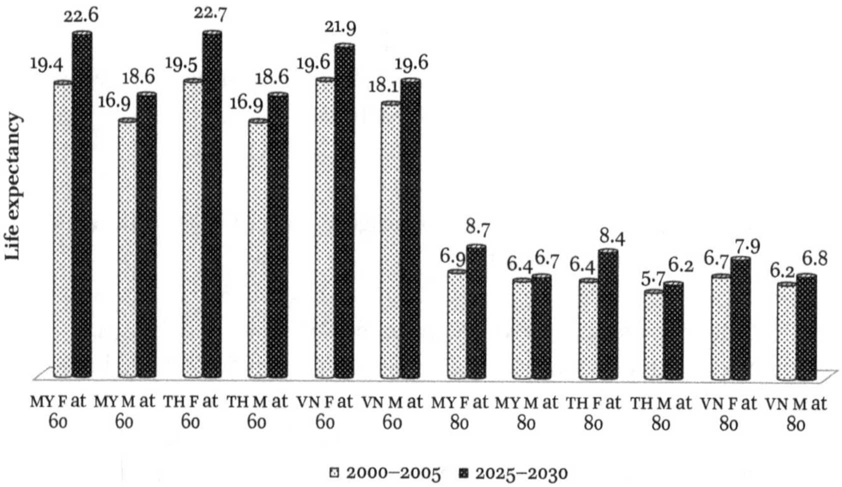

FIGURE 9.2 Life expectancy at age 60 and 80 by gender and country, 2000–2005 and 2025–2030.
Note: MY = Malaysia; TH = Thailand; VN = Vietnam.
SOURCE: CALCULATED FROM DATA FROM UN. 2001. *WORLD POPULATION AGEING 1950–2050*. NEW YORK: POPULATION DIVISION, DESA, UNITED NATIONS.

age 80 in Malaysia will be 8.7 and 6.7 years, respectively, during 2025–2030. This is compared to 6.9 and 6.4 years, respectively, during 2000–2005. Female life expectancy at age 60 in Thailand will be slightly higher (22.7 years) than that in Malaysia while that for male life expectancy will be the same as in Malaysia during 2025–2030. This is compared to 19.5 and 16.9 years for females and males, respectively, during 2000–2005. Meanwhile, life expectancy at age 80 in Thailand will increase to 8.4 for females and 6.2 years for males during 2025–2030. The increase in Vietnam will be a bit lower for both males and females. This probably reflects the poorer quality of life in Vietnam compared to that in Thailand and Malaysia, which suggests the need for a more proactive policy intervention to improve the Vietnamese quality of life. Without appropriate policy intervention to encourage a better quality of life with wealth accumulation long before ageing, increasing longevity implies a lengthening period of fragility/vulnerability for the elderly due to the risks of physical, social and economic disabilities. On the other hand, if they age healthily, actively, wealthily, such an increase in longevity would mean an increase in a valuable resource to the respective society as it ages further (Wongboonsin & Wongboonsin 2013, 2015).

The shift in the balance between the proportion of the younger and older population will also affect relations between different generations, for instance through the private and public transfer of resources from one generation to the next. This will further result in changes to the economy, health systems, and means of providing care (Wongboonsin & Wongboonsin 2013, 2015). Figure 9.3 shows that in years to come the three countries will experience an increase in the old-age dependency ratio. Given the notion of the old-age dependency ratio being the number of persons 65+ years per 100 persons aged between 15–64 years, there will be more and more elderly aged 65 and above who will depend on the working-age population in the three countries under investigation. Meanwhile, there will be a different trend of youth and total dependency ratios. The former refers to the number of persons 0–14 years per 100 persons 15–64 years, while the latter is the number of persons under age 15 plus persons aged 65+ per 100 persons aged 15–64 years. In other words, while the productive population in the three countries will experience decreasing pressure from youth dependency, they will still have to work hard to shoulder the burden of old-age dependency (Wongboonsin & Wongboonsin 2015).

Such a challenge is further reflected in the trend of the potential support ratio, parent support ratio, and familial support ratio by 2040. From the perspective of the potential support ratio, which is the number of persons 15–64 years per every person aged 65+ (United Nations 2017), the projection confirms that there will be less and less demographic availability of people

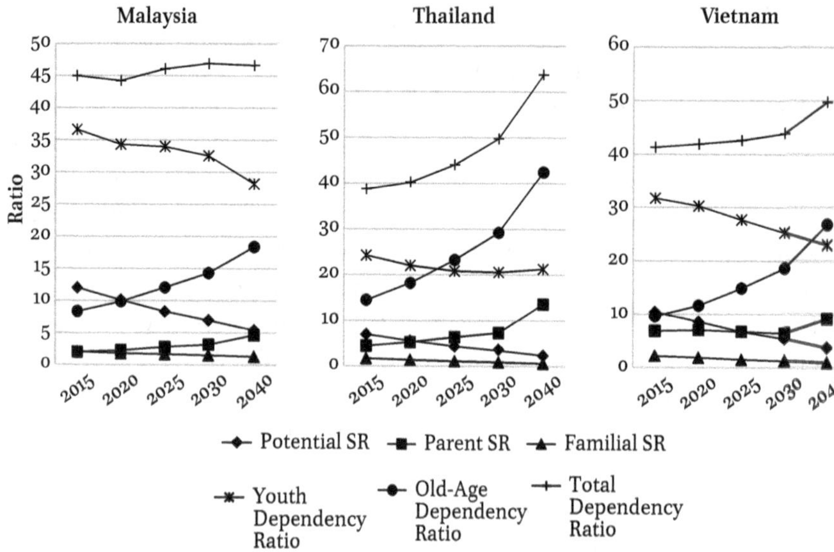

FIGURE 9.3 Support and dependency ratios of Malaysia, Thailand, and Vietnam, 2015–2040 (medium variant).
SOURCE: WONGBOONSIN AND WONGBOONSIN (2015), BASED ON DATA FROM UNITED NATIONS, DEPARTMENT OF ECONOMIC AND SOCIAL AFFAIRS, POPULATION DIVISION (2013).

in the productive age group to take care of the elderly aged 65 and above in all the three countries under investigation. Meanwhile, the demand for women aged 40–59 to provide care for their parents when they reach the age of 65–84 will be relatively stable, as shown in the familial support ratio. Given the increasing life expectancy, the demographic availability of adult children of elderly parents will remain relatively stable up to 2030 and will increase thereafter. This is reflected in the parent support ratio, which is the number of persons 85+ years per 100 persons aged 50–64 (Wongboonsin & Wongboonsin 2015).

3.2 *Fertility Decline*

While the proportion of the Malaysian population aged 15–64 years old will remain relatively stable at around nearly 70% of the total population until 2040, the Thai population of the same age group will decline from 72% of the total population in 2015 to 66% in 2030 and more drastically to 61% in 2040. The Vietnamese population in the group 15–64 years of age will remain at around 70% of the population until 2030, and then drop to 66% in 2040. In the meantime, all three societies will experience a decline in the proportion of the population at 0–14 years of age. It will reduce from 25% in 2015 to 19%

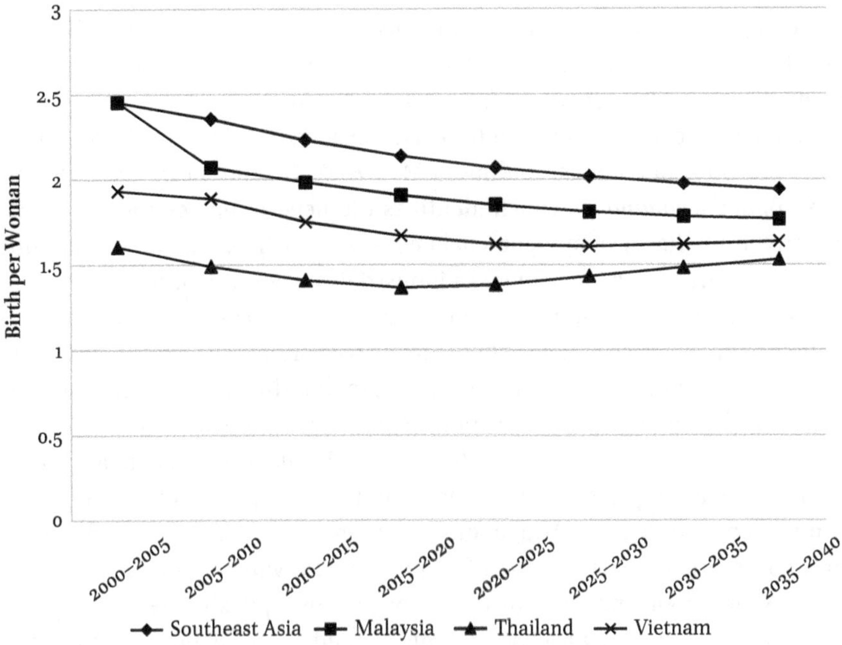

FIGURE 9.4 Total fertility rates: Southeast Asia, Malaysia, Thailand and Vietnam, 2000–2040 (medium variant).
Note: Data for 2000–2005 and 2005–2010 are estimates; data for 2010–2015 up to 2035–2040 are projections (medium variant).
SOURCE: WONGBOONSIN AND WONGBOONSIN (2015), BASED ON DATA FROM UNITED NATIONS, DEPARTMENT OF ECONOMIC AND SOCIAL AFFAIRS, POPULATION DIVISION (2013).

of the total population in 2040 in Malaysia, from 22% to 17% in Vietnam, and from 17% to 13% in Thailand during these respective periods (Wongboonsin & Wongboonsin 2015).

The above-mentioned demographic shift in the three countries under investigation is partly attributable to their declining fertility. Figure 9.4 compares their total fertility rate (TFR), or the average number of children a woman would bear during the course of her lifetime. As one may see, the TFR will be 1.9, 1.8, and 1.6 in Malaysia in 2015–2020, 2025–2030 and 2035–2040, respectively, while dropping from 1.9 in 2015–2020 to around 1.6 thereafter until 2030–2040 in Vietnam. However, the Thai TFR will increase slightly from 1.4 births per woman in 2015–2020 to 1.6 in 2035–2040.

3.3 *Impacts on Long-term Development and Old-age Security*

The demographic transition in the decades to come is a major concern to policy makers in the three countries under investigation (High Commission of Malaysia 2017; NESDB 2017; VGP 2012). This is based on the notion that the demographic transition into an ageing, aged and super-aged society will in the long term have an adverse effect on old-age security and the economic development process (Wongboonsin & Wongboonsin 2015).

Malaysia and Thailand aspire to reach the status of developed economies in the decades to come, according to Malaysia's *Transformasi Nasional* 2050 (TN50), and *Thailand 4.0* which identifies the need to unlock the respective country from its development challenges. Meanwhile, Vietnam's development goals are to become a modern industrialized country of middle income by 2020 and a developed industrial country of high income there after (High Commission of Malaysia 2017; NESDB 2017; VGP 2012).

Given the fading away of the 1st demographic dividend in Thailand and Vietnam, the demographic transition in years to come would be unlikely to contribute to a 2nd demographic dividend as Thailand and Vietnam further ages, unless appropriate policy interventions are in place (Wongboonsin & Kinnas 2005; Minh 2009; Wongboonsin & Wongboonsin 2013, 2015). As noted in the introductory chapter, the 1st demographic dividend, or a demographic window of opportunity for an economy to grow quickly, theoretically occurs when the working-age population expands at a higher rate than the general population. Whether the rapid increase in the elderly population negatively affects the economy or offers another demographic dividend depends on government policies (United Nations 2017). How to capitalize on the 1st demographic dividend and to pave the way for a 2nd one is a challenge for Malaysia.

According to a previous study in Thailand (Wongboonsin 2015), the shrinking population affects economic growth through many channels. Besides a smaller workforce, one may expect lower saving rates, as dissaving occurs during old age, which then impacts investment and capital accumulation. Moreover, a fall in aggregate demand can result as the pattern of consumption changes. Economic growth cannot be sustained if the number of children keeps on declining. The declining number of children adversely affects the size of the future workforce. The sheer increase in the ratio as well as the absolute number of the older population can be expected topose a real challenge for sustainable healthcare and social welfare provision.

Given the prevailing approach of policy making in the three countries, the fact that the elderly population is expanding means that the government will bear a higher burden for the provision of social protection, and that the sustainability of the system will be threatened. This will be exacerbated by the fact that a shortage of workers in the field of, to name a few, public health, eldercare, education and security, in the future is likely.

3.4 *Impacts on Families*

The demographic transition in years to come is expected to further adversely affect families. As noted above, the growth of the older population with the consequent increase in physical, economic and social inabilities and declining fertility will result in greater dependence, economically, socially and health-wise. Besides, as Thailand and Vietnam turn into aged and super-aged societies, and as Malaysia turns into an aging society with a low fertility rate, one may foresee a decrease in the proportion of the working-age population or adult children, a smaller family size and a further decrease in the capability of the family and kin in familial care. Such an impact could be ameliorated through changed attitudes among those of reproductive age towards family making, family planning, working, childbearing and child rearing. This is essential unless there are policy interventions for a re-establishment of families as social institutions that can solve social problems.

4 Policy Recommendations For Moving Forward

4.1 *Approach: Caring Societies with Sustainable Welfare towards a 2nd Demographic Dividend*

Based on current and future trends of demographic change, it is clear that Thailand, Vietnam and Malaysia are facing challenges to sustain their economic and social development. An on-going increase in the proportion and number of the elderly hinder such a prospect unless a 2nd demographic dividend is procured, or there is a strong commitment to increase capital accumulation and investment. As suggested by the United Nations (2017), a 2nd demographic dividend could be greater than the 1st demographic dividend and could contribute to sustained economic growth.

Meanwhile, the sustainability of both public and familial welfare must be enhanced for future generations to meet their needs. Taking into account the smaller base of the young population and more rapid growth of the older population, middle-income countries with limited reserves have to rely on more innovative strategies to help the working-age population to accumulate their wealth early in life and to a sufficient degree to fund public and familial transfers for social protection and welfare provision. In addition, it is necessary to prevent the diminished capacity and resilience of families in performing the vital function of caring for its members. Otherwise, this loss of precious but under-valued social capital may lead to higher government expenditure for health and welfare, while adversely affected societal well-being.

This chapter opines that the well-being of a society starts at the individual level. So far, the well-being of a person is left in the hands of certain members of his/her family, while care is regarded as personal consumption for personal benefits. It is necessary for policy making to be reoriented to encourage *societal well-being* in years to come, and to reflect *inclusivity* for all people of society, regardless of age and gender. Certain family members should not be left alone to perform the caring function for others.

Accordingly, care should be regarded as a *social investment*, in which other actors in society take their part in sharing the responsibility for the future of the society and in sustaining the economy for future generations. Such other actors are not limited to the state and kin, but should include the community and the private sector. Their engagement must be encouraged from the perspective of a *partnership* with the family. Corporate family-friendly policies, for example, can be part of social responsibility. State and corporate family-friendly policies should be a factor in the socio-economic contribution of the *intergenerational* relations between age cohorts as well as the *interdependency* of the different age cohorts as they are involved in caring over their life course. This is in addition to the notion that caring takes place across a family's entire life course and, as such, the notions of 'care giving' and 'care receiving' provide the concept of care with *reciprocal* connotations. Moreover, social investment in personal and familial care should be considered from the perspective of the quality and efficiency of *care time* and *active ageing* for the benefit of current and future generations.

The way to do so is multi-faceted while requiring long-term strategies and social innovations that respond to the changing needs of families in this changing context of care.

4.2 *Policy Measures for Future Old-age Financial Security*

Old-age security for the future generations of the elderly will be an important challenge. If the TFR keeps on falling, future children will become a less reliable source of financial security once the current working age population turns into the future elderly. In other words, the current working population/adult children will turn into the future generation of the elderly with less support from the future adult children. Also, as the future generation of older persons are likely to live longer after retirement while there are fewer children, one may expect a rising tendency for the future generation of older persons to live alone.

Accordingly, a family policy should not be limited to the elderly and children. The quality and well-being of the working-age population, or the sandwiched generation, should also be factored in. It is deemed necessary for the policy to encourage the current adult children or the working-age population to prepare themselves in financial terms before they retire. Examples of measures to increase savings include the dissemination of information on long-term financial instruments to the public, an adjustment of the mindset of people of working age such that they recognize the importance of being prepared financially for old age, and the establishment of a monitoring and a support system for community-based savings.

As noted above, an increase in the savings rate will facilitate a 2nd demographic dividend through capital accumulation and appropriate investment that can consequently promote growth. The government also should come up with fiscal incentives to further encourage savings, e.g. tax credits, etc. However as suggested by Wongboonsin (2015), such fiscal incentives should not be so generous that the rate of savings becomes too high, affecting consumption and investment in real terms–a phenomenon that is referred to as the "liquidity trap".

Long life expectancy, deteriorating health conditions and functional dependence are challenges that could have an adverse impact on old-age security. In addition to promoting household savings, the state's role should be oriented towards strengthening these three dimensions of old-age security: (a) financial security, ensuring that older persons do not deplete their savings before the end of life; (b) health insurance, providing curative care and preventive care for all older persons; and (c) disability insurance, facilitating active aging so that older persons without informal caregivers or adult children are able to perform the activities of daily living (Wongboonsin 2015). In other words, the respective governments need to fulfil their responsibility to provide a solid foundation for old-age security, drawing from the strength of these four actors in welfare: (a) the family network; (b) the market; (c) the state; and (d) the community. They should also ensure that an optimal balance among the four pillars is achieved.

Sound macroeconomic management by the government is required. Emphasis should be placed on the promotion of savings and long-term investment that can be used in old age, rather than on the stimulation of household spending. The government should also pay particular attention to interest rates and inflation rates, as these are critical components of old-age financial security (Wongboonsin 2015).

4.3 *Policy Measure to Minimize Impacts on the Family*

As mentioned in 2.3, the future demographic transition could further adversely affect families. It is accordingly necessary for the respective governments to campaign for a re-establishment of families as social institutions that could solve social problems. In particular, these three main issues should be addressed.

4.3.1 Work and Family: Work-life Balance

Conditions for marriage and childbearing often include whether a work-life balance can be achieved and whether children can be brought up to become adults who will later contribute positively to the economy and society. These conditions need to be met; otherwise people of reproductive age will choose to work rather than to form a family. To ensure that work and family are not competing choices, people of reproductive age need to be incentivized to have children. An example of such incentives includes the provision of parental leave. They also need to change their attitudes such that raising children is not viewed, culturally, as the sole responsibility of the wife but one that is shared equally between the wife and the husband. The fact that women are culturally expected to give up their work to have children and the mindset that only men can be breadwinners should be gradually changed, as these are known to delay women's childbearing.

It is accordingly necessary to establish a work-life balance so that there are more people of reproductive age willing to get married without delay and to have children as desired. Appropriate approaches to support childbearing, childrearing, and work-life balance that fit in each society should be explored.

4.3.2 Gender Equality and More Active Male Engagement in Familial Care

Gender equality should be nurtured while strengthening the family institution, familial care responsibilities, with a focus on an increase of men's role in familial care in practice. In a country where family-related leave arrangements are still weak, such as Thailand, the relevant state needs to provide incentive measures for workplaces to provide family-related leave arrangements, particularly elder parental care leave, parental leave, besides improvement of paternity leave and maternity leave.

Parents need to be able to spend quality time with their children. Particularly during their first few years of life, parents should be encouraged raise their children together, and if possible to live together. This may not necessarily be as spouses. Striking a balance in terms of parenting responsibilities between the two genders is deemed as important in societies in transition. Different stages of child development require varying inputs from the father and the mother (Wongboonsin 2015). More quality and affordable childcare and child development centers should also be provided.

4.3.3 Disadvantaged and Vulnerable Families

Building economic and social security among the disadvantaged and vulnerable family members is also deemed to be necessary. This includes those of limited financial resources, human resources, as well as time resources. Among others, intergenerational relations in communities should be promoted to strengthen collaboration in enhancing each age cohort towards a quality of life and resilience in weathering changes. Approaches and measures for social security should be identified to cover all jobs so as to mitigate poverty among elders. Moreover, well-balanced childcare and long-term care systems should be established to link major care providers together in a partnership approach: (a) the family network; (b) the market, including employers and market mechanisms, such as financial instruments; (c) the community; and (d) the state. The latter include policies and funds to strengthen such partnerships in the system of social welfare.

References

High Commission of Malaysia. (2017). *Fact sheet, Transformasi nasional 2050 (TN50)*. Bandar Seri Begawan: Ministry of Foreign Affairs, Malaysia.

Jittapunkul, Suthichai, Napaporn Chavoyan, & Jiraporn Kespichayawattaya. (2002). National policies on ageing and long-term care provision for older persons in Thailand. In David R. Phillips, & Alfred C.M. Chan (Eds.), *Aging and long-term care: National policies in the Asia-Pacific* (pp. 181–213). Singapore: Institute of Southeast Asian Studies.

Minh, Nguyen Thi. (2009). Dynamic demographics and economic growth in Vietnam. *Journal of the Asia Pacific Economy* 14(4), 389–398.

Mohd, Saidatulakmal. (2012). Welfare regime, social protection and poverty reduction. In Khoo Boo Teik (Ed.), *Policy regimes and the political economy of poverty reduction in Malaysia* (pp. 107–144). Hampshire, UK: Palgrave Macmillan.

NESDB. (2017). *The twelfth national economic and social development plan (2017–2021)*. Bangkok: Office of the National Economic and Social Development Board Office of the Prime Minister, Thailand.

United Nations. (2017). *Support ratios and demographic dividend: Estimates for the world*. Technical paper no. 2017/1. New York: Department of Economic and Social Affairs, Population Division.

VGP. (2012). *Viet Nam sustainable development strategy for 2011–2020*. Hanoi: Vietnam Government Portal.

Wongboonsin, Patcharawalai (Ed.). (2015). *Outlining appropriate approaches to reduce inequities in the Thai society amidst demographic shift*. Final report submitted to Office of the National Economic and Social Development Board by College of Population Studies, Chulalongkorn University, Bangkok: Chulalongkorn University Printing House.

Wongboonsin, Patcharawalai, & Joannis Kinnas. (2005). Maximizing the demographic dividend via regional cooperation in human resource development. In Kua Wongboonsin, & Philip Guest (Eds.), *The demographic dividend: policy options for Asia* (pp. 90–128), published jointly by College of Population Studies, Chulalongkorn University, Asian Development Research Forum, and Thailand Research Fund in cooperation with International Development Research Centre, Canada. Bangkok: Chulalongkorn University Printing House.

Wongboonsin, Patcharawalai, & Kua Wongboonsin. (2013). Demographic dividend and the future of Asia. In Emiko Ochiai, & Leo Aoi Hosoya (Eds.), *Transformation of the intimate and the public in Asian Modernity* (pp. 91–115), The Netherlands: Brill.

Wongboonsin, Patcharawalai, & Kua Wongboonsin. (2015). *Towards healthy and wealthy ageing ASEAN socio-economy*. Bangkok: Human Development & Migration Studies Center, College of Population Studies, Chulalongkorn University.

Appendix

TABLE A1 Who should be responsible for elder's livelihood?

	Bangkok Metropolis	Hanoi	Kuala Lumpur
	(1)	(2)	(3)
Middle Generation	−0.198	0.028	0.151
	(1.82)*	(0.22)	(1.62)
Old Generation	−0.171	0.188	0.060
	(1.47)	(1.33)	(0.51)
Female	−0.019	0.068	−0.053
	(0.26)	(0.79)	(0.94)
Married	−0.102	−0.216	−0.342
	(0.72)	(1.12)	(2.24)**
Some secondary education	−0.070	0.123	0.011
	(0.81)	(0.87)	(0.13)
Tertiary education or higher	0.191	−0.168	0.037
	(1.62)	(1.05)	(0.35)
Living standard: high		0.068	0.304
		(0.47)	(2.48)**
Living standard: middle		−0.005	0.062
		(0.04)	(1.03)
2 generation household	0.295	−0.037	0.158
	(2.36)**	(0.26)	(1.46)
3 gen, 4-gen, 5-gen, other types of household	0.268	−0.027	0.061
	(2.13)**	(0.19)	(0.53)
Total number of children	0.042	0.062	−0.011
Living with, or nearby to, at least one parent	−0.013	0.050	0.104
	(0.08)	(0.46)	(0.96)
Living with, or nearby to, at least one of spouse's parents	−0.052	−0.028	0.029
	(0.27)	(0.25)	(0.23)
Living with adult child	−0.006	−0.095	0.182
Living with adult child*Living with at least one married daughter	−0.263	−0.585	−0.005
	(1.65)*	(2.64)***	(0.02)

 | DOI:10.1163/9789004384330_011

TABLE A1 Who should be responsible for elder's livelihood? (*cont.*)

	Bangkok Metropolis	Hanoi	Kuala Lumpur
	(1)	(2)	(3)
Face-to-face contact with parents at least weekly	0.177	0.071	−0.142
	(1.19)	(0.74)	(1.48)
Face-to-face contact / spouse's parents at least weekly	0.049	0.242	0.124
	(0.32)	(2.45)**	(1.49)
Ethnicity: Chinese			−0.036
			(0.47)
Ethnicity: Indian			−0.038
			(0.46)
Pseudo R-squared	0.016	0.026	0.009
Number of observations	910	1118	1523

Note: Absolute value of z statistics are in parentheses. *, **, and *** denote significance at 10%, 5%, and 1% levels, respectively. The baseline groups are as follows. The baseline for generation is the young generation. The baseline for marital status is never married/divorced/separated. The baseline for education is primary or lower. The baseline for living standard is low living standard. The baseline for living arrangement is single person/1-generation household. The baseline for ethnicity is Malay. The following variables are controlled for but not reported in the table: married*received much financial assistance from parents, married*received some financial assistance from parents, married*received much financial assistance from spouse's parents, married*received some financial assistance from spouse's parents.

TABLE A2 Who should be responsible for elder's medical treatment and nursing care?

	Bangkok Metropolis	Hanoi	Kuala Lumpur
	(1)	(2)	(3)
Middle Generation	−0.182	0.126	0.174
	(1.69)*	(1.05)	(1.85)*
Old Generation	−0.058	0.240	0.138
	(0.51)	(1.77)*	(1.17)
Female	0.038	0.086	−0.032
	(0.52)	(1.04)	(0.58)
Married	−0.164	−0.158	−0.341
	(1.17)	(0.85)	(2.22)**
Some secondary education	0.049	0.145	0.032
	(0.57)	(1.06)	(0.37)
Tertiary education or higher	0.136	−0.224	−0.010
	(1.18)	(1.45)	(0.09)
Living standard: high		0.101	0.321
		(0.72)	(2.62)***
Living standard: middle		0.094	0.117
		(0.76)	(1.93)*
2 generation household	0.254	−0.028	0.185
	(2.05)**	(0.20)	(1.70)*
3 gen, 4-gen, 5-gen, other types of household	0.181	−0.101	0.115
	(1.46)	(0.70)	(1.01)
Total number of children	0.028	0.067	−0.021
	(0.74)	(1.97)**	(1.06)
Living with, or nearby to, at least one parent	−0.180	0.071	0.106
	(1.15)	(0.69)	(0.97)
Living with, or nearby to, at least one of spouse's parents	−0.199	−0.023	0.049
	(1.05)	(0.22)	(0.39)
Living with adult child	−0.053	−0.037	0.121
	(0.47)	(0.43)	(1.29)
Living with adult child*Living with at least one married daughter	−0.151	−0.199	−0.024
	(0.95)	(0.90)	(0.11)

TABLE A2 **Who should be responsible for elder's medical treatment and nursing care? (*cont.*)**

	Bangkok Metropolis	Hanoi	Kuala Lumpur
	(1)	(2)	(3)
Face-to-face contact with parents at least weekly	0.264	0.050	−0.130
	(1.78)*	(0.54)	(1.35)
Face-to-face contact / spouse's parents at least weekly	0.007	0.084	0.105
	(0.04)	(0.88)	(1.26)
Ethnicity: Chinese			−0.062
			(0.83)
Ethnicity: Indian			−0.062
			(0.77)
Pseudo R-squared	0.012	0.021	0.009
Number of observations	910	1118	1523

Note: Absolute value of z statistics are in parentheses. *, **, and *** denote significance at 10%, 5%, and 1% levels, respectively. The baseline groups are as follows. The baseline for generation is the young generation. The baseline for marital status is never married/divorced/separated. The baseline for education is primary or lower. The baseline for living standard is low living standard. The baseline for living arrangement is single person/1-generation household. The baseline for ethnicity is Malay. The following variables are controlled for but not reported in the table: married*received much financial assistance from parents, married*received some financial assistance from parents, married*received much financial assistance from spouse's parents, married*received some financial assistance from spouse's parents.

TABLE A3 Who should be responsible for children's rearing and care work?

	Bangkok Metropolis	Hanoi	Kuala Lumpur
	(1)	(2)	(3)
Middle Generation	−0.248	−0.080	−0.025
	(2.21)**	(0.62)	(0.26)
Old Generation	−0.163	0.007	−0.138
	(1.36)	(0.05)	(1.15)
Female	−0.150	0.098	−0.095
	(1.97)**	(1.10)	(1.65)*
Married	−0.043	−0.140	0.049
	(0.30)	(0.70)	(0.32)
Some secondary education	0.030	−0.012	0.004
	(0.34)	(0.08)	(0.05)
Tertiary education or higher	0.134	−0.033	0.111
	(1.11)	(0.20)	(1.03)
Living standard: high		0.125	0.280
		(0.83)	(2.24)**
Living standard: middle		0.098	−0.041
		(0.74)	(0.66)
2 generation household	0.175	0.156	0.147
	(1.37)	(1.05)	(1.33)
3 gen, 4-gen, 5-gen, other types of	0.233	0.265	0.128
household	(1.82)*	(1.73)*	(1.09)
Total number of children	0.047	0.027	0.006
	(1.22)	(0.75)	(0.29)
Living with, or nearby to, at least one	−0.087	−0.028	0.116
parent	(0.54)	(0.25)	(1.04)
Living with, or nearby to, at least one	0.280	−0.096	0.140
of spouse's parents	(1.41)	(0.83)	(1.10)
Living with adult child	−0.024	−0.079	0.126
Living with adult child*Living with at	−0.064	−0.565	−0.136
least one married daughter	(0.39)	(2.45)**	(0.62)

TABLE A3 Who should be responsible for children's rearing and care work? (*cont.*)

	Bangkok Metropolis	Hanoi	Kuala Lumpur
	(1)	(2)	(3)
Face-to-face contact with parents at least weekly	0.140 (0.91)	0.014 (0.14)	−0.103 (1.05)
Face-to-face contact / spouse's parents at least weekly	−0.100 (0.63)	0.159 (1.57)	0.010 (0.12)
Ethnicity: Chinese			−0.196 (2.56)**
Ethnicity: Indian			−0.057 (0.69)
Pseudo R-squared	0.013	0.013	0.011
Number of observations	910	1118	1523

Note: Absolute value of z statistics are in parentheses. *, **, and *** denote significance at 10%, 5%, and 1% levels, respectively. The baseline groups are as follows. The baseline for generation is the young generation. The baseline for marital status is never married/divorced/separated. The baseline for education is primary or lower. The baseline for living standard is low living standard. The baseline for living arrangement is single person/1-generation household. The baseline for ethnicity is Malay. The following variables are controlled for but not reported in the table: married*received much financial assistance from parents, married*received some financial assistance from parents, married*received much financial assistance from spouse's parents, married*received some financial assistance from spouse's parents.

TABLE A4 Who should be responsible for children's educational cost

	Bangkok Metropolis	Hanoi	Kuala Lumpur
	(1)	(2)	(3)
Middle Generation	−0.122	−0.158	0.020
	(1.13)	(1.33)	(0.21)
Old Generation	−0.035	−0.142	−0.108
	(0.30)	(1.06)	(0.90)
Female	−0.113	0.100	−0.102
	(1.54)	(1.22)	(1.78)*
Married	−0.021	−0.176	0.008
	(0.15)	(0.96)	(0.05)
Some secondary education	0.080	−0.073	0.007
	(0.92)	(0.54)	(0.07)
Tertiary education or higher	−0.050	−0.355	0.114
	(0.43)	(2.32)**	(1.06)
Living standard: high		0.054	0.277
		(0.39)	(2.22)**
Living standard: middle		0.104	−0.020
		(0.85)	(0.33)
2 generation household	0.109	−0.001	0.104
	(0.88)	(0.01)	(0.94)
3 gen, 4-gen, 5-gen, other types of household	0.176	−0.148	0.100
	(1.40)	(1.05)	(0.86)
Total number of children	0.029	0.046	0.004
	(0.77)	(1.38)	(0.21)
Living with, or nearby to, at least one parent	−0.104	0.117	0.093
	(0.67)	(1.15)	(0.84)
Living with, or nearby to, at least one of spouse's parents	−0.105	−0.146	0.149
	(0.55)	(1.38)	(1.17)
Living with adult child	−0.026	0.163	0.118
	(0.23)	(1.90)*	(1.24)
Living with adult child*Living with at least one married daughter	−0.182	−0.544	−0.160
	(1.14)	(2.54)**	(0.73)
Face-to-face contact with parents at least weekly	0.149	−0.041	−0.075
	(1.00)	(0.45)	(0.76)

TABLE A4 Who should be responsible for children's educational cost (*cont.*)

	Bangkok Metropolis	Hanoi	Kuala Lumpur
	(1)	(2)	(3)
Face-to-face contact / spouse's parents at least weekly	−0.057 (0.37)	0.139 (1.49)	0.028 (0.33)
Ethnicity: Chinese			−0.199 (2.61)***
Ethnicity: Indian			−0.085 (1.03)
Pseudo R-squared	0.005	0.018	0.010
Number of observations	910	1118	1523

Note: Absolute value of z statistics are in parentheses. *, **, and *** denote significance at 10%, 5%, and 1% levels, respectively. The baseline groups are as follows. The baseline for generation is the young generation. The baseline for marital status is never married/divorced/separated. The baseline for education is primary or lower. The baseline for living standard is low living standard. The baseline for living arrangement is single person/1-generation household. The baseline for ethnicity is Malay. The following variables are controlled for but not reported in the table: married*received much financial assistance from parents, married*received some financial assistance from parents, married*received much financial assistance from spouse's parents, married*received some financial assistance from spouse's parents.

Subject Index

www.ingramcontent.com/pod-product-compliance
Lightning Source LLC
LaVergne TN
LVHW020632300926
849161LV00004B/676